MW00583941

SEEING THROUGH

SEEING
THROUGH

A CHRONICLE OF SEX, DRUGS, AND OPERA

RICKY IAN GORDON

Farrar, Straus and Giroux
New York

Farrar, Straus and Giroux
120 Broadway, New York 10271

Owing to limitations of space, all acknowledgments for permission to reprint previously published material can be found on pages 467–468.

Library of Congress Cataloging-in-Publication Data
Names: Gordon, Ricky Ian, author.
Title: Seeing through : a chronicle of sex, drugs, and opera /
Ricky Ian Gordon.
Description: First edition. | New York : Farrar, Straus and Giroux, 2024.
Identifiers: LCCN 2023057425 | ISBN 9780374605728 (hardcover)
Subjects: LCSH: Gordon, Ricky Ian. | Composers—United States—
Biography. | LCGFT: Autobiographies.
Classification: LCC ML410.G64465 A3 2024 | DDC 780.92 [B]—dc23/
eng/20240110
LC record available at https://lccn.loc.gov/2023057425

Our books may be purchased in bulk for promotional, educational, or business use. Please contact your local bookseller or the Macmillan Corporate and Premium Sales Department at 1-800-221-7945, extension 5442, or by email at MacmillanSpecialMarkets@macmillan.com.

www.fsgbooks.com
Follow us on social media at @fsgbooks

1 2 3 4 5 6 7 8 9 10

The names and identifying details of some persons described in this book have been changed.

To Kevin Doyle, who may not read it,

but has certainly had to live with me while I wrote it,

no small feat

And to Lucy,

who brought immeasurable joy into our lives for ten full years.

12/28/23.

The job of the living is to be seen through.

—BRENDA HILLMAN, "QUARTZ TRACTATE," FROM *DEATH TRACTATES*

Contents

SEEING THROUGH

There is a Native American adage that says there are two wolves inside you. You have to decide which one you are going to starve and which you are going to feed. From the very beginning, there have always been two stories of my life being written side by side. At the age of thirty-three, I knew I had a decision to make. My dream of being a composer and creating a meaningful body of work like all the great artists I admired was a big one. I knew I was going to either feed that wolf or lean toward the profligate I was becoming.

One of my stories is about a little boy looking for a father, with a button inside. When pressed, it says, *This person is going to make you feel complete, whole. They will fill the abyss in you. They will relieve you of the constant gnawing pain that makes you feel empty, unloved, and unsafe.* But there's another story: that if you're important—if you are doing something necessary and meaningful with your life—this triggers my feelings of unworthiness and confirms my fantasy that being necessary and meaningful has always been a clear, straight, easy line for you.

Of course, you were a good student; you read a lot. You always knew what you were going to do with your life. If you were a man, you loved women. You loved your father, and he loved you. You played baseball with your father, went fishing, climbed mountains, and hiked together. You went to classes, studied, did your homework, graduated, got a master's degree, dined with your family, and discussed with civility what was on your mind. You went to bed feeling full and satisfied. You were good with the world, and it was good with you. You felt comfortable in your body, even liked it. And you were probably fairly confident of what tomorrow would bring.

This has never been my experience. I have sat through countless meals where deadly secrets were eating at my brain like bees, making it impossible to communicate. I have been smothered by my insecurities. All during the meal I've imagined: How can I get you into bed? You might have been hypothesizing about all the theorems and solutions you've come up with, your studies, your rites and rituals, the body of knowledge that is yours. Every word was a dart, and each puncture was a further diminishment. If all the people I have sat across a table from knew how often I felt terrible about myself, how alienated, in their company, they would be shocked.

What has been keeping me alive? Music. Music was when my house was emptied of its smoldering anger, frustration, and fear, and it was when I was happy. Some of my most joyous memories were when Lorraine and Susan, the oldest of my three older sisters, would both get out their guitars and sing all kinds of folk songs by Pete Seeger, Dave Van Ronk, Joan Baez, the Red Clay Ramblers, the Weavers, Peter, Paul and Mary, the Kingston Trio, Phil Ochs, and, of course, Bob Dylan, whom Lorraine later shared a bottle of wine with when he was Robert Zimmerman down at the Bitter End. She said, "You knew he was going to be something." Music was doing what it was supposed to do, creating community, breaking down walls, melting hearts. My father, anomalously, would beam with pride like he loved his family, and his life. The sarcastic sneer would disappear from his face, the opposition to anything and everything, and no one fought or hated each other. He even seemed to either not comprehend or ignore the lyrics to the songs that often expressed everything he was opposed to. My mother's face would relax with the temporary abatement of potential mayhem, and the highly unusual feeling that all was well charged the particles and fell over the room like light snow. My father complained that he had moved his family out of the Bronx to get away from the city, and now all they ever wanted to do was get back into the city, but if they hadn't, he wouldn't have had these cascades of music, these beatific oases, in our house.

We had a piano, a Krakauer upright. At the age of five, after hearing my sister Lorraine practicing a sonatina by Clementi, I sat down and played the piece by ear, so I was sent for piano lessons with Mrs.

Fox. There were two piano teachers in Harbor Isle: Mrs. Fox, who was more for the beginners, and Mr. Chaikin, who was for more advanced students. It was pretty much assumed you would at some point graduate from Mrs. Fox to Mr. Chaikin, and I did.

Mrs. Fox slurped coffee loudly from a mug that never seemed to empty during the lesson. She dressed in beige cashmere, summer or winter, had beige skin, beige hair, and in some ways, you could say she looked like a beige shar-pei, except for the angry eczema on her hands that was always red and raw. Mr. Chaikin drank a shot of brandy before every lesson, which meant he always had a sort of intoxicating sweet breath.

One day my mother was taking me to pick up my sister Sheila, the youngest sister, from her piano lesson at Mrs. Fox's. I heard some crunchy, crispy chords moving around in unexpected ways like I had never heard before. Someone was playing a sonatina by Dmitry Kabalevsky, a twentieth-century Russian composer. I remember staring up into the light as if I were Jules Bastien-Lepage's Joan of Arc hearing voices. The music was saying something to me about who I was, what I was supposed to do with my life. I felt a calling . . .

Music is the cause of most of my joy in life, as well as much of my unhappiness. Sometimes it's a bed of nails, at others, a field of clouds.

Words, too. Poetry, art, people who make art, who suffer as I do, who feel as bad about themselves as I do, but still insist on making something out of it. Nothing in me is a straight line. I have always been a hodgepodge; an assemblage of qualities I thought I was supposed to have. But always hidden in any performance of myself—the masquerade—was the stronger impulse to make something beautiful.

This is the lens through which I am asking you to read this book and, by association, my life—a life that comes out of chaos.

Toni Morrison begins her Nobel lecture with "Once upon a time . . ." because in the end it's all about stories, isn't it, what we share with one another?

The explorers wanted to see what was out there beyond the horizon, across the ocean, or on the other side of the earth. Before it's too late, I want to see who I am, beyond the secret stories I've hidden out of shame for as long as I can remember. I could never have told this at any other time in history. People say anything now—except that suddenly you also have to be careful: not sexist, not racist, not triggering.

I don't worry about that.

I am tired of judging myself.

You can judge me instead.

For me, it turned out both wolves needed feeding.

Wolf Lake, New York, October 11, 2021

On March 12, 2020, I was in the Lincoln Center Theater rehearsing for an evening preview of *Intimate Apparel*, the opera I had written with the playwright Lynn Nottage, based on her play. It was the third week of previews. We were slated to open in less than two weeks. The experience was both exciting and dispiriting. Exciting, because watching the show evolve under the stewardship of our director, Bart Sher, and our conductor, Steven Osgood, was deeply fulfilling; dispiriting, because the first cases of coronavirus started appearing in New York that January, when another opera I wrote, *Ellen West*, based on the poem by Frank Bidart, was being performed as part of the Prototype Festival in Brooklyn.

The virus didn't affect *Ellen West*. The disease still seemed far away, in a place called Wuhan, in China. But now, in March, the news was getting worse by the day. *Intimate Apparel* was sold out, but fewer and fewer people were actually showing up at the theater. I felt pathetic. I couldn't even fill a three-hundred-seat theater, but the circumstances were beyond my control.

As we rehearsed, every theater in New York started shutting down. We were practically last. There was talk about maybe keeping us open because of the smaller size of the venue, but I didn't want that. I envisioned a happy, healthy audience, not a dwindling one, masked and afraid. New York audiences are difficult enough without a global pandemic hanging over a production.

Finally, they shut us down too. We filmed the audience-less evening performance as a record for when we were back in the theater. We were proud of what we had made and excited to reconvene for the projected reopening date, April 23. Kevin and I packed up Lucy, our little rescue dog, and drove to our house on Wolf Lake in Sullivan County. Soon enough, it was clear, we were in an indefinite parenthesis; the projected reopening wasn't going to happen. Facing a great gap of unstructured time, a nightmare for my inner addict, I panicked. I decided to start a writing group. I wanted to take a break from music, explore other parts of myself, and writing felt like where I wanted to go, but I needed an incentive, an imperative to get anything done. I talked to my friend the poet Marie Howe, who thought it was a great idea. So, I made some calls.

In 1991, the writer/director Tina Landau and I were in Philadelphia, creating *States of Independence*, a musical about American history. One night, in my hotel room, Marty Moran, a cast member, and I were discussing embarking on separate journeys about a similar experience. Marty had been in a sexual relationship with a priest that started when he was underage. I had had several sexual encounters with older men starting from about the age of ten to the age of seventeen but never thought of them as damaging, feeling as if I instigated them, until I realized they were playing themselves out in my life in destructive ways.

When we got back to New York, Marty and I started attending a men's group at St. Luke's Hospital. Out of that work, Marty wrote a successful one-man show and book, *The Tricky Part*.

Meanwhile, I was not ready to deal with whatever the ramifications of what had happened to me were.

Twenty years later, my friend David Brunetti, seeing how I was struggling, in and out of sex and romance addiction meetings, making the same mistakes over and over again, told me about a program at St. Luke's. I went for an intake, not even remembering I had been there twenty years before with Marty.

The group consisted of me and five other men, as well as two therapists, Rommell and Louise. First, we were asked to tell our stories and bring photographs of ourselves at or near the age when whatever happened that led us to this group. When it was my turn, I cried uncontrollably.

What made me erupt that way? Whom was I crying for? A boy

looking for a father he thought he was finding in older heterosexual men. Perhaps the times and the prevalence of drugs precipitated these men having sex with me. Each encounter was overwhelming, unbelievably exciting, and devastating afterward, because they could not provide what I was looking for. I wanted more; I wanted them to love me. I wanted them for myself, but they had wives or girlfriends, and I felt gutted and alone.

I became a stalker of things I couldn't have, prizes bad for me to win. Each time, I felt lucky to obtain them, and then empty, hungry to either repeat those experiences or replicate them. Nothing excited me unless it was the impossible reward of a practically fruitless search.

After the group ended, I knew I needed to continue with the work. Louise called it abuse; she said I was victimized, even raped, and needed to see it that way, but I can't. I want them all back, everyone who was incapable of giving me what I needed. I want their love, their bodies. I want to continue attempting to win what I cannot have. Those men from the past are the source of all my fantasies, and I still see myself as the seducer, the perpetrator, though I was fifteen years old, or younger.

One day, I called Louise to ask her if she would start her own open-ended men's group. In that group, I started putting things together for myself. Eventually, I wanted to write about all the coils I unwound in it. After the whole world entered quarantine, and my writing group began to meet every Friday afternoon, the writing began to emerge.

The original writing group included Marie Howe, Sophie Cabot Black, Nick Flynn, Michael Klein, Donna Masini, Richard McCann, Marty Moran, Victoria Redel, and Royce Vavrek. Nick invited his friend Vievee Francis, and Marie invited the Irish poet Pádraig Ó Tuama, and they both joined. Richard McCann, who was working on a memoir about his liver transplant twenty years earlier, got sick and passed away while he was in the group. We were grateful to have had his avuncular warmth and shimmering brilliance for almost a year, and heartbroken when he died.

I knew from the start that what most excited me was allowing myself to be known and to say things I had never said before. It seemed like an instant excavation or exorcism. My first topics, because of the heat and the intensity with which they burned in me, were the sexual encounters. After so much time in my men's group, I knew more than I ever had about how those encounters affected me.

Of course, because we are all born into different environments, I started writing about my family. Sometimes I wrote poems and lyrics instead of prose—some, a reaction to what was happening in the world, and some about specific things that were coming up from the process of writing every day, even though my writing group likes to remind me that poems are not necessarily about "something," that more than anything they're about their "aboutness."

I started writing about the things I love and things I don't: music, foreign films, art, theater, my spiritual practice, recovery, and my body, which has taken up so much space in my head for as long as I can remember—this rental, which is only temporary, yet I seem incapable of remembering that.

Music, sex, and addiction have intersected or collided in my life, catalysts for confusion, beauty, and restlessness, which I hope I have been able to capture in these pages.

PART I

LONG ISLAND

221 Lincoln Avenue, Harbor Isle, Island Park, Long Island

I was born on May 15, 1956, after our name was anglicized from Goldenberg to Gordon, and named after Humphrey Bogart's character in *Casablanca*, my mother's favorite movie. I was two weeks late and weighed eight pounds, eleven ounces. My mother says pushing me out fixed her bad back. She was stooped every morning of my life, until the first jolts of coffee bolted her upright; before I was born, she had to be in traction for weeks in the hospital in order to stand straight.

In those early days of childhood, my mother would always say "Go out and play" after breakfast. On the little island where we lived, there was all kinds of trouble you could get into: stealing, vandalizing, throwing firecrackers, especially cherry bombs in mailboxes, egging, toilet papering, or climbing the scaffolding of new houses being built. But mostly, it was just playing, swinging on swings, jumping rope, swimming, the kind of fun you can have when you're young, brushing your hand along the tops of hedges while you're skipping and singing some stupid song you made up.

Running, playing "red light, green light, one, two, three," or tag, or hide-and-seek, saying obnoxiously, "I know you are but what am I," as a retort to anyone who called you something you didn't like, which often got me pummeled, or riding your bike up and down the street screaming, "No hands!" as if anyone cared. But for me, there was always an invisible audience. I felt I was always being filmed, because I was, no doubt, captivating.

At lunchtime I'd hear my mother's voice over everything, and from anywhere, calling my name with its special lilt. "Riiiiick," she'd call, "Riiiiiick," and I'd run home to eat. Sometimes my father was home for lunch eating the things my mother picked up from her Polish and

Russian parents, like bananas or blueberries with sour cream and sprinkled sugar, or pickled herring, or sardines in a salad, or blintzes, or stuffed cabbage, always with white bread and unsalted whipped butter. I didn't care that much about food then, amazing, considering how it lives with authority in my psyche even today.

After lunch, I'd stay out until I heard my mother's call again, and then I'd run home for dinner. You didn't hear about kids being kidnapped, abused, raped, or cut up then. The world felt safer. We didn't have "playdates" or get chauffeured around from here to there. We walked to school, we walked home from the train station, we walked everywhere. My mother always walked to town and back again with at least two full shopping bags over her shoulder. People stopped to offer her a ride, but she wouldn't take it. Walking helped her back, she said, and she was very proud of her comely legs.

When she was little, a boy in school pulled out my mother's chair as she was about to sit, making her fall, which damaged her back. She didn't get a driver's license until she was in her midforties. Her driving lessons began with my father, a catastrophe, given his patience and diplomacy. To keep a divorce at bay, she went to driving school.

She always looked too short for her light blue Chevy Nova, half her head peering out from behind the wheel like a twitching blackbird. But she was driving, even picking us up sometimes if we were trapped in the snow or something. She always drove too slowly, and people always honked at her or gave her the finger, but she didn't care. She probably would have been happier having a spinal tap than driving, but she had to do something to ease her sense of entrapment and need for autonomy. She had given up a lot for this life as wife and mother, perhaps too much, and the loss always seemed to encroach on her, like a tsunami that would wash her away. She at least *seemed* to feel freer once she could drive.

Anyway, you just went out until you came home, and what you did out there was your own business, and no one asked. Still, sometimes what you did had to come out, like when I was muzzled and tied to a tree and couldn't get loose. My mother heard my muffled screams a few yards over, so I had to tell her "it was a Cowboys and Indians game" gone awry, but usually it wasn't anything that dire.

Another time, at the Radcliffe Road school, when the gym was open for recreation, the parallel bars weren't adjusted properly and fell on my thumb, nearly cutting it off. I still have a huge scar straight across it. Even then I knew, on Monday morning, when Mr. Silverstein took my hand, looked into my eyes, and kissed my boo-boo, there was something not right about it.

Back to the subject of safety, someone might have said, "Don't take candy from strangers," but there was nothing menacing about it, and besides, I certainly would have taken candy because I really liked candy. But if I had to imagine in my own childhood the things happening to children nowadays, I never would have left my room. Certain "crises," like stepping on glass in the water at the beach and shrieking when the doctor sewed up my toe or getting my tonsils out at nine and everyone saying it would be fun because I would get to eat all the ice cream I could ever want, didn't make me feel unsafe in the world. But no one told me how painful something could be, or how you wouldn't even want one bite of ice cream because swallowing it felt like swallowing frozen razor blades.

My first memory is my mother washing me in a cement sink in the laundry room. The cement is coarse and prickly and harsh against my skin. This bath usually happens right after the beach and I have sand everywhere, including up my butt, and the whole thing feels like an alien invasion. Her bejeweled hands move quickly and have a life of acute nervousness all their own. My father looms a few feet behind her, a shadow of foreboding: the other. And it was that shadow, my father, who awakened an overpowering urge in me when I was allowed to go up to my parents' room and watch TV next to their bed—*Davey and Goliath, Romper Room, Just Around the Corner*—even if they were sleeping, which they usually were.

The urge to see, to touch, what was between my father's legs under the covers took over. I don't think I was even old enough to have an erection, so I don't exactly know how arousal played itself out. But that feeling of thousands of small animals running around in every direction in my chest as I stared at his genitals with the fascination an explorer might have had upon first seeing Niagara Falls, my mother's naked body barely occurring as a gray shape facing east, was impossible not to want to pursue. I don't know if I thought what I was doing was wrong, yet instinctively I knew I couldn't risk getting caught. There was immense danger doing this, but I absolutely had to do it.

Our house was a panoply of feminine energy with breasts and vaginas abounding. My sisters were strong personalities, well defined, mercurial. And so was my mother, Eve, the former borscht belt singer and comedian, for whom we were now the audience. Her first language was Yiddish. She could be a kibitzer, telling dirty jokes, gossiping, singing, and even dancing. It was like having Fanny Brice for a mother. If there is truth to the idea that inside the clown is crying, it was evidenced, in my mother's case, because, though she was deeply funny, there was something discomfiting about being witness to her comedy.

The humor could feel like a cover for something tragic in the deepest chamber of her heart. Supposing we are all reincarnated and traveling this long forever through countless lifetimes together, the moment I first heard my mother sing, I recognized her. Wherever she had been, I had been there, too. Her voice was the ancient air on which our destinies floated, the low hum of the mourning dove.

My mother became genuine when she sang. It was in her voice where you heard the truth, the sadness, the anger, the oppression, a kind of old-world Yiddish cry erupting from her singing like the cry of all Jewish people, both startling and disarming. Her singing reflected collective memory. It was the real deal—inviolable; you were in the presence of something holy. It was always a surprise for those who knew her only as someone funny, because singing was, in a way, the antithesis of her external personality. It was not funny; it was truth.

There was nothing in the least bit amateur about my mother's singing. Her voice was a lovely instrument, beautifully expressive. She had an ability to interpret and extemporize with it—sometimes, all of a sudden, talking a line with a cry in her voice, her unique phrasing, her taking a note up if she felt like it or repeating something for emphasis. She was an artist through and through. Singing was more honest than talking for her. She is the reason so much of the music I write is for the voice. It is also the reason that later on in her life, when reflux ground her singing voice to a halt, it was clear she felt like half a person.

My mother won a singing contest in Central Park singing "Indian Love Call" when she was fifteen. The great doyenne of the Catskill Mountains, Jennie Grossinger, who was in the audience, brought her up to Grossinger's with every intention of making her a star. Mom, or Eve Saunders, as she called herself, would come out in a tight red dress hugging all the right places of a well-developed, exceedingly attractive, charismatic young woman and sing about how hot she was. Then two comedians would come out from both sides of the stage and spray her with seltzer. "They put out the fire!" she loved to exclaim. She'd stand there all wet, which only accentuated her curves, giving her the va-va-va-voom she was clearly after.

Once she had them howling with laughter, my mother would sing with a blazing force, a turnaround in tone that was almost frightening, songs like "When a Gypsy Makes His Violin Cry" and "Take Me in Your Arms," and the laughter would give way to sobs. One of my mother's sheer instincts was knowing how to work a room. She knew she was a star.

My mother was born in Harlem in 1920, the youngest of four siblings, with brothers Sidney, Louis, and Buddy Samberg. Buddy, the one who had dragged her along to Central Park, was my mother's partner in crime, playing the guitar and crooning alongside her, but he knew he couldn't compete. Buddy had charm and talent—a poor man's Bing Crosby—but my mother had the heat and charisma of an acetylene torch. Later, Buddy made a living performing in a supper club in New Jersey, but was never entirely fulfilled or satisfied. Mom's brother Louis played the spoons fantastically, clickety-clacking them like a veteran vaudevillian. He played them at weddings, Bar Mitzvahs, even funerals. It didn't matter whether the occasion was solemn or boisterous, Louis played the spoons with an expression on his face that made him look like a more handsome Jimmy Durante.

Sid, the brother who was most sincere and most like my mother, died young. He was working on the subway tracks for the Metropolitan Transportation Authority when he started complaining that he was seeing double but put off getting his eyes checked. When a train came rushing toward him one day, he thought he was getting out of the way, but he actually moved straight into it.

Sid was my favorite uncle, because, as with my mother, I recognized him from a previous life. I saw love flying from his eyes at me like starlings. I laughed like a baby, only wanted to be around *him* when he visited. He was soulful, always seeming to get me. One of the greatest and most influential gifts of my life was the *Porgy and Bess* score Sid gave me. He found it on the subway. It was an unreturned library book. I learned every note of it.

In my twenties, I went to see Barbara Stabiner, a clairvoyant on Long Island. She told me that my mother had been a star in many lifetimes, and the reason it was relatively easy for her to give it up was that she *knew* she had done it before and it was time to master another scenario: a domestic one, being a mother and a wife. At one point (this is where you might throw this book across the room), the room got cold, and Barbara said, "Ohhh, we have a visitor." She said it was Mozart, and he had a message for me.

He said, "You can want to be a genius in this life, but you have to want to be a human being as well. You cannot forgo life in the pursuit of your work; it will come back to you." He continued, "Strive to be as good at being human as you are at being an artist." I will admit I rolled my eyes, but he made enormous sense. He said he was working on the human part where he was, growing in *all* directions, ignoring his "Mozart" incarnation.

Around this time, I had discovered numerology, and Barbara said I was surrounded by numbers. I said, "That's funny, I was just thinking of studying numerology because of a book I picked up last night," but she shook her head and said, "No, honey, you don't need to study it;

you already know it." We are all intuitive, right? Sometimes we find vehicles for our intuitiveness. When I look at people's numbers, I see and feel things that together create a map or a graph of that person for me, and I trust it all the more because of what Barbara said.

Barbara told me my father could have killed someone and, if not for my mother, would have. And finally, she said Uncle Sid was my guardian angel.

My mother and I were extremely close. No matter what I did, she thought I was a genius. Her relationships with my sisters were more complicated because, like her, they were women, and all the competitiveness that comes with that caused enormous friction in my family. My sisters solidly rejected my mother's acceptance of what they perceived as cowardice, powerlessness, and victimhood in her marriage.

One of my favorite things was watching the Academy Awards with my mother. She always remarked on who was up in weight that year, or down, Liz being the most frequent recipient. "She looks good," she'd say, nodding her head in approval, with the solemnity and pride one might affect at an inauguration. "Good for her. She lost weight."

Or she would say, "She looks heavy," the worst indictment you could utter, shaking her head, privately contemplating the difficulties Liz faced—the ins and outs about which she knew so much from movie magazines like *Photoplay* and *Modern Screen*. She always seemed to know when Liz and Dick were together or separated, speaking about their relationship as if they were dear friends she was always in a state of perpetual empathy for.

She loved the clothes, and she would always remark on the deformities whispered about in Hollywood. One such chestnut concerned the unfortunate Myrna Loy. "Bad legs," she'd say pityingly. "Thick ankles, that's why she always wears pants. You never see her legs in a movie, do you?" I didn't really know who Myrna Loy was, though I'd shake my head no, because I wanted to be in on it. But my mother could also explode like the top off a pressure cooker. Then she was the furthest thing from funny you could possibly imagine. These episodes involved smashing plates, running away from home, or sobbing hysterically, and they were almost always about having given up her singing career, or having four children with no help, or her marriage to a maniac.

My father was the second child of four, born in 1919. There was Aunt Sylvia, the imperious oldest, who liked to say things like "Rrricky, I wouldn't get into bed with him if he were the last white man alive"; my father; Aunt Blanche, the gym teacher; and Uncle Freddie, the jeweler. Freddie, born blond-haired and blue-eyed, which, in a Jewish family, is like being born with a crown, a scepter, and gold running through your veins, was very handsome and consequently treated like a prince. My grandmother was hard on my father, overwhelming him with expectations. During the Depression, he sold apples on the street to help her.

He had enormous native intelligence and discipline combined with an obsessive curiosity, but because of the exigencies of the times he missed education altogether. After the Depression there was the war, robbing six years from his youth.

Soon after my parents were married, before he went overseas, my mother went down to visit my father at Fort Benning, in Georgia. Because of his voracious appetite, they had sex so many times that she was sore and tired. He wanted to go at it again, but my mother tearfully told him, "I can't, Sam, I'm exhausted." He threw a tantrum so fierce she realized she would have to either leave him or never say no to him again. Because she chose the latter, my sisters and I grew up in a climate of intense sexuality—an atmosphere of forced complicity.

My father was stationed in Greenland during World War II. He said it was so boring that every night someone would have to be on twenty-four-hour patrol to prevent men from going out into the snow and freezing themselves to death, which, he said, was just like going to sleep. He made it sound so easy, even pleasant; I always keep freezing to death as my back pocket plan should things not work out. After Greenland, my father was sent to Europe.

After the war, because of all the nights in France his unit had to sleep outside on frozen ground, my father had to have surgery to remove a cyst at the base of his spine that had grown large and excruciatingly painful.

He did not leave the army honorably. He witnessed a superior officer making a virulent anti-Semitic remark to a private and, losing his temper, punched the officer in the face, doing considerable damage. He was dishonorably discharged. So, by the time my father came back from Europe to start a life and a family, he was a rage-filled mass of disappointments and a walking powder keg.

When he was stationed in France, my father was Staff Sergeant Samuel Goldenberg. He changed our name after the war to make it sound less Jewish because given the anti-Semitism at that time it was almost impossible to start a business that wasn't in the garment industry. My father's father, Papa Joe, for instance, was a furrier, making jackets, stoles, muffs, and hats for all the women in the family. But my father wasn't interested in fur. He wanted to be an electrician. Electrical work was considered extremely dangerous, and few wanted to take the risks, so you were almost guaranteed to make a living.

My father's pugnaciousness, combined with his strength and zero impulse control, was lethal. Outside the family, when others would find him fascinating and charming, or sexy and appealing, we crouched in horror over the part of the story they were missing. I think my father felt we were lucky enough just to be born. He was barely clothed and fed as a boy, so if we wanted more, we didn't deserve it. Why should we have what he didn't have? We should just shut the fuck up.

He was the antithesis of what a Jewish father was supposed to be— fostering the education of his children, proud of their learning and accomplishments, protective and paternal. He never even looked at a report card, didn't know our birthdays, never defended us, ignoring the neighborhood bullies, and basically left the parenting to our mother.

My father was easily threatened, so when it was obvious that one of his children might be advancing beyond him intellectually, he became jealous and enraged. My sister Susan seems to have been born brilliant, which made her electrifying in my eyes. But she lorded her intelligence over my father like a cudgel as revenge against his tyranny.

The tension of their not meeting until she was two, because he left my mother pregnant to go to war, and his being nothing but an intruder upon her happiness, meant they were always a land mine waiting to be detonated. The first thing she ever said to him was, "Don't you touch my mommy's pajamas."

Lorraine, a breech baby whose eyes were badly damaged, making her half-blind from a careless forceps birth, came into the world volatile and combative. She would say anything to anyone, and her relationship with my father was like setting off a hydrogen bomb.

Sheila, catching wind early that arguing and having a strong personality in our family brought you no good, shut up like a clam, suffering in silence with a never-ending array of stomach troubles that brought her in and out of hospitals and a lifetime supply of some horrible-tasting emerald-green medicine.

My mother's way of calming my father down was to have sex with him. They had sex day and night. You could always hear them: the breathing, the kissing. I walked in on them because there was no door to their bedroom. I don't know exactly what I saw, but I think it was a blow job, and that was enough to make me bolt from the room.

When I was born, my parents, after three daughters, had a son, momentous in a Jewish family. My father finally had a mirror. But being claimed and raised by all the females, I might as well have been a daughter as far as he was concerned, only more disappointing for dousing his fantasy about having a friend, an assistant, and even a confidant in the harem-like world he created.

When my father came home from work, I would run down the stairs, jumping into his arms and kissing him. He seemed happy to be greeted this way, until the day he recoiled, saying, "We don't do that anymore." His sudden inquiries into why I didn't have more friends who were boys precipitated his making me join Little League, where I was hit in the eye and practically blinded by a line drive during the first game. In an effort to turn me into a man, he took me fishing, but the loudness of the motor made me cry, and the smell of the fish and the motion of the water made me throw up, so that was a failed mission.

He would also bring me to work with him as soon as I was old enough to work. It might mean brushing rust off a huge shed with a metal brush, painting it first with a coat of Rust-Oleum and then with a coat of semigloss protective paint. He'd leave you to it, occasionally coming out to scream at you and tell you how badly you were doing it. He'd have me organize thousands of oily metal things, things he had pilfered from various demolition jobs—screws, nuts, bolts, sockets, switches—into a million metal compartments, which I found as interesting as Bartleby the Scrivener found the Dead Letter Office.

My father brought me to work at Mr. Kirchner's one day, a client who lived in a huge house in Great Neck, Long Island. At lunchtime, Mr. Kirchner let me play his huge grand piano. Hearing me, he yelled at my father for making me work with him rather than letting me spend my days making music. But my father would have none of it. It was only when I started making a name for myself as a composer that he started being proud of what I did.

When my father was in the house, there was always a cloud of danger or possible cataclysm. There were holes kicked through every door in the house. He could only half smile—one half signaling how stupid and disappointing you were and the other half waiting for you to prove him right. He would test you, knowing you wouldn't know the answer, so he could make you feel bad about yourself when you had the wrong answer.

One frequent test was sending you into the garage, *his* domain, stuffed to the gills with tools and all kinds of greasy smelly things, and asking you to bring something back, usually something you knew you'd never be able to identify but wouldn't dare ask for further information. "Go get me the monkey wrench." So, you'd go to the garage not knowing what you were looking for. After not being able to find anything looking remotely like a monkey, you'd go back empty-handed for the same humiliation over and over again. Sometimes he'd send you back again, saying, "Get me the chisel," with just enough description for you to bring back something similar but wrong. These little absurdist plays always had the same ending.

My father decided he wanted the bulkhead at the boatyard shored up with a mountainous pile of cinder blocks. Have you ever lifted a cinder block? When it's a six-foot pile of them, it is not a task to look forward to. On the Saturday I was supposed to do this, I told my father, "I don't feel well," and moped around as if I had consumption. I thought he bought it and that was that. I had no idea of the storm brewing.

At around 1:45, Peter called to tell me the Texaco radio broadcast of the Metropolitan Opera was about to start and it was one of our favorite operas of all time, Engelbert Humperdinck's *Hansel and Gretel*, with Frederica von Stade and Judith Blegen.

I met Peter Randsman one day, after his sister, Nancy, seeing how he was taunted on the bus, beach, and basically everywhere, sought counsel with my sister Sheila, knowing Sheila was friends with a lot of the taunters, and Sheila suggested, since Peter and I had the same problem (constant torment and an unstable relationship with what it meant to be masculine), we should be friends. Peter came looking for me one day and found me jumping rope behind Debby Sasso's house. He was so impressed with my sheer virtuosity at double Dutch and captivated by my penny loafers with actual pennies in them that he befriended me then and there.

Everyone needs a partner in crime. Peter was mine. When we met, dual lightbulbs went off. It wasn't just the as yet unknown shared sexuality that was the key; it was the sense that this person inhabited the same universe as you, as no one before ever had. With Peter, I finally had one person with whom I could stop hiding, who knew what it was to skulk the corners to avoid getting eviscerated. We laughed the laughter of the disenfranchised from the tender margins of outcast childhoods. His light has not dimmed in my life. Peter was God's gift to me so I could survive childhood.

Peter and I knew the shame and the fear of being the ones singled out in gym class who couldn't shoot a basket, or make it up the ropes, or do a push-up, or a chin-up, or a lap around the football field. Accordingly, at certain points in our burgeoning adulthoods, we transformed ourselves into musclemen, making up for lost time, becoming almost cliché-like in our masculinity. We became successful in our adulthoods because success was just an unexplored frontier; we already knew what it was like to lose.

Peter could not be woken up before 10:30 in the morning on weekends, which for me was like 4:00 in the afternoon. I would sit by the telephone, biting my nails, waiting for the exact moment I could call him to see what kind of trouble we could get into that day.

We would go to each other's piano lessons at Mrs. Fox's. One day, Peter was having his piano lesson and I was sitting on the couch by the window next to a bookcase. I randomly pulled a book off the shelf, which seemed to have light streaming and smoke billowing behind it, right out of a Harry Potter movie. It could have been called *The Secrets of the Universe*, or *Magical Powers and Wizardry*, but it was called *The Victor Book of the Opera*. It was filled with descriptions of various operas, at least a hundred, their plots delineated by acts, and for each one a photo from a production at the Metropolitan Opera, including those great pictures from Wagner's *Ring of the Nibelung*, where Brünnhilde always wears a breastplate and a helmet with horns. I look at it now, and I don't know what it was that so transfixed me, but I was a different person within the hour. My axis had shifted. The tectonic plates of what my life was supposed to be were altered radically, so naturally I think I was accessing a past life and no further explanation is necessary. When Peter's lesson was over, Mrs. Fox, seeing how hypnotized I was, gave me the book.

Peter, though a year older than me, admired and was influenced by me, perhaps because of the well-known sophistication of my dazzling sisters, my scary and imposing father, and my sexpot charismatic mother. The Gordon family had not yet entered the realm of scandal and destruction. It would be years before Susan became an addict, Lorraine, agoraphobic, before Sheila's first marriage disintegrated, sending her into a mental breakdown it would take her at least a decade to climb out of. I had yet to be torn too soon from the cocoon of my sexual innocence. My smoking, drinking, and taking drugs had yet to begin, and there was as yet no catastrophic acid trip.

Peter was familiar with the concept of opera, his aunt Betty being an aficionado, so immediately he told her of his new interest. This fascination quickly turned into an obsession, changing us radically. Sheila and Patrick, her high school sweetheart and soon-to-be husband, took Peter and me to our first opera, *Il trovatore*, at the Amato Opera, a tiny little opera company on the Bowery where they performed in a theater the size of a living room, with piano accompaniment only. The singers either had not yet emerged and were singing for exposure or were past their prime and hanging on for dear life. *Il trovatore* was a good first opera, because it prepared you for a lot of what you could expect quite often in the world of opera, great music, great singing, and dumb, implausible stories in another language.

To this day, Peter and I and our friend Arthur Levy, another childhood opera fanatic we met on the standing-room line, who grew up in Brooklyn, can talk for endless hours about voices: whose bottom is rich, whose middle is foggy, who is losing their top, who flats on any notes above the staff, who has the best pianissimi (Montserrat Caballé), who sounds blousy, who is too fat, too skinny, sexy onstage, can act, can't act, whose voice is steely, or dusky, or clarion, whose recording of *Turandot* is the best, who is the best mezzo. The names resounding through our heads when we were young were names like Leontyne Price, Victoria de los Ángeles, Birgit Nilsson, Franco Corelli, Mario Del Monaco, Joan Sutherland, Robert Merrill, Maria Callas, Zinka Milanov, Anna Moffo, Beverly Sills. These were the heroes and heroines of our youth.

I was struggling to find the station on my boom box, my treasured Bar Mitzvah present, when my father, apparently angrier than he let on about my feigning illness to avoid shoring up the bulkhead with the cinder blocks, burst into the room, his face so red and swollen he looked as though Medusa's snakes had overtaken him. He screamed, throwing me against the bookshelves, and looked as if he were about to have a stroke. My mother ran in to try to stop him because this was no ordinary anger; this was an episode of whatever psychological disease he had that was undiagnosed and unmedicated. He started screaming at my mother, too, and I was afraid he was going to kill us both. Peter was still on the phone, and Milton Cross was just beginning to introduce the opera, but I ran out of the house and hitchhiked to Sheila's apartment in Freeport. If she wasn't home, I could climb in the window, since she lived on the first floor and always left the window unlocked for me. I was never going home again. But after a few days of smoking pot, taking quaaludes, and drinking, I had to.

When I walked into the boatyard, no one was there, but next to the phone was a note from my mother: "Don't worry about apologizing, just get those cinder blocks into the water, and all will be forgotten." So, I just had to drop each fifty-pound cinder block into the water against the bulkhead until my arms felt as if they were going to break off and my hands were raw, red, and blistered. I have never heard *Hansel and Gretel* in the same way again.

There was no entry point for me into my father. When he took me to Rockaways' Playland on a night my mother was playing canasta so we could get out of her hair, I got sick after two rides. We went through the Man on the Moon, some weird amusement that was supposed to feel as if you were walking without gravity, but it was right after the Tilt-A-Whirl spun us around like the spin cycle in a washing machine, and I threw up all over the place. Immediately, we had to leave. My father could hardly manage one hiccup in the evening, much less two. He lacked the instinct to nurture. His scorn was palpable, as was my embarrassment.

Nothing about me seemed to please him. So just as my mother seemed to put all trepidation behind her when she was in bed with him, I, having interpreted that as the solution to getting along with him, wanted to have sex with him. Clearly, sex was the only way to win my father's love. My solution made sense to me. Having sex with my father would have meant having a father I could love who loved me in the only decipherable demonstration of love I (and he) understood. After forty years of therapy, I have, at least partially, begun to understand that my fantasy of having sex with my father had to do with trying to have a relationship with an intensely cold and rejecting man who terrified me. In my skewed little mind, which was clicking madly at every moment, I was trying to take in whatever information I could about how people loved one another, which in my house meant having sex with them.

Seeing my father naked in the house was what I wanted to see more than anything. When he was lying around after breaking his foot, and the blanket was not quite covering him, I stood transfixed where he couldn't see me, frozen and fascinated with desire. A testicle would fall out from behind the blanket, or the tip of his penis with its Cyclops eye. I saw my father's penis as a tap, or a breast, and it was his milk I wanted. That's how I would absorb him, digest him, become him, or at least become a man.

I drilled a hole in the hall closet adjoining the bathroom to spy on him, thinking it would be like a magnifying glass or a camera, but the hole I'd made was so small I could barely even make out the light. I would go through his underwear drawer when no one was home and put on his athletic supporter. The feeling of whatever he had wrapped around his penis and testicles surrounding mine was intoxicating, erotic in a way that folded me into the moment like a gigantic wave.

A Rendezvous was an annual summer event. A bunch of families would meet in their boats, tie up and anchor together for a few days, usually about a quarter mile from the boggy shore, and create their own little island. I remember it being off Short Beach on the North Shore near Smithtown. Coolers were filled with sandwiches, chips, cookies, fruit, beers, sodas, usually a bottle or two of scotch because my dad thought beer was a goyish drink, and off we went into our uncertain futures. It was a two-and-a-half-hour boat ride to get there, and I always sat on the front of the boat holding on to the railing and screeching when I got splashed. I was usually happy at the beginning of the trip. For the adults it involved a lot of sitting around eating, talking, and drinking, and for the kids, endless water activity.

I remember once being in the water about twenty feet from the boat and staring up at my father as if he were a sun god while my hand was down my bathing suit.

One day, around twilight, there was a full moon, so the tide was getting high. It was a beautiful scene, but I didn't think about the moon then, and we were already into the second half of the weekend, when I was no longer having fun. Marquis de Maximilian the Third, our Welsh corgi, needed to poop, so my father sent me with the dog to shore in the rowboat.

This was fine, except for one little thing: I didn't know how to row. I might have learned something about rowing at Camp Lenape, but it was not coming back to me now as the tide was pulling Max and me out to sea. My father's hysterical and insane screaming of perfectly useless directions on top of my mother's helpless gasps were becoming dimmer and dimmer the farther out the boat took us.

As general panic took over the Rendezvous, my father ripped off his clothes, dove into the water, and started swimming madly toward the rowboat. Everyone was watching from their boats. By the time he reached us, he was alternately spitting the water from his mouth and shouting words like "moron" and "idiot." Max's little stub of a tail was wildly wagging with delight at all the excitement, and unlike me he seemed genuinely happy to see my father.

As soon as he got himself into the rowboat, almost capsizing it and drowning us, I jumped out and swam to shore. I hung out in the sand marshes with the green flies for a long time, grinding my teeth and praying to God to kill my father. When I eventually swam back to the Rendezvous, I wouldn't speak to anyone, including my mother, my only ally. For the rest of the weekend, my dad and I were cautious, circling each other like angry cats.

I had no recollection of my father telling me to put my bike on the side of the house, but apparently he did, because from out of nowhere he ran out of the house, picked me up by my ear with one hand and the bike with the other while screaming at the top of his lungs, *"What did I tell you about this bike?!"* Once he smashed the bicycle down on the side of the house, wherever he dreamed he told me I was supposed to have put it, I fled from him because, among other things, being lifted by your ear hurts. He chased me into the house, and while my mother and sisters shouted "No!" they were helpless to save me. I lay down on the bed while he punched me in between my flailing legs, trying to kill me.

Everything my father liked, I didn't: cowboy movies, James Bond movies, adventure movies, or raw clams. I hated going to synagogue. Wherever he wanted to be, I didn't. And yet I dreamed of him getting on top of me, penetrating me, kissing me. I am aware how aberrant this may seem, but I was a child with an addled mind trying to make sense of my world and my place in it. Can something be construed as obscene if it is simply the body speaking from a mind that is not fully formed?

What started as a fantasy about my father later became a fantasy about Sheila's husband, Patrick. Patrick was Sheila's high school sweetheart. He was funny and mischievous but had a deep serious side I interpreted as poetic.

Once he took speed and stayed up all night doing an incredibly accurate drawing of Bob Dylan from the album cover of *The Times They Are A-changin'*. Another time, he assembled an assortment of pipes, screws, nuts, and bolts he swiped from his steam-fitting job at the Twin Towers, making me a sculpture that lived somewhere between the universe of Pablo Picasso and Louise Nevelson. He spray-painted it black, and it looked like both a robot and a satyr. It may be the most beautiful gift anyone ever gave me. It was lost or misplaced in the sea of my aimless moving, and I would do anything to get it back. I identified with Sheila loving Patrick because I loved him, too, at least as much as she did.

Patrick was nice to me, and my father wasn't. He was funny and lighthearted, and I would cry if I couldn't be with him, with them, as if I were part of their couple. He was, without a doubt, my first hero. I had a dream one night that I was literally drinking from his penis, suckling it like a nipple. But what made it different from the fantasy about my father was that the milk was bountiful, overflowing. And for the first time in my life, I felt full in a way I never had before. I felt such serenity that I never forgot it. It became fixed in my head as a kind of love I had never felt before.

Straight men, older or younger than me, respected or not, even the most impoverished, stand where my father stood, have something I never felt I had: power and cachet. I always feel smaller and weaker than them. Consequently, I have always laid enormous weight on my "talent," feeling it is the only thing about me that will get me love.

When I was fourteen, I saw the movie *The Boys in the Band*. It's hard to describe what I felt seeing that movie, having had no idea what the movie was about beforehand. If I had seen it yesterday, perhaps I could assimilate all the sadness, self-hatred, and loneliness the movie addresses and how out-of-date it feels. But in the time period the movie takes place in, everyone was closeted and spoke in code. You were either a "fem" or a "butch," and the roles were clear. Watching the movie, I wanted to see someone have sex with the hustler Emory bought Howard for his birthday. I didn't know how gay life played out among older men. All I knew was that being gay was dangerous, which I already knew firsthand because I was still trying not to get beaten up all the time for being effeminate.

I wasn't attracted at all to the insecure, frightened gay men I saw on-screen. I desired the men like my father. That was the wound I was trying to heal. I was looking for the opposite of a mirror. I started getting drunk in bars and having sex with older men when I was fifteen. So, coming out wasn't happy for me. What was I "coming out" to?

Gerard Shaeffer is older than I am. He is from Island Park, over the bridge, which means he is Catholic. I live in Harbor Isle, which is primarily Jewish. A lot of people, particularly anti-Semites, call Harbor Isle "Little Israel." Island Park is where you see trees in the windows at Christmas and houses festooned with lights. The Italians, especially the Girardis, have the most elaborate displays. My father calls Italians "Guineas." If he thinks the plumbing is bad in a house, or a door is put on wrong, anything badly done or on the cheap, he calls it "a Guinea job."

We run around at night during the holidays, quietly unscrewing the big old-fashioned bulbs, which makes a creaking whistling sound, and smash them on the ground. When they shatter, they make a cracking and satisfying explosion. Then we squeal with delight and run to the next house. It is thrilling, like shoplifting, or jumping from roof to roof of the cabanas at the beach club at night, or leaping off the boardwalk to get onto Long Beach free, or toilet papering the trees, or egging houses, or breaking in and vandalizing them, or setting a bag of dog shit on fire, leaving it at someone's doorstep, ringing the doorbell, and watching the unassuming victim stomp the fire out, sending shit flying everywhere.

Gerard has dirty blond hair and blue eyes. He might be attractive, but his personality makes him look scrappy and a little bit dirty like a feral cat. If I think about it now, Gerard is downright aberrant. He has a squeaky, snotty, effeminate voice with a strong sibilance and isn't someone I would ever take home to meet my family. My father would peg him for a *goyische feygele*, disliking him on sight, and my mother would mistrust him because she is part gypsy and has a sixth

sense about people. And there is plenty to sense and distrust about
Gerard. He is bitchy, catty, angry, and defensive, and his lips are always pursed, as if he were sucking on a lemon. But he is fun because
he is bad, inherently naughty. He is a secret friend, which adds an ele-
ment of menace. I am a member of his fraternity of evil, which seems
to have only two members.

We go to the lot at the end of Lincoln Avenue. Harbor Isle is still
new and undeveloped. When my parents first came to see it before I
was born, they were living with my three sisters in a crowded apartment on Hunts Point Avenue in the Bronx, which had become intolerable. This undeveloped sandpit surrounded by water, the occasional
house sticking up on stilts over the marshland, looked very promising.
It still has lots, reed-filled empty plots of land on the water. Filling it
with houses and the requisite sycamore trees of Long Island suburbs
takes a long time.

The reeds are so thick you can get lost in them. The crackling
sound of wandering through them, their panicles tickling your
face, mixed with the excitement they provide by forming a hiding
place, makes them thrilling. They seem to have a relationship with
the wind, singing as it blows through them, in what always seems like
searing commentary.

Where the reeds end, we have an encampment. A clearing hidden enough so we can smoke there. It is damp, salty smelling, and so
close to the water that at high tide, if a boat passes, the waves from
the wake crash up on your feet. At low tide, it just stinks, and we see
horseshoe crabs. We turn them upside down and watch their prehis-
toric black legs wiggle toward the sky as they struggle futilely to turn
themselves upright. We are like deer finding places to hide in.

There is nothing I like as much as smoking. Smoking is freedom.
It is adult and dangerous. I am already addicted, so much so that I get
a bad case of pleurisy from doing it. Everything seems to be about
getting cigarettes. I have to bribe my sister Sheila, or her friends, or
older people on their way into stores to buy me cigarettes. My babysit-
ter Erin and her boyfriend, Carlos, teach me how to smoke until I get
really good, inhaling and blowing smoke rings. Erin is from one of

the few Catholic families in Harbor Isle, the Logans, Carlos, from a family of gardeners over the bridge. The Logan girls, Caitlin, Maureen, and Erin, are the prettiest girls in Harbor Isle, but their parents, Edwin and Grace, are alcoholic and the family is woefully splintered. There is an air of tragedy about them, and something about their bloodred house feels forbidden. My sister Sheila is close with Caitlin, who is in her grade. Caitlin is tall, with bright red hair, blue eyes, and a cry in her voice. She gets pregnant and marries Dylan, a handsome, sloe-eyed, lanky Irish Catholic football player from Island Park who radiates a concomitant sadness. They have two kids pretty quickly, Tommy and Carrie, and move to a house over the bridge on Little Beach, the Catholic answer to Harbor Isle Beach Club, but without any luxuries like a concession or shuffleboard courts or sometimes even lifeguards.

Caitlin and Dylan divorce, and Caitlin dies of alcoholism so advanced she bleeds through her eyes. Erin is the black Irish in the family, a raven-haired, blue-eyed beauty with a smile like the white keys of a grand piano and dimples in all the right places. She chain-smokes and drinks. She and Carlos don't last. Erin ends up in Florida. Years later, when I visit my mother, Erin is our waitress at a Jewish deli in Boca Raton. She looks as if she has done time in an Iranian prison. Her voice is a smoky croak, her face cracked and dry, and she dies soon after of alcoholism as well. Maureen, the middle sister, an adorable gamine, marries Dean, the brother of Caitlin's husband, Dylan. I am strongly drawn to Dean. He is soft-spoken and shy, impish and beautiful, with a crooked smile and a pug nose. He seems to find me both fascinating and irritating. I only say this because he tells me one night when we are getting drunk at Pop's Bar that sometimes he thinks I talk too much. Dean is one of the various older men I have sex with at fifteen. Maureen and Dean became my sister Sheila's closest friends, but no one knew what happened between Dean and me.

If I can't get a pack of Marlboros, or Winstons, my favorites, I steal Susan's Parliaments with the recessed filters. They feel sophisticated in their elegant blue-and-white box, and I associate them with Vassar because that's where Susan goes to college. Or I find juicy butts on the street or in other people's ashtrays and collect them in used cigarette packs. I pick up used chewing gum and chew it. I call it ABC gum, "already been chewed." My cousin Carol smokes Kents. Her nickname is Precious because like Uncle Freddie, she is born with blond hair and blue eyes and doesn't look Jewish. Jews love it when they can "pass." It comes from a deep-seated fear of extermination, the same reasons Jews must have food, or love bargains, because you never know when it's all going to end. Precious comes to visit us, and all she seems to eat and drink is potato chips and Coca-Cola, neither of which my mother ever buys, so it's lots of fun. She is my aunt Sylvia's only child. Rarely exposed to anyone her own age, Precious seems to have been born at forty, and there is something terribly exotic about being with someone as old as my sisters but who looks, talks, acts, and dresses like a dogged and tenacious jeweler on the diamond exchange.

One night, my parents are away. They go away for two-week cruises to the Caribbean, places like Nassau (my mother's favorite), St. Thomas, and Jamaica. They also go to Puerto Rico, which is where Uncle Freddie and Aunt Sandra move, after their son, Irving, who is three years younger than me, and, you guessed it, blond and blue-eyed, even greater currency when you're a boy, runs out to catch a ball in front of their house in Brooklyn and gets hit by a hit-and-run driver who is never caught. He dwindles in a coma for a year and then dies, so they move to San Juan and never talk about him again, a roiling hysterical secret you are always painfully aware of. After it happens, his little sister Joni starts pulling her hair out in clumps.

My parents always get someone to watch us, usually my father's mother, Mama Yetta, who escaped Poland during a pogrom, fleeing over the mountains with her mother and her sister while her village was wiped off the map, only to get to America, where her older sister, who made it here earlier, turned her into her very own cleaning woman, so Mama Yetta is hands down the most depressed person I have ever met. She has photo albums of people who were all murdered, and every time you visit she takes them out to show you and cries, but when you're little, that kind of stuff is neither sad nor interesting. I like it when she puts a big hunk of rock candy in her mouth and drinks tea or hot water with lemon in a glass to dissolve it while watching Lawrence Welk. I love the clinking sound of the candy on her teeth with the slow slurping from the glass. Her cheeks stick out like a squirrel's full of acorns. Rock candy lives up to its name and takes hours to dissolve. Mama Yetta's scrambled eggs are always carelessly mixed and undercooked, so they look and taste like snot, but she makes delicious kosher pizza with Muenster cheese instead of mozzarella, and incredible apple cake in a pan I am fortunate enough to inherit after she dies.

My parents also go on weekend trips, and for these they trust me and Sheila, leaving us alone. Nothing is more exciting to me, because this usually means Sheila has tons of friends over for parties in the brand-new den my father has built and named Gordon's Hacienda. It has a bar replete with festive-colored lights illuminating all the pretty liquor bottles, a Castro convertible for company, and a stereo. It seems to me just about anything can happen there, and it does. I love Sheila's friends. Unlike all of Lorraine's and Susan's poetic, intellectual, often wan, plus a little bit smelly friends of every race and color from all over the world, Sheila's are the football players and cheerleaders, from Island Park and all points Catholic. They love to smoke, drink, take drugs, and fuck, *not* read. They live in their bodies and are sexy beyond all imagining. You always imagine they would look magnificent with their clothes off. At these parties, someone always ends up dropping their pants and showing their penis, usually Jeff S., my friend Richard's older brother, who, like Richard, has a formidable and memorable one. My father has a huge fish tank downstairs, which makes the whole house smell like turtles. Sheila's friends get drunk and throw things in it. Sheila gets in trouble when one of her friends carves the word "fuck" into the wooden paneling behind the Castro convertible in Gordon's Hacienda. If Sheila doesn't have a party, I have my own friends over to smoke and drink, cheap crap like Spanada, Boone's Farm apple wine, Tango, or Yago Sangria.

Sheila works at Jahn's, an ice cream parlor in Rockville Centre. One night she takes me to the Fantasy movie theater to see *Berserk* with Joan Crawford, about a circus in which a man gets a metal stake driven through his head and Judy Geeson gets sawed in half. Afterward we go to Jahn's for cheeseburgers, fries, and sundaes. Sheila keeps her tips in a big bowl on her dresser. I have a party while Sheila is working one Saturday night, one of the weekends when my parents leave us alone. Someone steals all of Sheila's tips. Gerard stays after everyone leaves.

Gerard wants to play a game. He says I should put my mouth on his penis, and he will put his mouth on mine. "Put your mouth around it." His personality changes, his voice gets quieter, higher, and squeakier, and his face takes on an expression I've never seen before. His eyes seem to indicate we are about to enter new territory where danger lurks a little closer. Why is it all of my memories pertaining to sex when I was little are more vivid and Technicolor than any other memories I have?

I say "ewwww" when I put my mouth on his penis, which just feels like soft, droopy flesh and very warm. Neither of us has erections or anything. I mean, mine must have been so tiny. It isn't at all erotic or exciting. When he puts his mouth on mine, it just tickles and feels funny, silly almost. The next day, we simply go back to smoking in the lot, and clandestinely ruining things. I could say the whole event is unimportant, but inside me, as soon as it happens, neon-red parentheses surround it, and still do. My chest tightens writing this, and my mouth is dry.

Soon after that, we are hanging out in an abandoned red house by the water that everyone calls the haunted house. It is our unofficial clubhouse. It is on a part of Harbor Isle that feels dissolute and decadent, like the setting for Eugene O'Neill's play *Anna Christie*. No one has lived here for as long as I can remember. The furniture is all broken and torn, hemorrhaging stuffing, with springs sticking out. The house is literally half fallen down, every floorboard creaking like the setting for a horror film, but somehow retains its deep crimson color and enough structure to get lost in. It is another exciting, damp and dank, salty, semen-smelling place where you can hide and do naughty things and grown-ups never think to look for you.

We are smoking before taking the train to Valley Stream, where

Green Acres is, the first mall on Long Island. We like to go there and shoplift. Sometimes my mother gives me money to buy things, like Day-Glo posters, but usually I just steal stuff. I am obsessed with posters. Sometimes I buy incendiary posters. This is the case with the one that gets me into trouble. It is the famous photo from the My Lai massacre in Vietnam. In the forefront, a terrified naked girl with burns from napalm all over her body is running toward the camera, and behind her are other families with children running for their lives from a bombed-out and decimated village on fire. In the top left-hand corner of the poster, in big letters, it says, "Question: And children?" And on the bottom right-hand corner it says, "Answer: And children." I think nothing of hanging it over my bed for decoration, making absolutely no connection with the horrifying content of the scene or what it means. It is just a poster and therefore cool. As soon as my mother sees it, she says, "Are you outta your mind?! Get that off the wall now!"

My mother also gives me money to buy my sisters presents. She always tells me exactly what to buy them, opaque panty hose, so I do.

One night my father brings me home a black light, which I want more than anything in the world, so I can see my Day-Glo posters in all their glory, a rare occurrence, because my father never buys gifts. Soon, though, after I begin lighting incense and burning candles in my room, he screams I am going to burn the whole house down. Suddenly the candles, the incense, *and* the black light are all gone.

Gerard wants to play the game again. By now, he holds a strange power over me, and I will do anything he asks. At that age, there is a kind of authority you ascribe to anyone who is even a year older than you. I worship Gerard like the older brother I yearn for. He puts his mouth on my penis, same tickle, same awkwardness. But this time, he lingers a little longer, as if he were suddenly enjoying it. I put my mouth on his, same revulsion, same warm, flaccid skin, but this time with an awareness of a stale smell radiating from his pubic hairs, no erections, no arousal, just mouths on limp penises.

When I write about this now, I am titillated. There is a part of me that wants to go back with all that I know now and correct it, enjoy it, but I knew nothing about sex yet. I hadn't even discovered orgasms or started masturbating. That begins one day when I get home from the Harbor Isle Beach Club. There is a lot of sand on the head of my penis. I am lightly rubbing it off while thinking of what Chuckie Hammer's penis might look like if it were hard: Would it stand up high enough to touch his belly button? Suddenly something inexplicable happens. The world changes, the earth shakes, my penis is suddenly very sensitive, and I am never ever the same again, chasing that feeling wherever it leads me, which is mostly into trouble. Nobody endlessly castigates men who are constantly eyeing women, who admit how frequently their minds are on "pussy" and "boobs." Or even if they do, it's often with eye rolling or amusement. But if you are a gay man thinking about "dick" all the time, everyone thinks you are a pedophile waiting to abuse their sons like the legions of priests in the legions of churches who preach the teachings of Christ while never once applying them.

But back to the game.

It has absolutely no significance at that moment, just something Gerard wants to do. Even brighter parentheses, though, close in around this moment. This is the day I learn a new word, "smolder," because when we get home from Green Acres, walking down Warwick Road toward Harbor Isle at dusk just after crossing the bridge, I see smoke and flames and the flashing lights of red fire trucks surrounding our haunted house.

Apparently, when I put my cigarette out on the damp mattress that afternoon, it smoldered until the house caught fire and burned to the ground. After that, Gerard tells everyone I "blew" him. I don't know what that means. I have never heard the term "blow." But I know it isn't good. Suddenly the world is considerably more dangerous.

I start getting beaten up all the time. Everywhere I go, over both bridges, in Harbor Isle and Island Park, at school, where everybody goes ice-skating, or in synagogue, people hiss, or they scream, "You blew Gerard." Out the windows of cars, "You blew Gerard, you blew Gerard." I am circled by groups of boys, closing in like hyenas on their prey. They kick and punch. I don't remember the physical as much as the psychic pain.

One time, I am with my mother when it happens, the passing car slowing down, the epithets "faggot," "fairy," "fem," the "You blew Gerard" in repetition like a poisonous mantra. I die, but she neither acknowledges their screams nor asks who Gerard is. She doesn't want to know, or she is protecting me because she feels my embarrassment. So, she says nothing, her hand perhaps clutching mine a little tighter, as if we were walking through a minefield.

I am terrified to ever leave the house again, afraid to turn a corner, afraid of dark rooms, of hedges at night, of closets, and nowhere, nowhere feels safe any longer. My ability to concentrate in school becomes considerably worse, and believe me, it doesn't have much leeway. I must wear my shame like a cloak, or a yellow star, because one night Peter and I are about to board the bus from Long Beach to Island Park when a group of boys run after us. They taunt us, and eventually (because I have a knack for saying the wrong thing at the wrong time and laughing when nothing is funny) they hold me down on the bus while the driver smokes in the parking lot so the largest of them can pee on me.

Another form of torture that starts in seventh grade is "Slam Books," notebooks that get passed around with a single page dedicated to everyone in the class. You are supposed to write little comments about whoever's page you are on. I sit out in the schoolyard going through it and come upon my page: "sissy," "cocksucker," "blew Gerard," "walks like a girl," and so on. I hand it to the next person, knowing they will see it and repeat it.

Gerard and I aren't friends after this. We never speak or even acknowledge each other. The only reason I can come up with for Gerard's betrayal is that he must be getting a lot of negative attention for his own sissyness and I am his scapegoat. What I learn is that sometimes there is no protection. No one can help you. You just have to walk through fire and hope you survive.

Later, when they finally know what happened to you, people ask, "Why didn't you say something? I could have helped you." It never occurred to me to tell anyone. I didn't have the language for it. When a dog is drowning, it doesn't know it's drowning. It doesn't get all upset, thinking, "How sad this is. I'm about to die alone." It just tries to stay afloat until it can't, which is what makes animals so poignant. They're innocent. They do what they're trained to do, or what their instincts tell them to. They don't editorialize.

One summer I come home from Carnegie Mellon University and Peter takes me to Pal Joey's, a new gay bar in Bellmore, Long Island. Gerard is there. Peter only knows about Gerard, he was not there when it was happening, Gerard and I happened in an isolated bubble of swamp gas. I feel sick when I see him. He is dissolute and seems prissier and homelier. Disappointment, frustration, years of abuse and abusing, have made him embody his own acid tongue. In a bar full of vain, tanned, worked-out gay men, he looks unkempt and out of place, like a bruise on an apple.

People avoid him, but I can't muster up even a shred of empathy. He is Judas, as far as I am concerned. I don't talk to him. Years later, I hear that Gerard has died of AIDS.

Weeks after Gerard's betrayal, when I have become a full-blown pariah, I light a match at the lot where we used to smoke. I am with Peter and a new group of disenfranchised boys who, like me, are going nowhere fast. I want to see what will happen if I light the fluffy top of a dry reed. The field quickly erupts in flames, racing through the lot with a dangerous crackling sound. It is all we can do to make our way out of there without igniting ourselves. We fly back to my house, laughing and cursing in utter panic. We hide in the basement with the blinds drawn, listening in terror to the sirens until they cease and we're sure the fire is out. My mother comes home with groceries and asks if we have heard about the fire, but we feign innocence.

Psycho |≡

Peter moved through the world as if the only thing to do in it were to get boys to take their pants down. He would proudly recount how Bobby S., or whoever, let him jerk them off. Bobby S. was in my class, and it was from him I first learned there was something that came out of your penis if you rubbed hard enough, but we weren't old enough yet.

One night Peter and I were with an older boy, Sherwin R. We were drinking in the backyard of Dr. Sussman's house, which was frequently abandoned and consequently the site of a lot of activity that felt forbidden. Once we even broke in. We didn't do any damage that night; it was just such a strange house we wanted to see what it looked like inside. I guess you would call it 1960s modern, but it wasn't like anything else in Harbor Isle. This night, we were slobbering and drunk guzzling Spanada and Tango.

At one point Peter and I were sitting on either side of Sherwin, and Peter started feeling Sherwin's boner, squealing to pretend he thought it was gross, but I could tell he was doing exactly what he wanted to do and pretending Sherwin was making him do it. He cajoled me into joining the game, and of course I was in the world I would inhabit for so much of my feral childhood, confused, aroused, and not in much need of cajoling. I didn't want to stop, and for weeks I replayed it over and over, wanting to be back there, exploring unabashedly without having to pretend I didn't like it.

Another night, Peter and I were at Billy V.'s, another boy who somehow ended up in Harbor Isle, though I have no idea how. Billy was also older than me by two or three years. We were high. My elbow was resting on Billy's hard-on. There is no way he wasn't aware of what was happening. It was a silent agreement that my elbow was rubbing him in the right way and turning him on, and I wasn't going to move it, and he wasn't going to let on to the others that he and I were basically having sex. I couldn't have been more than nine or ten at that time.

If there are boys who grow up wanting all the girls in the neighborhood, I wanted the boys—not all, but some, and that was never anything but dangerous. There are so many names of boys from the neighborhood, Ron S., Richard S., Jeff S. (simply because of what he looked like naked when I slept over at Rich's), Michael L., that had a charge for me, names filled with fantasy and possibility.

Peter brought Michael L., who was older than both of us, over as if he were the Papa Bear teaching his cub to hunt. We played a game on the bed in my bedroom. If Peter or I lost (the game seemed to be rigged so that we always did), we had to play with Michael's penis. During the event, Michael got up to go to the bathroom to pee. Peter and I waited back in my room. We didn't talk, because there were no words; this was only about the body. Michael walked back in. The sight of this man who was no longer a boy, entering the room naked, with his heavy, lumbering penis, one small droplet of pee dangling from it, has played over and over again in my mind, drifting forever in and out of my lifelong fantasies like one of those tape loops in a peep show.

In porn, you always see when a man is trying to come. He closes his eyes, looking back into the cauldron of memories to recall that moment, the dangling pee, the fantasy-filled memory that never fails to seal the deal, bring him to climax. I might have been reading Dr. Seuss, doing something innocent and childlike. Instead, I was learning how to jerk Michael L. off with Peter, my mentor.

When I was eleven, Peter took me to see *Psycho*. I was distressed the moment the movie began. In a somber black and white, after the most terrifying film music, a depressed and fidgety Janet Leigh, in her bra and whatever state of undress she is in that reminds me of my mother, looking as if she were chewing on a nail she just bit, is getting ready nervously after making love to John Gavin. The atmosphere is eerily ominous in a way I had never seen or known. The fact that she has stolen money and is feeling guilty while driving somewhere alone and already scared in the car really upsets me. But then she checks into this awful motel where Anthony Perkins, who seems to be chewing on a nail as well, takes her to her room, which is as lonely and faceless as possible, and you know this is the horrible room she will die in. She even flushes something down the toilet and you think, "She will be flushed down that toilet too." Then the shower scene happens. The horrifying music, the strings screeching, the frightening old woman, the huge butcher knife, Janet Leigh looks so defenseless she is even crying. I was 100 percent freaked out. It was as if we were watching a snuff film and it was really happening. I felt sick and started to shake and cry. I begged Peter to leave, but he said I was being a baby and we didn't. I had never experienced anything like it. It felt like terror, sadness, and depression colliding in a catastrophic accident inside me.

When I got home that day at dusk, it was winter, and no one was there. The house was dark until Sheila came home. I remember feeling desolate, abject, bereft, as if I were no longer young. I felt awful, alone, in a cold universe, cut off from the rest of the world. I see that I was severely depressed after that movie and had entered entirely new territory for myself.

The Trip

In 1968, I was twelve. I was jealous of everyone taking LSD. I wanted to hallucinate, wander through the forest with my arms outstretched, see colors exploding, clouds morphing into creatures, flowers coming alive, all the stuff Peter Max was painting and Grace Slick was singing about in "White Rabbit." I wanted my "mind blown" and a "whole new perspective," though it is hard to imagine what kind of new perspective I might have wanted, because I had *no* perspective at all.

Island Park was one town away from Long Beach, where the boardwalk was. You could buy any drugs you wanted on the boardwalk. Nobody ever asked you how old you were. So, one night, before a party at April Blume's house—she lived with her father, Chuck, in the apartment above his boatyard, Chuck's Marine—I went to Long Beach in search of LSD. It was dusk and the sun was almost down but for a sliver of orange on the horizon. The night felt pregnant with possibility, and my stomach was aflutter with butterflies. The guy who sold it to me said only, "Don't take the whole thing at once." When I got to April's, I swallowed the whole thing.

We smoked pot and drank Boone's Farm apple wine, the cheapest booze you could buy. I was standing outside and realized it was kicking in when a ringed corona began circling the full moon, its prismatic colors brighter and more vivid than anything I had ever seen in the sky. I went back inside to share my excitement. In April's bedroom, we got the giggles, that pot-induced hysteria which is one of the best reasons for getting high, out-of-control, heaving, raucous laughter.

Suddenly, like a jump cut in a Godard film, I stopped laughing. A thought entered my mind like a marauder: "I need to get out of this room." My blood seemed to be rushing through my veins so fast I could hear it. My heart began to beat out of my chest, and my limbs no longer felt as if they belonged to me. Abruptly, I rushed into the living room. The place was boxy and rectangular, like a coffin. Ironically, two years later, my father bought Chuck's Marine, renaming it S.G.E. Marine (Sam Gordon, Electric), but when my father bought it, he blew out the whole wall facing the water and made it glass so you could stare for hours at the barges passing through the channel and into the bay. I was fourteen when we moved there.

As soon as I sat down, I had two thoughts: first, "I need to get out of this room *too*," and the second, right out of Sartre's *No Exit*, and strangely existential for a twelve-year-old, "There is no escape." Sweating and trembling wildly, I entered into a blind panic. Quickly spiraling out of control, I started screaming, crying, and rambling incoherently. April slapped me hard across the face, a gesture straight out of some movie she had seen, thinking it would help. It didn't. It was decided I had to leave because I was bumming everybody out, bringing them down. Jimmy Policara, who was there without Johnny, his identical twin, was elected to walk me home. I had a crush on Jimmy because he was nice to me, protective, like an older brother. He was a year older than me. The Policara twins were unusually handsome and muscular for boys their age; consequently, they radiated confidence and were kind because they had each other and they liked themselves. (They both died young, though, from overdoses, so liking themselves didn't stop them from destroying themselves.)

I kept my hand on Jimmy's shoulder as if I were going blind, as if I were making my way across broken glass barefoot, or I were a dainty woman wearing perilously high heels. He was comforting beyond his age, almost spiritual in his selflessness, and I didn't know what I was going to do when I left him. It was surreal to walk past the suburban homes, normalcy spilling out of them like milk, while I was having a psychotic episode. When we arrived at my door, I thanked Jimmy with a wish he'd come inside and quiet me with his body, shakily muttering goodbye as if it were my last sane moment on earth, and ran inside, bolting for my room. I grabbed our Welsh corgi, Max.

I held him in front of me, staring into his eyes as if he were my

savior, a role he seemed comfortable filling, opposing his usually insane, out-of-control nipping at your heels or jumping up, showing his
teeth, and biting your balls character. It was as if he were suddenly
possessed by God or a dead relative's spirit and knew his job was to
save me. Max was the dog my uncle Freddie bought my grandmother
Mama Yetta to keep her company when she was living alone in Jackson Heights, but Mama Yetta tried to control him by beating him
with a broomstick and deranged him, so we had to take him off her
hands.

Suddenly I heard the door open downstairs. Disaster. My father
was home. I thought he was upstairs in the bedroom wrapped around
my mother with his hands clutching her breasts, the way he always
slept, but he must have been at a Masonic meeting. In 1970, my father
became a master in his Masonic lodge, so he spent a lot of time during
this period memorizing some little black book and going to meetings. I doubt, though, anything in the Masons prepared my father
for his twelve-year-old son freaking out on acid. I got out of bed to
assure him things were normal, trying to head off an unmanageable
confrontation at the pass, but as soon as I got up, the room started
spinning, or I did, and I projectile vomited in all four directions, coat-
ing everything in the room with puke. He rushed in to see what was
happening. I told him I drank too much at a party and I would clean it
up. He could have gotten angry, but he seemed to know to step away
rather than do anything to make matters worse, as out of character as
Max's intentness, but everything was topsy-turvy that night. When I
got back to bed, I was changed. A door in me had opened, the wrong
door, Bluebeard's door where all the bodies were kept, and there was
no closing it ever again. When I awoke the next morning, rattled and
unsteady, it was one of those late spring days when the wind is blowing
through the silvery leaves so aggressively it confuses the senses. It
seemed out of season, neither warm nor cold, spring nor summer,
just jostling and unsettling. My mother was out on the porch. I could
barely look at her. Usually, her chirping presence in the morning with
offers of coffee and whatever I might possibly want for breakfast could
snap me out of anything. This morning, she seemed like a stranger, as

if my life story had been rewritten overnight and she were no longer my mother, like *Invasion of the Body Snatchers*. I looked out at the trees wistfully, with a grave and wholly unfamiliar sadness, and thought, "My youth is over."

This set off something irrational and horrifying in me. I was afraid everything was laced with drugs. I could eat and drink only at home. If I inadvertently forgot the rules and accepted a piece of gum or a cigarette from anyone outside my house, I would immediately start to panic and have the whole trip all over again. In these states, I felt as if I had unknown and dangerous strength combined with a fierce desire to destroy myself, as though my blood were rushing through my veins too quickly, with intense speed. If I took a knife and stabbed it through my heart, the force would be so great it would go through my chest, through the earth, and plunge straight out of China. I would have to hold on to the bed or the chair, shaking so badly everything around me would shake too, as if there were an earthquake, and pray until it was over. It was always followed by the same doomed end of youth and innocence feeling, all joy and energy drained from me.

A couple of weeks after my first trip I had a piano lesson. I was friends with my piano teacher Mr. Chaikin's son, Danny. Peter and I would sleep over in the basement at Danny's all the time, doing things like playing "Revolution 9" from the Beatles' *White Album* backward on the tape recorder, looking for signs to verify that Paul was dead. After my piano lesson, Danny's parents went out for the night, and we decided to smoke pot. It was a mistake. The pot provoked a reoccurrence, only ten times worse. I had auditory hallucinations, as though my thinking were so intense it was making my hair singe. I could hear, smell, and feel it singeing, so I threw water on my head.

Mr. Chaikin and his wife, Fay, came home and found me in their bedroom in a state of disarray that was so concerning, they called my parents. I don't remember any admonishment or even a lecture; this was out of my parents' wheelhouse. A future riddled with drug-addicted children was still ahead of them. But the next day my mother took me to our family physician, Dr. Forest, who had one leg—irrelevant, but worth mentioning. He told me, perhaps to scare me, that the drug I

took takes at least a year to leave the system. This was a disaster because it meant that for at least a year, because what he said suggested it,
I had a reoccurrence every day.

The only people who could talk me off the ledge were my mother
and my sister Lorraine, who also freaked out on acid and tried to kill
herself in her therapist's office. My mother, hearing my screams, would
have to come down late at night and talk me down, or I would call
Lorraine in torment from a public telephone booth, and she would just
breathe with me.

This journey into madness carried into my adulthood and continues
today in myriad ways whose manifestations I imagine will find their
way into this continuing saga.

The Three Sisters

Susan had an aura of brittle brilliance around her, like the highest harmonic on a tuning fork. All of us were named after movie stars. Susan Carol Goldenberg was named after Susan Hayward. She was twelve and a half years older than me, born November 14, 1943, so when she left to go to college, I was five. I have always had a thing about the whole family being together. In group therapy, if someone is missing, I think the whole session should be canceled. When a plate chips, I want to throw away the entire set. So, when Susan left, it was a blow, like having a limb removed.

The whole family convened to drive her up to Vassar, probably the last if not the only time we ever went anywhere as a family. Susan and my mother both wore sweaters my mother had knit, my mother, her favorite peach-pink mohair cardigan, and Susan, a pattern from an Irish sweater catalog, cable knit, a depressing turd brown with leather buttons.

In the photos, Sheila looks miserable. What was wrong? It might be from that period when all she did was hide in her room listening to "This Boy," by the Beatles, and crying. Lorraine too, I'm sure, had complicated feelings. She knew she would never get into all the colleges Susan got into, trailing behind her, silhouetted by her glittering spotlight.

Vassar had a stunning campus; it was the quintessence of what a college campus should look like. My father, after much consternation about the tuition, was happy that day, finally proud his daughter was going to Vassar, excited about all the social events described in the catalog for parents when they visited, an opportunity to mix with people above his station, he thought, which never materialized.

None of my relatives thought a girl either needed or deserved to go to college, much less Vassar, which they considered a "goyish" bastion. They shamed Susan about wasting my father's hard-earned money. At Vassar, she and her best friend, Deborah Michaelson, whose father, a doctor, kept Deborah and Susan supplied with diet pills to stay skinny, wanted to fit in, which meant looking Waspy instead of Jewish. They wore headbands, Capri pants, Pappagallos, and Fair Isle sweaters. They sought to emulate the characters in *The Group*, Mary McCarthy's scandalous novel about Vassar girls.

I have a memory in my Susan catalog that sits high above all the others. It is insignificant, and it is everything. Susan came home from Vassar for the winter holidays. It was nighttime, and I was already in bed. I heard the excited greetings and wanted to run downstairs to hug her. But then I heard her climbing the stairs to my room and was overwhelmed with excitement. It was me she really wanted to see. I was her favorite. She gave me a kiss, her extremely cold nose almost stinging my face, and sat down next to me. She still had her coat on, wet with snow.

This was how she introduced me to poetry, sitting on my bed every night lulling me to sleep by reading Edna St. Vincent Millay, dropping poetry into my lap like a bag of gold coins, changing me forever. She got into Barnard and Radcliffe, but Millay didn't go to either of them, so she picked all-girls Vassar. She tried to get Millay's room, but they wouldn't give it to her.

She gave me a recording of Millay reading her poems, so I hear her voice in my head with her crystalline New England accent, as well as I hear my sister's. Susan started to read earlier than most children and could read two books a day. Precocious and uninhibited, she'd stare out the window or across the aisle on a bus, pointing and shouting loudly, "Look, Mommy, there's one white person and one brown person!" Striking, with almost jet-black hair and piercing eyes, she had an intelligence that made her fascinating but terrifying, especially for men who are threatened by women smarter than them.

Those glamorous photos of the poet Anne Sexton always remind me of Susan—the crisp intelligence, the beauty, wit, and tragedy, and the lit cigarette smoldering between her fingers. Susan was a Scorpio. She had a stinger with a lethal dose of poison in it, enormous charisma, and a huge sexual appetite. Fathered by my father, she was destined for complicated and uneven relationships with men.

That night she entered like a snow angel, bringing the cold in from outside, sparkling with a few crystals of snow. She looked different from when she had left, sophisticated, grown-up, self-assured, and confident. She said she had bought a present for me in Poughkeepsie, which seemed to me like the most exotic place in the world. I shivered with anticipation. It was a box of big round lollipops, swirling with every color of the rainbow, hypnotic and magical, exquisite in their box. I gasped. Many of my happiest moments when I was little were when I was on the rides at the carnival, orange, yellow, red, green, pink, purple, and blue rides, so I have a thing about color. If I had my way, the whole world would look like a carnival. These lollipops were the perfect present.

When I was four and Susan was sixteen, she was a cashier at Waldbaum's, the local supermarket. Before she left for work one day, she was in front of the house on the top stair of the cement stoop, and I was standing in the driveway looking up at her. She seemed to have a cloud encircling her, trapping her in its vapor. I will never forget her expression. Though I had no vocabulary to express such things, in that moment she looked like the saddest person I had ever seen, as if sadness were a throbbing, impenetrable fortress and she couldn't get out.

Only later did I realize it was a part of who we were. Other families had beliefs, boundaries, rituals, and principles they adhered to. We were renegades. It was exciting to be part of a family that was different from everyone else's, where everyone had such vivid personalities and operated outside the lines, but it was also isolating and created a divide, a fracture in all of us. We believed nothing collectively. We were free-standing trees with no forest.

What I saw in her face that day I saw in my own later. I saw it in my father's rage, my mother's singing, Sheila's smoldering silence, Lorraine's agoraphobia, and Susan's murderous self-destructiveness.

We were different, but not always in a good way. Often, we were terribly sad.

After Vassar, Susan married Michael Lydon, whom she'd met at Yale. She went there her last year of school because Vassar threw her out for having too many boys in her room and Yale had just turned coed. They moved to London, where Michael was the London correspondent for *Newsweek* and Susan became the editor in chief of a magazine called *London Life*. Susan developed a British accent, wore Mary Quant makeup, and shopped on Carnaby Street in her white Courrèges boots, Betsey Johnson miniskirts, and big op-art earrings like the famous models of the time: Veruschka, whom David Hemmings was lasciviously photographing in Michelangelo Antonioni's tremendously successful masterpiece from 1966, *Blow-Up*; or the rail-thin Twiggy; and Penelope Tree with her pouting lips and oval eyes. Sometimes Susan and Michael brushed up against the Beatles, and Susan would send me the English versions of their albums with different covers that were soft instead of hard and always had an extra song omitted from the American releases—*Rubber Soul*, for instance, had "Drive My Car"—making me an instant celebrity with my friends.

My sister Lorraine Marsha Goldenberg, born December 13, 1946, named after the actress Lorraine Day, was a Sagittarius: intuitive, empathic, and elusive. Need and insecurity made her cut and paste her personality accordingly. Her way of speaking—cadence, tone, accent—could change so often it was sometimes hard to peel away the layers and find her.

But when I was at my most abject, Lorraine was the one I turned to. She understood on the deepest level what catastrophe felt like, violently half blinded as she was by the forceps at birth, so she always intuited exactly what I needed to hear to feel better.

Lorraine seemed happiest when she was pregnant or had a baby suckling at her breast, when a look of extreme serenity lit her face as in Piero della Francesca's *Madonna del parto*. She had four children from four different fathers, only three of them husbands, and breast-fed each until they were at least four.

The most volatile of us, she was the least afraid of barking back at my father. She would purposely goad him, "What are you going to do, kill me? Go ahead, kill me." She brought home a Japanese boyfriend when my father still called Japanese people "Japs," and a Black boyfriend when he still called Black people *schwartzes*, so we were always on eggshells. He threw her out of the house once in a blizzard without a coat. She ran down the block to the house of her best friend Ellen Levy, who was the double on *The Patty Duke Show*. Whenever you saw Patty and Cathy together, the one whose back was turned was Ellen.

It was hard to tell when Lorraine really loved a man. Was it an act of defiance, charity, a show of strength, or need?

Lorraine got pregnant at sixteen and married Bobby Shapiro, whom she'd met at a Vietnam War demonstration. I loved Bobby because he helped me with my piano playing, and in 1964 he carried me through the World's Fair on his shoulders in the snow. His mother married a Black man, and they had a house upstate in Haines Falls, New York, where I went and played with all the Black kids during the summer, so much nicer to me than any of the white kids I knew.

Lorraine and Bobby moved to Willett Street on the Lower East Side, into an apartment that fascinated me because if you touched a poster on the wall, thousands of cockroaches scurried out from all directions and back again. Turning on the lights in a dark room created a flurry of activity the likes of which I had never seen. There was a sound of rustling and an odor you only smell in apartments where cockroaches flourish. I wasn't scared or repelled by insects but fascinated. I held them in my hand and caught them with jars and nets.

Lorraine took me to a leather store in the Village where a cobbler measured my feet and made me the most beautiful leather sandals, which got softer and more comfortable every time I wore them. She took me to the Fillmore East to hear bands like the Fugs and the Who. The Fugs always had curse words like "fuck" in their songs, so that was pretty rousing. The light shows were spectacular, but it was always too loud, and I couldn't wait to go home. She also took me to see movies with subtitles at the Japanese cinema, like Kinugasa's *Gate of Hell*, which won an Academy Award, but I couldn't understand or read it. I remember only the dazzling Eastmancolor and someone getting stabbed.

Before Lorraine and Bobby's building was condemned while they lived in it, whenever my mother sent me to visit Lorraine to make her feel better about living the way she was, away from home, with a baby and a husband so young he sometimes had a runny nose and didn't even wipe it, my friends, a Puerto Rican brother and sister named José and Sondra, and I would climb like monkeys through the abandoned and crumbling buildings that lined much of the decrepit block. Lorraine took José and Sondra and me to a school auditorium where a man demonstrated how he could make anything in the world out of balloons, elephants, giraffes, horses, bunny rabbits, and he sent us all home very excited with various balloon animals. Then my niece Maggie was born, in 1964, when I was eight. I helped name her. I picked Magdalena, so she was Magdalena Shapiro.

When Bobby and Lorraine came to Harbor Isle to visit, I would corral Maggie the whole time, whispering stuff in her ear. I adored her. I wanted to mold and shape her as if she were my project. I would scream and howl inconsolably when they went home. I was the youngest, so Maggie brought something out in me my sisters must have felt when I was born: protectiveness, tenderness, and a feeling of power and strength I rarely felt in the world. I felt these things later in life with Jeffrey, which may be why I cried for five years straight after he died.

After Lorraine and Bobby broke up, which was soon after Maggie was born, my mother watched Maggie while Lorraine flew to London to visit Susan and Michael. I was sad and missed Bobby. Lorraine had developed a speed habit. She had sores all over her arms, and she smelled. She inherited my father's temper, which speed exacerbated, and Susan was pregnant, which made her irritable, so after Lorraine left, they didn't talk for a long time. Maggie unfortunately developed trench mouth in Harbor Isle and had to be treated with gentian violet, so she screamed constantly in her high chair through a deep, gaping purple mouth.

Susan found out in the midst of her pregnancy that the baby was dead, but she had to carry it to term. After the dreadful birth, when she came home from the hospital, Michael hadn't changed the sheets she had bled on. It is hard to imagine it was a deliberately insensitive move, but something died in their marriage that morning, though there were several years still to follow.

One time Susan and Michael came home from London so Susan could nurse Michael, who had terrible hepatitis and was so jaundiced that not only was his whole body bright yellow, but his eyes were as well. I had never seen or heard of such a thing.

Soon, they moved to San Francisco. Susan wrote for all kinds of cool magazines like *Ramparts*, *Eye*, and *Avant Garde*. (My very first poetry setting, a bloody, ghoulish, and horrifying poem about a heroin addict, was from *Avant Garde*. When my parents were showing 221 Lincoln Avenue to potential buyers in 1969, my mother, proud of everything I did, asked me to sing and play the song for a couple who might as well have been George and Laura Bush. They looked horrified when I was done, something my mother was completely oblivious to.) Susan and Michael became acquainted with Jann Wenner and started *Rolling Stone* magazine together. In the early days there, the men got all the interesting assignments, and the women got things like the home economics stories one associated with women's magazines like *Woman's Day*, *Family Circle*, and *Redbook*. It infuriated Susan, who felt she was as good a writer as, if not better than, Michael. She thought Michael would stick up for her, but he openly admitted he felt competitive with her and grateful that his sex gave him advantage over her, further inflaming their disintegrating marriage.

When my niece Shuna was about to be born in 1968, my mother took me to San Francisco. I had never been on a plane, and I was beside myself with anticipation. San Francisco was dazzlingly different from New York, with hills so high they had steps. They lived on the top of Telegraph Hill, so the views were thrilling, though I was disappointed the Golden Gate Bridge wasn't gold.

Susan took me to the most beautiful shop I had ever been in, Design Research, in Ghirardelli Square, which all the delicious chocolate is named after. Jimi Hendrix was singing "Purple Haze" over the speakers. I stared in wonder at all the beautiful and colorful Marimekko fabrics. Susan's friend Barbara Garson, newly famous for a play she wrote called *MacBird*, came to lunch. Barbara was the first and only person I had ever seen suck the marrow from chicken bones. They let me go to the pier by myself, where I went to the Wax Museum and Ripley's Believe It or Not! How exciting it felt to be out at eleven years old knocking about San Francisco alone.

Michael took me to a Laundromat to help with the now voluminous diaper-filled laundry. I liked Michael and never thought of him as impermanent, because, other than Bobby and Lorraine, all the comings and goings with men hadn't started yet in the lives of my sisters, and therefore mine. I was having fun opening and closing the dryers. Michael might have said, "Stop it," and either I didn't hear him or I didn't want to hear him because what I was doing was too much fun in the boring Laundromat. So, I kept doing it until he abruptly slapped me quite hard across the face and screamed, "I told you to stop doing that!" It was the second time he'd ever hit me like that. The first time was in Harbor Isle when I thought I was doing him a favor by washing his red Mustang convertible, but one of the windows was open. That time, he felt so ashamed for hitting me he cried.

I don't know the exact circumstances of their separation and divorce. Susan showed up at Lincoln Avenue one summer with a man named Luke who had a scar that went from the nape of his neck clear down his back. At a party in the hills of Marin County, sitting on a wall over a high cliff tripping on LSD, he fell backward and broke his neck and back. Shuna called him Lukie. They had driven across country in a Volkswagen through places like Appalachia collecting patchwork quilts, old reindeer sweaters, and vintage clothes to sell. I wore one of the reindeer sweaters she gave me until it completely unraveled. Michael was deeply wounded by the breakup and moved north to a town called Elk.

After Lorraine and Bobby broke up in 1965, she lived for a time with her friend Danya, smoking cigarettes and experimenting with heroin. When I visited, I slept on the floor on a little mattress with Maggie. I got Lorraine in trouble when I told my mother about the drugs and the needles I saw. She threatened to take Maggie away. I ran to Peter's house to tell him and his mother, Bernice, about all the drama and excitement in the Gordon household, and she forbade Peter to ever play with me again.

Lorraine was a copy editor for Dell Publishing Company, editing, among other things, Eldridge Cleaver's *Soul on Ice*, which everyone seemed impressed by. She moved to Masaryk Towers on Columbia Street by the Williamsburg Bridge and formed a band called Goldflower with her friend Bev Grant. They opened Randall's Island, the three-day festival following Woodstock, with a feminist diatribe, "I'm Tired of Bastards Fucking Over Me."

One weekend, Sheila called my mother and said Lorraine was acting strange and there was an empty bottle of pills next to her bed. Lorraine had attempted suicide. My mother rushed into the city and took Lorraine to Bellevue Hospital and, after her stomach was pumped, had her committed to the psychiatric ward against Lorraine's will.

Sheila's response to the climate in our house, watching my mother say yes to a man who publicly humiliated her all the time, calling her "stupid" and rolling his eyes practically every time she opened her mouth, was to hide her sexuality. She never wore anything revealing, like my "sexpot" mother, never showed her cleavage or wore anything tight. She was not going to peddle her wares. As Sheila saw it, sex had led to my mother's fate, having sex with someone on demand no matter how awful they were to you. If I became obsessed with sex as a way of getting love, especially with heterosexual men I could turn into my father, Sheila was wary, hauling the baggage of my mother's exhibitionism and submissiveness like a millstone around her neck.

Sheila Claire Goldenberg, named after Sheilah Graham, the British actress and writer who ended up being F. Scott Fitzgerald's last girlfriend, was born September 12, 1949, a Virgo and an earth sign like me, a Taurus, so she and I were at least *supposed* to be grounded. Since I fell in love with everything about Sheila, including her husband, Patrick, we were deeply bonded. It was as if Susan and Lorraine belonged to the Goldenbergs, and Sheila and I to the Gordons. We needled Sheila, with her teased hair and pencil skirts, calling her the "teen queen," Long Island's answer to Lesley Gore, because she strove to be "normal," which was familiar to me. I craved acceptance just as she did. The more I fit in, the less likely it was I would be killed. Lorraine, caught between an older sister she felt eclipsed by and a younger sister who chose a path she could never have accommodated, struggled miserably in the margins.

Within the confines of our house, in her self-imposed exile, Sheila was isolated. There had to be *somewhere* she could emerge, and she knew that would never happen if she was as "weird" as Susan and Lorraine. Susan and Lorraine could barely open their mouths without inciting violence, driving my father to extremes like ripping radios and telephones out of the wall to hurl at them, nearly killing them, hence the holes through every door. They were incapable of fitting in. Sheila and I wanted to survive, subsuming whatever cradled itself inside us to be hidden for use later. Earth signs are practical. Sheila and I *played* at cool. Susan and Lorraine *were* cool. Susan and Lorraine were jealous of how close Sheila and I were. After I was born, when my mother brought me home from the hospital, Sheila cried, "I thought you were bringing me a puppy." That's what I was, Sheila's obedient puppy, panting, wagging my tail, following her around, while waiting for a bone. Susan left when I was five, Lorraine when I was seven, so I had Sheila the longest. She drew me bubble baths for my birthdays, made me all my favorite things to eat, bought me fabulous origami sets and watercolors, and allowed me to tag along with her wherever she went, treating me like a friend, rather than a little brother. She was my favorite person in the world.

Fifteen

I loved these men.

I have tried to be completely honest about how vividly I remember things, and this does not preclude sex, because so much of what happened not only shaped me but implanted itself in my mind like acutely detailed movies, rolling at all times. Sometimes, it feels as if my head might as well have been a peep show booth in Times Square.

Numerologically, I am a five, which is all about freedom. The challenge inherent in the number five is to learn the proper uses of freedom, versus the destructive aspects, like being unmoored and amoral. Since five represents the senses, until I got my senses in check, until I put certain things down, the "toys of childhood," I was led to many places where I most probably shouldn't have been. This is all to say, this chapter may be particularly shocking.

DEAN

One night I was having dinner with Sheila, Patrick, and a bunch of their friends at a restaurant called Lenny's in Long Beach. Lenny's was one of those seafood restaurants with aquamarine-colored walls festooned with old crab traps, nets, anchors, conch shells, and plastic blue-claw crabs and bright red lobsters, all held in place by a rope net that looked authentically inauthentic.

Sheila's male friends were Adonises from over the bridge in Island Park. They were football heroes, lovers of the outdoors, with lungs full of fresh air and muscles developed naturally and effortlessly, who lived securely and confidently in their bodies like Greek gods. They didn't worry about what they ate. They didn't exercise to stay in shape. They didn't have any trouble taking off their clothes and showering in front of other men. Their penises were heavy and sat comfortably, though a little crowded by the enormous testicles in their underwear. They radiated health, youth, and robustness. They showed no signs of neurotic behavior whatsoever. In short, they weren't Jewish. Still unable to call myself what I was, or even know what I was, I knew that Sheila's male friends ended up in my sexual fantasies with great frequency.

That night, at a big wooden round table, there was a lot of drinking. After much joviality, in the light and easy style they were used to, never seeming to worry about whether they were interesting or not, which made them interesting, the men got to talking about how they could see themselves having a homosexual experience. It was playful drunken banter, suggestive, maybe even meant to provoke or prove their broad-mindedness, this being 1971, still the sexual revolution. Their faces would scrunch up into little balls when they were talking about it like children, deliberately trying to be coy and cute, but never losing sight of the unwavering confidence they had in their masculinity. Men like them could do whatever they wanted and still be *men*. I certainly never lost sight of it. They had an openness that was disarming and unusually candid. There was even mention of a hot tub and a fantasy one or two of them had when they were in one together, which, in my fifteen-year-old virginal state, was especially titillating, almost overwhelmingly so. Just imagining the steam coming off the bubbling water and the hands and mouths pulling, sucking, eating, my little head was exploding. It was the last conversation you would ever expect to be hearing at this particular table.

Strangely, the wives seemed amused, rather than aghast, rolling their eyes or half-fascinated, as if the openness of their husbands were droll and modern, and not in the least bit threatening. What was happening?

At that point in time, they were all steamfitters working on the

Twin Towers, which you could see being erected across the water, giant penises like dots on the skyline, from the boatyard we moved to when I was fourteen. As a matter of fact, it never occurred to me until now, I saw them go up, and I saw them come down. I knew people who built them, and I knew people who died in them.

The waiter brought the food, but I wasn't hungry. I was sitting bolt upright in my chair with a hypervigilance cataloging every word of the conversation with my heart practically heaving out of my chest. I'm sure my eyes were darting while I busily stored this information, this time bomb, that would tick inside me until I could act on it. About a week later, I was given the opportunity.

There was a picnic at a place called Wildwood State Park, a beautiful stretch of preserved beach and steep sand hills on the Long Island Sound. You could run straight down the hills, hitting the water with enormous excitement and velocity. It was thrilling, but you had to watch you didn't get snagged by the scrub and the knotty underbrush on the way down, or you'd tumble as I did, all the way down to the water. Luckily, I was so high I just laughed and shook it off. I had way more important business to attend to. Sheila and Patrick weren't there that day, so I went in the car with Dean and Maureen. Sheila would occasionally stay away from events like these so she could read *The New York Times* to expand her mind. She was more ambitious intellectually than her friends, and sometimes she would demonstrate this by individuating, reading, thinking, going to museums, seeing foreign movies. She might have belonged to Long Island more than her sisters, been more comfortable in its suburban cocoon, a semi–prom queen, but she was still the sister of Susan and Lorraine Gordon, intellectuals, beatniks, denizens of folk clubs in Greenwich Village, antiwar and civil rights activists, and radical feminists who no longer shaved their legs or their armpits, and now and then she had to assert it.

At this moment in time, Maureen was Sheila's best friend, and probably mine too. Maureen, like Dean, was adorable. She was always so happy to see you, a puppy with her tail wildly wagging, she'd seem to burst out of herself with joy, her voice a kind of squeal with delight. She was so pretty and delicate, gamine-like, with her blazing-red hair, pursed lips, freckled skin, and bright blue eyes, like a beautiful and grown-up Pippi Longstocking. It's a little thing, but it fascinated me that she would always stop off after work and buy herself a tuna fish sandwich on rye toast with lettuce and tomato to have for dinner. I loved the adult agency about it: that you could have a sandwich for dinner when you grew up and no one cared. She and Dean always had beers and cigarettes going, can in one hand, cigarette in the other. Neither of them was very tall, and both had the kind of beauty that is disarming because it sits at the threshold of youth and adulthood, accessible and untouchable at the same time. Neil Young's album *After the Gold Rush* had come out the year before. I was obsessed with Neil Young, and that album was the apotheosis of all that was great about him. I loved the mellowness of "Harvest" and the rock-and-roll thrum of "Cinnamon Girl," but *After the Gold Rush* had it all, the energy, the art, and the melancholy. I even liked it better than *Sugar Mountain*, the live album I bought one day on the black market when I was stoned and wandering through Central Park instead of being in school. One of the cover photos was of Neil's jeans with a million patches on the knees and thighs, which I decided I needed to emulate. Susan sent me beautiful patches of fabric from a fabulous notions and trimmings store in Sausalito, California, and Maureen helped me sew them on.

We all took quaaludes, muscle relaxers, which anybody can tell you made you feel as if all your nerve endings were tingling, and had hands that were reaching out tremulously for another body. Plus, we were drinking. Everyone had dispersed, swimming, playing ball, or running with the dogs along the water, dappled by the sun, like photographs from fashion magazines, Island Park's greatest beauties.

At one point, Dean and I were alone. We were sitting on a picnic table. I was looking down at the redwood, fingering it where the paint had chipped, killing time and nine months pregnant with what I was about to say, until, nervously, I looked up. "Dean, do you remember the other night at dinner, at Lenny's, when you said you could have sex with another man?" I asked. "Yeah," he said, looking into my eyes in a new and unfamiliar way. There was every possibility he could have either denied it or not remembered, because there was a lot of drinking at the table that night, and he could easily have been in a blackout, but he seemed completely open, even happy I asked, unsurprised, almost as if he were baiting me all along. "Who were you referring to?" I asked. My heart was beating out of my chest. He named his brother Paul, first, who was married to Maureen's gorgeous older sister, Caitlin. Paul was very tall and handsome, dirty-blond floppy hair, the requisite dazzling blue eyes, though either affectless or apathetic, and certainly depressed most of the time, so his beauty, for me, was marred by a fatal lack of joie de vivre. Then Dean named my brother-in-law, Patrick, whom I had immense and complicated feelings about. Patrick was wildly charismatic, extremely handsome, of Irish and German descent, with Medusa-like ringlets of blond hair, blue eyes, and a tall lanky body with arms and legs that were like the limbs of a Great Dane finding its way for the first time. He was the Billy Budd of this set. You could imagine his beauty and charm arousing the murderous jealousy of a Claggart. I have his high school photo hidden in the photos on my iPhone because I still cannot quite manage how handsome he was. He was at least a foot taller than Sheila, and she always seemed to have her head nuzzled under his arm if they were next to each other.

I always wanted to be where Sheila and Patrick were. If I couldn't, if we had plans, for instance, and they canceled on me—I am thinking of one particularly rainy and miserable Sunday—I would writhe on my bed, groaning in agony. This infuriated my mother, who couldn't bear feelings she didn't understand and couldn't fix, especially, I think, because she didn't like me wanting to be anywhere with anyone more than her.

Dean hesitated, looked up at me, and with a puckish smile said, "And you." Pause. I felt all of the blood drain out of my head. The moment is fixed in time as sure and as solid as Mount Rushmore. It was what I wanted to hear, what I was looking for beyond all my wildest dreams, but also, almost too exciting for my fifteen-year-old brain and body to process. All my nerves screamed, "Yes!"

I would like to say I was in love with Dean from the very first moment I ever saw him, though how could I have known then what love was? I don't know if I even know now. I don't like the word "crush," though, which diminishes the size and weight of what I was feeling, framing it in a kind of *Bye Bye Birdie* light, teenage girlish, and I certainly didn't feel like a teenage girl. Dean was boyish and a man at the same time. He seemed to embody a casual shrug. Nothing ever seemed to miff or ruffle him. With his pug Irish nose and crooked Charlie Brown smile, his walk, or shuffle, which was both shy and deliberate, as if diffidence were his routine, his beautiful hazy blue eyes, which always had a smile, a smirk, and a little judgment in them, his lazy half-drunk eyelids, and his mouth, his beautiful mouth, with full moist lips that always twisted into a comic book squiggle and begged to be kissed, he seemed to me made out of clouds and moon dust. Because he was a steamfitter, his shoulders were wide and coat hangerish, so T-shirts hung from them like an Abercrombie & Fitch ad. His hair was a little above the shoulder, brown and silky, floppy, like his brother's, and some of it often hung in front of his right eye, blowing lightly like a lace curtain in the breeze.

Dean, Maureen, and I would hang out together, getting high and drunk. I'm pretty sure they found me exotic and fascinating with all my talk of classical music, poetry, Joni Mitchell, foreign movies, and operas. We Gordons sort of played that role, the hothouse wildflower, the exotic bloom in every public garden, the interesting Jew. Though Dean had humiliated me at Pop's Bar, telling me he thought I talked too much, stinging me so hard it made my cheeks burn. That didn't matter at this moment now, at this moment, when we were sitting on a picnic table in Wildwood State Park, and he had just told me he could have sex with me.

By now I had carved a little hole in the table, and my fingertip hurt from the nail engorged with blood-colored paint and sawdust. "Why don't we then?" I asked, half timidly, not wanting to betray a desire my body and head were about to explode from. "Okay," he said, smiling at me, and he climbed off the table as if he knew exactly where we were going. "Come on." He set off and I followed him. We walked down a sandy path surrounded by tall reeds. Well, I walked, Dean ambled, like my big brother escorting me to my life. It was a beautiful day, sunny, but with a breeze that made the reeds wave and crackle, as if they were singing.

It was curiously isolated for a public park. You had no sense anyone was around, no concern anyone might see you. It was timeless, for me, that infinite space where critical events get frozen and burn into your memory like hot stones. The sun was high, so it was about two o'clock. I felt dizzy, sensing something new was about to happen to me and my life was about to change. Trembling, I was faint with desire, almost crazy.

Dean stopped, so I stopped. He grabbed me and started kissing me in a way I had never been kissed. Well, I had never been kissed, period. He was about my height, and the fit was perfect. The sensation of his tongue madly moving around inside my mouth forcefully—the delicious intrusion, the taste of beer and cigarettes—the tightness with which he held and caressed me, the sensation of something hard in his pants pressing against me, no one had ever held me this way. He was looking straight into my eyes. Most of the time, when men looked into my eyes, it was to say nasty things, or scold me, or humiliate me, and my default was to avert my gaze. But not now. We were staring at each other. This kind of love, or attention, or whatever you'd call it, and tenderness from a man was entirely new to me, much less someone I had done so much fantasizing about. I felt completely intoxicated. I can see, feel, and taste him right now as I write this.

I don't remember our removing our clothes, but the next thing I remember is Dean kneeling, taking my pants down, and sucking my penis.

I want to take a moment here to say I am not comfortable with the nomenclature of sex. Using words like "cock," "dick," and even "prick" feels inappropriate, because in this story I am back where I was when it was happening, unsophisticated, too inhibited to use the slang and lexicon of adulthood. It's almost as if I were stuck in an anatomy book of boyhood where only the scientific terms that are used to describe what is being seen for the first time have the ability to arouse with their air of forbiddenness.

Dean's sucking my penis was a whole new ball game, not the revulsion I felt with Gerard at eleven, the tickle, when my body was not yet alive, when I hadn't even had an erection yet, or one I can recall. This was as if every nerve cell had its own mind and there were a ticker tape parade of rejoicing happening inside me, replete with applause and confetti. The word "pleasure," previously dead on the page, was being redefined as the most important word in the English language, and I was being given a demonstration of its many details, intricacies, and fine points. This was an awakening.

Then we lay down in the sand, in a sixty-nine position. I had only seen this position in pornography, but I knew what it was called. I had never had a blow job. I had never given one, notwithstanding whatever aberrant thing happened with Gerard. The painful thing about this memory is, I had no idea how to have sex, what was expected of me, how I was supposed to perform. Once we were lying down, I don't remember anymore how what he was doing to me felt, or what it felt like to do anything to him. I remember the position, my head between his legs. I remember relishing having his penis in my mouth along with what was swirling in my head, "This is Dean! This is Dean's penis!" but it feels lonelier, less activated in my memory, more robotic. We were no longer face-to-face, so perhaps the fact that we were now into the mechanics of sex and beyond intimacy made it less memorable. I don't even think I was aware of any bodily sensation, just an overwhelming sense there was something I was supposed to do and didn't know how. Even now, it is harder for me to accept pleasure than to give it. I always feel as if I have to be doing something. In my fantasies, I am rarely anything more than a mouth, an orifice, never a whole person, or rarely. Maybe it is only in disappearing myself, who I think I am, who I have constructed myself to be, who I believe I am supposed to be, what I think I look like, divorced from my voice, my opinions, that I can actually become a body, a penis receiving pleasure. I would never even attempt phone sex because I couldn't imagine affecting a sexy personality or voice; I would simply sound like Ricky, and anybody would know who I was. Maybe this is why so many people prefer masturbation or those weird anonymous glory holes. "So many people": Am I afraid of saying "I"? You don't have to be anyone in masturbation, or when you are shoving your penis through a hole in the wall. You don't have to be talented or have made any kind of impact. You don't have to be clean. You don't have to brush your teeth. You can feel fat.

I must have figured something out, though, accessed some kind of innate talent for pleasuring, because Dean moaned and came in my mouth, and I swallowed it. It tasted odd and salty. Not necessarily a good taste, but it seemed that was what I was supposed to do; otherwise, what were you supposed to do with it? If it were now, I would have relished it. Now I know, I have admitted to myself, I have a fetish about cum. I believe it is directly related to the fact that I wasn't breast-fed. My mother had inverted nipples, so we never bonded in that way. So, the need to suckle, the thirst for mother's milk, combined with my father's fierce and aggressive loathing and rejection of me, somehow made me crave something from him, and in my mind I turned his penis into a breast and his cum into milk, father's milk. I craved my father's milk. Of course, I didn't know all of this yet, that day with Dean. I hadn't had time yet to fully cultivate the shape and parameters, the machinations, of my desires. I reiterate, I was fifteen.

Now we arrive at the part I am still terribly ashamed of. I notice my left hand clenching into a fist even as I write it. After Dean came, which tasted strange, like nothing I had ever tasted before, and I can't quite put my finger on how utterly strange that moment was, where I had no idea if what I was doing was terribly right or terribly wrong, I thought I was supposed to be done. I didn't even know how to ask for an apple, much less take someone's time for my own pleasure, so I was suddenly faced with having no idea what to do. I faked an orgasm, pretended I was done. I sighed and moaned, making noises I imagined you were supposed to make, perhaps like something I heard in a movie. I remember giving the performance and feeling half-ridiculous, but it seemed like the only thing I could manage to do. Dean said, "You didn't come," with a puzzled look on his face. He was right, I didn't, but I said I did. Dean, being an adult, knew of course that I hadn't. I didn't realize men can't fake orgasm, or really, anything men could and couldn't do. I knew nothing. I don't know how I got the faking-an-orgasm thing, but I could feel Dean's disappointment in me. What was he disappointed in? Did he want my cum? Was it actually turning him on to turn me on? I was clueless. I just didn't know what my role was. He kept saying, "No you didn't!" every time I insisted I had come. I knew I had done something wrong, and it hurt, because this was the first time anyone had ever made love to me. I felt love, or whatever you would call it, and confounding beyond anything I had ever known, and I felt like a failure. Somehow, though, I didn't think I could just say, "I didn't come." I had never in my life uttered anything about coming or not coming, so how would I have language for the protocols of sex? I was both lying and knowing I was being caught in a lie. Just as I couldn't tell anyone about what happened between Gerard and me when I was eleven. Gerard lived inside me like scissors trying to cut their way out of me. I simply did not have the language.

We walked back through the reeds, on the hot sand, and we were quiet, as if something almost wonderful had almost happened, but didn't, because of me. My chromosomes felt different, and the air particles felt charged, but everything was tinged with the sorrow and sadness of failure. I am sixty-four, and I still want to go back and fix it. I'm stuck there, in that pain and confusion.

Now I was determined to get Dean back into bed, because I hungered for his kisses and his body again, but also to amend my mistakes. I vowed I would perform like a real pro this time, a world champion in bed. I vowed I would be *hot!* One night Dean and I went out drinking at Pop's Bar, which, by the way, was right off Little Beach. Everyone went there salty and sandy after being in the sun, or in lieu of. It was one of those nights where there was wall-to-wall people, but Dean and I were in a little booth by ourselves in a protective bubble where nothing could get in, no sound, no intrusion. It's amazing they never carded me. I looked older than my age with my long hair, my half-boy's, half-man's body, a look of constant consternation, and peach fuzz on my chin, but still, I was fifteen. Things were more relaxed in those days.

We decided I was too drunk to go home, so I would sleep over at their house. Maureen was already asleep when we got home. Dean went to bed with her, and I was by myself on the couch in the living room. I prayed he would come in. We could start over again, and this time I'd get it right.

But when I woke up, it was to Dean sort of fucking my face. His penis was in my mouth, and he was moving up and down. It was nothing I had ever experienced before. I can't say it felt like rape or violation, because it was certainly some twisted version of what I was hoping would happen, but I was more shocked and confused than anything. Why wasn't he kissing me? Did he just need a warm mouth around his penis? Who was I to Dean at that moment? Was he going to leave Maureen for me? I didn't get an erection, because I was even more flummoxed than the first time about what to do; also, I didn't know then, as I do now, that I require a little warming up. I need to kiss, to talk, and to feel connected in order to become aroused. My plans for amending what had happened at Wildwood State Park went straight out the window because it was just a sort of chaos of penises and mouths and drunken bodies and lips that didn't know where to go. It was basically just drunken groping, me, fumbling with my hand on my penis, trying to get it hard, and Dean, trying to use my mouth to get off. We didn't even kiss. No one came; no one connected.

When he went back to bed with Maureen, or rather careened back to bed, I felt bereft and empty. I cried. I stared out into the desolate night, astonished at how badly my second chance had gone; I was able to neither orchestrate nor engineer anything. I was even *less* in control. It was almost as if he didn't even know who I was when he came to my bed that night. I felt confused and humiliated. I felt hopeless, and I feel it now, in the retelling of it, after forty years of therapy. This ended up being the last time he and I had sex, or whatever you would call it, the casualty, I imagined, of my ineptitude. I had lost very quickly whatever allure I might have had for Dean.

My feelings for him remained intense for a very long time. I guess they still are. I lived to see him and always tried to look my handsomest, thinking I could say or do the right thing to reel him back in. What is odd is that here we are, almost fifty years later. I have been in recovery for sex abuse (or whatever you call it) for many years. I know this was not a good and healthy thing that happened to me. I was a boy, Dean, a man, but I never quite get over the confusion of it having been something I wanted, and whatever happened being my fault, because I made it happen. I feel as if I engineered it. I know the adult is supposed to know what is right and wrong, but I can't forgive myself. I can't forgive myself for not coming when he blew me at Wildwood State Park and lying about it, or for not getting an erection that night in bed, which made me feel like a little boy, or even a girl, rather than a man with him. It's as if I pushed him away with my inadequacy, interrupting the scenario in which we walk off into the sunset and love each other forever.

From Dean I learned something that has caused me enormous pain many times over. Just because a straight, married, heterosexual man finds you attractive, intriguing, exotic, and thinks fooling around with you might be fun once or twice, especially if you perform well, which I didn't, doesn't mean they are going to turn gay, fall in love with you, and leave their wives for you. At most, you are a dalliance, an experience, a notch in the belt, a demonstration of their breezy open-mindedness, a taste, a different flavor. If they happen to be the first person who touches you, or kisses you, in a way that feels like love, the first tenderness, they will create a little compartment, a drawer inside you marked permanent desire and permanent hurt, that never closes and never goes away.

To this day Dean's name still makes me want to cry. I still desire him. I still feel hurt, embarrassed, and all the rest. I even thought of writing him and telling him—but why? What could I hope to achieve, a mercy fuck? Make him feel bad for having sex with a minor fifty years ago? It seems fruitless. What happened between Dean and me was probably the damaged leading the damaged. I heard he is a born-again Christian now, with a new wife and kids. A few years later, I was home from college for a summer, and I got a call from Dean saying there was a man who worked with him at a steam-fitting job he wanted to fix me up with. I felt sad and strange it wasn't a call about Dean wanting to see me, but I also fantasized about him sending me a steamfitter who could be for me what Dean couldn't. I met the man, Francis, at the Wildwood, a gay bar on Columbus Avenue. It was one of those old places from the 1970s that stink of beer and cigarettes. Huge bowls of peanuts lined the room, and the shells mixed with the sawdust all over the floor made a crunch and rustling under your feet. On the phone, Francis had a sweet and appealing voice, almost like that old actor who always played the kind Irish priest in those movies from the 1940s, with a ball at the end of his nose: Karl Malden. But in person, he seemed old, sad, and sweaty, pale and pasty, and needy, and it was all I could do to get the hell out of there. After that I just ignored his phone calls until he left me alone. It was so painful that Dean's "replacement" failed the test, dashed my hopes.

Recently, I found Dean on Facebook. He is a shrunken gray-haired version of himself. His wife looks like the little blond shiksa Robert Redford marries in *The Way We Were* rather than marry Barbra Streisand. I requested his friendship, and he accepted. Why? Very occasionally, he likes something of mine, but in general I wonder whether he sees me on Facebook as a braggart, tiresome, or the one he said "talks too much" in Pop's Bar, one night months before we went back to his house drunk and I woke up with his dick in my mouth.

CARL

Carl, my brother-in-law Patrick's brother, was tall and lanky, swarthy, and handsome. There is no getting around it: these boys were blessed. Darker than Patrick, with a Jack Nicholson mischief in his eyes and a leering, salacious smile, he was sex in a bottle, a satyr, made of flirtation, raised eyebrows, suggestion, and swagger all at once. Carl would sit on the beach and talk about his sexual exploits, what he had done to women, or what he wanted to do, with such relish it's almost as if he presented himself as a walking, talking erect penis. As he gawked at women walking by, you could see him getting an erection under his shorts. He clearly had an insatiable sexual appetite. I had heard him talk once about his dalliance with a man, a guy named Joe. I remember him almost joking about Joe's scratchy whiskers when they kissed, the first time he kissed a man. It clearly made an impression on me. But as his appetites usually demonstrated, he was decidedly heterosexual and, at this point, divorced from his first wife and with a daughter. I liked him because he was funny and sly and treated me as if I were special, a genius or something but definitely a peer. Sometimes when he looked at me and his eyes would linger maybe five seconds longer than I expected them to, it would totally disarm me.

On one of the times when my parents were away on a cruise, there was a party with Sheila's friends at the boatyard. After what had happened with Dean, a gathering of Sheila's and Patrick's friends now felt rife with possibility for me. I might have been fifteen, but I no longer looked like a boy. I looked the way teenagers look when they have passed through their pimply puppy dog awkward period and suddenly they are all clear-skinned walking and talking desire, with pheromones firing like lasers.

At the moment the quaaludes kicked in and everyone was sufficiently drunk, Carl, in what now seems to be some kind of planned ambush, asked me if I wanted to go home with him. I was astonished, shocked, and surprised, and my heart practically leaped out of my chest. Of course, I said yes. Like Dean and Patrick, Carl was a steamfitter, working on the Twin Towers. He had a lithe, beautiful body that screamed strength and confidence.

Meanwhile, Patrick approached Peter and said to meet him in the laundry room. I am recounting this as Peter told it, and I need to say that, because Peter can be hyperbolic. Patrick moved the bed in front of the door and asked Peter if he had ever been with a man before. Aside from various hand jobs for neighborhood boys, he hadn't. Patrick sat Peter in the middle of the bed, asking him if he had ever had a dick in his mouth. Peter was at eye level with Patrick's crotch as Patrick began manipulating his fly. He eventually got the zipper down, revealing his formidable penis, which looked "ten inches long" to Peter, who described Patrick's testicles as "cantaloupes." Peter was careful to express how gentle Patrick was when he pulled Peter's face into his crotch, put his penis into Peter's mouth, and pushed it gently deep into his throat, moving in and out until he came so much, Peter said, "it came through my nose." Patrick asked if Peter had ever kissed a man. Peter of course said no. Patrick pushed him down on the bed and lay down beside him, and they kissed "long and passionately."

Carl drove me in his black Volkswagen to California Street, in Long Beach, where he lived with his girlfriend, Susan, so we could have sex. In the car, he described how no one was ever disappointed with how much he came when he ejaculated. Why was he telling me this? Had I said something that made him think he should tell me this? When we got to his house, he went to pee while I lay down on the bed. What a strange feeling it is, exhilarating and lonely, before something you really want to happen is about to happen and you are scared and excited all at once. I stared at everything in the room with new eyes. Fantasy was about to give way to reality, and I didn't know what to do with all of it.

I don't remember taking my clothes off, but I remember him coming in and immediately unzipping my pants and starting to suck my penis. I wasn't hard yet, but it felt so good I got hard pretty quickly. I think what was new about that moment was how desirous he seemed of me. Then we kissed. My head was swimming, and my skin was singing from the quaalude.

Carl was even older than Dean and Patrick, maybe by three or four years. So, if I was fifteen, he might have been twenty-five or twenty-six. He was a very different experience from Dean, more feral, like a wild animal. He kissed forcefully so it was invasive and made you aware of your size, he being at least a foot taller than me. From kissing, we somehow found ourselves in a sixty-nine position. Though I marveled at the size of his enormous penis and testicles, I had no idea what to do with them. I was all desire and absolutely no know-how. As with Dean, I had no technique. I remember, because of the angle, I was staring straight at his asshole while I was sucking on his penis. I was not grossed out by it, though I had never thought of that part of the body as sexual before. I just didn't know what to do with it. He wanted to fuck me, but I wouldn't let him, because I feared he would kill me putting anything that large up inside me. I had no thought of receiving pleasure myself. It's as if, in all these experiences, an inner geisha was unleashed in me. If I managed to be pleasured at all, it was inadvertent, because I thought I was simply there to please the other person. What was I supposed to do to make him happy? Who did I need to be?

Finally, because I ran out of ideas and my fear and inexperience began to dominate, I told him to jerk himself off and then, when he was about to come, to let me know and I would swallow his cum. I did and it was a lot. Why did I even think to do that? Where was I getting my information from? At that moment, it was not an act that was sexy to me. It was what I thought I was supposed to do in my skewed, inexperienced mind.

In the car on the way back to the boatyard he said not to tell anyone. I felt strange and excited, but also disappointed, because again, I was in a situation that was so completely beyond me. I had just had sex with Carl, someone I'd known since childhood, someone to whom I was still at least close to being a child. I didn't know what to think or feel. But I added him to the list of men I could now sexually fantasize about, having added information to my arsenal. Once again, I hoped it would happen again so I could get it right, know what I was doing.

I feel ashamed writing this. Why wasn't I studying, reading, anything other than having sex with these men I had sexualized for so long, a parade of fathers. I was high all the time, obsessing about older heterosexual men for whom I was a momentary road out of the ordinary, some kind of lure or catnip. It is painful now to know all of this was wrong and did me harm in numerous ways, but telling the stories still arouses me, and I would do anything for most of them to happen again.

I remember, after the Michael Jackson documentary, *Leaving Neverland*, when the two men who came forward with allegations of abuse against him expressed their confusion, because to this day, essentially, they feel as if what happened were something they wanted to happen, or didn't know was bad, ruinous in fact. They were doing whatever it was they were doing with their hero, making him happy, giving him what he wanted. They were close to him, special to him. That's how it was with me. I was kissing, making love, or trying, with these men who were my heroes. But then the tables turned, and I suddenly seemed to have power, though what it was and how I was supposed to use it were mysterious to me. It was the most exciting thing in the world, having sex with these objects of desire from my childhood, once Sheila's friends who dined out on teasing me, now the naked men in my arms, or I in theirs, and probably that is what was so damaging about it. Nothing could ever compare, or be that exciting again; I would forever be relegated to seeking to duplicate those experiences, for how could anything ever compare with those thwarted doors into the impossible, the incomplete, the wished for but inappropriate. I was simply too young for those doors to be opened.

Back at the boatyard, I knocked insistently on the door of the laundry room, sensing what was happening. Peter says, "No matter how much I entreated you to go away, you wouldn't." I was heartbroken, burning with envy that Peter had had sex with my brother-in-law, the man I loved most in the world. As far as I was concerned, Patrick was married to my sister *and* me. There was no one I fantasized about more than my brother-in-law. But I had just gotten home from having sex with Patrick's brother Carl and needed to tell someone. It was so strange, wild, curiously full, lurid, and empty all at the same time.

Afterward, Peter and I ran breathlessly downstairs and compared notes like madly chirping birds in our forever altered states.

PATRICK

We were at Carl's house on California Street. We were again high on quaaludes and drinking, very high. Sheila was in the hospital getting her tonsils out, so Patrick and I were hanging out. I was going to sleep over at their apartment in Freeport to keep him company. It was a Friday night and Patrick made one of his "Friday Night Specials" for everybody, which consisted of ziti, tomato sauce, and cheddar cheese and would probably be considered disgusting now, but at the time, and especially when you were high and drunk with the munchies, was like ambrosia. On the way home I did what I was planning to do all night, as if I had conquered several mountains but not Everest, and it was time. I cajoled him, persuaded him to have sex with me. I reminded him about my friend Peter and the laundry room, and said, "If you could do it with Peter, can't you do it with me?" I pulled out every manipulative stop I had.

It wasn't too hard to convince him. He agreed to it. I could barely contain myself. I felt like a conqueror, a conquistador, luring whatever I wanted onto a gold plate. When we got home, undressed, and got into bed, I started kissing him. I couldn't wait, the anticipation made me feel like a wolf about to enter a henhouse, so I became the aggressor.

We made out for a while. He started sucking my penis, but then he leaned back for me to pleasure him. I went down on him, where, again, the gift of size that clearly ran in that blessed family revealed itself to me in all its splendor like the monolith in *2001: A Space Odyssey*. I was definitely, at that point, a boy with an unlimited credit card at FAO Schwarz. While I, still burdened with all desire and no know-how, tried to figure out what to do, where to start, he fell asleep with my head between his legs.

He was still erect. He smelled clean, and there was a faint hint of baby powder, which made him seem both man and child. I was confused. It was too large an experience, too many answered prayers at once. I was overwhelmed. All of my nerve cells were an explosion of desires met. For a few moments I didn't know what to do, whether to continue while he slept, or what? I sort of jerked myself off while manipulating him in various ways, and when I came, I went into the bathroom to clean myself off.

It is hard to describe how strange I felt looking in the mirror. My sister Sheila and I have always looked somewhat alike. Sometimes, it is beyond us being close; it's as if we were the same person. In this way, we easily lift each other up, and we easily hurt each other. I seemed to be staring at both of us, only this time it was I who had slept with her husband, while she was in surgery having her tonsils removed.

The next morning over breakfast, he told me it would probably be better if I didn't tell Sheila. He didn't really need to say that; I wasn't *that* stupid. For the rest of my life, in some ways my head has been stuck between Patrick's legs with his huge hard-on staring at me and my confusion about who I was and what to do with it. There you go, fifteen, one thwarted experience after another, all ending with me in what felt like love, not knowing what to do with my feelings, and waiting forever for something to happen again that shouldn't have happened in the first place, casting a pall of expectation and disappointment over everything in my life that would follow, making love and sex never as exciting, never as cloaked in the atmosphere of the forbidden, never as dangerous, damaging, and impossible as my half-fulfilled fantasies were then. I was still a boy, inflamed with getting what I wanted, amoral without meaning to be, unbound, unguided, and in that way, in many ways, these experiences almost ruined me, but I am a phoenix. I prevail.

PART II

CARNEGIE MELLON

Peter met Richie Laeton when he moved to Long Beach, switching high schools, and we became a happy triumvirate, three gay teenagers navigating the craggy fear-filled terrain of being one's true self. A prodigious artist, Richie was obsessed with Barbra Streisand, making meticulous pointillistic drawings of her repeatedly with a Rapidograph that bore an astonishing likeness. His parents were reluctant to take him to Las Vegas for her big concert engagement, so he enacted a five-day hunger strike until they relented. He cajoled a stagehand into getting an astonishing assortment of the drawings to her hotel room, but rather than an invitation to meet, or even an autographed photograph, she sent a curt "Thank you" back, which crushed him.

A year ahead of me, when Richie went to Carnegie Mellon University in Pittsburgh to study design, I visited him there.

After seeing two handsome and elegant-looking gentlemen striding across the campus holding hands while walking two Afghan hounds, that Bergman's *Wild Strawberries* was showing on campus that night, and that a production of *The Threepenny Opera* was planned, which Richie was particularly excited about, because it starred Donn Simione, a triple-threat actor/singer/dancer from Toledo whom Richie was obsessed with, I decided I needed to be there. Donn was so old-fashioned-movie-star handsome he was cast as one after college, dancing elegantly with the Grace Kelly of Broadway at the time, Rebecca Luker, and he appeared in a rather lengthy and revealing *Playgirl* spread.

I had to be at this bustling cauldron of intellect, imagination, and talent where men like Donn Simione roamed freely, and I needed *out* of high school, so at sixteen I auditioned for the music department, playing Hindemith, Schumann, Scarlatti, Bach, Brahms, Beethoven, and two modernists, Peggy Glanville-Hicks and Leo Kraft. I don't know if it was my playing, my enthusiasm, or because no one had ever played pieces by Peggy Glanville-Hicks and Leo Kraft to audition before, but I got accepted. I left high school in December, and in January, I was at CMU.

At the time of my audition, I was obsessed with three pieces of music: Ned Rorem's incredible 1971 song cycle, *Ariel*, for soprano, clarinet, and piano, uses Sylvia Plath's poems, finding a musical equivalent to Plath's words, the desperation, the danger, the audacity, the icy intellect, and her standing at the edge of a precipice, with such genius and clarity that I was bowled over. In "Lady Lazarus," he used the time signature 11/4, which I had never seen or heard anywhere else. It was perfect for the off-kilter, unsettling rhythm of the words, and I listened to this dazzling work over and over again until I could sing every note of it! I would make people come to my room and listen to it. I walked around singing Sylvia Plath's brutal words in my head, a bizarre inner soundtrack to my life, and even came home from college when, for Rorem's fiftieth birthday, he was being honored at Alice Tully Hall. I knew Phyllis Curtin would be performing these songs, so I got a ticket in the second row. I had never seen a singer cry onstage. I could barely speak after the performance.

Shostakovich's shattering 1969 Symphony No. 14, for soprano, bass, and chamber orchestra, dedicated to Benjamin Britten, using poems about death by great poets like Rilke, Apollinaire, and García Lorca, which, in my humble estimation, is a superior piece to Mussorgsky's *Songs and Dances of Death*, which he had orchestrated. I would play sections of it, like "Malagueña," with its sizzling strings and castanets, and "On Watch," with its rattling death bones impersonated by the xylophone, over and over again, marveling at its endless invention. Both of these works, the Rorem and the Shostakovich, demonstrated such careful attention to text setting in their perfect marriage of words and music they were clearly paradigms for what I would later seek to emulate myself as a composer. But then, all that I was was nascent. Outside the great art I loved, I had no idea who I was. I was only what I was inviolably drawn to.

The third piece was Stephen Sondheim's crackling, earth-shattering musical *Follies*.

Richie and I moved in together at Hamerschlag Hall, where I could use the communal shower only between the hours of 3:00 and 5:00 a.m., lest the unbelievably handsome Mark Leone enter and I would get a boner looking at him.

One night, Richie and I go out to the Holiday, the gay bar on Forbes Avenue, festooned in all our disco finery. Donn Simione, clearly waiting for Richie to leave my side, walks over and says, "Can I see you alone sometime?" Seeing Donn in a gay bar is somewhat astounding. His old-Hollywood-movie-star handsomeness sets him absurdly apart. Barely able to even look at him, stunned, flattered, and astonished, I of course say, "Sure!" knowing this will cut Richie to the quick. The night of our date, we meet at his apartment overlooking the Holiday on the corner of South Craig Street and Forbes Avenue. Richie knows but hasn't let on the full extent of his anguish. I am still young, seventeen, and very scared. Yes, Donn is wildly handsome, but I have no idea what to do about it. I am still so inexperienced at sex, other than whatever you would call my prodigious underage sex life with older men at fifteen, I feel like a lamb going to slaughter. I stare out the window before we undress, wishing we could just go get drunk at the Holiday. I don't remember kissing him, or doing anything that might have been pleasurable or fantasy fulfilling, say, blowing him, or something that seems fun in retrospect. All I remember is the pain of Donn plunging himself inside me, my legs all the way over my head and touching the wall behind me, his twin bed, and the shower afterward in his bathroom, which was the first time I ever remember so much semen coming out of my rectum.

Donn and I go to dinner afterward, and I don't know what to say. What I feel, besides embarrassment at my ineptitude, is that he is out of my league. When I get back to our dorm, Richie is sitting on the floor, leaning on his bed, his neck elongated like an angry swan. His lips are pursed like a spurned Loretta Young, and he is surrounded by lit candles, listening to Barbra Streisand sing "The Way We Were." He is threatening to slit his wrists with an X-Acto knife, the chief tool of his trade and precisely the right thing for him to kill himself with. No apology will dampen the hurt, though, apparently, he wants to hear the details more than he wants to die, so I recount the evening, giving him every lurid detail. I thought Donn was my new boyfriend, but it was over before it even began. For a little while, obsessed with him, I skulk around early in the morning to catch glimpses of him on the way to Dynamics, the obligatory morning exercises for actors, but clearly he is not pining similarly for me. We have one more date. He gives me a necklace, a Star of David, and breaks up with me. Did he break up with me because I was a Jew? It will always remain a mystery.

In my first semester as a pianist, something felt wrong. Sitting in a practice room all day to perfect a Chopin nocturne when I knew I would never in a million years be good enough to make it as a concert pianist seemed futile, and I did not feel I was able to express who I *was* as a pianist. Stephen Sondheim had just written his dazzlingly elegant score for Alain Resnais's movie *Stavisky*, and I listened to it over and over again. My fingers wanted to make something like *that* happen and with the director of *Muriel*, *Last Year at Marienbad*, *Night and Fog*, and *Hiroshima mon amour*. I was so obsessed with his *Follies*. I ached to express the same brokenness, derision, and disappointment he expressed in that, or Ingmar Bergman expressed in all of his movies. I wanted to *be* the music, not just *play* the music. I wanted to make something great, profound, and moving. I was discovering new composers like Olivier Messiaen with his swirling, nattering birds and profound unequivocal devotion, and Hans Werner Henze with his post–World War II ferocity and angularity. Music was taking hold of me in a new way, devouring me. There was a blind pianist named Lynn who was obsessed with Shostakovich. "Shostie," she called him. She could play anything of his on the piano, and she *was* the music; there was no separation. I envied her. Being a pianist felt wrong, so I found out what was necessary to enter the composition department and over a school vacation, to the amazement of my father, who always harbored the idea I was lazy, wrote about a hundred pages of music. I switched majors and became a composer. Besides getting sober, it was probably the single most important decision of my life: finally, a road, albeit bumpy and filled with doubt and crippling insecurity, but a road. I walked into my own light.

My first compositions were settings of all the poems I loved, and some by the poets I met at school. I took writing classes to learn how to write my own poems and lyrics. I wrote awkward Sondheim imitations where everybody was in failed, miserable marriages as if I knew anything about such things. I modeled myself after Sylvia Plath, Anne Sexton, and Robert Lowell, writing confessional poems, though I had no idea what to confess. I wrote an awful poem about Marilyn Monroe, replete with the alliteration "mannequin manic maniac," about the perils of notoriety and her lurid exploitation at the hands of careless men. But by deciphering the architecture of a poem through attempting to create its musical equivalent, I started figuring out how to construct things, how to build containers for my thoughts and feelings.

I befriended a teacher in the drama department, a former mime named Jewel Walker, who asked me to write music for his exquisitely nuanced productions of William Inge's *Picnic* and *Bus Stop*, and then other directors enlisted me to write scores for plays by Christopher Marlowe and Bertolt Brecht.

I remember little of what any composition teacher said about my music, except at a piano lesson one day with Colette Wilkins. After I played and sang for her my setting of Dorothy Parker's poem "Threnody," she said my music had an "energetic melancholy." I find it the most accurate thing anyone has ever said about my music.

Richie left school, so I got a house off campus in Shadyside, an elegant neighborhood within earshot of the highly subsidized Shadyside Presbyterian Church with tree-lined streets and Victorian mini mansions and chic boutiques, cafés, and restaurants. Other than the fact that the city was still a steel town with a booming industry in the 1970s and stank like rotten eggs at various hours throughout the day, it was in many ways, scenically, a lovely city, surprisingly verdant and landscaped. I rented a house on Filbert Street with a designer named Doug Turshen, an affable fellow who was always helpful, calm, and disarmingly sincere and never got angry, a perfect foil to my always close-to-the-surface hysteria. He was about my height, nice looking, with black wavy hair and a surprisingly turned-up nose for a Jew, and dressed in that way Jews started dressing when Ralph Lauren came onto the scene and taught them how to dress like WASPs and get away with it. I got the upstairs room in the front of this Victorian house, a great room where the ceiling had all kinds of wonderful angles. After sharing an ugly cement rectangle of a dorm room with Richie, and communal bathrooms and showers, I was excited to have my own room. I painted the walls a vintage salmon and the floors a shiny black lacquer. I hung patchwork quilts and my beautiful John Graham poster. Doug helped me to mount bookshelves by the door for my plants, records, and stereo. I put a large goldfish bowl on them with about ten darting and undulating goldfish. On the first night I slept there, I was awakened by what sounded like an atomic bomb. I am afraid of loud noises and easily startled, so I jumped up, stood on my bed, and began involuntarily shrieking. Doug ran in and turned on the lights. Apparently, the goldfish bowl was too heavy for the walls and tore down the shelves and everything on them. Goldfish were flopping up and down, and everything was floating in this new lagoon. I was useless and in shock, but Doug said, "Oh, well," smiling and shrugging his shoulders, and slowly cleaned everything up with enormous composure. He even saved the goldfish, putting them in a plastic bag with water until we could figure out their next home.

After two years in the composition department, during Christmas vacation I swallowed some diet pills, Black Beauties, and then took the train into the city by myself to see Martin Scorsese's movie *Taxi Driver*. Bernard Herrmann's score welling up over the smoke-filled garage, and Robert De Niro's performance, were overwhelming. On the way home, I resolved I needed to give up music and become an actor. This is something I did a lot. To be attracted to someone didn't always mean I had to *have* them; sometimes, it meant I had to *be* them. I had to be Robert De Niro! I decided to audition for the drama department. Acting suddenly seemed the only art that would access my inner intensity. I didn't tell anyone, but for the rest of Christmas vacation I hid away in my room and memorized Sammy Goldenbaum's monologue from William Inge's *Dark at the Top of the Stairs*. He seemed a perfect character for me, an insecure, shy half-Jew boy who kills himself. My obsession with foreign movies paid off. When I got back to school and auditioned for the drama department, I delivered the monologue with the intensity of Bibi Andersson or Liv Ullmann in Ingmar Bergman's *Persona* and was accepted immediately.

The theater department at Carnegie Mellon had a stellar reputation. It was notoriously hard to get into and to survive the rigorous scrutiny and the physical discipline, so it was easy to imbue the often glamorous and charismatic "dramats" with magic powers. In my first semester, I was out to dinner with a group of them, actors *and* directors, and because I had assigned them so much power and authority in my head, sitting at a table in a restaurant beside them was intolerable, and I collapsed, my head falling to the table, just missing my food. When I came to, they were ashen, thinking I had died. I assured them I was okay, but they drove me home and never invited me out again. Ironically, two of them, after college, when they moved to New York, were responsible for *Moose Murders*, a play on Broadway that has the reputation of being the worst flop in Broadway history. If I had known that that night, the information might have saved me.

With the help of speed, I was a very diligent actor in the drama department. Impressed with myself for being accepted, I worked hard. Dynamics—basically, yoga, stretching, and rigorous exercise for all the actors from freshmen to seniors every morning at 9:00—were required, and if you missed three, you were out.

But then I met Brian Frank. He had been a drama major at Ohio University a few years before. While there, he noticed he was having trouble singing on pitch at a chorus rehearsal and his legs would suddenly give out underneath him as if they were made of rubber. Clowning around, demonstrating this in the cafeteria one day for friends, he suddenly collapsed. He was intubated and rushed in an ambulance to the hospital in Columbus with a strange syndrome called Guillain-Barré involving paralysis. He is the worst recorded case in history, having lost the use of everything all at once. For a year, all he could do was click his tongue to communicate. His mother had to move from Baltimore to Columbus to be near the hospital. Recovery took a year and was miraculous, because usually even someone with a milder case ends up with some paralysis, but Brian recovered everything, though he had to be retaught to walk, talk, and breathe on his own without a respirator. At the orientation in the Kresge Theatre at 6:00 p.m., when the students and the faculty get acquainted, since I was now an *actor*, I thought I'd make a splash wearing a pair of rhinestone-encrusted cat sunglasses housewives in the 1950s wore or French movie stars like Brigitte Bardot. Brian singled me out, saying, "We have to be friends." After such extreme paralysis, he needed to make up for lost time, and we started having a lot of fun together. I became a bad student, while he *was* one from the start. We started smoking pot together, getting the munchies, eating too much, and fucking off. There were serious actors in our class like Holly Hunter, who talked out of the side of her mouth with such a thick southern accent you would never in a million years have guessed she would become a star, and Linda Kozlowski, from Fairfield, Connecticut, who was gorgeous and looked like Greta Garbo. After school, Holly was nominated for an Academy Award for *Broadcast News*, and Linda got cast in the Broadway production of *Death of a Salesman*, with Dustin Hoffman, playing one of the tarts in the bar scene. Dustin thought Linda was a "star" and told her to go out to L.A. and make movies. He even offered her his house. She was soon cast in the movie *Crocodile Dundee*, starring opposite Paul Hogan, an Australian megastar in his first movie. The movie was a megahit, pulling in fifty million dollars at the box office. Paul, a former bridge worker with a wife and five kids, was responsible for making an Australian accent fashionable. Linda and Paul fell in love, and Paul divorced his wife and married Linda. In the tabloids, there was an attempt to denigrate Linda, blame her for Paul's behavior, cast her as the dumb blond home wrecker, the brazen harridan; nevertheless, she was now rich and famous, and we were enamored. Brian and I were neither raving beauties nor exceedingly talented as actors, so this foray into the Carnegie Mellon drama department lasted only a year. To prepare for a scene, I would take speed and do fifty push-ups before I went into the room. I did a scene from *Fortune and Men's Eyes*, where I was Rocky, and Brent Barrett, who became a Broadway star in musical comedy, was Smitty. I liked the idea of being butch and mean and saying things like "I like my boys clean," but that character existed in me only if I was drugged. I did a scene with another actress, Kristin James, from *A Taste of Honey*, and decided that day to see if I could act without speed. John Ulmer, the acting teacher, said it was the worst thing he had ever seen. Brian and I would go out to gay bars and discos every night. I dated the thug bartender at the Holiday bar, and one time he came over to have sex after a barroom brawl. Thank God it was pre-AIDS because I remember the metallic taste of his blood when I kissed his split lip.

After three and a half years, three different majors, and a degree in nothing, I left Carnegie Mellon University.

In the summer of 1977, Brian and I, after quitting school, had just finished a stint in a theater company with a bunch of actors and directors from Carnegie Mellon. In residence at Lake Erie College in Painesville, Ohio, it was boiling hot, and we were living in un-air-conditioned dressing rooms with mattresses strewn on the floor: women in one and men in the other. It was a verdant, pollen-filled, overgrown part of Ohio, and there was so much dust on the floor and mold in the old costumes from years of repertory theater in these not very hallowed halls that my allergies went mad, and I was miserable with red eyes and a constantly running red nose. My twenties were a time when I had very little idea what my body wanted or needed, so I would go to Howard Johnson's for breakfast with Brian, order chocolate chip pancakes, put a ton of butter and syrup on them, and then wonder why I felt so disgusting and wanted to sleep for the rest of the day. I was writing music for Jean Anouilh's *Waltz of the Toreadors*, as well as playing Father Ambrose, the deus ex machina character who runs in at the end, connects all the dots with a very long monologue, and runs off again. On opening night, with eleven people in the audience, including our friends Tom and Lorraine, I ran out to do my monologue, sew everything together for this poor audience that could have cared less, and I forgot the entire thing, every word. I looked at Brian, hoping he might give me a clue, but he looked at me and shrugged, mouthing, "Sorry, no idea." I blathered whatever I could muster and ran off the stage utterly humiliated, because nothing that happened previously in this unbearably long play made sense without what I was supposed to say, and everyone wanted to kill me. I was preoccupied with the makeup backstage all night, and my costume, one of those black friar robes that has ten thousand buttons, had just been finished that day, so I spent so much time trying to get those fucking buttons buttoned, and my rouge correct, I never went over my lines in my head. It was a total disaster, even for the actors who *remembered* their lines, because no one in Painesville, Ohio, was interested in Jean Anouilh, or theater, and our little theater company disbanded quickly.

On weekends, our friends Tom and Lorraine, mercifully, would come get me and Brian out of the aptly named Painesville and drive us into Cleveland, where I started understanding how five bottles of wine with dinner were better than one. Just as Carlos and Erin had taught me to smoke, Tom and Lorraine were teaching me to drink. I have had so many good teachers in my life.

After Ohio, I was living with my parents at the boatyard in Long Island, and I called Tom in Cleveland and Brian in Baltimore and told them I thought we should live together in New York City. They liked the idea. I searched the listings in the *Times* and found an apartment on West Seventieth Street. Our friend Andrea Wolfson came with me to see the apartment. The super, Mike Colon, while showing us the apartment, tried getting us to become Jehovah's Witnesses, but we just kept asserting, "We're Jewish!" I took the apartment.

When Tom, Brian, and I moved in together, my lifelong habit of shoplifting paid off. Seeing as we were always broke, there was a supermarket, Food City, between Sixty-Ninth and Seventieth on Columbus Avenue, and I would steal steaks by putting them under my overcoat. I usually got away with it, but I must have had a look about me, because once, at another market, Pioneer, I was pulled over when I hadn't even stolen anything. I became irate, as if crime were the *furthest* thing from my nature. A few mornings after we moved in, I got a call very early in the morning from my mother. "They got him." "Who?" I said. "Son of Sam."

One day, Tom, Brian, and I were at the Riviera Cafe on Sheridan

Square. We were getting drunk on martinis when Robert De Niro came in with some friends and sat at a table across from us. I knew I had to do something. At one point, when he got up to go to the men's room, I followed him and stood against the bathroom wall like a hustler waiting for a trick. When he was done, I mauled him, telling him how I became an actor because of him, recounting the saga about *Taxi Driver*, the speed, Carnegie Mellon, and the Sammy Goldenbaum monologue: an aria of praise, a paean, recited at the tempo of Rimsky-Korsakov's "Flight of the Bumblebee." He put his arm around me in an act of great charity and walked me back to my table in the most older-brotherish way, greeting my friends warmly and wishing us a good night. Brian and Tom, their jaws on the floor, were speechless.

For much of my life, I have been prone to obsessions. When I became inexplicably fixated on a person, sometimes it felt like youthful ardor, others, like being crushed in the jaws of a vicious animal. Sometimes they were brief; sometimes they lasted for years. Sometimes they were people I didn't even know, and never got to know, so they were merely whatever it was I projected onto them.

It was when I first visited Carnegie Mellon. I saw Timothy Calligan descending the stairs of Skibo, the cafeteria, in a red puffy down jacket. His hair was dirty blond, and his eyes, a grayish almost cobalt blue behind his wire-rimmed glasses. He looked like if Linus in *Peanuts* had grown up and had the same countenance, serious, a little harried, lonely, and studious. His cheeks puffed out slightly, like a squirrel accruing acorns.

Timothy was an architect. The architects seemed to flicker at another vibration than the rest of us. They stayed up the latest and worked the hardest. They seemed grown-up, ruggedly individual, as if they were born at thirty and had no room or time for the superfluous. It was Tim's seriousness and integrity that hooked me, aspects of an imaginary masculinity I failed to understand or express, or if I did, I didn't know it.

He seemed to me a romantic figure out of Brontë or Austen. I don't remember a single time seeing him with anyone, and he seldom smiled. He did later, when I had him over for dinner, after considerable scheming, and it was a kind smile, a quiet, contented smile, but not a happy smile. It was as if the puppeteer had pulled the strings on both sides of his lips.

There was a very strange kid at CMU at that time, a pianist whose name was Jack. The first person I ever met with obsessive-compulsive disorder, he washed his hands so often they were cracked, dry, and bleeding. It was hard to imagine how he played the piano with those bloody stumps. Jack felt the need at one point to tell me he saw Tim showering in the bathroom of his dorm and Tim had big balls, which, though the messenger was slightly repellent, was nevertheless invigorating information. Then and now, I feel aberrant being let in on that kind of intel. I want it, and I'm afraid of being the person who wants it, like everyone's delight when Stormy Daniels describes in detail Donald Trump's small mushroom-headed penis. One time I was having dinner with an agent for opera singers in New York. I asked him out because I thought he was attractive and seemed interesting and I was lonely. At dinner, we were talking about Peter, who is also an agent, and he leaned across the table, looking both ways to make sure no one was listening. "Can I ask you a question?" he asked. "How big is his meat?" I nearly fell off my chair. "Are you really asking me that?" The date was over. I understand the impulse. If we weren't civilized, we might go around asking, "How big is your penis? Can I touch it? Can I suck it? Sing to it?" Or, "You have great tits! Can I put my head between them and move it back and forth?" I love how dogs say hello by sniffing each other's butts. But we *are* civilized, so we don't. I hate myself for recounting what Jack said and for even letting it in when he said it, but he did and I did and there you have it.

If we are drawn to people for different parts of their personalities and how they reflect our history, Tim was more like my father. I was a fuckup at Carnegie Mellon. I got some work done in the interstices between chasing desire and getting high, but Tim was the model student, the older brother who could teach you morals and good behavior. If I was in a practice room, supposedly practicing piano, I was more than likely sitting on the windowsill staring out, waiting for a sighting of Timothy in his red down coat to ignite my longing, like

Jay Gatsby with the green light across the water. Even now, just the thought of him sets thousands of hummingbirds fluttering in my stomach. Timothy.

I was living in a carriage house behind a mansion owned by the Currys, a wealthy Pittsburgh family, right across from Shadyside Presbyterian Church, a beautiful jewel box of a house with ivy growing up the sky-blue stone walls. When you opened the bright cherry-red door, you walked up a flight of three pinewood stairs. I remember what it smelled and felt like, the cool air of its containment, my quick beating heart, the excitement, mystery, and agency I felt having my own house. There was a big living room, a little room off it that I rented a piano for, and a lovely little kitchen and bathroom. Out every window were lush Boston ferns. My fantasy house, if I could carry it in my pocket and plop it down wherever I was in the world, it would always be where I wrote, dreamed, and felt happy. I built shelves across the windows in lieu of curtains and lined them with rosary vines, or strings of hearts, because they were the favorite plant of all three of my sisters, and since I worshipped them, I had to follow in their footsteps.

I painted the living room robin's-egg blue and hung a huge red, white, and blue Missouri star quilt my sister Susan had given me from her journeys across Appalachia on which she would buy patchwork quilts, old clothes, and reindeer sweaters to sell. I had a million records, a great stereo, and tons of philodendron, snake, and dieffenbachia plants in the kitchen. It was the year the cast album for Sondheim's *Pacific Overtures* came out, and I played it over and over again.

You were allowed to live in the carriage house for a year, and then you had to pass it on to the next inhabitant of your choosing. Lisa Pleskow, a fascinating and affable artist who worked in quilted textiles, passed it on to me. After I befriended Tim and made him dinner one night, which to me felt as if we had taken a giant step toward finally loving each other, I decided to pass it on to him. Dinner with him was memorable because I was so excited to have him in my house I nearly exploded, though I wish I could remember what I made, or even one thing we said. His manner was earnest, calm, kind, courteous, and grounded, without in any way being staid, and I felt vindicated in my obsession.

In EST, a rigorous and confronting training founded by Werner Erhard I did in 1975, after you paid $250, you were promised you'd get "it," the meaning of life. You were humiliated, forbidden to use the bathroom, broken down, and eviscerated from your ego to your id, in order to imbue you with the concept that you are responsible for your own life and you create your own reality, I learned the value of telling the truth. Immediately following the training, I wrote to my father, telling him I was gay. I never heard back. A few years later, Barry Plumlee, a straight playwright I was obsessed with, still at CMU after I quit, wrote that he wanted to visit me in New York.

He looked like Jackie, the tough guy from *The Little Rascals* with an appealing scowl and sneer, like he had just been in a fight, or was about to incite one. His eyes would squint like he was a mountain lion stalking you. He was clearly seeking to emulate Bertolt Brecht, writing satirical, what he hoped was scorched-earth prose, but he wasn't worldly enough yet, so his satire could be flaccid and uninformed; but he had something too, and you imagined a bright future. He came over to the carriage house one day. We decided to cut school for the whole afternoon, a common occurrence for both of us. We got wildly drunk, so drunk that when I went to play for chorus rehearsal in the early evening, I was late, fell off the piano bench, and was kicked out. I waited for weeks for Barry to show up again at my door, aching for him. We were about as unlikely friends as there could possibly be, but he was a crystallized version of my father's rage, sarcasm, and condescension, and perhaps what my father might have been like if he were educated, and he was enamored of me, thinking I was a real artist, squealing with delight at my New York Jew culture and intelligence. A mutual fascination had us circling each other for a while which I took to mean love. He was handsome, enigmatic, and compelling like Jack Kerouac, and I just thought we could throw in a little bisexuality the way it floated around the Beats, Neal Cassady, Allen Ginsberg, and William Burroughs.

So, I replied with the ultimatum, "Only if we sleep together." And then about a week later, I received a postcard: "You blew it faggot."

Unbelievably, we remained friends, writing each other continually for years, tomes, through our various travails.

The last time I saw Barry, he came to see *Sycamore Trees*, the musical I wrote about my family for the Signature Theatre in Arlington, Virginia. I was really excited to see him; for him to experience a piece I was so proud of. My obsession never waned. His looks were grizzled and gone. He had very long hair and looked like one of the men who showed up for the recent Trump-instigated insurrection at the Capitol. Alcohol had pulled the weight of his face downward, and it looked unnaturally long, which his hair only exacerbated. At dinner after the show, he was moved and impressed by the piece and we were having a lucid conversation, but he started drinking, after telling me he was sober. I had to lie in order to extract myself, when his personality took the extreme turn alcohol enabled in him, and I suddenly felt trapped and frightened the evening would never end, claustrophobic even.

Barry died of throat cancer, like my friend Tom, who also drank himself to death. Two talented writers felled by addiction.

I came home to Island Park on spring break. I made Tim a lovely painting, no doubt invigorated by the speed I was ingesting all the time so that I never slept once that whole vacation, and with the impulsive daring and lack of forethought drugs enable, I wrote on the back of it, "I love you," and sent it to him. I never heard back from him, and he never once mentioned it.

On the morning I was moving out of the carriage house, before summer vacation, while packing, I accidentally dropped a bottle of Oil of Olay into the toilet, which broke straight through, leaving a huge hole and a pile of broken porcelain all over the floor. It was just above the water line, so water didn't come streaming out, but clearly a new toilet was going to be necessary because flushing it would be disastrous. Panicking, I didn't know what to do, so I did nothing. I just left. Tim had to buy a new toilet when he moved in.

Back at school, when I saw him in the cafeteria line after the summer, he yelled at me with rage and hatred in his eyes, really yelled, and never forgave me.

I don't understand why I did that. Maybe I was afraid of having to pay for the toilet or having to ask my parents for the money, or just plain getting into trouble. Timothy's sternness was in keeping with the seriousness he projected. Clearly, with him, wounds ran deep, and when transgressed, he was blood red intractable.

A few years ago, I won an alumni award at Carnegie Mellon. It was me; Rob Marshall, the director; Ted Danson, the actor; and Ann Roth, the costume designer. I finagled someone in the administrative department to give me Tim's address. I thought I would do a ninth-step amend ("made direct amends to such people wherever possible, except when to do so would injure them or others"), so I wrote Tim a long letter of apology. I never heard back.

Susan Klein, a talented writer I met in the English department, was a whip-smart, naughty, and very funny Jewish girl from New Rochelle. Her father, Richard Klein, was the principal of the High School of Music & Art, her brother Jon, at one point, was the head of CNN, and her sister Debra was a journalist Kevin hired to write for both *Condé Nast Traveler* and *The Wall Street Journal*, so I have karma with the Klein family. Susan and I shared a proclivity for obsession. She was obsessed with an obviously gay actor named Stephen Joseph (as Romeo, when he uttered the line "Juliet, thy beauty hath made me effeminate," an unfortunate titter filled the hall) and wrote endlessly about him in poems of deep longing. "Orestes, Doomed"—"When I heard them rouse me to go to sea, a babe of maybe three, sat swaying in another mother's arms, in the quelling of a five-day storm, in the muted cries of foreign waters"—is one of the first poems I set to music in my foray into art song. Susan spun mythologies just as I did. This bound us.

So, it is particularly poignant that this morning Susan Klein sent me Timothy's obituary. "Have you seen this?" I hadn't. He died in 2020 of something called Lewy body disease, which I had never heard of. It is a devastating disease that slowly takes your mind and body away from you, much like Alzheimer's, before it finally kills you. I read about Tim's life, how full it was, how brilliant, heroic, and self-sacrificing he was, and I mourned for myself and the limiting lens I was only able to see him through.

PART III

MUSIC

If you asked me what for me was the most charged and powerful word in the English language, I would answer without delay, "Opera." After Mrs. Fox kindly gave me her copy of *The Victor Book of the Opera* and I enlisted Peter in what would become our shared lifelong obsession, Peter and I started going to the opera all the time, waiting on long lines early in the morning on weekends to get standing room tickets. People would leave after the first act and then we'd scramble around like mice for seats. Sometimes people took pity on us and handed us their ticket stubs before leaving at intermission. But mostly it was trying not to get caught by the ushers, which felt familiar, like the anxiety and excitement of shoplifting, or entering adult bookstores, or stealing from my mother's pocketbook.

I started getting into twentieth-century works, like Douglas Moore's *The Ballad of Baby Doe*. The recording starred Beverly Sills, whose voice then was like a gleaming ball of mercury. The soaring voice, the extravagantly beautiful music from influences I could already identify, and the lovely poetic words were balm for a burgeoning creator. Somewhere inside me, the idea of words set to music was marinating.

Jack Beeson's *Lizzie Borden*, with its fascinating horror movie score, was like nothing I had ever heard. It was truly terrifying and beautiful all at once. Right at the top of the opera, you hear a chorus of boy sopranos, which should denote innocence, but with the combination of what they are singing, and the subtext in the underscore, it is more like *Lord of the Flies* on steroids. You know something horrible is imminent from the first notes. Brenda Lewis played Lizzie, and I became a huge fan of hers because of her recording of Mark Blitzstein's

Regina, his adaptation of Lillian Hellman's *The Little Foxes*, wherein she played Regina Giddins, the wildly ambitious, greedy, and murderous central character who barks out things like, "It's gettin' late. Wha doncha awl go home!"

In an old Chinese silk–covered journal I was keeping when I was twenty-six, the same journal wherein, after one of my first therapy sessions, in a moment of openheartedness born of unburdening myself, I wrote the entire song "A Horse with Wings," on the local train from Christopher Street to Seventy-Second Street, there is an entry about what I want to do when I grow up, what kind of writing I want to emulate. I cite various ensembles from operas I was obsessed with, "What Would You Like to Harvest," from *Lizzie Borden*; the final quintet, "To Leave, To Break," from Samuel Barber's *Vanessa*; "Make Our Garden Grow," from Leonard Bernstein's *Candide*; "Do Not Torment Me," from Michael Tippett's *The Knot Garden*; and "You Bring the Gift of Love," from Marvin David Levy's *Mourning Becomes Electra* as the heights I was hoping to achieve as a composer for the musical theater. I would still hold them up as pinnacles of beauty today, and I would add "From the Gutters, Why Should We Trouble at Their Ribaldries," from Benjamin Britten's *Peter Grimes*; "We've Made Our Own Investigations," from his *Albert Herring*, and the quartet for the lovers, "I Swear to Thee," in his magnificent setting of Shakespeare's *A Midsummer Night's Dream*; Hugo Weisgall's great fugue in *The Tenor*, "Get Rid of Her, Gerardo"; "Oh, What a Lovely Dance" and "In Endless Waiting Rooms," from Gian Carlo Menotti's *The Consul*; "The Rain Quintet," from Blitzstein's *Regina*; and "Oh Bess, Oh Where's My Bess," from Gershwin's *Porgy and Bess*.

I was already writing a musical about my family, out of which would come Don Katz's book *Home Fires*, and eighteen years later, my *Sycamore Trees*. The first records I bought were Bizet's *Carmen*, starring Victoria de los Ángeles; Puccini's *Madama Butterfly*, starring Leontyne Price; Borodin's *Prince Igor*, because of the incredible choral music; and all four operas in Wagner's cycle *The Ring of the Nibelung*. One time, I was sleeping over at Peter's house. I was terrified of the dark, and he kept his room pitch-black, so I always begged to sleep on the inside, closer to the wall, so when the axe murderer came, they would get Peter first. He was being particularly difficult and stubborn about moving that night in a sadistic sort of a way, so I had to agree to give him my recording of *Das Rheingold*, conducted by Georg Solti, before he would change places with me, a huge sacrifice, but necessary and worth it if it meant saving my life.

There was a store near Grand Central Station called Music Masters where you could buy live performances of operas from all over the world. That's how I got the recording of Samuel Barber's *Antony and Cleopatra*, from the opening night of the new Metropolitan Opera at Lincoln Center, in 1966, as well as Marvin David Levy's *Mourning Becomes Electra*, live from the Met in 1967, and the world premiere of Ned Rorem's *Miss Julie*, live from the New York City Opera in 1965, the failure of which occasioned the funniest thing I think I ever heard Ned say: "When you bomb with opera, it's an atom bomb."

I begged my parents to send me to Chautauqua, the summer community in upstate New York where intellectuals went to lectures, concerts, plays, operas, and ballets all happening simultaneously, and world-class teachers trained kids like me in every discipline. I was sure it was what I needed. I went as a pianist with Peter, who went as an actor. The whole time I was there I was reading another book that changed my life: *You Might as Well Live: The Life and Times of Dorothy Parker*, by John Keats, which had just been published.

(In 1991, I got a commission to go to Opera Omaha for their Fall Festival and create a new piece with Angelina Réaux, Michael Sokol, her husband, a terrific baritone and singing actor, and the English opera director Keith Warner, using the poems and short stories of Dorothy Parker. We created a piece called *Autumn Valentine*. Angy and Michael memorized whole stories, acting them out with all the "he saids" and "she saids" intact, playing on both of their unusual strengths as actors able to speak *as well as* sing, which is unusual for opera singers. I set a bunch or Parker's poems as sort of set pieces and commentary, and I was onstage as the pianist, so it was a three-performer evening. While in Omaha, I was staying in a house with the composer Hugo Weisgall, who was there because his opera *The*

Gardens of Adonis was being done in the festival. Hugo was a thorny man, but it was easy to tolerate because I have loved his music since I was a little boy. At one point, I even got in touch with Hugo, and went up to see him at the Jewish Seminary, where he taught, to see if he would take me on as a student. I had already approached Dominic Argento, whose music I *loved*, from his song cycle "From the Diaries of Virginia Woolf," which won a Pulitzer in 1975, to his opera *Postcard from Morocco*, which is one of the nuttiest and loveliest fractured narrative collage operas out there, to see if he would teach me, and he suggested Hugo. One of the first things Hugo said to me was, "MY GOD, YOU'RE GOING BALD AND YOU'RE SO YOUNG?!" Which endeared me to him right away. He seemed to be tired of teaching and suggested I talk to his student and friend Bruce Saylor out at Queens College, so I did. Nothing happened in terms of Bruce and I becoming student and teacher, but we became friends which is even better. The night Hugo came to see *Autumn Valentine*, he came backstage afterward and said to me, "If you can write like that you don't need to study with me." Now I'm sure some critics would differ with that assessment, but it was enough for me, and I stopped running all over the place looking for a teacher and just settled into the business of being a composer.)

Chautauqua was an inappropriate place for me at the time. I was, I am sure, undiagnosed with ADHD, and certainly not a candidate for the kind of practicing my piano teacher Ozan Marsh expected. Because it was a religious community, someone was always telling you to speak softer. I was always getting yelled at by Elizabeth Rae Gappan, the dorm manager, for coming home too late and having to wake her to unlock the door. Peter liked it because the theater department was fun, not as austere as the music department.

I met a soprano, Laura Skolnick, there and we would complain about the place together while eating serving after serving of pumpkin pie, a delicacy previously unknown to me, at the little diner on campus. Laura later married Raymond Menard, the head of stage management at the Metropolitan Opera, and I was the Lamaze coach for the births of both of their daughters while Ray was traveling.

One night, there was a water bug on my pillow at least two inches long and after screaming bloody murder, I knew it was time to go home. I go there often now to coach young singers on my songs and do concerts, and I find it charming, the colorful Victorian houses, the lush gardens, the lake around which everything is built, but all that charm was lost on me when I was younger. What I remember most of all, was one of the pianists working on a set of five piano pieces by a then-contemporary composer named Peter Mennin. I became obsessed with those pieces. Almost immediately, upon returning home, I made a pilgrimage to my favorite place in New York City, on Fifty-Sixth Street behind Carnegie Hall, Patelson's Music House, and bought the pieces. Hard as they were, I played what I could, reveling in whatever strange, crunchy, and wonderful chords and unusual skittering counterpoint I could work into my hands.

Patelson's was an august and beautiful space, with walls of dark wood, endless bins of music, and soft spoken, intelligent, and impeccably dressed salespeople. There was a handsome man who worked there. He had jet-black hair and very pale skin, which made both extremes shimmer, and a perfectly trimmed mustache and beard. He he had very red lips and deep kind eyes, and I would dream about kissing him. He may have been a catalyst for my going there so often. He wore little wire-rimmed glasses like a sexy bookworm, and always dressed in elegant conservative tailored clothes—cashmere sweaters, wool pants.

Years later, when I worked at the Gay Men's Health Crisis doing intake for AIDS patients to get into the system in order to be eligible for the services they offered, he was one of my first cases. He walked in and immediately we recognized each other, and it was an unbearably full and sobering moment. He was thin, his face slightly deformed and sunken in from the meds, and his looks were gone, but the same kindness rushed from his eyes. It happened more than once, someone I idolized from my past, showing up and needing my help.

My first published music was four songbooks, "A Horse with Wings," "Genius Child," "Only Heaven," and "Finding Home," published by Rodgers and Hammerstein/Williamson Music. By far, the most thrilling thing for me was seeing them in the bins at Patelson's, at first, under "G," but soon enough, under "Gordon."

Once a piece of music became important to me, I would read everything I could about the piece, the composer, buy the score, study it, and play through it. I was, and still am, a big researcher.

We are irrepressibly who we are when we are young. No one has to tell us who to be or what to like, we just are, and we just do. It is only when others shame us for our choices that we begin cultivating alternate people-pleasing personalities, in order to impress, or get love.

Lucia di Lammermoor

Sheila's friend Leslie gave me a ticket to see Roberta Peters in *Lucia di Lammermoor* at the Metropolitan Opera.

It was 1968, during one of the worst snowstorms in New York history. I was dying to see *Lucia*, because everyone made it seem like a freak show where the soprano sings so high it's practically impossible. I loved Roberta Peters singing Zerbinetta on a recording of Richard Strauss's *Ariadne auf Naxos*. Zerbinetta seemed impossible enough, so I think I imagined she would levitate and spin off into the sky like a dirt devil.

First, I walked in the snow, which was about three feet high, to Rabbi Babroff's for a lesson on my haftorah in preparation for my imminent Bar Mitzvah, but when I got home, it was snowing so hard my parents forbade me to go to the opera. There was no way I wasn't going, so I ran away from home. I got to the city on one of the few Long Island Rail Road trains running that day.

Roberta Peters, after she murders Arturo and gets blood all over her pretty white gown, sang the mad scene. It was beautiful and exciting, but it was not even as high as Zerbinetta, so it was one of those experiences where my expectations exceeded reality, though it was thrilling to be at the Metropolitan Opera for the first time and to see Roberta Peters, who looked like one of the pretty moms of Harbor Isle, only famous.

Afterward, it was snowing so hard you could barely see two inches ahead of you. No trains were running. I called Sheila panicking from the phone booth in the Empire Hotel across from Lincoln Center, not knowing how I would get home or where to stay, and she had Leslie pick me up and take me to her apartment. I don't remember how long it took me to get back to Long Island. The city was immobilized for days.

Joni Mitchell

On April 20, 1969, in *The New York Times*, there was an article about a then not very well-known singer-songwriter named Joni Mitchell:

> Her music has a haunting, unearthly quality produced by the strangeness of the imagery in her lyrics, the unexpected shifts in her voice, and the unusual guitar tunings she uses. She is one of the most original and profoundly talented of all the contemporary composer-performers . . . who have evolved folk music into art-rock.

It was written by my sister Susan.

In my most probably hazy or made-up memory, there was a photo of Joni Mitchell walking among the trees with her friend Judy Collins. Judy had put Joni on the map by recording her song "Both Sides Now" and making it a hit. Notwithstanding my mother's short but stratospheric stint in the borscht belt, Susan and Lorraine's impassioned folksinging, and Sheila's short-lived piano lessons, because I showed signs of what they considered an extraordinary ear, and because I was the only boy in a Jewish family where sexism was written into the hierarchy, music was ceded to me. Susan told me I needed to hear this woman's music because I would love it. I worshipped my older sister, so I registered what she said and asterisked it inside myself as very important.

Nineteen sixty-nine was also the year the movie *Alice's Restaurant* was released, based on Arlo Guthrie's song of the same name and starring him as well. My niece Maggie was four at the time, too young for almost anything that happened in that movie, but my sister Lorraine took us to see it anyway. At one point, a speed freak careening down the highway on his motorcycle crashes and dies instantly. At the funeral a woman with a guitar sings a song I knew immediately had to be a Joni Mitchell song. It had the strangest, most exotic harmonies, nothing I had ever heard in folk or pop music. They were spicy chords, neither major nor minor, almost modal, and they were unpredictable in where they led. That was what was often disappointing in folk music, though I couldn't have put it into words at the time: I always knew what the music was about to do, and even if the words were complex, expressing rich ideas including paradoxes and ambivalences, the music was not. But "Songs to Aging Children Come," which was indeed by Joni Mitchell, shocked me, haunting me for the rest of the movie.

Joni and Susan were born in the same month of the same year, so they were both, at this point, twenty-five years old. I was twelve. I asked for the album the song was from, *Clouds*, and became transfixed, mesmerized, completely and overwhelmingly obsessed with Joni Mitchell.

At that point, all that was available were her first two albums. *Song to a Seagull* is quiet, its sorrow is gentle, genial, it feels like having your tarot cards read over a cup of tea. *Clouds* is darker: a failed marriage, an a cappella protest song. Both albums are iridescent, like the underside of a butterfly wing, or the inside of an abalone shell. Susan gave me Joni Mitchell's address in Los Angeles, on Lookout Mountain Avenue, in Laurel Canyon. I started writing to her and sending her presents, like pictures I drew, to accompany my impassioned letters of adoration. I would even decorate the envelopes. One day, I was shopping on St. Marks Place in the East Village and bought a record of an astrology reading for Scorpios. I sent it in her next gift package. I received a letter postmarked December 11, 1970. It was in a small, nondescript envelope, but I recognized the handwriting immediately. I almost had a heart attack. It was written on paper hastily ripped out of a notepad, its edges frayed.

Hello Ricky,

Thank you for all your letters and thoughtful things. I love things you make yourself. I haven't played the record yet

because thieves ripped off my record player. I'm on my way
to San Francisco to sing on a friends record and to get out
of the L.A. air.

Goodbye,

Joni Mitchell

Her handwriting in a bright blue Sharpie spilled off the page as
if it were about to jump in the water. The record she was on her way
to sing on was Carole King's *Tapestry*. At the time she was seeing
James Taylor, and they were singing backup on "Will You Love Me
Tomorrow?"

When I was in seventh grade, Mr. Gary, the gay music teacher,
allowed me to teach my own class on Joni Mitchell, though I included
two Donovan songs, "Isle of Islay" and "The Magpie," as well as the
Cat Stevens song "Into White," which I felt entered the exalted place
where, as far as I was concerned, Joni's work belonged. I had learned
that Saskatoon, Saskatchewan, where Joni grew up, was noted for a
kind of Canadian yodeling. That explained her ease with registers,
how she could go from singing in her chest to soaring in her head
voice instantly, and fluidly, like a yodel; think "Oh, Ca-na-daaaa" in
"A Case of You" or "CaliFORnia, I'm coming home" in "California"
or "He was walking along the ROAD" in "Woodstock."

By this point, I was as in love with poetry as I was with music, and
in particular the confessional poetry of Sylvia Plath and Anne Sexton.
Joni Mitchell, Donovan, and Cat Stevens in the songs I mentioned
seem to have settled on a kind of contemporary art song. Their lyrics
seemed like poems—in Joni's case, often, confessional ones—and the
music circled the words in a perfect enmeshment of mood and tone, as
unpredictable as the lyrics.

If I were to mention the songs I was most enamored with, though
I could name every one, on *Song to a Seagull*, there would be "Mar-
cie," which still tears my heart out whenever she sings "To the sea,"
holding "sea" through what seems like at least five changes of land-

scape and playing with the words "red" and "green" in the most imaginative way, allowing them to represent over time the colors and flavors of candy, the changing seasons, and the stop and go of traffic lights. On *Clouds*, it would be "Songs to Aging Children Come" and "I Don't Know Where I Stand," though even as I write these titles down, "The Gallery" drifts into my head, admonishing me for leaving it out.

When I was a boy, my sister Susan would lull me to sleep by reading Edna St. Vincent Millay poems to me. I knew "The Ballad of the Harp-Weaver" so well it seemed to be my story; the poor sad little boy who awakens to a pile of golden clothing while his mother is frozen dead at the harp she wove them on. Joni's lyrics were like Millay's poems, formal and deep but also playful, wry, and funny. She never repeated anything randomly, she told stories and her lyrics evolved in the course of a song, or sometimes the lyric was nonnarrative, conjuring up a universe with a complex spell of sounds and associations, as if words were dancers. She was original and thoughtful. I had never heard songs like that, and all from just a woman and her guitar. They were so simply done and so hair-raisingly intimate.

But then, with her next album, *Ladies of the Canyon*, she exploded out of herself. She brought in a new instrument, the piano, and an occasional obbligato instrument, like the clarinet in "For Free," and in songs like it, "Woodstock," "Willy," and "Blue Boy" she seemed, for me, to enter a place no previous songwriter had ever entered. She carved a world of sonorities and words that were wholly contemporary but rooted in historical tradition, complex enough to be a part of the classical music canon. This was the work not just of a troubadour whose music was simply a vehicle for the words but of a true poet and composer.

It is interesting that she began as a painter, because she certainly knew how to paint with notes and words. Just listen to the first four bars of "Ladies of the Canyon." Where have you ever heard guitar chords like that before? She made them up, invented her own tunings, taught herself to play the guitar according to her own ear.

I first heard a song from *Ladies of the Canyon* on the radio when the album wasn't out yet. It was "Willy." "Willy" conveyed so many emotions at once. I called all the radio stations and badgered my sister to see if anyone could get me an advance copy; I even thought of pestering Joni! But I had to wait like everyone else. In some ways, it is my favorite of her albums, because it is where, for me, she catapulted herself into a whole new language. But then came *Blue*. Now she introduces a new instrument, the dulcimer, but not the way anyone else plays it; she reinvents it. From the very first notes of "All I Want," the first song on the album, you are thinking, "What is that sound? Is it an Autoharp? What are those chords? What is that instrument?" And in one song after another there is unbearable joy, unendurable sadness, and the baldest candor anyone could imagine. With songs like "All I Want," "A Case of You," "Carey," "River," and "California"—all of them really—she has created her own genre, her own universe. For me she was now as much a genius as Benjamin Britten, Kurt Weill, Alban Berg, Samuel Barber, and all the other composers I idolized at the time, as important a poet as Millay. I didn't distinguish between "serious," "classical," "pop," and "commercial." I just loved what I loved ardently.

The albums by Joni Mitchell seemed to have a *feeling* that floated through each song like smoke, making them feel almost symphony-like in their ability to invoke emotions and images, as if each song were a movement, a part of a whole conceived in one burst, one explosion.

I wanted to know her; I loved her as tenderly as if she were my closest friend. I dreamed about her, thought about her day and night, couldn't shut up about her. She was going to make her Carnegie Hall debut in February 1972. I wanted to do something big, a grand gesture to exceed everything I had done for her before. I had taught myself to embroider, and I got really good at it. I was intoxicated with the huge palette of colors you could find in the shimmering silky threads. I became a habitué of craft shops and dreamed up patterns and designs. I would draw scenes, figures, flowers, and butterflies on fabric and fill them in with all the stitches I had learned: backstitch, split stitch, satin stitch, French knot, chain stitch, the Lazy Daisy stitch. I decided I wanted to make Joni Mitchell a dress.

I enlisted my friend Maureen to help me. Someone had to make the dress. My sister Susan said Joni was her size, and if I made something that fit her, it would fit Joni. I bought several yards of a soft chocolate-brown muslin. Maureen found a pattern for a sort of caftan with a drooping neckline and sleeves that belled out, something that would be comfortable and easy to throw on, very hippie chick flower power. She made the dress, and it fit Susan perfectly. I started embroidering it all around the hem, up and down the collar line, around the sleeve ends, and here and there all over the bodice: birds, autumn leaves, wildflowers, bumblebees, and sunsets. When I was done, it was beautiful. Excitedly, I wrapped it in brown paper so I could paint on the package, and I painted a portrait of Joni.

On the day the tickets were supposed to go on sale, I got up at three in the morning to get the train from Island Park into the city. I was determined to be the first person in line and I was. It was a freezing-cold January morning. The second person was my new friend from ninth grade at West Hempstead High School, Jodie Siegel, a fellow Joni aficionado, though an amateur compared with me. No one could rival my devotion. Finally, at 10:00 the box office opened. Excitedly, trembling and half-frozen, I walked up to the ticket booth. I could barely get the words out. "Front row center seat, please." I had never been first in line, in the privileged position of being able to ask for exactly what I wanted. There was a delicious power to it. The lady in the booth smiled as if she knew my type; the crazy wide-eyed first-in-line fan who would do anything for their adored idol. She went straight for the ticket, pulling it out from the rubber-banded VIP bundle, with a smile of satisfaction knowing how happy she was making me.

My mother, who clearly had never on her own bought a ticket for a concert or a show in New York City, had given me a check from our bank, the National Bank of North America, and I handed the check to the ticket seller. She looked at it and then looked at me.

"We don't take checks."

"What?" I said.

"We don't take checks, honey. Cash only."

"But that's all my mother gave me! I don't have anything else."

"I'm sorry," she said. "You'll have to go get cash and come back."

"Can you save the seat for me until I get back?" I pleaded.

"No. I'm sorry. We're not allowed to do that." She pitied me, but she was granite, unyielding.

I cried, railed, and bargained but to no avail. She would not take the check or save the seat, and by now my insistence and hysteria were wreaking havoc in the line. Jodie had cash, but only enough to buy her own ticket, and I even imagined I saw a faint gloat on her face that she was in fact going to have a better seat than I was. Suddenly I wanted to kill her.

Abject and miserable, I bolted from the line. I had to run around Fifty-Seventh Street wildly and insanely looking for a National Bank of North America, which, believe me, was not as omnipresent as today's Chase or Citibank. When I finally found one, I had to beg them to call my mother and our branch in Island Park to vouch for the amount so they could give me cash. However long this took, which felt like an eternity, by the time I got back to Carnegie Hall, it was early afternoon, and there was now a line around the block, and I had to get on the end of it. I was heartbroken, shattered, and lost. I wept, bit my nails, and ground my teeth feverishly, until finally I got up to the ticket booth again. The same gravel-faced gargoyle who seemed hell-bent on ruining my life stared out at me with contempt and antipathy. I wish I could say she had kindly put the front row center seat aside for me and was waiting for me to come back, but she almost seemed to relish my misfortune.

I secured a ticket, though not in the front row, but in the center section somewhere toward the back of the hall. I never scolded my mother or even held it against her, but the wound was deep, and when I think of it now, I could murder her, but she is dead. Until that moment, I had never been so crestfallen in my entire life. However, all was not lost. Jodie Siegel got the center seat in the front row, next to Neil Young.

The night of the concert, I had dinner with my three sisters before the show somewhere in the vicinity of the hall, though of course
I could barely eat. My stomach was in knots from the excitement.
When we got there and found our seats, I knew I could not sit where
we were. It was just simply too far away. I marched up to the front of
the auditorium with my package under my arm, begged Jodie to move
over, which she happily did, knowing something good was going to
happen, and we squeezed into one of those tiny Carnegie Hall seats
together. Of course, I was astounded to see Neil Young next to us, but
it was Joni whom I was there to worship.

The lights went down, and the concert began. I had never had an
experience like this before. I had never so deeply loved a living mu-
sician, a living performer, and the experience of her being so close to
me, about ten feet away, was overwhelming. There she was in all her
radiance, her implausibly high cheekbones, her endearing overbite,
her hair the color of wheat reflecting the gold of the spotlights, her
crystal-like vulnerability, her little giggle, and that voice, even more
soaring in person, filling the hall.

After about an hour of ecstatically worshipping her, I felt it appropriate to approach the stage. She had put down her guitar and was
sitting with the dulcimer in her lap. While she tuned it, just before
she started the patter into the song "Carey," the fourth song on side 1
of her magnificent new album, *Blue*, I went up to the stage and whispered meekly, "Joni. I'm Ricky." Unbelievably, she looked up and replied through the microphone, with the kindest familiarity, "Ricky
Gordon, my old pen pal!" I nearly collapsed. Everyone who knew me
in the hall screamed. I was shaking as if I were at the pearly gates
face-to-face with Christ. "I made you something," I said, and shoved my
package across the floor toward her. She looked at it, the pretty painting on the brown paper, the elaborate wrapping, and said, just as she
had said in her letter, "I love things you make yourself." "It's a dress,
Joni! Wait till you see it!" I murmured. Satisfied and beaming, I sat
back down with Jodie, who clutched me tightly to her as I gloated. I
buzzed for the rest of the concert like a happy bumblebee.

I wish I could say she opened the package, looked at the dress, oohed and aahed, and showed it to the audience. I wish I could say she tried it on so all of Carnegie Hall could marvel at my exquisite handiwork. But sadly, I never heard from her again.

The next day, in high school, news had spread about Joni Mitchell talking to me from the stage of Carnegie Hall, and everyone treated me like a movie star. I have no idea if she ever saw the dress, tried it on, or anything. The truth is, that night was sort of the grand finale to my Joni Mitchell story. At first, I was somewhat heartbroken and horrified at not hearing from her, but I had exhausted my idolatry, and with each new album I identified less with her work. The next album was *For the Roses*, which she wrote in a self-imposed exile from the world, feeling wrung out, hurt by celebrity, its fickleness, its ups and downs, in need of unbroken space and time. I liked that album very much, and I recognized some of the songs because she had premiered them that night at Carnegie Hall, but something was missing; she had become less transparent to me. I no longer found myself memorizing the lyrics, or essentially even always knowing what the songs were about. I couldn't even tell you now the order of songs, other than that "Banquet" started side 1 and "See You Sometime," side 2. The title song specifically about the pain of stardom, I didn't understand; I mean, how could being a star be painful? It sure looked fun to me!

In ninth grade, I was at the helm of a sort of revolution wherein we started a free school under the auspices of the legitimate high school for students who felt hamstrung or incapacitated by standard educational procedures. In a classroom deep in the margins of this quarter-of-a-mile high school with thousands of students, I painted a huge black-and-white mural of what looked like the face of the disenfranchised, and we called ourselves SAFE, which stood for "Student and Faculty Education." For me, this meant I could pursue my major obsessions at the time, foreign film, in particular Ingmar Bergman, and music, in particular twentieth-century music. There was a revival movie house in Chelsea called the Elgin, where I saw thirty-eight Bergman films at a festival, and then I would amble into SAFE to talk about them with my teachers, whom I called by their first names. Art (Sherin), Claire (Dorogusker). I learned Ravel's *Le tombeau de Couperin* on the piano, to play for my classmates and teachers.

I had a drug problem. Before this, no doubt, I was precocious. I smoked pot, there was the drug catastrophe at twelve, I drank, but this was different. It began because one day in ninth grade, I was talking to a lot of my closest friends in school, and they were talking about something they were all members of, honor society. Not being a member had never bothered me before; in fact, it seemed almost boring and nerdy to *be* a member. Until this moment. They were throwing names around like Fitzgerald and Hemingway, and not only did I feel left out, but I had a terrible and painful realization: I didn't read enough; well, I didn't read. I felt it in the pit of my stomach: shame. I was different from them, less than them. I suddenly felt this almost insane need to catch up. I simply couldn't trail so far behind these people, that would not do, I was too competitive to be a loser. But, though I hadn't been diagnosed with attention deficit disorder, I knew there was definitely something wrong with me. I would go to read something, and the first sentence would repeat itself over and over again in my head as if it were on a tape loop. I couldn't get past it, and it didn't make sense to me. This is why, I understand now, school was so hard for me. I couldn't do my homework and I did terribly in class, usually relegated to the slow class—people called it the dumb class—because I had trouble reading. I was always the kid without my homework, spouting the lamest "the dog ate it" sort of excuses. My parents would constantly get called into school, where they'd be told, "Ricky isn't performing up to his potential," but they never applied any pressure. They held little faith in educational institutions. If anything, they had contempt for education, having never finished their own. Feeling easily threatened by those they deemed smarter than them, they were particularly contemptuous of teachers and anyone in authority. The principal in junior high school called my mother in because of my smoking, but he was smoking while he admonished me. "We'll talk when you have quit smoking," she said. "Until then, I'm not interested in what you have to say about my son!" If my parents felt anyone was putting on airs, they immediately had utter derision for them. My mother's case, though, was different. She knew from the day I was born I would amount to something, and she didn't really care how; she was just sure of it, even giving me what she felt was a stage name. "Ricky Ian Gordon" was a concoction she was very proud of. If excelling in school was not my path, she didn't seem to care much. Interestingly, I never had any trouble reading about what interested me. I could read endlessly about the composers and filmmakers I loved, and I already loved poetry, but if it was something I had to read, and I wasn't interested, forget it. But now, I wanted to fit in with my peers, read what they read, know what they knew, talk about what they talked about.

I don't remember where I first got it from, but I discovered speed, Benzedrine, Black Beauties, one pretty blue-speckled capsule called Fastin, and eventually my mother's diet drops, which were prescribed for her by a diet doctor named Datlof who eventually ended up in jail. Speed made me feel miraculously normal, as if I could finally concentrate. I was taking speed to stay up all night and read. I was in a bookstore one day, and there was a trilogy of books by Sartre called *The Roads to Freedom*, which I thought if I read it, I'd be really smart, so I did. I remember nothing of those books. Nothing. I think one was called *The Reprieve*. I read Camus and Thomas Mann; I went crazy, making up for what I thought of as lost time. But then I would have to take downers, like Seconal or Valium, to sleep. Sometimes I would smoke pot to calm down or to get engaged on a deeper level, though sometimes it just gave me reoccurrences of my bad trip. Later, I added drinking as a reliable way to sleep, but nothing ever worked as well as barbiturates. Speed took away my appetite as well, so I didn't have to worry as much about what I could or couldn't eat. It was sort of an all-purpose drug.

I couldn't stand high school. I barely went to classes, even after I spearheaded the revolution from which the "free school" was formed. I was often crashing or high. I would nod out in class or have to go to Mrs. Killoran, the nurse on the first floor, where sometimes I'd climb out her window and hitchhike places, like to Sheila's apartment in Freeport. In the 1973 West Hempstead High School Yearbook, I am often photographed outside in the parking lot smoking. I was incapable of living inside the structure everyone else was living in. I had few morals or ethics. I didn't really know right from wrong. Religion was haphazard and had not caught fire inside me, so whatever structure it might have imposed was lost on me. In short, being normal was alien to me. I was a feral animal on my own track, following no rules, guided by what appealed to me, what interested me, and what I wanted, and nothing else. Perhaps I was an artist being made, an iconoclast? It felt great sometimes, following my every whim, but it also felt lonely, and it was often disastrous.

When I got to CMU in 1974, the album of that moment was Joni Mitchell's *Court and Spark*. Though I remember it as remarkable, and played it all the time, and though the very mention of it roils all the feelings and memories of my first year of college—the freedom, the independence, the exaltation, the sex, drugs, and alcohol, the longing, the obsessions—Joni was no longer a solo instrumentalist; she had a band. There was electricity, arrangements, and drums. I no longer felt as if she were speaking to me alone. There were too many people in the room. The whispered intimacy and dailiness of *Song to a Seagull*, with sweet songs like "Sisotowbell Lane" and "Michael from Mountains," the risky, quiet, searing a cappella protest of "The Fiddle and the Drum," and the dried flowers of *Clouds*, the old neighborhood clattering of *Ladies of the Canyon*, and the harrowing heartbreak, the Plathian confessions of *Blue* had given way to a more "global" and "universal" sound. She was more commercial, more pop, more accessible, still fascinating, but each time, incrementally, a little more *gone* from me. She was less vulnerable and no longer needed me. She no longer broke my heart.

Then came her experimentations with jazz, where her songwriting style became more freestyle, meandering, and formless. She got hip. When I listen now, it is a strange kind of hip, as if being who she was weren't bringing her what she wanted so she invented a new persona. Is being cool good for art? Cigarettes eventually robbed her of her soaring head voice, her purity, so she began to growl like a jazz singer, a trombone instead of a clarinet. Sometimes, she even sounded high, faraway, and distant. Though I didn't lose interest, I definitely became a more impassive observer, curious but less involved. I almost always bought an album when it came out. I liked *The Hissing of Summer Lawns* and *Hejira* very much for their urbanity, their glittering surfaces—but the "very much" of interesting, the "very much" of "ah, yes," not the "very much" of crazy love. They were still brilliant, but for another audience. *Mingus, Wild Things Run Fast, Don Juan's Reckless Daughter*, and *Chalk Mark in a Rain Storm* were less and less my style, and even, at moments, I thought, less focused, and not necessarily good. I didn't get them. As far as *Dog Eat Dog* and *Taming the Tiger* go, I didn't even purchase them. I didn't purchase them? The distance from where I started to where I ended up is almost alarming. I couldn't go on the journey with her; something I never thought I would say about Joni Mitchell. It was a painful loss of innocence. But then, finally, after years, a veritable desert, she surprised me with *Turbulent Indigo* and especially *Night Ride Home*. I *hated* her setting of Yeats's seminal poem "The Second Coming," just as I loathed her song "Love," which uses sections of 1 Corinthians 13, but I think "Cherokee Louise," "Borderline," "Turbulent Indigo," and "Night Ride Home" are truly great songs. I *loved* that "Night Ride Home" started with a chirping cricket. She seemed activated, quirky, and impassioned again. Honest. Connected to the world. She had made peace with the limitations of her voice. The smokiness was working in tandem with the subject matter; it was all of a piece. She was angry, and jaded, but pointedly so, and lyrical again. Once again, I could feel the form, the skeleton, the clarity. I felt invited back.

But I have never returned to the place where I started, in the blush of first love. Funny, this morning, in my meditation, a thought drifted into my mind: I miss wanting things so much, loving things so much. I miss the ache of admiration or desire on a level that feels as if it could exalt or destroy you. Maybe it's age.

Joni Mitchell is a magnificent artist, entitled to as many phases as she likes. Who am I to judge which of these stages was meaningful or produced better art? But I am writing here about me as well. My tastes, my aesthetic, in many ways were shaped by her and by all the other artists I loved. But we change. Our tastes change. Our needs change. Our friends change. Joni was back, she was great, she just wasn't my best friend anymore. Sometimes, we will go anywhere an artist we admire takes us. I love all of Benjamin Britten's music, truly I do, but his last opera, *Death in Venice*, based on Thomas Mann's great novella, is my favorite opera of his. I love Beethoven's late quartets most of all his work, and Fauré's late music is some of the most beautiful music ever written. Witness the way Bertrand Tavernier in his exquisite film about an aging painter falling out of fashion with the times, *A Sunday in the Country*, uses Fauré's late music to parallel the painter's situation. His final piano trio, string quartet, and quintet for strings in this astonishing movie are inseparable from the film, and now the music is inseparable for me from the images of the water pouring over the rocks in a quickly rushing stream and the late dusk light of the French countryside with which Tavernier captures its heartbreaking humility. Fauré, too, fell out of fashion, his light dimmed and eclipsed by impressionists like Debussy and Ravel, just when he was writing his loveliest, most aching music. Stanley Kunitz ends his final poem, "Touch Me," in a body of work impossibly profound and beautiful, with the lines "Darling, do you remember / the man you married? Touch me, / remind me who I am." And what of Sylvia Plath? Are not her last poems her most powerful? In "Words," she writes, "Years later I / Encounter them on the road—// Words dry and riderless, / The indefatigable hoof-taps. / While / From the bottom of the pool, fixed stars / Govern a life." A whole city could rise and fall on the power of those lines.

Alas, we love what we love when we love it, and living is worth all of it, for those flickers, however long they glow.

When I moved into the world as an artist in my own right, when writing music and words became my life's work, in some ways I had to kill my heroes. They were crowding me out. I needed them to fan the flame of who I would become, but then I had to let those birds fly free. I had to soar in my own orbit.

There is a later chapter to this story, poignant and circular. In the early years of the twenty-first century I met Judy Collins. Stephen Holden, the critic from *The New York Times*, became a fan of my music and he put us together, thinking Judy might want to sing some of my songs. I sent her a bunch of recordings and scores. She was lovely and very complimentary, getting back to me right away, and we became friends. One day after lunch at a café on my corner, she came back to my apartment. She sat down at my Knabe upright and began to play and sing her stirring song from 1989, "The Blizzard." "This is Judy Collins," I kept saying to myself over and over. "Judy Collins is in my house, playing and singing at my piano!" I felt awed and honored. A few years ago, Judy was performing at Café Carlyle. She included my song "A Horse with Wings" on her program. She sang it beautifully. All I could think of, the whole night, was that photograph in my sister's article in 1969 of Joni and Judy wandering through the woods, which I realize now I may have imagined, and how magical, generous, and utterly unpredictable life is.

Joni Mitchell's letter from 1970 hangs over my piano, framed in gold. Even the envelope is framed. It may be my most valuable possession.

Laura Nyro

Madonnas weep for wars of hell
They blow out the candles and haunt Noel.
—from "Christmas in My Soul," by Laura Nyro

It wasn't *Eli and the Thirteenth Confession* that hooked me. I mean, I knew Laura Nyro was unique and special, and "Luckie" is a spectacular song, but she seemed to take a deep long journey inside herself for her next album, *New York Tendaberry*, and it is as if she moved from great to genius in one giant step. There was a new interiority to her writing, and, like Joni Mitchell, she seemed to have completely entered her own world with that album. She let go of any standardized form of songwriting, no longer strophic, no longer ABA; now she was rhapsodic, fantasia-like, her songs could go anywhere, and they did, unexpectedly and surprisingly. What is the form of *New York Tendaberry*? It is like an art song, like a poetry setting. It goes where it needs to go, where the words go. She follows her own rules, not any dictates laid out by the gods of pop music. It is like when Joni Mitchell on *Blue* let go of pure form in her song "The Last Time I Saw Richard." She lives in the skeleton, but the words, the flesh and bone, go wherever they want.

Joni Mitchell rang personal to me. Laura Nyro, at least when I fell in love with her, rang political. She cared about the world like a mother about her children. She gathered up the evil that harrowed the world and wept for it with her voice.

If I had to pick one song to talk about on *New York Tendaberry*,

it would be "Gibsom Street," the first song on side 2. When I first
heard that song, I thought it had the depth and the portent of a Bertolt Brecht play, like *Jungle of Cities*. Brecht says, "A man doesn't get
finished off at once, ever—they want to have at least a hundred goes
at him! Everybody's got far too many chances." There is, in "Gibsom
Street," a terrible tremble from the first note to the last. I had never
heard a pop singer sing a song like that. It was full of warning and
trepidation, like a horror movie or even a Jacobean tragedy.

> *I wish my baby were forbidden*
> *I wish that my world be struck by sleet*
> *I wish to keep my mirror hidden*
> *To hide the eyes that looked on Gibsom street*

What happened on Gibsom Street?

> *They hide the alley cats on Gibsom Street.*

You know something awful has happened there, with visions of
infanticides, serial murders, or overdoses, but she never actually tells
you what happened. It is a perfect song brilliantly done. On *Eli and the
Thirteenth Confession*, there is certainly that full-blooded heartbreaking perfection in the songwriting, but it's as if something happened to
her, and whatever it was happened on "Gibsom Street" as well. Someone grew up, found out what the world was *really* about, was woefully
hurt by it. Even the "aboutness" in the lyrics, rather than any striving
toward pure narrative, feels like pure poetry:

> *Where is the night luster, past my trials?*

And it is a perfect example of the unique pyrotechnics of her singing,
she goes from pianissimo, almost a whisper, to wailing like a banshee.
Listen to the section

> *In my sorrow oh my morning*

It is so forceful and bone-chilling, even terrifying, it comes out of her guts as if she were keening.

And just technically speaking, where is she putting these incredibly high notes, because they are too stratospheric for the chest and too heavy and rich for the head? There seems to be no end, no limit to her voice, like Joni Mitchell, with her roots in Canadian yodeling, and yet no evidence of something called technique, vocal technique, just instinct and prowess, necessity and danger. There is menace in her music, and celebration, and rejoicing and transcending. There is whisper and catcall. She is all over the place yet totally contained in her own particular logic.

In *New York Tendaberry*, and then the next one, *Christmas and the Beads of Sweat*, she caught me at that place where you play the album so much the vinyl almost melts with your insistence. You tell me the form on the last song on *Christmas and the Beads of Sweat*, which, by the way, how about that album title? What does it mean? To be that elliptical, to trust your voice that much, in pop music. But listen to "Christmas in My Soul." It could have been written yesterday.

> *I love my country as it dies*
> *In war and pain before my eyes*
> *I walk the streets where disrespect has been*
> *The sins of politics, the politics of sin*
> *The heartlessness that darkens my soul*
> *On Christmas.*

She chants the words "Christmas in my soul" at the end of the song as if there were never tinsel, never lights, never mistletoe, but only a savior being born, a way out of this mess mankind has made. Her voice is unleashed, as if grief has unmoored her from safe harbor, swept her out to sea. It could be sung now for Ukraine.

And she seemed to know exactly who she was, as if she came out of the womb dressed like Laura Nyro, with huge black brocaded dresses and red roses, throwing her big black mane of hair around, as if she were caught in a spell, and howling.

Sheila and Patrick took me and Peter, who more or less went along with my forays into Joni Mitchell, Neil Young, and Laura Nyro like a devoted friend, but never held them with the same ardor I did, to see her at the Fillmore East in 1970. I've always said Miles Davis opened for her that night, but now I know, he was just on before her. Miles Davis was too important to "open" for anyone. I didn't know who he was, and I feel guilty writing this, but I dismissed him because all I wanted was her. Jazz was still way off in the future, and I was in no way an appreciator of it yet. But he set the tone, the scene for the ungodliness that was about to happen. I will never forget, I think she was singing "Captain Saint Lucifer," though it could have been "Mercy on Broadway," and somehow, during that song, she got up from the piano, ran around it, ran into the audience, and ran back onto the stage. What was she doing? It was as if she had jet fuel rushing through her veins. She was electrifying. If other performers were using drugs at the time to get to such ecstasies, I don't think she was. She looked too full and wholesome, like a healthy Jewish girl whose music pulsed off the softness of her body.

I want to tell you about a scene and a time I go back to when I hear *New York Tendaberry*.

Sheila and Patrick were living in Rockville Centre with a couple named Susan and Kenny Wilson and their little boy, Kenny Jr. I loved that house. I loved being there beyond anywhere I had ever been. For one thing, there was no one on earth I wanted to be with more than Sheila and Patrick, so anyone who was there, where they were, I loved too. Kenny kept snakes, so he had two *huge* pythons that fascinated me, especially when you got to see one stalk, attack, and eat an unknowing rabbit. The atmosphere in this house was, you were somewhere you could say or do anything, and it wouldn't matter. The furniture was welcoming like a warm lap, the pictures on the walls all felt mystical, like mandalas, and everywhere there were colorful fabrics draped over everything that could easily be turned into a sari, a sarong, or a blanket for warmth. I guess it was a little like a commune. It was a shame-free zone. It was the time of free love and dried flowers and incense, and anything can happen. It was a happy

time for Sheila. She and Patrick loved living there. Sheila bought a
Nikon camera and documented their lives in beautiful photographs
glittering with amber light. She hung her jewelry, her earrings, her
necklaces, from the mirrors with complete trust that nothing like a
robbery could ever happen there, in such a beatific atmosphere. It
might have been the happiest they ever were when they were together,
so much so that when they broke up, it punctured the membrane that
kept Sheila tethered to the world, and for at least a decade she was
deranged with sadness. One night, I was at the Wilson house. Sheila
and Patrick went to a party. I don't remember why I didn't go with
them, maybe I wasn't invited, but I stayed home with Kenny, and we
smoked really strong hash and got crazy-ass high. We were tripping
out on *New York Tendaberry*. I was hearing everything including the
arrangements, the brass, the chimes, the breaths, and the piano in a
whole new way, as if it were live in the room. When you are young
like that, you can give yourself over to music, like being underwater,
because you are always looking for a way out, out of your body, out of
your broken heart, your rattled mind, and music, music is the escape
hatch. Only as you grow older do you develop all the controls you
need to keep everything out, including beauty, including love. Kenny,
who, with his wavy, shoulder-length golden hair and his beard and
mustache, which were slightly darker but no less luxurious, looked
like a Viking, or the soul of Ireland, fell asleep on the floor. I was
overstimulated in that way you get when you are so high you can stare
at the corner of a room for hours completely amazed, saying "Wow"
every ten seconds. Well, here I was in a room on a chair listening to
Laura Nyro with Kenny asleep on the floor facing the ceiling, and
I felt as though I could stare at him, examine him brazenly, eye his
crotch for even the least imperceptible movement, imagine devouring
him. I was a Peeping Tom, and my subject was two feet from me. I had
a very erotic couple of hours just staring at him, undressing him with
my eyes, living in the wild reckless abandon of the imagination Laura
Nyro and her almost shamanistic implicitness conjured up. It was one
of the most powerful sexual fantasies I have ever had. Kenny and I
were in the same room together, and the freedom of being able to look

at him and not be seen was perhaps, besides the moments of staring at my father naked under the covers as a little boy, my most powerful experience of pure unabashed voyeurism. I even remember the corduroy pants he was wearing, the way the fabric defined every rumple and curve, every bulge of the terrain of his masculinity. I wanted to take his clothes off, ravish him, bury my face in him, eat him, drink him, do anything I wanted to him.

Susan and Kenny both died of alcoholism, their beauty giving way to rootlessness and ravagement. Alcohol and drugs, the waving banner of the times. Sometimes, we would all go out onto the lawn in front of the house, get drunk and high under the stars, and stare at the VFW across the street, talking and laughing, making up stories about everyone who passed, Laura Nyro singing inside wantonly. We called it Vinnie, Frank, and Willie's. Nowhere else in my life could I feel such camaraderie.

This morning I woke up with the song "You Don't Love Me When I Cry" moving mournfully through my head. There is a particular loneliness Laura Nyro addresses that plays somewhere in my heart like a solo muted trumpet, taps, for everything that is gone.

Two mainstream die
You don't love me when I cry

How would Laura Nyro and Joni Mitchell fare now? Neither of them was slick or packaged. They were authentic, poetic, compositionally complex with more than major and minor chords, they could really sing, without pitch stabilizers, and they were vulnerable and honest.

After the Beatles, Peter was not part of my forays into pop music. He was connected to classical music, the voice, opera, and then musical theater. It was probably through me that he cultivated a taste for twentieth-century music and then symphonic music. He is astonishingly well rounded now.

Food of Love

And the solitary cord of sea lutes.
—Guillaume Apollinaire, "Singer"

Music is like poetry. Sometimes there is only one line you really love in a poem, or one poem you connect with in a collection, but you will love that line or poem enough to say you love that poet, to use it to exemplify your life's meaning and your personal philosophy, to quote when you are in love, to order your confusion, to hang over your workplace or on your refrigerator, to tape onto the bathroom mirror, or to lull you to sleep. You can love a moment in music so much it becomes synonymous with the way you feel and experience the world. A turn of phrase, a chord, an orchestral color, can so roil, so unseat you, they can become as powerful as food, air, or water. You cannot imagine life without them. Without music, poetry, painting, architecture, literature, I would not want to be here. The natural beauty of this God-given earth is astounding in itself, but sometimes, for me, it is when it is ennobled by a great artist that it becomes even more so.

When I was at school at Carnegie Mellon, I would take my watercolors to Carnegie Library on Forbes Avenue and listen to and discover all kinds of music previously unknown to me while I painted. Two of the pieces I discovered in that library are Ravel's *Shéhérazade*, sung by Régine Crespin, and Alban Berg's "Der Wein," sung by Jessye Norman, both sensuously, dizzyingly beautiful.

There is a moment in the first section, "Asie," of Ravel's *Shéhérazade*. Just before the singer sings the words "I'd like to see earthenware pipes stuck into pursed mouths wholly surrounded by white whiskers," there is a three-note motif, C-sharp, A, B, in the strings; the clarinets hold a G-sharp octave after the third note is sounded, and we are into a passage that is perhaps one of the most beautiful moments in all of music, and I have never *not* felt that way, every time I hear it. Ravel masters the orchestra so as to allow every instrument to speak as it was meant to be spoken, to grab your ear, saying, "Listen to me!" Every pluck, every blow, every inhalation, is a personal gesture like the beating of his heart. In every piece, he leaves you stimulated and shaken, as if coffee were percolating, rushing through your veins. But there are millions of earth-shattering moments like this. Only now, I thought of Robert Helps's simply exquisite piano piece "Hommage à Fauré," and I found it on Apple Music to play. As soon as it started, my heart cracked like glass. Or in Bach's *St. Matthew Passion*, when the bass sings, "Mache dich, mein Hertze, rein":

> *Make thyself clean, my heart,*
> *I will myself entomb Jesus.*
> *For he shall henceforth in me*
> *For ever and ever*
> *Take his sweet rest.*
> *World, begone, let Jesus in!*

This moment is so beautiful, so wrenching to me, it could almost make this Jew convert. It may be the pinnacle of music. It is beyond the notes, inexplicable, ineffable, unbearably humble. At first, in a rolling but restless 12/8, the two oboes double the violins in a melody that, though in a major key, has the full spectrum of depth and sadness that someone asking for a kind of purity and beauty elusive in life might have. The melody starts on the second beat rather than the first, which creates a kind of tension, representing the need of the request. Then, in the middle, the B section, major becomes minor, as if representing the world that must be cast out, the unclean, the bitter. "World, begone, let Jesus in!" It must be Bach's version of a journey into hell, and it is a moment sparer, more halting, less lyrical than the first section. Then, after the world *is* cast out, we are back to the beatific, the slightly uneasy serenity, a boat upon the water before the next storm approaches.

There is a kind of faith that is so radiant it is inviolable; we know it is real, and we feel it in our marrow. I met the Dalai Lama when my opera *The Tibetan Book of the Dead* was premiering in Houston. It was the first time I understood the word "embodiment." I had been setting these Buddhist teachings to music every day for more than a year, and here, standing before me, the Dalai Lama, the embodiment of Buddhism. He held my hand and transmitted the teachings to me in a way I couldn't understand before meeting him. Suddenly joy, kindness, and simplicity were solid objects I could hold in my hand. Here were the principles of Buddhism in all their radiance. Bach seems to embody his faith in his music. He asks, "Make thyself clean, my heart, I will myself entomb Jesus," with the humility of a supplicant and transfers in the beauty of his music his faith to us. It is his gift.

Music is a language that never stops talking in my head. When I was growing up, I just loved what I loved, and life was simple. But when I claimed the mantle of composer, music became not always a pleasure but an indictment, a gun, an arrow to pierce my confidence or a lance to free my envy and jealousy. That said, most of the composers of these pieces are dead, so I am not competing with them, and I have made peace with their genius.

Vanessa, by Samuel Barber, with a libretto by Gian Carlo Menotti, is an opera that completely intoxicated me when I first heard it. Barber's achingly precise music combined with Menotti's Chekhovian libretto concerning three women of different generations either eagerly awaiting, longing for, or shunning love, having already been destroyed by it, is an opera of such luxurious beauty and sensuousness even the reading of a menu at the top of the opera is exquisite. Barber was a master, a perfectionist, and the architecture of the score, of all of his music, its pristine unarguable construction, his impeccable sense of theater, make his music feel utterly trustworthy. It is written so well for the voice every role is instantly indelible, and no matter how many times I see and hear it, I am always excited to hear how a new cast will navigate its virtuosic vocal terrain. The recording conducted by Dimitri Mitropoulos,

and starring Eleanor Steber, Rosalind Elias, Nicolai Gedda, Regina
Resnick, and Giorgio Tozzi, may be one of the most beautifully sung
recordings of all time. There is a story about Rosalind Elias. The opera
was rehearsing for its premiere at the Met, and she felt her character,
Erika, Vanessa's niece, needed more, a beat was missing; well, or she
just wanted more to sing for the sake of impact. She had the balls to
call Samuel Barber from the office of the dapper and acerbic general
manager of the Metropolitan Opera from 1950 to 1972, Rudolf Bing,
and ask for an aria for her character. In response, he wrote the tender
and brooding "Must the Winter Come So Soon?," surely one of the
most popular arias for mezzo-sopranos of all time. Almost fifty years
later, after we had cast her as Granma in *The Grapes of Wrath*, I got an
invitation to tea at her apartment, and instinctively I knew what was
coming: "Ricky, I promise I won't ask much of you, but can't you just
write Grandma a *little* aria? Not too big, just a *little* aria?" I felt so proud
and honored to be in the same boat with Samuel Barber, and of course
I called Michael Korie, the librettist, and happily we wrote her a lullaby
to lull Granpa to sleep after she has dosed him with her soothin' syrup,
the same lullaby Ma later sings to her as she dies in the back of the
truck. Roz was one of the warmest, most generous people I have ever
worked with. Of course, when I was in her living room, all I could think
of was Peter, who would probably faint dead away knowing I was in
Rosalind Elias's living room. My mother was frail and could not make
it to St. Paul to see the opera, and my father was gone, so Roz would
smother me with kisses and tears, becoming both parents at once. "Isn't
your mother so proud of you?" she asked me one day, after we made it
through a reading of act 1. When I went to Florida after the world premiere, I played my mother a recording of the opening, "The Last Time
There Was Rain," and she quietly said, "holy," when it was over.

   Lulu, by Alban Berg, based on *Pandora's Box* and *Earth Spirit* by
Frank Wedekind, is probably my favorite opera, because I never get
entirely used to it. It is always revealing something new, surprising,
and tantalizing to me, and it is mysterious, wildly out of reach to as-
pire to. It's like a person who can never be known so they become the
only one you want to know. The story of this woman, an object of

desire for all who are destroyed when they finally attain her, is such a potent deterrent illustrating the adage "be careful what you wish for." Also, with my proclivity for obsession, this woman who becomes whatever anyone projects onto her, imagines her to be, wants or needs her to be, is thoroughly captivating to me. Berg manages to make the twelve-tone system, which can be rigorous and systematic in a way that can seem arid and cold, warm, melodic, and gorgeous. Moment upon moment of sheer invention, color, texture, detail, and brilliance makes this a work I would see every performance of, everywhere in the world, if I could. The integration of words and music, every nuance in the story pitch perfectly depicted in the music, is unparalleled. The furious and intelligent way the orchestra sings, burbles, belches, and breathes with distinction and personality, as if every instrument right down to the triangle were a character in the opera. Berg was a dramatist through and through. It is also the only opera I know of that is truly chilling and terrifying. The music after Lulu is murdered by Jack the Ripper, following her bloodcurdling scream, which Peter and I listened to over and over again to the absolute disdain of his mother, Bernice, does make your blood run cold. The range for the singer who plays Lulu is stratospheric, making her almost out of reach, a little beyond comprehension, though it is eminently singable as well. It is an adult opera about adult themes, and there is not a moment when its being an opera robs it of its dramatic impact. There was a moment just after I got sober, when the singer Teresa Stratas, who is, for me, the greatest Lulu ever, and perhaps the most talented and committed singing actress of her generation, wanted to make an album of my songs, "Stratas Sings Gordon." One day, during that time, I ran into her at the end of my run in Central Park, sweaty and exhausted. I screamed, "I'm listening to you! Your *Lulu* from Paris!" I was indeed listening to her magnificent recording of the full three-act version of the opera directed by Patrice Chéreau and conducted by Pierre Boulez. She was just about to be murdered by Jack the Ripper. She looked at me as if I were crazy, and said, "Why are you listening to *that*? And while you are running?" The album never happened, but I saved every message she ever left me, including the ones where, if I wasn't home, she would just sing the whole song for me over my machine. I call it "The Almost Teresa Stratas Album." Interestingly, she was Roz's best friend, and after every rehearsal of *Grapes*, Roz would call Teresa to kibitz on the phone. It always tugged at my heart a little. When I wanted the album to happen, she was always a little bit out of reach. She almost drove me to drink. No one canceled as much as her. She could be a bag of tics and neuroses, but onstage she could tear your heart out and hand it to you, bloodied on a plate.

Gian Carlo Menotti's *The Consul*, a three-act opera set around a mysterious consulate somewhere in Eastern Europe, constructs a bleak and somewhat hopeless universe, perfect for opera, in which a family's desperate attempt to flee totalitarian rule is met with an indifferent and overwhelmed bureaucracy. Sound familiar? It could be the Mexican border right now, or Afghanistan, or Russia, or . . . Menotti used his love for, and knowledge about, Italian grand opera to write a complexly viable and devastating piece of music drama that actually ran on Broadway for eight months. Menotti was himself an Italian immigrant to the United States and wrote the opera as a response to refugees fleeing Europe after World War II. As an Italian citizen living in the United States during the war, Menotti was considered an "enemy alien." When I discovered it as a boy, I found it deeply stirring. I loved the fact that Menotti, as a moving tribute to Mabel Mercer, a singer he loved, opens the opera with a recording of her singing a song he wrote especially for her that we hear through the window, "Tu reviendras et voudras," which must be rented, every time the opera is performed, so it is always her. Menotti's musical language, which I loved in all his works, from *Amahl and the Night Visitors*, *The Medium*, and *The Telephone*, to *The Saint of Bleecker Street*, was astounding in its imaginative insertion of dissonances and "wrong notes" into such inviting and seductive melodic language. In one gorgeous aria or ensemble after another, it had a spikiness mixed into its beauty, sad and happy all at once, that made me listen to these pieces over and over again until I knew them backward and forward. I had the scores, and I played and sang through all of them. His orchestrations always included the piano in a way that made sense to me as a pianist, percussively and

harmonically, often gluing the various textures of the orchestra together the way Stravinsky does in a piece like Symphony in Three
Movements, which is one of my favorite pieces of all time and for
the record one of my favorite Balanchine ballets. Also, and I say this
without any irony, being as obsessed as I was with Sylvia Plath, this
opera, which ends with a woman overwhelmed, destroyed, and out of
options, putting her head into an oven, got all mixed up with my sense
of who was who and what was what and sometimes I almost felt as if I
were listening to an opera about Sylvia Plath. *The Consul* won both the
Pulitzer Prize and the New York Drama Critics' Circle Award, and
the idea that Broadway was at one time a place where operas by someone like Menotti could get produced and have decent runs is perhaps
where I got the crazy notion to attempt such an impossible task. Gershwin's *Porgy and Bess* was produced on Broadway in 1935, the Menotti
operas I mentioned, the double bill of *The Medium* and *The Telephone*,
in 1947, *The Consul*, in 1950, and his *Maria Golovin*, in 1958. Leonard Bernstein's *Candide* was produced in 1956, and Kurt Weill's *Street
Scene*, in 1947. Broadway was an arena open to great invention and in-
novation. Then Stephen Sondheim came along, spinning one complex
and intelligent masterpiece for the musical theater after another. So
many of us wanted to believe, later, that Sondheim was an open door
into a new musical sophistication on Broadway. But he was not, he was
an aberration, and in many ways the Broadway musical seems to have
regressed musically, not grown up. It's about the money, of course.
Everything is more expensive to produce, so the margins for exper-
imentation over commercialism have narrowed. Perhaps it is a form
designed to speak to its time and that is a good thing, but I am not of
this time, and it rarely, if ever, speaks to me anymore.

Richard Mohaupt's *Double Trouble*—now there's a rarity—may be
one of those pleasures you discover when you are young that gets
into your heart before you have the powers of discernment. It may be
a cheap thrill, it may be sexist, or a guilty pleasure, or it may be an
undiscovered masterpiece, but I will always love it unabashedly for
the moment I discovered it. There were record labels that recorded
new music when I was little. They were always my favorite record

labels. One was Desto, one was CRI (Composers Recordings Inc.), and one was called First Edition Recordings, which the Louisville Orchestra recorded with. I would be surprised if even one person reading this book knew this opera, and I wonder, if I had discovered it now, what I would think of it, but I happened on it when I was a little boy, and though even then I cared very little about its convoluted plot concerning mistaken identity, I loved the music and the singing. I am grateful for the quality in myself that propels me toward things I don't know, in a hoarding obsessive-compulsive kind of way. I can't see *one* Ozu movie; I have to see all of them. I have to be a talking head expert on them. I had to know everything recorded by these labels, so by the time I was, say, seventeen, I had already heard a shitload of contemporary music and had plenty of ideas about what I liked and didn't like. I mean, how many of you out there could right now, on cue, sing the entire opening of William Bergsma's *Wife of Martin Guerre*, or George Antheil's *The Wish*, or Peggy Glanville-Hicks's *Transposed Heads* and *Nausicaa*? Even Mark Bucci's *Sweet Betsy from Pike*, or Karl-Birger Blomdahl's space opera *Aniara*, with the lead character named Daisi Doody, or even Lukas Foss's *Jumping Frog of Calaveras County*? Go on, hum me a few bars. I could! I mentioned before Menotti's opera *Maria Golovin*, about the tragic story, the blind Donato, who falls in love with Maria, a woman who comes with her little boy, Trottolo, to stay in his mother's boardinghouse during the war; it ran for a very short time on Broadway and was considered a failure. Not to me. I know every note!

There were so many pieces by Ned Rorem I loved, that influenced me as a kid. When I first moved to West Seventieth Street, my next-door neighbors were a couple, Pat Cerza, who worked as an agent for the great impresario Sol Hurok, and John West, a respected operatic bass. John told me Ned Rorem lived on our block, and he would be happy to introduce me. Ned invited me over for drinks one night. I had just set Anne Sexton's poem "Three Green Windows" to music in a rather long setting that almost made it like a solo cantata. What could I have understood of that poem at the time: "I have forgotten that old friends are dying . . . / I have forgotten the names of the literary critics." Ned asked me to play it. I gave him the score, and I played and sang the entire piece from memory, which impressed him. Ned always liked my voice. He liked it, but he said the song had "too many notes." Over the years, Ned and I became friends, and he always showed up at what I did and was very supportive. He wept backstage at Cooper Union after Tina Landau and I organized a staged concert version of our show *Dream True*, a piece so suffused with my love for Jeffrey and my grief at losing him that it refreshed Ned's grief for his lover of many years, Jim Holmes. When Ned lost Jim, I had already lost Jeffrey. He asked if we could have dinner. It was surreal comforting a composer thirty-three years older whom I have been listening to most of my life, whose books I have read, whom I have thought about over and over again. Some of Ned's pieces that I love are the following:

"Some Trees": poems by John Ashbery, for vocal trio and piano. John Ashbery's poems can be difficult because they don't necessarily have a narrative logic and can seem like an assortment of fragments beautifully strung together, but always, the language is intoxicating, meticulous, and radically mysterious. Ned finds a way to make the individual strands glitter, and we hear the poems for what they are, above anything, scintillating breezes of ideas blowing by.

Poems of Love and the Rain: settings of various poets, for mezzo-soprano and piano, but a dazzling conceit; after the last poem, the whole cycle mirrors itself, backward to forward, with each poem set a second time but completely different. It is a technical feat Ned achieves beautifully.

Ariel: Five Poems of Sylvia Plath: a brilliant cycle for soprano, clarinet, and piano; dizzying settings of harrowing poems gloriously captured in the music, full of the same fever the poems have. Ned's interweaving of the clarinet and piano with the voice are nothing short of ingenious, and the words are set with such clarity you practically memorize the poems as you hear them.

For pure, simple, and beautiful early Ned, when he was living in France with the Vicomtesse Marie-Laure de Noailles, his Second Piano Sonata is elegance personified; it is Frenchified French music and sheer loveliness written by a man who was clearly overwhelmingly handsome, desirable, and tanned. It is such a part of me, having listened to it so many times, with the beautiful playing of Paul Jacobs, who died of AIDS. Music, like no other art form, I think, can place you immediately back in time, to exactly where you were when you first heard whatever it was you fell instantly in love with. It is a bookmark, a placeholder like a pressed rose in a letter from across the sea. I found Ned when the tiny seeds of being a composer were taking root in me, and his music formed inner models that would later emerge when I started seriously putting notes on paper.

One thing I learned from Ned too: you can love the miniature as much as the grand, and a piece's seeming inconsequentiality should never deter you from loving it dearly. My late friend the painter Duncan Hannah always said this too. So many of the painters he loved were the sorts of little-known, under-the-radar painters who just stayed in their studios painting beautifully without trumpeting themselves, Walter Sickert, Henry Lamb, and Edwin Dickinson, for example.

Dmitry Shostakovich's Symphony no. 14, settings of poems about death by Lorca, Apollinaire, Rilke, and Wilhelm Küchelbecker, for soprano, bass, and chamber orchestra, is a dark, brooding, ferocious piece of music, dedicated to Benjamin Britten, where every note feels weighted with Shostakovich's oppression under Stalin, his dread of imminent death, and his monumental engagement with the necessity of words. Moments like "Malagueña," galvanizing in its intensity, "The Suicide," overwhelming in its mournfulness, the cello solo that begins it is truly pure grief in notes, and "On Watch," so anxiety provoking you want to jump out of your skin, are upsettingly beautiful in a way that is unparalleled, somehow distilling all of Shostakovich's genius down to a few bold gestures, and that is a lot of genius distilled. This piece is indeed bone-chilling, a fact illustrated with the use of xylophone and castanets. There is so much beauty, mischief, raucousness,

naughtiness, rage, oppression, and wrenching heartbreak in Shostakovich it would take lifetimes to mine all of it.

I want to say something about the great composer Hugo Weisgall,
without googling him, just trying to describe what it is that captivated
me about his music. What could be more subjective than someone's
taste in music? Music is ephemeral, a series of notes strung together,
noises that cohere into a whole that either you like or you don't. There
is something about Hugo's roots. The fact that he was European and
ended up in America at age eight, but unlike Kurt Weill, whose music
instantly became American sounding when he moved here, which for
me means less interesting, because I loved his expressive, decadent,
and gritty German music better, Hugo retained his roots. America
makes its way into the notes, as does his devoutness, his Jewishness, and
his thorny contrariness, and in his dramatizations too, so especially in
the three operas, *The Tenor*, *Six Characters in Search of an Author*, and
The Stronger, he has an impeccable sense of theatrical timing, and often
an astounding ear for melody, but the complexity, the Europeanness
of the music remains, so you have something hybrid that is totally
unique. Weill had a geniality, a need to be liked, and an extraordinary
knack for fitting in; Weisgall did not. He didn't care if you liked him. I
admire his stubbornness in holding on to who he was. His writing for
the voices is so exciting, with huge leaps and dangerous tessitura, and
his orchestrations are unique, his own, a sound that is hard to put my
finger on, with jazzy wind riffs mixed with impassioned, tart, and astringent strings, but somehow European with a nod toward America
at the same time. There is nothing ingratiating in his music. Just listen
to the opening of *The Stronger*, first piano, then trumpet, then sax,
then clarinet; is it crazy mixed-up jazz, or what? What is this music?
Each instrument seems to be expressing something cynical, cajoling,
questioning, and bitter, a fascinating array of attitudes.

The Tenor is about a huge star tenor, Gerardo, one of the rare tenors who can sing Tristan in Wagner's *Tristan and Isolde*, so he is worshipped as a god, something the opera universe specializes in, or used
to. Weisgall deftly weaves themes and textures from *Tristan* in and
out of the piece, both orchestrally and vocally. Gerardo's manager,

Maurice, a young fan girl hiding behind the curtains, and Helen, who has left her husband and children after sleeping with Gerardo in order to be with him forever, are all embroiled in the illusion his stardom stirs. It is, for me, about the falseness of celebrity, the self-centeredness and ego that come with it, the fantasies we project onto "stars," those who benefit from them, and those destroyed by them. It hovers about the fact that what people fall in love with on the stage is not necessarily the same off the stage, and in this case that artifice has disastrous consequences. The characters are so well drawn, specific, funny, mean, naive, and tragic they seem perfectly etched from life, realistic and harrowing. The libretto is clearly by a great poet (Karl Shapiro with Ernst Lert, after a play by Wedekind) because the words are rich, dense, and packed with subtext and meaning. Even an aria about folding a coat is ingenious. The only reason I can come up with for why it's *never* done is that it requires a tenor on the level of a *Tristan*, and that kind of tenor is going to concentrate on *Tristan* rather than a contemporary opera they may get to sing once or twice and never again, the tragedy of modern opera. Interestingly, I was just doing some research on the piece, and I saw the first review of the opera in *The New York Times*, which began, "'The Tenor,' a very bad one-act comic opera by Hugo Weisgall, had its first performance by Opera '55 at the Provincetown Playhouse last evening."

And it made me remember how sickening and heartbreaking it can be to put anything out into the world sometimes. Poor Hugo, to have a work of such beauty so entirely dismissed. The critic later goes on to say, "The principal shortcoming of 'The Tenor' is ineptitude."

I don't even know what to say. I'm glad he didn't kill himself, though I know, for him, there was a lot more where that came from. Hopefully, that critic is swimming in the water of his own ineptitude for all eternity. As Leonard Bernstein said, "I've been all over the world and I've never seen a statue of a critic."

Weisgall's *The Stronger*, with a libretto by Richard Henry Hart based on a play by Strindberg, is an opera for two women: one sings, and one listens. Estelle runs into Lisa at a bar while shopping for presents on Christmas Eve. She begins to talk and, in the course of the twenty-five-minute opera, cannot help revealing entirely too much about herself, how competitive she has always felt with Lisa, how inferior, her pain and her rage about that. She has always known Lisa was in love with her husband; she gloats about possessing him herself. Is Lisa jealous of her, or vice versa? The question, in the end, is, who is the stronger, the one speaking or the one listening? There is a line in *All About Eve*, Addison DeWitt says it to Eve in his sublime dressing-down of her in New Haven; it is about Karen, the role Celeste Holm played: "I had lunch with Karen not three hours ago. As always with women who try to find out things, she told more than she learnt."

Perhaps the most beautiful review I have ever received was from Hugo Weisgall's daughter, Deborah, who wrote an exceptionally loving and wonderful book called *A Joyful Noise: Claiming the Songs of My Fathers*. I was in Rockport, Maine, in 2016, at the Bay Chamber Concerts festival, directing Jesse Blumberg and the Aeolus Quartet in my opera *Green Sneakers*. On the day of the opening, July 15, I collapsed and had to be rushed to the hospital. I was very sick and was in and out of the hospital for a month before I was strong enough to get the necessary surgery to correct the problem. The show went on without me, after which Deborah wrote to me in the hospital, where I drifted in and out from massive doses of morphine:

Dear Ricky—

That was an astonishing, beautiful work. It was simple, straightforward, unsparing: words and music intertwined so that they were impossible to separate. It overflowed with sentiment and there was not one sentimental moment. It celebrated the ordinary in a most extraordinary way.

And the performance—Jesse [Blumberg] embodied confusion, loss, tenderness, and—I don't know how he did it—the luxury of impatience. And the quartet—they did all of that, too.

Here's more: the "luxury of impatience"—that's a phrase to live by. Once again, your way with words: you hear the

music in them. "He dressed beautifully, and he shopped copiously." It is your sense of how the small things illuminate
us: you notice.

As for Benjamin Britten, well, I love everything. There can be
stretches of Britten that may feel uninspired, note spinning, but
there will *always* be a moment that knocks you over the head, and they
are *always* worth waiting for. Recently, Kevin and I watched Claire
Denis's great film *Beau travail*. It was my second time seeing it, and
one of the reasons I wanted to see it again was to hear the music Britten had written for his opera *Billy Budd* woven into the film. There
is a moment in the opera where all the men on the ship are so over-
wrought, at a boiling point over the injustice they have just witnessed,
they literally moan to the music in an almost unbearable rising and
falling. In context with the opera, it is a truly disquieting moment.
The opera is, for me, so unsettling that I decided, the last time I saw
it, with my friend Nathan Gunn magnificently playing Billy at the
Met, I could never sit through the opera again. In the opera, evil and
impotence win. A man is destroyed because of the power of unchecked
desire and envy in the character of John Claggart and a spineless Captain Vere, who lets it all happen, obeying decorum and law rather
than his conscience. Unfortunately, I sort of feel the same way about
The Turn of the Screw, where every note of the score is pure genius and
invention in the form of a theme and variations but the story centers
on child abuse and can be incredibly icky to sit through.

Britten's last opera, *Death in Venice*, written with the librettist Myfanwy Piper, is my favorite. An adaptation of Thomas Mann's novella
in which a renowned older writer, Aschenbach, travels to Venice for
refreshment and inspiration and becomes captivated with the beauty
of a young Polish boy traveling with his family. What becomes a fixation for Aschenbach goes from invigorating him to destroying him.
There is so much in the score that is mysterious, from the murkiness of
the lagoon, always gurgling and roiling or quietly exploding like bub-
bles forced to the surface from the muck, to the great swirling force
of Aschenbach's obsession, I am always awestruck. Moments of such

exquisiteness in the music, from the journey to the Lido, conveyed in swirling uneven strings, an off-kilter barcarolle, to the splendor of Piazza San Marco, with its magisterial brass and bells, and moments of such quiet heartbreaking intimacy, Aschenbach barely able to murmur the words "I love you," make it so that I never tire of it.

Peter Grimes is another endlessly inventive masterpiece, and this time it is not the Venice lagoon but the Suffolk coast where the central character is outcast and destroyed, a favorite theme for Britten. It differs from *Billy Budd* in that he may actually deserve it, but that is up to us to decide. Even the widow, Ellen Orford, who has elected to give her heart to him, must face the eventuality of his prevailing violence and the sorrow he has wrought. The *War Requiem, Les illuminations, Nocturne, Serenade for Tenor, Horn, and Strings* are all such stunning and beautifully crafted pieces I marvel at them in awe. It makes me think of an architect friend I went to school with, Paul Aferiat. After he visited Frank Gehry's Guggenheim in Bilbao, he called it "one of the seven wonders of the world," and I remember thinking how rich it was to see someone admire and praise the work of a fellow architect with such generosity of spirit, for I think that to lay claim to a title, composer, architect, painter, writer, poet, performer, is to touch the sleeve in reverence of all before you who have done what you are doing, or attempting to do, and those brief moments when the individual ego is set aside and an artist can appreciate with humility the beauty in the creation of a colleague are true transcendence. For just five minutes of your time, close your eyes, and listen to Britten's setting of "A Shepherd's Carol" by W. H. Auden.

"O lift your little pinkie, / and touch the winter sky. / Love's all over the mountains / where the beautiful go to die." It is a small work of such variety, quietude, and distinguished power it always overwhelms me with emotion.

It is Easter. Last night, Kevin and I watched Luchino Visconti's *Death in Venice.* I last saw it when I was fourteen. My father, mother, and I had just left Mama Yetta's in Jackson Heights on a Sunday night, which means we were probably plied with enough chopped liver, brisket, matzoh ball soup, and apple cake to end up in the hospital for quadruple bypass surgery, but for some reason my father decided we needed to go to the movies. He saw the word "Death" in the title, and thought it was a Western, though I'm not sure what kind of Western happens in Venice, but we went in. He fell asleep for the whole movie, my mother for three-quarters, and I stayed awake and just thought, "What the . . . ?" for two and a half hours. It turns out that there are moments of staggering beauty including both the entire opening sequence and the entire ending, accompanied by the magnificent Adagietto in Mahler's Fifth Symphony, but whereas in the book the moments when Tadzio notices Aschenbach, or smiles at him, are few, monumental, and earth-shattering, in the movie Tadzio is practically a hustler luring Aschenbach on every fifteen minutes, and the scenes between Dirk Bogarde and Mark Burns where they discuss aesthetics are unbearably pretentious. What Visconti gets right, he gets painfully right, though, and the moments of searing beauty are many and well worth it.

But—and this is the point of bringing all of this up—what Visconti misses in the film, I feel Britten and Piper get brilliantly. With all the male protagonists except Aschenbach and Tadzio played by one singer, the inexorability of Aschenbach's fate, in the face of one guide, tormentor, or perpetrator, in several different disguises, becomes all the more haunting. Also, with music, you can create undertow, subtext, so when the strolling players are performing, for example, the subtext of plague horrifies underneath the entertainment, like rotten fruit. In a way, to me, its myriad multifaceted corners, like the carats of a diamond, are the work of a man on his deathbed who is at the edge of knowing everything.

I am listening to the great and glorious *St. Matthew Passion* as I write. Christ has risen.

I discovered Marc Blitzstein when I took a double album on CRI of *The Cradle Will Rock* out from the library. In 1937, in Steeltown, U.S.A., Larry Foreman attempts to unionize the town's workers and combat the villainous, greedy businessman Mr. Mister (Donald Trump except with a brain), who has a bent toward autocracy and controls everything, the factory, the press, the church, and the social organization. The piece is almost entirely sung through, like an opera, but it is more like a musical in the way the scenes and musical numbers are shaped. Blitzstein was adroit in all styles, so the score is fantastic, a wildly eclectic and theatrical Brechtian hodgepodge. John Houseman produced it originally for the Federal Theatre Project, while Orson Welles directed it. The Works Progress Administration temporarily shut down the project a few days before it was to open on Broadway, locking up the theater and making everything suddenly inaccessible. So, to avoid government and union restrictions, the whole audience and the whole cast marched down to another theater in defiance, and the show was performed on June 16, 1937, with Blitzstein playing piano onstage and the cast members singing their parts from the audience.

At one point I could sing and play through this entire score, and would, often.

When William Hoffman and I were working on *Morning Star*, we heard a fascinating story about *The Cradle Will Rock* from Sylvia Regan, who wrote the play we were basing our opera on. She and her husband were great friends of Marc Blitzstein's. Blitzstein had them over when he was done writing *The Cradle Will Rock* and sang and played the whole thing for them. They thought it was a masterpiece and told him so enthusiastically. When they were invited to a preview, they thought he had completely ruined it with the orchestration, prettifying it and softening its edges, so they thought God had saved the piece and Marc by shutting down the theater and making it so that it had to be experienced in the same bare-bones way they heard it, and even better, with the halo of political pariah around it. Having recently heard the orchestrated version, I agree. She told another story as well, not apropos of music, but too interesting not to tell. Her best friend growing up was the playwright Clifford Odets, who wrote, among other things, *Waiting for Lefty*, which I was impressed by because we were always doing scenes from it at Carnegie Mellon University during my short-lived stint in the drama department. Clifford gave her an idea for a play once, and she went away and wrote it. But he wrote it too and got it produced on Broadway, while her work was suddenly redundant, and she had wasted years writing it. She never spoke to him again and told the story as if he were Benedict Arnold.

The Cradle Will Rock, combined with Blitzstein's brilliant adaptation of Lillian Hellman's play *The Little Foxes* into a more formal opera, *Regina*, made him one of my favorite composers and a role model,
with his seamless and effortless blurring of lines between operas and
musicals, his ability to write coruscating texts, and his need and ability
to both connect to the times and say something meaningful and rele-
vant. Also, he loved and was influenced by Kurt Weill, as I was, which
only added to my adoration. He came to a terrible end. While working
on an opera for the Met about Sacco and Vanzetti, he went down to
Martinique and apparently tried to pick up three sailors in a bar who
feigned interest but then robbed him and brutally beat him to death.
The first story in Truman Capote's *Music for Chameleons* is about this.

In 1977, I saw a poster for a movie called *3 Women*, and I thought
it was the most striking, intriguing movie poster I had ever seen. It
was a new style of graphic that seemed to be borrowing from contemporary art in its vocabulary: three loose, hand-created boxes, almost
like a graph, containing intriguing raw, unfiltered photos with their
edges showing, a kind of elegant script for the font, on an off-white
opaque matte paper, and in blue, what appeared to be handwritten
diary entries. Robert Altman, the iconoclastic director whose movies
were like no one else's, was already an exemplar of mine, with people
talking over one another, improvisation, and a visual style that was as
unique as the directors of the Nouvelle Vague. The movie *3 Women*
ended up being my favorite, not only because the constellation of three
women (*Three Sisters, Cries and Whispers, Hannah and Her Sisters*) had a
particular resonance for me, or the strange circumstances that threw
these women together into a surreal and dreamlike fractured narrative reminding me of Ingmar Bergman's *Persona*, but because more
than anything it had an ingenious score like nothing I had ever heard
by a composer who was new to me, Gerald Busby. The movie seems
to grow out of the score as if the score were the roots and the trunk of
the tree, and the movie, the branches and the leaves. Its combination
of woodwinds, brass, low strings, and snare drums is so odd and indelible, so wonderfully, unabashedly dissonant, I had to know everything
about this composer. This was a movie with real music in it! There

was not a lot to find out. He was cast in Altman's *Wedding*, but that was later. Paul Taylor commissioned him to write a score for dance, and he wrote "Runes," a piece for solo piano, which was terrific.

Another composer whose music I was introduced to in an unusual way was Donald York. In the early 1980s, I became friends with the choreographer Jonathan Hollander and his then wife, Noelle Braynard. They were dear friends of my friend the artist Kit Grover, who would bring me down to their loft, where they were always eating some yummy pie Noelle had baked. They were kind and welcoming, and they seemed to have such a sweet life. Jonathan had his own dance company, Battery Dance, and Noelle, his muse, was the lead dancer as well as the costume designer, and their meals always ended with pie. Of course I always thought, "How are they not fat?" Jonathan, hearing my music, asked me if I would write something for the company. I loved the idea, but it scared me because I had never written for dance before. I knew he admired the work of Paul Taylor, so I went to see every piece Paul Taylor's company did that season at City Center. I never before appreciated dance this way.

I fell in love with his sexy, athletic company and his incredibly varied selection of works; even *Lost, Found, Lost*, a piece scored to live Muzak, floored me. But always, my favorite pieces, *Polaris* (a brilliant concept where the same choreography is danced to two completely different scores), *Syzygy*, *Diggity*, *Snow White*, and *Last Look*, seemed to have scores by the handsome man conducting in the pit, Donald York. "Who is this man and why can't I marry him?" I thought. I developed a whole relationship with him in my head. Don was different from Gerald, whose music was unlike music I had ever heard, as if it had crawled out from the mud without any influence whatsoever. Don's could be reminiscent, but in the best form of homage, with *Diggity* nodding to Copland and *Snow White*, to Stravinsky, but *Polaris*, *Syzygy*, and *Last Look* are bold in construction and wholly original, and gorgeous, and phenomenal pieces on their own, inspiring astonishing choreography from Paul Taylor.

Then I attended the New York City Ballet, where I was dazzled by so many of Balanchine's collaborations with Stravinsky, including

Apollo, Orpheus, Symphony in Three Movements, and *Perséphone.* Finally, I wrote *The Caste System* for Jonathan, a three-movement solo piano piece that I, like Gerald, played onstage whenever the piece was done. The ecstasy I felt at seeing dancers on a stage leaping, twirling, and doing pas de deux to my music was as addictive as crack, and I wrote three more pieces for Jonathan: *A Nickel and a Song; The Anyone's Ballet,* inspired by the great E. E. Cummings poem "Anyone lived in a pretty how town"; and *God's World,* using poems by Cummings and Millay.

If I am at all threatened by other composers, I befriend them, or they loom so large in my imagination I am subsumed by them. Don and Gerald became friends.

I found Gerald living at the Chelsea Hotel, and after I showered him with compliments, he gave me signed scores of pieces I consider as great as anything I have ever heard. Don and I met on Facebook, and we became pen pals until Paul Taylor's 2020 season, when he came to New York and we finally hugged in person.

Kurt Weill and Bertolt Brecht's *Rise and Fall of the City of Mahagonny* is a work of pure audaciousness, a primal scream against everything in a country about to erupt into perhaps the most corrupt world power in history, but it has been viewed as a critique of American society as well. Whatever it is, it is a stroke of lightning by two geniuses that shook the world to its foundations when it premiered, similar to how Stravinsky's *Rite of Spring* did. In a way, it is like one long, three-act, very entertaining sneer, a huge "Fuck you" to everything, capitalism, tyranny, and all seven sins. To me, when done well, it has never lost its power to incite, when the historical context is understood, and everyone working on it *gets* it, because it can also seem silly and blustery if everyone in it is just posing, performing their *idea* of what decadence looks like, and the inner life of the piece is wrong. *Mahagonny* has the strength and power of certain reactionary pieces that grow out of political unrest. There is danger and necessity in every word and note that make it feel like a pyre on which all artifice and superfluousness is burned. At moments, it is like a pile of junk, lit up and clattering, and at others, like a hideous and tragic emergency. Whatever it is, it is one of my favorite pieces. Two highlights: "Alabama Song" and "Benares Song."

I loved Paul Hindemith growing up. Playing through his piano pieces, I would revel in his use of fourths and fifths, the spikiness mixed with the beauty, the impeccable use of classical form with a thoroughly modern sensibility. I would endlessly play through his three piano sonatas, with my absolutely favorite moment always being the fugue at the end of the third, which is spectacular and such a fitting way to end this cycle of sonatas, much in the same way the fugue at the end Samuel Barber's stunning piano sonata provides such a dizzying grand finale.

I loved Hindemith's earlier and *much* more dissonant *Suite "1922"* and the entire book of preludes and fugues, his *Ludus Tonalis.* His symphony *Mathis der Maler,* inarguably beautiful and probably his most famous and recognizable piece, his *Kammermusik* no. 2, so wonderful, crisp, skittery, and deliciously bristling even Balanchine had to choreograph to it, as well as his *Four Temperaments.*

If you knew the bombast of the fugue at the end of Piano Sonata #3, then you would understand why my waking my sister Susan and her boyfriend, David Getz, at 6:30 in the morning in his house in Fairfax, California, in order to practice it might have been somewhat unnerving. I'm pretty sure I played so loud Susan's collection of rhinestone crucifixes over their bed nearly leaped off the wall. When my parents loaded up their camper in the mid-1970s and made their way across country to see their daughters in California, Susan forgot to remove the crucifixes for my father's visit, and he groused about it until the day he died.

The English composer Michael Tippett is basically the *other* English composer who was writing at the same time Britten was, so most people know Britten and not Tippett. There is a reason for this, I think. Michael Tippett, for one thing, wrote all of his own libretti, and they can seem (okay, they often *are*) convoluted, or mired in the psychology, jargon, or jingo of the day, so they can seem (okay, they *are*) dated, but when his howls of protest and love come together and work, like in his tremendous opera, *The Knot Garden*, it is overwhelming. I had, until the point I discovered him, never heard music like his. Just listen to the opening bars of *The Knot Garden*. What is he doing?

It is like that from start to finish! So detailed and unusual texturally, like organized pandemonium, impassioned, committed, and new! And nothing like Britten, his tasteful compatriot. His use of brass, those huge crunchy chords at fortissimo, his astringent *molto intenso* strings, the electric guitar, and his screeching woodwinds; I love this opera. At its center is Shakespeare's *Tempest*, but that is just a departure point for Tippett's take on race relations, homosexuality, deformity, and the maiming effects of war.

Tippett's Second Symphony, with its pounding Vivaldi-on-LSD opening spilling into the most delicate and stirring second movement, which boasts an exquisite theme of such hesitancy and poignancy, is thrilling. His music sounds like no other, but that is what it's all about, right? Voice, an original voice.

Olivier Messiaen was a devout Christian, with a faith that was so unshakable he filled his notes with the same love of God as Bach. Whether you like his notes and his particular language, the chirping and cackling of birds, their songs as well as their mad chaos, the stillness of stars and their imagined explosions, the majesty of mountains and canyons as well as what it might have sounded like when they were formed, ice breaking and clouds moving, sunrises and black holes, is subjective, but I tell you this: His music is real. It is holy. It is the truth. The place it comes from is pure and clear. What he has seen, and where he has been in his own *interior castle*, is magnificent, and to go on the journey with him to his peculiar, mysterious, and rattlingly beautiful universe is a privilege. If I had to pick some pieces by him to cite, though there is something in everything he writes, his massive piano work, *Vingt regards sur l'Enfant-Jesus*, his *Trois petites liturgies de la Présence Divine*, for thirty women's voices, and his three incredible song cycles, all with his own texts, the *Poèmes pour Mi*, *Chants de terre et de ciel*, and *Harawi*, are like nothing ever written before or after them. His particular and wholly original uses of rhythm, repetition, and interruption are singular, and his writing for the voice, from howling, extolling, to intoning and growling, and then just pure opulent crystalline lines, is breathtaking. For me, it sounds as if Christ were sitting on his shoulder picking the notes for him the way a bird plucks worms from the dirt, to glorify his uncertainty, his splendor, his mystery, his violence, his illustriousness, his wildness, and his power all at once. Messiaen's music is anointing; it is like Spikenard oil, or the loaves and the fishes.

William Bolcom is just, for me, the guy who did it. He took popular music at its most popular, and contemporary music at its most contemporary, meaning at its thorniest, and managed to mash them all together into a language that allows for anything, music that is wholly all his own, encompassing and incorporating his encyclopedic knowledge of everything ever written, his clear love of theater, his taste and discernment, his worship of the great American songbook, and his uninhibitedness! He will do whatever he has to do to make the moment work, period! In a way, what Bernstein began in his *Mass*, Bolcom continues in his Blake settings, *Songs of Innocence and of Experience*, and the three operas he wrote with his brilliant and witty collaborator Arnold Weinstein, *McTeague*, *A Wedding*, and *A View from the Bridge*, as well as his cabaret songs, marvels of his particular brand of eclecticism. Bill is the Frank O'Hara of music. Frank took whatever he saw, felt, and thought, "this and that," and included it in the poem. Nothing was excluded from his watchful and intuitive eye and heart. This is Bill. Bill is also a friend and a generous colleague, as is his wife, Joan Morris, who is a gifted singer and interpreter of twentieth- and twenty-first-century song, as well as Bill's music. Now that it's legal, I have to tell you something funny. When I was doing *The Grapes of Wrath* at Minnesota Opera, Bill invited me to breakfast one day. He was in Minneapolis doing something with Phil Brunelle, the choral conductor. Anyway, we were having a lovely time, but then I found out the *real* reason he wanted to see me. I laughed! He wanted to know if I knew where to score some pot! I said, "Bill! I'm clean and sober!" I love Bill. He has had an enormous influence on me.

The music of Béla Bartók is situated in time and place, like a big jewel-encrusted box of Eastern Europe. One of my favorite pieces of music of all time is his Divertimento for String Orchestra, because it was one of the albums lying around at my sister Lorraine's apartment on the Lower East Side and when I first listened to it, it ran through me like a thousand spiders. The music is beautifully crafted, deeply heard, completely enmeshed in Bartók's Hungarian heritage, awash in themes and threads that you sense are from somewhere you have never been, utterly exotic, and all of it imbued with the dread of encroaching autocracy, oppression, and then, strangely, pure ecstatic joy. There is a beauty and an anxiety in Bartók's music, as if he were a nervous, jittery man who was always hungry and music was his meal, his lifeline. There is a reason Stanley Kubrick opens *The Shining* with Bartók's *Music for Strings, Percussion, and Celesta*. It is icy, bone-chilling, and menacing in fact, but also astoundingly beautiful. The Concerto for Orchestra is basically just one sublime melody after another with what feels like unceasing inspiration, giving every instrument in the orchestra bar none something to chew on and delight in playing. It is awe inspiring like a cliff face. One is always aware of a serious nature, an austere background, an unhappy childhood, and every note tells the story. When I was little, one of my favorite pieces to play was Bartók's *Allegro barbaro*. And I would listen over and over again to his *Contrasts* and *Hungarian Folk Songs*. Now I love his three piano concerti and his opera *Bluebeard's Castle*, but it is always changing. For a recent brilliant use of his music in film, notice how Joanna Hogg uses *Bluebeard's Castle* in her film *The Souvenir*.

As an aside. Something else lying around at my sister Lorraine's was an album by the Incredible String Band, and I was obsessed with a song of theirs called "Cousin Caterpillar," as well as a version of the Christmas carol "Ríu ríu chíu" on an album of New York Pro Musica's.

I have written elsewhere how I first, at least knowingly, heard the music of Hans Werner Henze at the end of William Friedkin's movie *The Exorcist*. I say "knowingly" because I had seen all the movies that employ his music, Schlöndorff's *Young Törless* and *The Lost Honor of Katharina Blum* and Alain Resnais's *Muriel*, but I didn't know any of his other music, and when Friedkin uses a movement from his *Fantasia for Strings*, I had one of those moments that are rare, like my Kabalevsky Joan of Arc moment, where I am reminded in my bones of how important music is to me. He became a revelation and an obsession with me. Henze's music can be angry, violently so, but then it can be luxuriously sensuous. It is impossible to exactly point to where it springs from because, again, his voice is so strange and distinct. The *Fantasia for Strings* is an expansion of his music for *Young Törless* and travels between some ineffable place of mournfulness and rage. The *Cantata della fiaba estrema*, for chorus and soprano soloist singing so unbelievably high it is unfathomable, uses the beautiful poems by the Jewish Italian writer Elsa Morante and is otherworldly, magical, and exquisite. His music in *Being Beauteous*, from a poem by Rimbaud, and *Whispers from Heavenly Death*, which uses poems by Walt Whitman, goes from achingly tender to fierce, atonal to tonal, and supernatural to transcendental. Inexplicable.

The great jazz singer Sarah Vaughan's voice is a freak instrument with endless color and astonishing versatility. It goes everywhere and anywhere and seems to bounce off the Grand Canyon of her bones with its resonance. In particular, two albums she made later in her career for Pablo Today, the *Duke Ellington Song Book One* and *Two*, are incredible. If you need instant cheering up, just listen to her recording of "Everything but You" on the second of those albums. Dinah Washington, with her wonderful fast vibrato like an oriole, Dakota Staton (the most beautiful recording of "My Funny Valentine" ever), and the smoky and hip Chris Connor were also the singers I listened to over and over again. The great singer/songwriter Neil Young, whose "The Needle and the Damage Done" is one of the saddest and most empathetic songs about addiction ever, bewitched me with his strange falsetto twang like a cat in heat. Talk about self-invention, where did he get that sound? The profound effect Bob Fosse's movie of Kander and Ebb's *Cabaret* had on me when it came out cannot be underestimated, Liza Minnelli might as well have been the Buddha during that period, and the Broadway musical *A Chorus Line* essentially changed my life, making it easier to own my sexuality and planting the seed for my wanting to write for the theater, where you could suddenly be confessional and entertaining all at once. It would not be incorrect to say that at the moment I saw it, *A Chorus Line* was the most powerful thing I had ever seen, period. Bernstein and Sondheim's *West Side Story*, Maury Yeston's *Nine*, Michael John LaChiusa's

Wild Party, and of course all of Stephen Sondheim's shows were also beacons on the path, still are.

Speaking of Leonard Bernstein's *Mass* (libretto by Stephen Schwartz), I attended every performance of it at the Metropolitan Opera in 1972, developed a crush on the singer who played the Celebrant, Alan Titus, and stalked him, following him home one day. He was very nice and talked to me a lot about his wife . . . Bernstein's *Mass*, for a kid my age, was monumental, earth-shattering. It was everything, an event, a concert, a religious experience, and ultimately a unifying experience, where I felt at one with the entire audience by the end. It might have been my first holy experience. My favorite moment, musically, is the entire "Sanctus" section. I do not react anymore with the same fervor when it comes to the eclecticism of the *Mass*. Some of the rock sections seem silly to me now, pandering. But they were perfect for who I was then, and I have no need to trample on them, just to say, we grow, we change, our tastes shift, and that is where I am now.

When I saw Meredith Monk's *Quarry* at BAM in 1977, the combination of music, dance, theater, and spectacle was overwhelming to me. I saw it many more times and consider it seminal in terms of my own development as an artist. Meredith is unique in that she found everything she needed inside her body. Everything springs from her voice, a multifaceted sapphire shooting off shafts of light in a thousand directions, each sound a crystal-clear brainchild. Meredith is one of the great iconoclasts of the twentieth century, and *Quarry* is the quintessence and the last word on a multidisciplinary masterwork.

In 1981, there was a French film festival at Lincoln Center. I had just run seven miles in the park in the rain, and was getting ready to go see Alain Resnais's *Last Year in Marienbad* and *Hiroshima mon amour*. I came out of the shower and turned on the radio. WNYC had a program about Steve Reich's new piece *Tehillim*, his setting of Hebrew psalms. I was mesmerized instantly by the piece, and I became so obsessed with it I wore it out, and now I don't know if I can ever hear it again, but wow. What was it? The overlapping of voices, the clapping, the harmonies, the repetitions? This is a strange thing to say, but it sounded so natural to my ear, from start to finish, I almost felt as if I were listening to a piece of music I had written myself. The second movement, when the piece slows down, was so beautiful I remember sitting naked on the arm of the couch shaking my head. It had an inevitability, an innate sacredness that made me feel the undeniable reality of my own heritage. I was acutely aware of something new on the horizon, and I was very excited about it. It was a relic, history before it was written, and indeed I was right to be excited, because he still hadn't written *The Desert Music* or his *Octet*, which are also metamorphic.

In 2005, I was up early in the morning getting my breakfast before I started writing. I was listening to WNYC on the radio, and they mentioned something about a "Must Have Festival." They were asking listeners to write in describing the one recording they would take to a desert island with them if they could take only one. I liked the challenge, remembering how one thing I loved in one of Ned Rorem's published diaries was how Poulenc's Stabat Mater was his desert island piece. I went to my computer immediately and wrote to them about my favorite recording: Sir John Barbirolli conducting the Mahler song cycles *Songs of a Wayfarer*, *Kindertotenlieder*, and *Rückert-Lieder*, with the great mezzo-soprano Janet Baker. I explained how the music on the recording seemed to be sprung from a rock, as if there were no singer, no conductor, no orchestra, just simply music that was always there as God had meant it to be, whole, intact, celestial, the music men and women were supposed to hear when they were either being born or dying. In fact, I said, when I was dying, I wanted to hear "Ich bin der Welt abhanden gekommen" from this recording as the angels were ushering me into the mystery. I won! The prize was, I got to hang out with one of the disc jockeys, David Garland, at the station one night and for two hours play anything I wanted to play, including my own music. They were two of the most pleasant hours of my life, playing a considerable amount of the music aforementioned in this chapter in an eclectic evening of music. I played Joni Mitchell, and Blitzstein, Bach, Berg, Britten, Barber, Rorem, Shostakovich, and Gordon.

I listen to music when I walk, and I have a ton of music on my iPhone. Often, I just put it on shuffle, and an incredible variety of music enters my ears like darting, skittering swallows, but every time something by Stravinsky comes on, every time, my eyes widen from what always feels fresh, as if it were written this morning. Just this week, it was the "Chinese March" from *Le chant du rossignol*, a teeth-grindingly anarchic little piece of staggering fucking genius that is so mind-blowing you want to explode out of your skin and run backward on water! Stravinsky uses the orchestra in ways that could only be Stravinsky, as if they were playing with saws, hammers, swords, and butterfly wings. It is literally as if the whole world started singing, farting, screeching, moaning, laughing, crying, and howling all at once. The sheer generosity of invention in Stravinsky, the variety, the ingenuity, the tickling, stabbing sound universe is unparalleled and overwhelming. The image I have in my head of him is sitting next to a window at his out-of-tune upright piano, drawing, not composing, drawing, painting with notes, God guiding the brush that is his hand. Stravinsky had it all, as far as I am concerned, everything, hook, line, sinker, anchor, motor, door window, cavalcade. Explosion. I have to stop, listen, and marvel at being alive in a universe that created such a being. I didn't get it at first. When I was a kid, he made no sense to me. But when I got it, wow, I got it. All hail Stravinsky.

Elsewhere, I intend to write about the creation of some of my own key works, but I wanted to write about music I have loved and lived with first. We are what we digest, no?

Kevin is away for three days visiting his family in Ohio. I ate dinner while watching a documentary about William S. Burroughs, and then, only moments ago, I received this text from my friend Jessica Molaskey:

Hey Rick,

I hope you are well. I can't wait to see you in person and be in the presence of your next gorgeous opus. I hate to bring you bad news, but I thought you should know instead of reading it somewhere online. My dear Don York, one of the great loves of my life passed away today at 4:00 pm from complications of a heart attack and then stroke. He was such a great artist, friend and human. Just very sad. That's all. I love you and the fact that somehow, we both found our way to him. Xoxox

The last time I saw Don was when Paul Taylor had his last season in New York at the New York State Theater (I still can't call it the Koch Theater) in 2019. We had coffee before his show that night. He was, he said, ready to move on from Paul Taylor and concentrate on composing (that'll kill anyone), and he was already working on a musical. I had a sense of wonder around me that night because we had become friends. I still felt everything I felt about him from the first time I saw him conducting, only now I was encouraging him, because, like me, he had a resounding solstice point regarding his own gifts. I loved him and looked forward to seeing him again and hearing whatever treasures he was working on. Don York is dead. Death is all around us and so close, why not take the risk of being known. The only alternative is not being known. Who wants that?

AFTERTHOUGHT

I don't know why, some may say (will, or already have) it's a lack of talent, or education . . . but always accompanying my life of being a composer has been a fantasy of leaving it behind . . . the pain, not the fun part . . . not the having written, and the seeing and hearing my

works performed, not the engagement with people who are making
my music, the creating of community that forms after you have spent
all that time alone in a room writing it . . . there is so much good. But
the painful part . . . every time I hear music, *any*, thinking it's good, or
bad, or I *could* do it, or I *couldn't* do it . . . watching movies or TV . . .
hearing the incidental music and either indicting myself or patting
myself on the back . . . pretty much all the music I hear is an invitation to either like myself at its expense or loathe myself in the face of
it. I don't know where this comes from . . . my fantasy is, if I went to
Harvard, and knew everything there is to know about music . . . if I
could even tell you right now what a Neapolitan sixth chord was, if
I could play every instrument and knew its ins and outs as well as I
know the back of my hand . . . if I could analyze every piece of music
ever written with an encyclopedic mind, if I had perfect pitch, if I
had done my homework, if I had read all of Shakespeare, Tolstoy, and
Proust . . . if I could, basically, just start over . . . start from scratch . . .
never drink, never take drugs, never have sex with men so early in my
life that sex became a priority over everything, education, morality,
spirituality . . . if I could wash away the sins, everything that has ever
gotten in the way of my essential *being* swimming toward my essential
beauty . . . the light that is mine . . .

But my story is like those little alligators hatching from their
shells with nothing but an instinct to make it to the water, unaware
of the dangers that will most probably prevent them from getting to
it. I made it to the water without getting eaten, which is something
to be grateful for, and I have definitely gotten to do, much of the
time, at least since the age of thirty-three, what I love, or at least
what most interests me, what I most want to be good at. But what
threatens all of it—and I mention it only in case you feel the same
way, if it helps you to know—is self-doubt. I'm not sure I'm any good,
and I could name scads of others who are better, but I won't, because
that would be *too* self-destructive (do I really need to give you the
opportunity to decide I am right?) . . . and I haven't been entirely dis-
honest about my *envy* in this book . . . but at my best moments, when

the clouds part temporarily, when the meds are working . . . when I have just meditated and for a moment there is nothing in me but silence, wind, and maybe even God's love, I can tell you this: I see genuine beauty in what I have made, genuine beauty out of the shards of glass that are my life.

PART IV

SECRETS

My Body, or Shit

When I first met Swami Muktananda in 1980, he made us all promise we would never believe the lie that we are our bodies.

The last things anyone likes to talk about in therapy are money and feces. I think this may come from Freud.

It feels as if all of my life, anything of value, what I have written, whom I have befriended, what I have read, what I have seen, whom I have loved, have all happened in the interstices between when I am not engaged in some sort of secret activity that has to do with either my obsession with sex, my obsession with someone inappropriate, my obsession with my body, or pornography.

I was in second grade. Peter was a grade ahead of me. He brought over *Flossie in Bondage*, a 1935 hard-core novel published in Paris describing sex between a man and a woman with photos that made me feel like a ravenous tiger at the zoo, just before raw red meat is thrown into the cage. The man in the picture had black socks on and reminded me of my father, and the photos were sepia tinted, so they looked like his photographs from the war. This was the first time I read about a woman swallowing semen, or anything pertaining to what men and women did in bed, and in highly descriptive, florid language, unlike anything I had ever read.

Whatever I felt, seeing fantasies that had been rolling around in my head depicted in images, and words, became my first drug. I was so aroused I was sweating. *Flossie in Bondage* conjured the atmosphere engendered in my house growing up—the unintentional and loaded atmosphere of incest.

The first time Peter and I were allowed to go to the city by ourselves, I was eleven, and he was twelve. We were beside ourselves, jubilant to finally see the great houses of the culture we so worshipped: the Metropolitan Opera, which was brand-new, having just opened in 1966 with Samuel Barber's *Antony and Cleopatra*; the New York City Opera, also new, having moved from City Center to Lincoln Center; and Broadway! Peter's father hadn't been to the city in so long he thought Broadway was still Forty-Second Street. When our train pulled into Penn Station, we made our way to the IRT as his father told us to do, took the express train to Forty-Second Street, and ascended from the subway like the three sailors in *On the Town*. Immediately, we found ourselves right smack in the middle of countless porno shops and XXX movie theaters. This was 1967, and Forty-Second Street was a pretty raunchy mélange of call girls, hustlers, and pimps.

We walked by window after window of hard-core magazine covers with photos of naked women on one side, men on the other, and all with black tape covering their genitals. Suddenly I didn't have to be a spy drilling holes in the walls; it was all here. I was trembling as if I had been plugged into a socket. Every store had signs that said BE TWENTY-ONE OR BE GONE. All day, we scurried in and out of one shop after another like rats trying to dodge the sentries, getting thrown out and doing it again, until it began to get dark and we had to go home.

We were silent on the hour-long train ride back to Island Park, staring out the windows, imagining our uncertain futures with whatever comprehension our little brains could muster. The fact we were both *only* interested in one side of the windows hung in the air like soot. Something had irrevocably changed.

That day, we didn't see any Broadway theaters or Lincoln Center or anywhere operas were performed or music was sold, just the dimly lit corridors of our troubled souls and an odd assemblage of genitalia. From then on, every time I went into the city, *a* city, I would try to get into every adult bookstore I passed. Just the words "Adult Bookstore"

promised more to me than if it were called "The Actual Secrets of
the Universe Including an Actual No Kidding Appearance by God
Shop."

I could always find at least one kiosk where I could buy *Screw* magazine, which was always reliable for a penis or two in its pages. Inevitably, my mom would find it, no matter where I hid it, and get rid of
it, but she would never mention it, a mercy on her part.

I have always been afraid of my body, its desires and its functions.
When I was a little boy, I was dressed, undressed, my hair was combed
and cut, I was put to bed, and I was bathed by my mother and my three
sisters. Basically, being the only boy and having been born much later
than my sisters, I was their baby doll. Their hands would brush by
my penis and my testicles with a casualness, as if they were a hand
or a leg, as if they had no significance at all, or as if I were flat there,
like Barbie's boyfriend, Ken. Consequently, my genitals didn't have
any significance in my mind. I had no sense for a long time that they
were for anything of real importance other than pee pee or poo poo.
They even had a little word for my penis. It was called "pootsie." They
would touch it and flick it and laugh and say, "Pootsie, pootsie," as if
it were a kitten or a bunny rabbit, and the notion that it defined me
as different from them or the same as my father, who did not have
anything anyone called a "pootsie," was imperceptible to me. As soon
as I was aware of even having a body, I wanted to cover it up. When
we would go to the beach, I would wear a T-shirt and I wouldn't take
it off, not even to swim. When it was wet, it would hug my little body
in all the wrong places, quite unattractively, and become transparent,
which looked worse than not wearing it at all. My mother would say,
"You look like a bag of groceries! Why don't you take that shirt off? It
looks terrible!" but I wouldn't and that was that. I didn't have a body
like my sisters or my mother, but I didn't have a body like my father
either. I was chubby, so sort of had boy boobs, and very late to the
game hair-wise, so without knowing what to call it, I sort of felt like

a pseudo-hermaphrodite, a term I only learned when *Fellini Satyricon* came out in 1969, the year of my Bar Mitzvah.

What did a role model look like to me? We did not have *Will & Grace* on TV when I was growing up. There was no discussion of sex change. No one was identifying as anything other than what they were, male or female, and if you felt outside the parameters of what those identifications meant, you were in trouble, and you hid it. If you were male and you did things like look at your nails with your fingers outstretched rather than in a fist, or you crossed your legs all the way like a girl rather than one leg halfway crossed masculinely, or you weren't an athlete, or you liked theater and classical music, especially opera, if you spoke with even the slightest sibilance, mentioned fashion, or played with dolls, there was a plethora of names you could be called: sissy, fag, faggot, fem, queer, fairy being the most common, at least in my case, with an occasional pansy. Girls usually had fewer choices: tomboy, dyke, and sometimes with the added qualifier, like fortissimo rather than forte, bull, bull dyke. No one talked about pronouns.

I would watch my sister Sheila get dressed every morning. Since Susan, my oldest sister, and then Lorraine, the second oldest, had left home, it was Sheila's bed I would crawl into every morning at around 3:00. Sheila, I'm pretty sure, from birth, wore makeup every day. She knew the ins and outs of it, the subtleties of the ritual, its gravity, its seriousness, as if it were in her DNA. Even now, she says with great conviction, as if she were reciting seminal parts of the Constitution, "I'm sorry, but women of a certain age [I'm not sure what age that is] *have* to wear makeup." After she got her hair out of curlers, she would bend over and brush it forward and back vigorously until she got the perfect Patty Duke flip. I stole Sheila's copy of Truman Capote's *In Cold Blood* and read it way too early, and all I could think of was poor Nancy Clutter, brushing her hair a hundred times a day, only to end up murdered by Dick Hickock and Perry Smith.

I have no memory of any of my sisters ever being in the bathroom to poop, only to beautify. They never talked about what their bodies did, nor did my mother, and I never remember them farting. They seemed to live above the clouds in Olympus, and whatever happened when the bathroom door was closed was a mystery to me. They all got something called a period, which I thought was a stomachache because they talked about cramps. One day, after walking halfway to elementary school, I decided I couldn't bear to face the combination of schoolyard taunts, violence, and humiliation. Also, being the only one who never had my homework ready and couldn't sit still or shut up made school unbearable. Holding my stomach with a manufactured grimace of extreme pain on my face, I turned around and ran the mile home. Throwing open the front door, I found Sheila and my mother sitting at the breakfast table sipping coffee. I screamed, as if in agony, "I am getting my period!" which I thought would immediately exempt me from a day of school the way it always did my sisters. "What?! You're a boy, idiot! Only girls get their periods!" my mother screamed.

As for my body's functions, they confused me as well. My mother would always stand outside the door and say "make for me" when I went to the bathroom, so I always felt I was giving her a gift when I made a "doody," as she liked to call it. They all liked to call it that; even Daddy, without anything they called a "pootsie," called a bowel movement a "doody," turning him from a dangerous, unpredictable, rage-filled homicidal maniac into a silly little boy for a fleeting moment. Consequently, I couldn't shit anywhere but in my own home, where my mother awaited her gift. If I had to go at school, or I was on the way home, I would just go in my pants. The feeling of something warm and lumpy spreading around inside my pants was physically a relief but mentally exhausting. I spent a lot of time trying to hide the evidence. I would avoid and dodge everyone, skulking in corners like a fugitive, lest someone smell and suspect me. Public bathrooms were simply out of the question.

When I was eight, my parents sent me to Camp Lenape, in the Pocono Mountains, because I was getting beaten up all the time. Camp Lenape was supposed to be my respite, or rescue for the summer. Most of the boys and the counselors had been there before and knew each other, so they were excited to be back. I was lonely, homesick, and terrified of bats, which were plentiful, and our cabins had no windows, so I could only sleep under the covers because I imagined them giving me rabies at night, so it was a critically unhappy juncture for me, not filled with relief, just a new kind of torture. One day, we were by the lake for swimming and rowing activities. All the boys and counselors were running back and forth with oars, canoes, and little Sunfish sailboats. In the great hubbub of activity, all I could think about was the disaster, which was about to befall me, which could only be exacerbated by being submerged into water surrounded by a hundred boys. I had to make a "doody." I ran into the woods far away from everyone and dug a hole so deep you could bury a small body in it. When I got back, all the activities had begun, and I had to sneak into the water and somehow fit myself in unobtrusively. That was probably the first time I shit at Camp Lenape, and I had been there at least three weeks, so needless to say, shitting, where it happens, when it happens, how it happens, and everything else related to it, has always been fraught for me.

There was a boy named Neal G. in Island Park. He, along with another boy, Jay B., was pigeon-toed. Considering how insecure I already felt about myself, being a prominent target for violence and jeers on the playground, boys like Jay and Neal, with actual, visible physical deformities comforted me, because at least I wasn't them. One day, I walked into the boys' room, a terrifying place of torment for me anyway, and some boys were standing on two sides of one of the booths staring over the divider into the booth in the middle. I joined them because joining them was the safest thing I could do. I certainly couldn't go to the bathroom; I couldn't do that with *anyone* in the bathroom! Or, given a choice, the building! So, I looked down into what they were looking at: poor Neal G., already, in my mind, vulnerable because he walked funny, and there he is with his pants down trying to poop with at least six boys staring down at him. He looked so pale, helpless, and embarrassed, the smell of shit wafting up from the toilet, the whiteness of his naked buttocks was burned into my mind.

Something happened when I was twenty-four. I saw the movie *Ordinary People* and was overwhelmed by it in every way. I wanted to be Timothy Hutton's Connie, the boy who couldn't save Buck, his brother, from drowning in a roiling sea after a boating accident in a sudden squall left them tethered to a small piece of wood. I lived in a constant state of pain and anxiety, and I wanted to suffer legitimately and handsomely like him. He had a huge reason for suffering and was back from the hospital after a suicide attempt. I wanted to kill myself, but be discovered and live, so then everybody would know how much pain I was in and treat me with deference, like him. I bought the same exact winter coat he wore in the movie, cheap buckskin with a fake-fur lining. I wanted to stare across a table at Elizabeth McGovern. I didn't want a mother like Beth, played by Mary Tyler Moore, chilly and judgmental, but I would have taken being her, because she *also* suffered legitimately, thin and impeccably dressed, losing a son, Buck, the one she liked, and being left with the suicidal one, Connie, whom she didn't like. "We just want you to be happy!" her friend Ward says one day at the golf course.

"Happy! . . . Ward, you tell me the definition of happy, huh? But first you better make sure that your kids are good and safe, that no one's fallen off a horse, or been hit by a car, or drowned in that swimming pool you're so proud of! And then you come to me and tell me how to be happy!" I took my mother to see it. She would take the train in from Island Park, and I'd meet her at Penn Station. We'd go to a nearby coffeeshop for breakfast and then either shopping at Macy's or to a museum, a Broadway show, or a movie. I decided she needed to see *Ordinary People*. After the movie, she told me, "Your father finally admitted he understands why you would need therapy." Something about my father's acknowledgment of my confusion or suffering made me burst into tears, which scared her. "Maybe we shouldn't have seen that movie." I didn't try to reassure her, because I knew she wouldn't understand.

I knew I needed a Judd Hirsch, who plays Connie's loving therapist, in my life as well, the warm Jewish father I never had. The father who cared about me, read my report cards, knew my birthday, and even, later, my phone number. My father was unaware of anything about me. I could have turned Judd into a surrogate father and then fantasized about having sex with him, or maybe even seducing him, which would have checked a lot of boxes. I knew I needed help; that was 100 percent clear to me.

I was cleaning houses for a living and paid for therapy with that money. Okay, let's be real: I was a burgeoning drug addict and alcoholic, so I both earned the money and stole the money. Let's say you were my client. I was cleaning your apartment, hanging your clothes, and I found money in your pocket, say a twenty-dollar bill. I would give you two weeks to realize this, but if after two weeks, which seemed like a proper grace period in my addled mind, the money was still there, the money was mine. Sometimes, I found things, like a rack of gold fillings in a box of assorted objects I had decided were meant for the trash, so I took them and sold them. In this way, I paid for my first trip to Europe and my first shrink, Richard T. Instinctively, I knew it wouldn't be right to ask my parents for help paying for therapy, because how can you be honest about the people who fucked you up when they are paying the tab? I had to be completely honest for the first time in my life. I knew that was the only way I would get better, and believe me, by then shitting in public bathrooms was not my only problem.

Dr. T.'s office was in a building on the corner of Barrow and Hudson in the West Village. I saw, at my very first appointment, that Robert De Niro lived in the building, which added a spark of excitement.

I knew that if I were going to get better through therapy, which I had to clean houses (and steal) to pay for, I had to tell the truth, and I really wanted to get better.

Two hard truths were these:

It was impossible for me to be honest about my feelings if I thought they might hurt or affect someone. If someone was attracted to me, I felt as if I had to give them what they wanted. Consequently, being liked was a spotlight that trapped me in its glare. I slept with people who repelled me and never had the courage to say, "I don't like you back," or "I don't feel the same way you do."

I was not attracted to Dr. T. My fantasy of falling in love with my dynamic Judd Hirsch therapist was not to be. I knew I had to tell him, to say something *not nice*, see what it felt like. One day, I blurted out, "Richard, I have to tell you something." "What?" he said, gently smiling at me. It stuck in my throat. "I am not attracted to you. I think you are ugly!" I felt as if I had just stabbed him in the stomach, as if the only thing anyone can wholly take pride in is their physical allure. Take that from them and they are nothing. He didn't look in the least bit hurt. There was even a hint of a smile on his bearded, Freudian, inscrutable face.

Then, and this is infinitely more cataclysmic. There was a small bathroom in the waiting room of Richard's office. Before every session, I would pee. One day I walked into the bathroom. I almost collapsed. There was a shit in the toilet. A huge turd was floating around in there like a proud, happy sailboat. This was perhaps my biggest nightmare! Was it his? Was I looking at my therapist's shit? I mean, it was enough to find him physically repellent, but was I now staring straight at his shit? Now what was I going to do? Of course, I had to tell him. How could I possibly *not* tell him? How on earth could he forget to flush? If it were me, I could never look at him again. I'd probably have to avoid the whole West Village. And here he was, *blithely* leaving his shit in the bowl like an artifact! I never even imagined it was anyone else's, another patient's, for instance. I walked into his office completely traumatized. I could barely see. He asked how I was. "Not good," I said. "Not good at all." "What's going on?" he asked. I took a deep breath and asked, "Is that your shit in the toilet?" "What?" he asked, with a furrowed brow, as if he might have to call the medics to bring the straitjacket. "There is a huge turd floating around in the toilet! Is it yours? Did you forget to flush?!" I asked accusingly. He was completely unmoved, never even admitted it was his shit. Clearly, as far as he was concerned, we were standing straight in the eye of the hurricane of my problems. Shit! "What is your fantasy about it being my shit in the toilet?" "My fantasy? My fantasy," I replied. "My fantasy is, I'd probably have to leave the country if it was mine, or at the very least, kill myself!"

There is a moment in *Sex and the City* when Carrie has finally gotten Mr. Big, the amazingly handsome, ripe-red-lipped sex god Chris

Noth, into bed. They are now officially dating. At the start of the episode, the camera closes in on their bed in the morning, a beatific view of rumpled white sheets, sunlight pouring in, and entwined bodies sleeping, two exceptionally beautiful people in their lucky life. Suddenly we hear a fart. It is Carrie's! She literally wakes herself and Mr. Big up with the sound and vibration of her own fart. Abruptly, she jumps out of bed and runs into the bathroom to dress and leave. She doesn't look Mr. Big in the eyes or mention what has just happened. She is faced with a catastrophe, and this is most likely the end of the relationship and possibly her life. He thinks it's funny, but for her it is a humiliation on the level of Greek tragedy. I could feel her burning shame. I spent my whole life not wanting anyone to know I farted or did anything that smelled. If I felt I had bad breath, I would quarantine myself until it was over. I would certainly not talk. I'm surprised I even have any gums left with the way I floss and brush my teeth as if my task were to get the sin out: Lady Macbeth with the blood on her hands. After days of her not returning his calls, Mr. Big asks Carrie over to dinner. There is an elephant in the room. She skulks the corners like a fugitive, traipsing around in her Manolo Blahniks, to feign the appearance of one who doesn't fart, trying to put the awful and terrible past behind her. Big is gentle and deferential, avoiding uncomfortable topics. He has made a romantic Italian dinner with candles and red wine. He speaks sotto voce, as if he were Romeo, and she, his Juliet. Carrie acts super soft and feminine. Surely, she has spritzed herself with several sprays of Lovely, Sarah Jessica Parker's fetching signature perfume, a floral, woody musk fragrance, to distract Mr. Big from what he surely smelled the last time he saw her. When they sit down to dinner, there is the sound of what seems like a nuclear explosion. Mr. Big has put a *whoopee* cushion on her chair! It is hysterical. We laugh, blessedly relieved of the tension in the air.

My mother always sprayed so much Lysol after she was done in the bathroom I thought maybe she shit Lysol! I never once heard her fart, though I always heard my father fart. Lillian Hellman wrote, in *The Little Foxes*, "There are people who eat the earth . . . Then, there are people who stand around and watch them eat it." That was my father, eating the earth and then shitting, burping, and farting it out unabashedly. If he ate an apple, he ate the whole thing and at the end spit a clump of seeds, core, and stem into his hand, putting it on the napkin where you could see it, like someone vomiting proudly on the table. He talked with a full mouth, and when he ate walnuts, the cracking of them, the picking the pieces out of the shell, the getting of the walnut fragments embedded into his nails and all through his teeth as he chewed them, and the general mess he left behind for someone else to clean up spoke volumes of his sense of entitlement.

No, I was not going to be like him. I was going to be like my mother and my sisters, thoughtful, reflective, cultured, non-farting. How often in my life have I felt as if I were going to explode but wouldn't even dream of farting or shitting in anyone's bathroom but my own? Or been in a house and looked for the bathroom that was as far away from people as possible, defying the boundaries they had clearly set for where guests were welcome. Or run the water loudly so no one would hear me doing anything that might be you know what. Or lit matches and then sprayed something to eliminate the smell of the matches so no one would even think I had lit matches or shit or farted! Or been in bed with someone I just had sex with or wanted to have sex with and forcing myself to stay awake all night so I wouldn't inadvertently fart, whether I was attracted to them or not! Or always saying I have to go pee no matter what I have to do so no one will ever know I actually defecate like the others.

We must have discussed it for at least a year, but honestly I don't think I ever got over it. I *still* have PTSD about that lumbering turd in Richard T.'s toilet. Recently, Kevin bought me an eight-hundred-dollar toilet seat. It comes with a remote control. It heats when you sit down. After you have done your business, it shoots water up your butt at various speeds and temperatures, so you can have an anus as clean as the one you were born with. It has a function that dries your ass and then one that deodorizes the bathroom after the whole affair is over. No evidence whatsoever. Now I ask you, could there be a better present?

My whole life seemed to be dedicated to hiding anything about myself that set me apart or that I might be embarrassed about, bad breath, smelly farts, dirty hair, smelly armpits, acne, or any conceivable human imperfection or sign of aliveness.

At the time I started losing my hair, which was pretty young, my midtwenties, my friend Gary, a Jesuit priest and a theater director whom I befriended at Carnegie Mellon University, was the head of the theater department at Regis College in Denver. He brought me out there as an artist in residence. We were going to turn Bertolt Brecht's brilliant antiwar play *A Man's a Man* into a musical. I was living with the then state senator Dennis Gallagher, his wife, JoAnne, and Dennis's incredible mother, who would knit me bootees because it was the middle of a particularly snowy winter and freezing. It was a big, beautiful, drafty Victorian house with all kinds of secret stairways. I wonder what they were thinking when I was spending hours in the bathroom every day, filling entire hot water bottles and shooting them up into my body over and over again, until I felt there was literally nothing left in my body but clean water. I was taking speed to starve myself. And here, this thing started to happen to me I couldn't control. My hair was falling out! My whole life was about being cute, alluring, and now the worst of all things was happening. I was going to look older and, even worse, like a man, not a boy. I had never figured myself a man like my father. I was stuck in being a boy, the precocious boy who lured straight men into his bed. I had magic powers, and this was about to fuck everything up. I was going to be gay and bald! It started a long period of despair and helplessness, like thirty years. I felt if I was going to lose my hair, everything else had to be perfect, and I worked relentlessly at this impossible task. I heard Albert Einstein would have given back all his knowledge including the theory of relativity to get his hair back. I totally identify.

One day, God spoke directly to me in my state of despair, laying out an obvious and devastating parable right before my eyes. I had just played an audition for a sexy young baritone with dark, brooding looks and a cleft chin. I was attracted to him, which exacerbated my insecurity about my looks that day. Afterward, I was walking down Central Park West. It was a bright, sunny day in summer, so the light was shrill and piercing. You had to squint to see. I had forgotten my self-hatred for a moment, and there was a jocularity in my step, something you might construe, erroneously, as self-esteem, when suddenly I looked at my reflection in a window and the bright, stinging light went straight through whatever hair I still had left on my head, making me look as bald as a pool cue. I wanted to fall through the sidewalk into a sinkhole, wipe myself out, erase myself. Out of the corner of my eye, a scene came into view, catching my attention. An older man was getting out of a black car and stepping onto the curb. He looked up, breathing in the dazzling beauty of the day, the warm and fragrant summer air. Then he looked down to see what stood before him. There was a little girl on the sidewalk, greeting him. It was clear from her body language she was ecstatic to see him. He looked at her with such burning love, as if the kind and blinding light of Jesus were emanating from his eyes. I saw the girl only from behind. She was wearing a beautiful robin's-egg-blue silk dress with crinolines that made the skirt fan out like a parasol. On her little feet were black patent leather Mary Janes and white anklet socks, and her blond hair, with angelic curlicues and ringlets as if it had been set the night before, danced in the breeze with a big blue bow in it. I imagined her mother dressing and primping her for the treasured arrival of her beloved grandfather. There was so much love emanating from this beatific scene it seemed like an apparition. As I was walking past, I looked back. I couldn't wait to see the little girl's undoubtedly adorable face. I had an idea her joy might invade me, imbue me with what I was lacking in that moment in my homely gay bald state, gratitude and love. I was so shocked at what I saw I almost fell down, as if a car had just slammed into me. She was the most deformed human being I have ever seen. She must have had what the Elephant Man had because her face was so badly misshapen you could barely tell where her features were. Her face was a lumpen, frightening disfigurement. If she were smiling, you wouldn't be able to discern it, but her body was smiling. This made the love passing between her and her grandfather, the way he looked at her as if she were the most beautiful little girl in the world, almost unbearable, as if I were no longer walking in the sun; I had entered it and I was burning alive. Dumbfounded, I stared at the grandfather's face, searching for some sign of pity, but there was none. To him, she really *was* the most beautiful and perfect little princess in the world, nothing less than an angel. I walked briskly, trying to hold back a torrent of tears, but I couldn't. I sobbed all the way down Central Park West.

If only the lesson of that moment lasted forever. At sixty-seven, I am still trying to hide my head. I had to stop wearing hats all the time because it feels worse to think that people think I wear hats out of shame for my baldness rather than because I think they are cool. It is okay with me to have an affectation, an eccentricity, and I like the way I look and feel in hats, but I don't want to be seen as ashamed of myself.

Yesterday, I called the psychopharmacologist. I want to wean myself off the antidepressants. I want to see who I am without them. Do I still need them? It is directly related to "Hello, world, I fart, I shit, I am bald, and I am depressed." It is a week later, the "getting off the antidepressants" experiment was a disaster. I am back on them and good riddance!

Money and feces. Shitting and farting. What is it I hope to rid myself of, so to speak? Or hold on to? Well into my teens, wherever I went, I would spend everything, including my money to get home. Once, I thought I could outwit some guy playing the game where they hide a quarter under one of three cups, and you have to guess which one it's under. When I lost, I chased him all over the city pleading for at least enough money for train fare. I was always begging for spare change to get onto the Long Island Rail Road at Penn Station or hiding from the conductor in the stinking train bathroom until we got to my stop or giving him a sob story until he agreed to take my address and write my mother for the money.

All of my life I have been in love with beauty: the beauty of music, of art, of poetry, of foreign films, of moonlight on the snow, or of the romantic sadness in the face of an unrequited love. I thought I needed to mirror such beauty. Bad smells and fat had no place in my exacting aesthetic. This is why I had to make an opera out of Frank Bidart's "Ellen West." I identified with this woman whose ideal is crippling her, who feels degraded by her body, who only in death feels grace. She says, *"The only way / to escape / the History of Styles / is not to have a body."* Where did I get the notion that I had to reflect outwardly what I was trying to achieve inwardly? Beethoven certainly wasn't hampered by this idea with his always full and stinking chamber pot and his abysmal digestion. No wonder Rossini sobbed after visiting him, lumbering down the steps in the pouring rain. Those Dutch painters knew to put insects in their still lifes, or rot on the leaves, to remind the viewer of what lurks beneath the surface in the dirt, beyond or behind the beauty. Perhaps by writing about shitting, farting, bad breath, body odor, and baldness, I can get to a deeper place in myself, a place less inhibited by what it may reveal about me or my body. Though probably not.

PART V

AIDS/JEFFREY

AIDS |

I wish I could say I understood my homosexuality. I have never known where I fit in. When I started losing my hair, which, to me, meant losing my looks, I became even more confused. It seemed like a culture based solely on appearances. I once said at my gay AA meeting, "Gay people used to want to be Michelangelo. Now they just want to be David."

I seldom went into the world as a gay man feeling it was other gay men I wanted to have sex with. I was often repelled by what I construed as femininity, which I associated with my mother and sisters, who loved me too *much*, needing me to be their *good* husbands, boyfriends, and confidants, roles that sometimes made me feel more eunuch than man, so I looked for nourishment from the *other*, trying to fill the fatherless, brotherless, male-less space, which got all mixed up with sex and sexuality, so the whole topic has often been one big cauldron of confusion, subterfuge, and pain.

And I have never been comfortable identifying myself as a top or a bottom. I didn't always know what I wanted. In the movie *Brokeback Mountain*, when something sexual finally happens between Ennis and Jack, Ennis, furiously, thrusts himself into Jack, quickly lubricating his dick with spit as if he has been doing this forever. There is no tenderness. Even in the countless movies where drunk couples ravish each other on elevators standing up, or on kitchen counters the moment they enter the apartment like rapacious animals devouring each other. I've never looked at another man and thought, "I want to fuck him." I have little experience with the motion men make, thrusting or shoving themselves into someone with the urge to penetrate.

Some of this confusion may be why I am still alive. A lot of my friends in the 1970s frequented bathhouses and back rooms in bars where men were just randomly having sex in the dark. I was too scared.

SNAPSHOT NO. 1, 1981

Daniel Katz moved to New York City from San Francisco to work for Perry Ellis, the clothing designer, in the early 1980s. There was no one else like Perry Ellis in the fashion industry. His line was small and exquisitely crafted, classic yet elegant with a new spin. It wasn't about the clothes; you were investing in your charisma when you bought his clothes. His shirts were expensive with their pleated shoulders and French cuffs but so beautiful and well made they were easy to justify buying. They made your shoulders look broader, and the cotton they were made from was so soft they made you want to caress yourself or whoever was wearing them. He lived down the block from me in a gorgeous town house on Seventieth Street.

I met Perry when Christine Barker had a huge Christmas party in her loft in Chelsea and Perry was there with his lover, Laughlin, Christine's brother. They met when he became Perry's lawyer. Christine had been in *A Chorus Line* on Broadway for years playing Kristine, the one who couldn't sing. I was her vocal coach and accompanist, as well as friend. She was not a great singer, but adorable and a great dancer and character in the tradition of Gwen Verdon. She could put over a song because she had so much moxie. Christine would take a helicopter every Saturday night after her last show of the week to Perry and Laughlin's house on Shelter Island. I was jealous. It all seemed so Waspy perfect and glamorous, and I felt like a bursting-at-the-seams Jew.

Daniel Katz grew up in Kansas, which seems strange. Jews in Kansas? But they were not religious. Coincidentally, I knew his sister, Susan. She was friends with *my* sister Susan in the Arica School. She was beautiful and chic with her black wavy hair cut in a bob, piercing dark eyes, and delicate hands she waved around like sparrows. She was a singer, a chanteuse with a moody voice and jazzy delivery in the Piaf vein, and I used to coach her on Thelonious Monk's "'Round Midnight." Daniel was exceedingly handsome, another one of the rare

Jews with blond hair and blue eyes and a little nose. He had a wide-open midwestern face like a cornfield and a very attractive serenity and dignity about him that made him immensely appealing. I'm sure Perry Ellis hired him the moment he laid eyes on him.

I met him because he became friends with my roommate Daniel Glynn, who was also in the fashion industry. Glynn (I will call him Glynn to avoid confusion), of Davenport, Iowa, had been a male model. He was a tall Irish Catholic who laughed quietly with his mouth closed and was just the slightest bit standoffish and snobby. I came home one night from doing a concert, and my roommates Tom and Brian had an exceedingly handsome man visitor. Glynn, Tom, Brian, and I went out for drinks on Columbus Avenue. He played footsie with me the whole time under the table. We slept together that night and for a week, but we had no chemistry and were clearly just meant to be friends. When Tom and Brian moved out, or when I kicked them out because I was afraid I'd never get any work done with them around, because all we did was party, Glynn moved in.

Glynn's parents would come to visit, his father, out of place and agitated as if there were nothing but danger and decadence outside Iowa and he might turn gay or worse, Jewish, if he left the apartment, and Glynn's perfectly coiffed, very thin, tanned, and bangle-braceleted mother, who was fine as long as she had a Bourbon Press in her hand. Her vowels were so wide it was hard to tell where the consonants were hiding. Glynn had a streak of darkness in him and had attempted suicide at one point. He had the scars of uneven and clearly hysterically placed slashes across both wrists. He worked for all the top Italian designers, so when he lived with me, it was great fun to have a million-dollar wardrobe for nothing. My favorite things were two Valentino suits. They were cotton and striped; one was blue with black stripes, the other, red and black. They fit me like a glove and made me look somewhere between an Italian gangster and a gondolier.

I loved drinking and snorting cocaine with Glynn. We would go downtown to cop from a dealer named Fay in her apartment. There was so much cocaine in the air of her dark-wood, closed-shades lair, as well as all of the paraphernalia for weighing it, packaging it, and selling it, you got high just by stepping over the threshold. Fay, who was about six feet four with bright red hair, had snorted so much cocaine that her hairline was receding. She looked Elizabethan. She also looked as if she hadn't seen daylight or breathed fresh air since the 1960s and was two or three weeks away from a serious coronary event. She always allowed you to sample the merchandise, so I lived for these excursions.

Glynn and I would often dine at Cafe Luxembourg, down the block from us, on Seventieth just off Amsterdam. The restaurant was owned by Keith McNally, the famous restaurateur who started One Fifth and Balthazar. Our friend Don Palladino, another exceedingly handsome man, was the manager, and I loved his stories of shopping in Paris for all the appointments. Cafe Luxembourg looked like one of those great Parisian bistros on the left bank, La Coupole or Les Deux Magots, and was *the* restaurant, the moment it opened, filled with movie stars, publishers, and cognoscenti of every stripe. It was hard to *ever* get in, and we *always* did.

Daniel (Katz) was one of the many incredibly handsome men in the fashion industry Glynn brought into our lives. One Sunday, a few weeks after Easter, it was crisp and sunny, and Daniel and I had plans to go to the flea market on Columbus Avenue at Seventy-Fifth Street. I was hoping we might kiss and took hours getting dressed after doing three hundred push-ups, chin-ups, and sit-ups. About two weeks before, I had performed in a cabaret of my music produced by Ira Weitzman, who had put together a series at West Bank Cafe under the auspices of Playwrights Horizons. It was me, playing and singing, along with Jack Eric Williams, the original Beadle Bamford in Sondheim's *Sweeney Todd*, and Diane Sutherland, née Fratantoni, who was in *A Chorus Line* at the time. She was accepted into the national tour as Morales, who sings "What I Did for Love," while still at CMU. We were all insanely jealous and in awe that Diane was in the hottest show in the world and getting credit for it. Daniel Katz had attended the cabaret, and as we were about to cross Columbus Avenue on Seventieth Street, he said, "You are so lucky that you get to do what you love for a living." I said, "What do you mean, Daniel? Don't you love what you do?" He said, "No, I mean, it's all right, but it's just . . . fashion." It was my second sign that something was wrong, though I thought he was the luckiest guy in the world and totally happy.

The first sign anything was wrong with Daniel, though I didn't register it as such, because I wasn't looking, no one was, it hadn't even been named yet, Daniel took me to a somewhat intimidating Easter brunch at an icily elegant interior-designed-within-an-inch-of-its-life airless apartment, forbiddingly decorated in blacks, grays, and whites, as if color were outlawed. All the guests seemed to be immaculately dressed *in modo* like mannequins to match the decor: meticulous hair, bulging muscles, and so on. Even the food was impeccable. Even the place setting! I had an attitude the whole time we were there, fidgeting while overindulging in the champagne. I couldn't tell Daniel I wasn't having fun, because I was his guest, and I was firm in the mission of making him like me. I felt like Woody Allen as Alvy Singer in *Annie Hall*, envisioning himself a disheveled Hasidic Jew in the company of Annie's perfectly contained WASP family. Afterward, we stopped at Daniel's apartment on the East Side before heading west to my neck of the woods. He needed to use the bathroom. When he came out, he looked pale, almost green, and an odor filled the apartment that was beyond the usual smell of a just-used toilet; something was wrong, it smelled like sickness, like a miscarriage, even death, but I had nowhere to catalog it yet. I just knew, it was the first dissonance in what I perceived to be a beautifully constructed chord.

So, this Sunday, we are crossing Columbus and I am still marveling at the fact that ravishing Daniel thinks I have a better life than him, when he complains that his back is hurting and asks if we might just go back to my apartment instead of going to the flea market so he can lie down for a little while. "Of course," I said, and we did. He went to sleep in my bed for several hours, noticeably longer than a little while.

A couple of days later, he was in the hospital with pneumonia. I was taken aback, but I understood how pneumonia can cause back pain because of the lower lungs filling with liquid, so I was glad he was properly diagnosed and could get treatment. I knew he'd be his old self again, and I could try once again to kiss him.

Then he called to say the doctors had recommended he get a therapist. "A therapist?" I said. "Why would you need a *therapist* for pneumonia?"

He was discouraged after his first session. I tried to explain, old pro that I was, "You need to give it time, honey. The beginning is just the honeymoon period. Once you get *past* your 'story,' the relationship with the therapist forms, and that's where the *real* healing takes place." I was assuming he had all the time in the world. "No," he said. "I can already tell. I think she'll have real trouble understanding that I'm going to die." "What?!" I balked. "Die?! Are you kidding, Daniel? Don't be so dramatic! You just have pneumonia! What you need is antibiotics!" But he seemed to know something I didn't, and robotically, without a shred of emotion, said, "No. I'm going to die."

When I visited him in the hospital a week later, it was shocking how quickly he had deteriorated. He was losing his beautiful blond hair, his cheeks were sunken in, and his bright blue eyes had dulled to a pale gray. They were calling it either gay cancer or GRID, which stood for "gay related immune deficiency." We had not arrived at AIDS yet.

I never saw him again.

SNAPSHOT NO. 2, 1985

I was volunteering at the Gay Men's Health Crisis. By now it was impossible not to know someone who wasn't sick and dying. The most important things I did there were intake for new clients with AIDS or working for the 500 Men Initiative. At one point, there were plans afoot to make a film, so I even got to be a film composer for a little while.

Chance of a Lifetime, from 1985, was the first instructional safe sex porno film, and I wrote a charming (I thought) chamber music score for various reeds and piano to accompany the numerous sex scenes. At one point, the director, John Lewis, and I had to interview some porn stars to be in the movie. We went to the apartment of one of them,

in Chelsea, whose nickname was Stan Eleven, which tells you everything you need to know.

His idea of an interview with John and me was he wanted to have
sex with both of us. He took off his shirt, and his nipples had been so
overly manipulated they were about an inch long and I was repelled. I
was curious to see what the eleven represented, but not curious enough
to get past those nipples. I stayed in the living room, perusing his
coffee-table books, which surprisingly, and a pleasant surprise, were
all hard-core pornography, occasionally going out onto his terrace to
overlook smog-filled Chelsea and its denizens, while John encountered
whatever the "eleven" stood for.

SNAPSHOT NO. 3, 1986

A new show is opening on Broadway, *Rags*, with music by Charles
Strouse and lyrics by Stephen Schwartz. I am excited to see it because
the great opera singer Teresa Stratas, a riveting presence on the stage,
is starring in it. My friend Mark Fotopoulos is in it.

After the show, Mark takes me backstage to meet Teresa, but there
is a sign on her door that says, I LOVE YOU ALL. IF YOU LOVE ME, YOU
WILL LEAVE ME ALONE. So we do. When Mark is done getting out of
costume and makeup, we are standing in the lobby.

Mark was a beautiful dancer and singer I'd met when he was in *Sophisticated Ladies* with Terri Klausner on Broadway. She and I started
doing nightclub acts together, and he would often be around. He was
a Greek god, with jet-black hair, chiseled features, the stature that
dancing brings, and a robust and beautiful leading man baritone voice.

The late afternoon sun is pouring in from outside on this autumn
day; crisp fresh air, the smell of moist fallen leaves, the rush of co-
lognes and perfumes, and the fumes of cabs waiting outside for the
elderly matinee crowd leaving the theater invade the senses. Mark
emerges from backstage. I see a small dark spot on the side of his nose
just over the nostril, which he has tried to cover up with makeup,
clearly without much success. I don't say anything, you don't have to.

You know by this point how it will end and you know he does too, so I just feel sick and sad.

Mark fought long and hard, becoming active in Act Up, but he finally had a nervous breakdown because the continued stress of trying to be the poster boy for longevity with AIDS, trying to hold back the catastrophe of losing his looks, his voice, and his body, got to be too much for him, and then he died, looking the way so many beautiful young men ended up looking then—gaunt, hollow-eyed, spotted, with mouths white from thrush, and frightened.

SNAPSHOT NO. 4, 1986

Perry Ellis and Laughlin Barker both died of AIDS. Laughlin went first, so Perry died of a broken heart *and* AIDS.

After they died, whoever took over the Perry Ellis trademark transformed the company from a boutique company, particular and exquisitely selective, the expression of one man's genius, to an entire line of clothing and fragrances that were sold in department stores and would look at home remaindered at Filene's Basement, so it almost felt as if Perry died and then Perry Ellis died.

SNAPSHOT NO. 5, 1986

One of the men I dated was a designer for the ad firm BBDO, right out of *Mad Men*, named Rich Martel. Having grown up in Maine and gone to Bowdoin College, he looked as if he had just stepped out of the L.L.Bean catalog and exuded a sort of lumberjack masculinity that I thought was sexy. He had that kind of really fine thin hair that is fun to run your hand through because it is like new spring grass.

He had a big dog, which was impressive, not only because it took up about a quarter of his tiny apartment, but also because the fact that anyone could live alone, take care of a dog while managing a forty-hour-a-week job, and go to the gym regularly seemed formidable.

He was bigger than me, which seems to be a theme, so it was easy to feel consumed by him. He had noticeably thin lips (my mother

always said, "Never trust a man with thin lips": What did she mean?)
and a protruding lower jaw that made him look slightly Neanderthal
but handsome.

One night, I was finished performing on Seventy-Second Street,
at a club called Steve McGraw's, and I called him to ask if we could get
together. He lived right down the block, so he invited me over. Perhaps I was looking for emotional support when I called, to be taken
care of, to be the son of a father, which was odd and I'm sure con-
fusing. I was still a boy looking to be saved, not a man. When I got
there, we kissed and had sex. Rich was well endowed and beautiful
with his clothes off, and I was turned on but inept mechanically. I let
him fuck me that night, not because that is what I wanted, but because
I didn't *know* what I wanted. Rich let me know it was over soon after it
began, saying he'd rather be friends. I was sad and felt inadequate and
disappointed.

I called and asked if we could have coffee and proceeded to ask
him all kinds of desperate and awkward questions like "Is it because
my dick isn't big enough?" I don't think he even knew because he did
like me. He made me a set of drawings, the most beautiful male nudes,
exquisitely drawn with yellow and blue Magic Markers. What I think
was that we couldn't be equals together. He wasn't looking for a son;
he was looking for another man. It took me a long time to understand
the weight of the needs I brought to potential relationships. Rich
ended up with a handsome blond, blue-eyed man named Chris who
was even taller and bigger than Rich. They looked good together,
right, compatible, and I was jealous of Chris.

Chris died first. The last time I saw Rich, he was living on Seventy-
Ninth Street in a tiny studio. He called to ask me to come over because
he was cold and couldn't get his socks on. He had neuropathy, and
his feet and ankles were horribly swollen. He couldn't sit up. It was
summer but he was wet and shivering as if it were February. I was as
gentle as possible, seeing he was on a precipice. He was grateful and
cried, and the weight of the tragedy, of all of it, including the cruel
and strange reversal of roles, was overwhelming. He died soon after.

I was newly sober and would get crushes on all the men who were nice to me in AA. Alcoholism and drug addiction are isolating, but all of a sudden I was surrounded by all kinds of people, many of them handsome men giving me their numbers and being nice to me. "Are you kidding?" I thought. "What have I wandered into? This is an oasis."

One of these men was a dentist named Russell Arndt. Russell was also very masculine, like Rich, and looked as if he spent a lot of time at the gym. He was kind, shaking your hand, looking you in the eye, and wishing you well, but he was also just recessive enough to be mysterious, so I was smitten. If Dustin Hoffman hadn't been cast in *The Graduate*, he might have been. The day I went to Rich's memorial service at the big church on Seventy-First Street, I saw Russell. It turns out he knew Rich and had dated him as well. I sat with him. Afterward, I walked him to the subway. I was, I'm sure, flirting, when he said, with gravity, turning the car in a whole other direction, "It felt so strange being there." "Why?" I asked, as for me, it could've been the third memorial service that week. "Because I know I'm probably next." "What?!" I said. "You look like a billboard for robust and perfect health!" "I'll be next," he said. "You have AIDS, Russell?" He shook his head yes, and his eyes became glassy. I wanted to look away.

He died within the year. He disappeared himself, so he wasn't one of the ones we watched disintegrate bit by bit, just one day we heard it was over, no visitors, no nothing. As a matter of fact, by then, in the rooms of AA, men were dying left and right. Every five chairs or so was either vacant or occupied by someone whose cheekbones were a little too prominent, on their way to, or already *at*, gaunt-like thinness, sometimes spotted, mouths grotesquely whitened by thrush, wide-eyed, then dead.

You were always visiting them in the hospital, or in the makeshift hospices their homes had been turned into by their lovers, or at their memorial services. I have a whole set of songs that were appropriate and moving to perform at memorial services, suffused with grief, because grief and terror were the only two emotions you felt, the two clouds you walked around in. One time, I went home to the boatyard to visit my parents. Late at night my mother heard me crying in the kitchen.

She walked in and said, "Maybe you need to get outta that GMQ . . . or whatever they call that place! It's tearing you up inside." But she couldn't possibly understand: it wasn't the GMHC, it was everything, everywhere, and it was potentially everyone, including me.

SNAPSHOT NO. 6, 1988

It was December 1988, very close to Christmas. I had a bulimic episode, bingeing and then purging myself, so my system was completely empty. It is hard to define what would bring on these episodes—frustration, feeling ugly, feeling unheard, unexpressed, or suppressed, depressing people, impotence in a situation, which could mean, at that point, death all around me—but it would always end in my trying through any means possible to get rid of everything in my body. I totally understand what I have read about bulimics trying to get rid of feelings. Only then would I feel cleansed, as if I could start over.

I was invited to two Christmas parties. The first was on Fifth Avenue at the home of a beautiful society matron, Kit Gill, whose name made her sound as if she should have been a good friend of Truman Capote's. She had been a big fashion model in 1969 and was still quite striking looking. I have absolutely no recollection of how I met her. That night, I drank a lot and ate some terrible Italian finger food in her fabulous living room. Apropos of nothing, I loved the way Kit smelled and went searching through the town house for her bedroom so I could see what her fragrance was. It was J'ai Osé by Guy Laroche, and it was dusky and beautiful. I bought myself a bottle and wore it for years on special occasions, like when I performed at the Ballroom with my friend Angelina Réaux. I would meditate, do push-ups, and then apply a few drops of J'ai Osé before I went onstage. The second party was a cast party for Charles Busch's *Vampire Lesbians of Sodom*. When I arrived, it appeared to me that everyone *but* me had just come from the gym, so my insecurities about my looks skyrocketed. I was already pretty lit from Kit's party, and a bunch of us were standing around in the kitchen, when a pipe with unknown contents was passed around. I emptied my lungs so I could get as big a hit as possible and inhaled as if my life depended on it. Almost immediately, I had that horrible familiar feeling. "Uh-oh, I have to get out of this room, here we go again." Twenty years later, the trip again. My blood started rushing through my veins, and I could feel and hear it. My limbs started feeling both tense and jellylike, as though they were no longer mine. I knew what was about to happen, and I had to take any measures to reverse it. I careened out into the street and sat on the stoop. It was freezing cold. I was breathing deeply, trying desperately to get myself down from the ledge, but I was already pretty far gone. It was Hell's Kitchen before any kind of cleanup, and I noticed some shady activity on the street and felt unsafe, so I got myself back inside by clawing at the walls. Someone at the party who had decided he needed to sleep with me approached me and was slobbering in my ear. He was groping me in the stairwell hall while I felt death approaching. I jumped up to get away from his smothering me when everything began to swirl, and in what seemed like slow motion, I swiveled, cascading down to the floor. I don't know how long I was out, or how I got onto the couch back in the apartment, but I heard a voice over me asking, "Should we call an ambulance?" and from somewhere inside myself, though I was unable to open my eyes, I shook my head yes because I knew I was in trouble. I was wheeled out on a gurney by two emergency workers, an oxygen mask strapped to my face, wearing my brand-new Andrew Marc leather coat, which cost more than any item of clothing I had ever purchased, so I was hoping and praying they would handle me and my coat gently. I noticed that all color had drained from the scene. It was as if I had passed through a threshold, and I was now in an episode of *The Twilight Zone*. Everything was black and white. On the way out the door, Charles Busch was arriving, fashionably late. I murmured a quiet and friendly "Hi, Charles" from behind the mask. He looked at me, mystified, raised an eyebrow, and shrugged, in that 1940s female movie star manner of his. "Daaahrling, what an exit." Then they rushed me off to the Roosevelt Hospital emergency room.

When I arrived, they gave me blood tests and blood pressure tests but mostly asked me questions about my drug and alcohol use. I balked, throwing words like "negligible" and "minimal" around as if

I had been coached by Courtney Love, but then I had to go to a cardiologist. The cardiologist, after stress tests, EKGs, and sonograms, told me I had a really slow pulse, great for being an athlete, but not so hot for drugs and alcohol, because my heart didn't need to run any slower. This explained my lifelong history of collapsing. It took a few more of these enchanting four-in-the-morning trips to the emergency room to finally get the message. I got clean and sober on Halloween of 1989.

A man named Bart Gorin took to me right away and became my guide and protector in AA. Bart looked almost like a cartoon character. He had a long face and he was tall, but his body wasn't naturally tall; it looked as if it had been stretched out on a rack. His voice was as distinctive as the way he said my name, holding on to the *i*, "Hiiiii, Riiiiiick." In Chinese there are characters that don't just express a word; they express the history and the time the word was born. Bart said my name like that, as if my name included everything he knew about me and everything he had made up in his head about me.

Bart would ring my buzzer at 6:30 every morning to get me to a 7:00 meeting called Fast Break. There I found everything I was looking for when I drank, all the interesting, colorful, sexy, slightly dangerous people who were speaking intimately about their feelings and listening when you spoke about yours. He was my savior.

Bart had a set of cockamamie rules he lived by, which he asserted with enormous zeal. We were at a meeting one day, when a woman walked in wearing—well, there is a Yiddish word—*ungapatchka*, which means "overly ornate, busy, ridiculously over-decorated, or garnished to the point of distaste." She was wearing rainbow socks, polka-dot pants, and a plaid blouse and was blinding to the eye. Bart turned to me and with utter seriousness whispered, "The best dresser in AA."

One of his most important rules was "Gossip keeps you sober," which is in direct conflict with AA's suggestions for living, but he took it quite seriously. He would sit next to you at meetings like a translator and all through the meeting with great earnestness whisper little tidbits about everyone into your ear, quietly pointing, things like "murdered his lover in a blackout," or "jumped out a window and landed on a sprinkler," or "hit man for the Mafia . . . avoid at all costs."

Bart's story was illustrious. He dealt heroin to John Lennon and Yoko Ono. My favorite detail from his story is when he worked for a while doing odd jobs for Greta Garbo. He was friends with the artist Ray Johnson, a modern-day dadaist, who swam off a pier in Port Jefferson, Long Island, one night to kill himself. When I was in Philadelphia doing *States of Independence* with Tina Landau, the Philadelphia Museum of Art was planning a Ray Johnson show. The entire show ended up being the correspondence back and forth with the museum about the show that Ray would decorate, draw on, paste things onto, cut up, make paper planes out of, and so on. It was genius and hilarious. He would also make Joseph Cornell–like boxes that were beautiful. Bart would send Ray Garbo's used cigarette butts with her lipstick on them, and Ray would incorporate them into his boxes.

Bart lived upstairs from Duncan Hannah, a handsome dandy of a painter who resembled and modeled himself after Alain Delon, dressing and wearing his hair like him, even sporting the striped boat-neck T-shirt Delon wore in René Clément's *Purple Noon*. We would all hang out and go to meetings together. Duncan had Bart's wryness with a healthy dose of sarcasm as well. One day we were walking down Seventy-Second Street, and we passed a "bum" lying next to a building, slobbering, singing to himself, and chugging from a jug of cheap wine. Duncan said, "Not one of Fireside's success stories." Fireside was the celebrity-filled meeting we went to every day at lunchtime. I howled with laughter.

I heard about Duncan before I met him. One day I was at my friend Alan Kleinberg's apartment, and he had a beautiful little painting of Ned Rorem, one of my heroes, on his wall. "Who did this painting?" I asked. How did Alan Kleinberg know who Ned Rorem was? Duncan did.

Duncan and I bonded because of our love for foreign movies and all things introspective and melancholy. I loved his work. I filled my apartment with his muted, nostalgic childhood paintings, drawings, and collages, and they ended up adorning the covers of many of my CDs and books.

Everyone had a crush on Duncan. His hair was so thick it was as if his scalp were having a follicle festival, inviting all the hair everyone else, like me, had lost, to the party. His wardrobe was decidedly cinematic, based either on English movies about disaffected youths Tony Richardson might have directed, fops like Oscar Wilde, or movies by Godard, Truffaut, or Melville. Lou Reed even wanted Duncan to poop on him when he met him—that's the kind of adoration he inspired—but in general Duncan was straight. I was the only attendee at his wedding to Megan Wilson, a wonderful woman from England, a designer of, among other things, book covers for Vintage/Random House and other publishers. On June 11, 2022, Duncan was watching a French movie with Megan in their house in Cornwall, Connecticut. Megan went down to the kitchen for something, and when she came back upstairs, Duncan was in a coma. He had had a heart attack and died that night. He was sixty-nine years old. The last time I spoke with him, we had a long conversation about this book, comparing notes (his memoir, *20th Century Boy: Notebooks of the Seventies*, came out in 2018). For me, another bright star in the galaxy of my life has gone out.

At one point, Richie Berlin came into the meetings. Richie was Brigid Berlin's sister, the Brigid who was Andy Warhol's best friend, and Richie was a major Warhol character. She had the personality and elocution of someone who had grown up with great privilege on Fifth Avenue but had then been put through the wringer. She was tanned and grizzled and wore just enough gold on top of her casual running clothes to let you know she was rich. She carried around a tiny white fur ball of a dog named Boomer. She pronounced it "Beeoouuumerr" with as much Upper East Side hauteur as was humanly possible. Her father was chairman of the Hearst media empire for decades, and their lives were filled with movie stars, politicians, and royalty. Highly committed to thinness, Richie was addicted to speed like Brigid and me, so she ended up in our meetings when she finally bottomed out on speed and alcohol, grinding half her teeth out of her head.

Richie was generous and took pity on me with my never-ending, pathetic money problems, so she was always slipping me hundred-dollar bills. A humble millionairess, she worked as a bicycle messenger. She would stop when she saw me and throw money at me. She instituted an event every Thursday night in Bart's honor because he had AIDS and was not long for this world. He could eat wherever he wanted, see whatever he wanted to see, buy whatever he wanted to buy, and invite whomever he wanted on these expeditions. Often this included me. It could be fun, but Richie was volatile and had a terrifying temper, and if she blew up at whatever or whomever in your presence, it was hard to recover from. She easily reactivated my PTSD when she made a scene. We were having dinner one night and something Bart said made her angry. It was one of the ugliest, most frightening outbursts I had ever seen, with about seventy years of entitlement, neglect, and hunger for love to back it up.

One time I had her speak at a meeting I was chairing. Usually, the speaker tells their story, which lasts a maximum of twenty-five minutes. Then there is a secretary's break where business is discussed and money is collected. Then people raise their hands to share. Richie talked for the whole hour. The secretary had to quietly hand out the contribution baskets while she kept talking. I was mortified. At forty minutes in, even though no one was fidgeting and everyone seemed rapt, I ran to my friend Danny in the back of the room to ask what I should do. "Just let her talk. She's fascinating," he said.

Another time I brought Ned Rorem to speak. I had had so little time and so little sober experience and just wanted everyone to be impressed with my famous speakers. I knew Ned hadn't had a drink in twenty-five years, so I assumed he knew the protocol at meetings, but instead of telling his drinking story, he told the story of his life and career, peppering it with anecdotes and any number of famous names like Jean Cocteau and Francis Poulenc, assuming this ragtag room full of drunks and addicts would know whom he was talking about. But they didn't. When he was done, he got up and took a huge bow as if it were Carnegie Hall. Then, when people were sharing, he kept interrupting them to have conversations or to flirt with them, and they would scream back at him, "There is no cross talk at this meeting!" He had no idea what they were saying and instead of feeling bad persisted in having conversations with them!

One time I got Barbara Cook to speak and invited my friends

including my mother and sister to the *anonymous* meeting to hear her. Needless to say, it took me a while to grasp the concept of anonymity.

Bart was a sex addict and would stand by the window in his apartment and play with his formidable dick while watching construction workers. He was in the Sexual Compulsives Anonymous meetings too, which I wouldn't mention here if he were alive.

Bart died on Valentine's Day in 1991. He would call me from the hospital to discuss what he should wear in his coffin. The conversations were so macabre they were funny. Richie had bought him a flashy hand-knit orange sweater he loved, and he settled on a new pair of black corduroy pants for the bottom. I thought his choice was a little Halloweenish, but he liked the idea, thought it was appropriate, just the right amount ghoulish.

SNAPSHOT NO. 7, 1974/1989

My first real sex, tender sex with an equal my own age, was at Carnegie Mellon, with a singer, a tenor named Danny Cronin. You would never have known he was gay. He dressed like one of the Little Rascals, with torn pants and two T-shirts at a time, both ripped. We were in eurythmics class together with Marta Sanchez where you ran and danced around the room to learn rhythm with your body. If you walked into one of our classes, you would wonder why we weren't all dressed in white gauze with dandelions in our hair being led by Isadora Duncan. It was helpful to me as a composer later because it made writing rhythms, breaking them down on a page, easier, because you had installed them in your body. Danny, with his vivid blue eyes and leprechaun smile, was terrible in that class, which he seemed to delight in, a disaster at polyrhythms. He had the same record as me of missing classes because of hangovers, or just because. He grew up in an Irish Catholic home and had a million sisters, all with the middle name Mary, so everybody just called him Danny Mary. I learned he had an incestuous relationship with his mother, when, years later, we found ourselves in recovery for drug and alcohol addiction. Doug and I decided to have a party one night. It was one of those beer keg and chips parties with wall-to-wall people. At the end of the party, all the stragglers ended up in my room. When one by one they were leaving, Danny, ambling down the steps, said something to indicate he might be gay. I said, "Wait. You're gay?" He laughed, and said, "Yeah." "Wanna stay over?" I asked, and he did. Sex with Danny that night was sweet and innocent. We were just kids at college, drunk and fumbling around, exploring each other's bodies. It didn't herald the start of a relationship, neither of us wanted that, and I still awakened with the terrible feeling I would always have waking up in the morning with someone I didn't know well enough to wake up with, but it was the beginning of a long friendship, terribly fraught by the end when he died after a long and protracted battle with AIDS, because I think he was angry at me for not being sick, for continuing to live my life when his was nearing its end. He was angry at my ambition, my momentum, my forward movement, while he was forced to stand still. It was painful, the way he'd wave me off like an insect, but also unbearably forgivable. At points, our friendship was uncommonly beautiful. No one helped me more when I got into recovery. I could call him anytime, day or night. He taught me how to pray and what prayers to use. I called him once early on, after a masochistic marathon of movies all centered on alcoholism, *I'll Cry Tomorrow*, *The Lost Weekend*, and *Days of Wine and Roses*. He just listened, while I howled into the phone.

PHOTO MONTAGE

Don Palladino disappeared from Cafe Luxembourg and died.

Daniel Glynn was down in Florida working in a bodega in South Beach before he died. The last time we had spoken, he was living in Hong Kong for business. He cheerily said, "I've already had my Monday."

His onetime boss from the clothing company Henry Grethel, Jack Ethridge, who ended up in AA before he got sick, died, as did our friend Michael Jacobs, another beautiful man who had moved from San Francisco to New York when Daniel did.

George Anton and George Nowicki, who were angels to me when I first came into AA, died. Bruce Steier, even though until the end he looked as if he were still going to the gym, great in his tight white T-shirt, died. Frank Fedornock, my sponsor Adam's sponsor, thus my grand sponsor, died. I visited him in the hospital, and it was almost comical how *un*vain he had become. He had a Q-tip and was cleaning the thrush out of his mouth, a Sisyphean task, while he was talking to me. Frank had been tall and handsome, though by now he looked like Mr. Green Jeans from *Captain Kangaroo*. I had great admiration for him because one time, when he had been asked to tell his story at a meeting, he couldn't think of anything to say and sat on the steps silently for twenty-five minutes. Unbearable, but I couldn't believe anyone could be brave enough to not say anything if they had nothing to say. If my mind goes blank, out of nervousness and panic, I talk a mile a minute.

Adam S., my sponsor, told me on my third anniversary that he just wanted to make it to his tenth anniversary, and I burst into tears. But happily, he got the cocktail, and he is still here. Michael Jeter, not long after he won the Tony Award for *Grand Hotel*, died. He came to our Monday night AA meeting and crowed, deservedly so. Billy De Acutis, whose scenes playing William Hurt's doting gay assistant were all deleted from *Broadcast News*, though James Brooks was nice enough to send him a reel with the deleted scenes, died. Frank Mauser, a friend and the historian for the gay movement, died. My friend Danny Cronin, the first man I had sex with at college, stopped talking to me a year before he died. Rock Star Michael from the meetings died.

My friend Dennis Koontz, once a champion figure skater from Johnstown, Pennsylvania, who was a great artist at Carnegie Mellon doing strange things with graphs, dead flies, live goldfish, postage stamps, and tape, before I ever saw anybody do work like that, and who once, when we lived together and I was practicing piano, put his erect penis in my right ear, died. Dennis was a satyr. At one point, Danny Cronin put out an all-points bulletin that he was interested in anal sex and was looking for a volunteer to deflower him. I suggested Dennis, and Dennis was happy to oblige. Bill Turner, who was the director and composer at Carnegie Mellon who wrote a score for Bertolt Brecht's *Jungle of Cities*, which was the best score I have ever heard for the theater and the reason I write for the theater in the first place, died. It opened indelibly, with Calvin Tsao, who became a famous architect, in a spotlight, dressed in drag with whiteface, singing a twelve-tone aria/prologue that began, "You are in Chicago in 1910. You will witness an inexplicable wrestling match between two men."

Roy Phelps, the midwestern tenor who lived on the fifth floor of my building, and his dark Mediterranean lover, Eliot Fortè, who painted their entire apartment Day-Glo pink and green, every room, including the ceilings and the moldings, died.

Brad Gordon, the handsome, doomed-looking photographer who took my picture when I was very young at my yellow rented piano, died. The couple that lived upstairs in the penthouse, Royce and Joe, who had a pet squirrel that would leap at you, clamping onto your arm with its claws, died.

Tim Walsh, who went to school with my friend Mary O'Connor at McGill, whom Tom Piechowski, my first New York City roommate, fell in love with, died. Sometimes, Tom, Tim, and I would take quaaludes and have sex.

Tim died at home in Pittsburgh. Tom visited him, but Tim didn't know who he was. It seemed like every other gay man you knew was dying gruesomely.

DOMINIQUE

I was cleaning the loft of Antonia Polizzi, an artist who looked like an Italian princess with full lips, a deep voice, and wild black wavy hair and who wore big glasses like Sophia Loren and had a voice and affect like the great filmmaker Lina Wertmüller. Her bathroom was huge and tiled in black shiny tiles that showed streaks no matter *what* you cleaned them with, so I always wanted to kill myself when I was there, but that was not uncommon in those days. I always put Steve Reich's *Music for 18 Musicians* on because it made me feel better, like a bee tending to a hive.

I bring it up, because a "doctor" who was treating a bunch of us, Dominique Richard, made his office there and I saw Antonia and Dominique quite often. Dominique treated me, and eventually many of my friends, because he was one of the few "doctors" who could get rid of parasites without toxic medicines like Flagyl and Atabrine, which were basically like swallowing insect repellents. Parasites were supposedly an early sign of a compromised immune system, or they could compromise your immune system, making it easier to contract AIDS, so you had to get rid of them quickly.

Dominique was an iridologist. He would examine the irises of your eyes and come up with a thousand things you needed treatment for, so you'd have to buy at least twenty bottles of herbs, tinctures, and drops to put under your tongue or in warm water at night, or in the afternoon, or in the morning, or every ten minutes. You had to give up coffee and sugar while you were being treated by him, which for me was a fate worse than death, but in those days you could have submitted me to anything because I was always looking for a door out of my confusion and misery. It was expensive, but I trusted him, and he did, as I said, get rid of the nasty parasites of my friends Arthur and Peter by using things like geranium oil. I didn't get parasites, because

I was afraid of all the places you could pick them up, like bathhouses, sex clubs, and back rooms. I was like Little Bo Peep when it came to that stuff.

Dominique told a lie about himself to inflate his magnetism, a big one. He said his mother was Jeanne Moreau. Catherine in *Jules and Jim* was his *mother*? I would ask him endless questions about her. "How did she like Truffaut?" "Oh my God, Antonioni?" "What did she say about Louis Malle and Jacques Demy? Marcello Mastroianni?" "Did *you* meet them?" Stupid questions. He would answer evasively, making me feel silly and shallow for caring about celebrity when it was no big deal. None of us ever suspected he'd made it up. He sort of looked like her, was French, and did not seem like a charlatan. Plus, who on earth would make up a lie that was so easy to disprove? He was very professional, the setup looked real, and with the thousands of little brown bottles with droppers in them all over the place, you really felt as if you were in a laboratory.

One week we went to some house upstate that was supposed to be his country house, and we were all getting treatments of some kind or other. It was winter, so there was snow on the ground, and I was happy, because winter with snow on the ground in upstate New York is my favorite weather and favorite place to be. Rich Martel was there attached to some contraption in the bathroom that was giving him special enemas of bitter melon and coffee. It was odd to see big, powerful Rich with tubes coming out of him in such a compromising position, but I truly believed this would make him better.

I was disappointed, because supposedly we had arrived just after Jeanne Moreau left and I couldn't believe I'd missed her. Allegedly, she had been there for a week and had to get back to Paris to begin filming a new feature. I bring this up because it is sort of a perfect illustration of the kinds of offshoot treatments, snake oil salesmen, cranks, and "healers" who cropped up all over the place, and the desperation that allowed everyone to put their faith in them. When you are this close to the possibility of death, you are susceptible to anything, and while I didn't think Dominique was a quack, I certainly wouldn't have recommended him, or spent hundreds of dollars on him myself, and I don't think he would have had such a booming business feeding people geranium oil and giving them bitter melon enemas if it weren't for the AIDS crisis.

AFTERWARD

During the entire time of the AIDS crisis, the Pride parades every year were strangely exultant. I think it was because we were celebrating ourselves for taking hold of a situation it was clear the government didn't care about. President Reagan took far too long to even *mention* AIDS, much less *do* anything about it, and the same for Mayor Koch, who was gay, which made it even more galling. We cared for our own. We fought for them, advocated for them, tended to them, visited them, memorialized them, wrote about them, sang about them, made quilts about them, raised money for them; wept for them, distributed their ashes, buried them, and grieved for them. We were a harried, damaged, and broken generation, and we would never again be the same. Ever.

And then we had to make our way back to a place that no longer existed, where innocence was trounced, our hearts were permanently broken, and everything looked, felt, tasted, smelled, and sounded different.

We were, thousands of us, Lazarus. We had to rise from the ashes. We didn't have to rebuild our lives; we had to build new ones.

Jeffrey

When Adam Guettel's song cycle, *Saturn Returns*, premiered at the Public Theater in 1998, I took my friend Michael Klein to see it with me. Toward the end of the show, there is a song called "Awaiting You." I was listening, already teetering on the edge, when I heard the lyric "And what about the child who cannot breathe" (Adam had a brother, Matthew, who, when he was four, ran into his mother's room and died in her arms in the throes of an asthma attack) "or the gentle sage who won't see the age of thirty-two," who was Jeffrey.

I held it in and kept breathing. But when it was over, I bolted out of the theater, and Michael followed me, mystified. I fell into his arms and sobbed uncontrollably for the rest of the night. I was inconsolable. It wasn't that Adam had co-opted something that was mine but that I hadn't even figured out what *I* needed to say about it yet, how to shape my own grief into something, and in one line Adam had brought Jeffrey back to life and mourned him before I had.

For me, Jeffrey's death was the apotheosis of the AIDS crisis. I had worked at the Gay Men's Health Crisis doing intake for years. I had lost friends, lovers, collaborators, heroes. But then I fell in love with Jeffrey, whom I met through his friend Dan. Dan was unbelievably handsome and guileless. He admitted freely to having read only two books in his entire life, biographies of Elvis Presley and Muhammad Ali. I thought for sure Dan was straight; I would have bet my life on it, until he had a party and played Liza Minnelli and Barbra Streisand continuously, over and over again—dead giveaways.

In 1992, Jeffrey was walking across the room with Dan at one of the meetings. Dan had always talked about his friend Jeffrey, his friend from the American Academy of Dramatic Arts, where they both studied acting. Something strange and inexplicable happened. When I saw him, my head seems to have been encoded with a bomb that was designated to explode at that moment. He looked like one of those Picassos from the period where all the figures look primitive, with big, deep-set, almost black eyes, olive skin, and roundish features. Part Colombian and part Italian, he seemed to be part water sprite as well.

When he laughed, it was half-adult and half-infant, and he could look so joyous it dwarfed what you already knew as joy. Dan had a New Year's Day brunch, and I went because I figured Jeffrey would be there. He was, and we spoke all day. I felt as if I were hovering above my body. I called Dan that night and told him to ask his friend Jeffrey if it would be okay if I asked him out. Jeffrey liked the idea, and we made a date.

But he canceled on me twice, and I thought he was trying to blow me off. So, I ignored his calls for a while to punish him. Finally, he got me on the phone and said he really *had* been sick and really *did* want to go out with me, and could we reschedule? Begrudgingly, I said yes, and we planned to meet at my house on a Sunday. When our date came around that week, I was a few minutes late and Jeffrey was standing at my buzzer. When I rounded the corner and saw him, he seemed so happy to see me.

Once, after he died, I wrote in a poem, "It was a part of my story before it ever happened." I was watching videos of him as a boy. His father took videos of him, his older brother, Gary, and his younger sister, Paula, opening gifts every Christmas morning. I would watch them, feeling I had always known him, even though we had technically only met when he was twenty-eight.

When Jeffrey was eleven, Gary, who had gone from high school baseball star to teenage alcoholic in the span of a year, died a violent death on Christmas Eve. The Grossis lived in Wilmington, Delaware, and Gary was invited to a Christmas party in Baltimore. His volatile Italian American father, Frannie, was at this point deeply upset with Gary, who had put on tons of weight and was squandering his talent as a baseball player and his looks.

His father screamed at him, making him promise he wouldn't get into the car of a drunk driver after the party. Gary agreed, so instead, at the end of the party, Gary tried to walk home on the highway by himself, at one point attempting to cross the divider to call his parents, when a car hit him, killing him instantly. Yvonne, Jeffrey's mother, and Frannie had to drive to Baltimore and view the body, while Jeffrey and Paula waited alone at home.

There is a harrowing video of Jeffrey and Paula opening their presents the next morning with a pile of Gary's unopened presents right next to them. Yvonne and Frannie sent Jeffrey to live with his Colombian grandmother, ChiChi, who liked to ply him with "whickey," as Jeffrey would call it (hence, my meeting him in AA), while his mother stayed in bed for a year.

The parents' marriage slowly disintegrated, ending within the year, and a permanent cloud of grief and trauma filled the lives of the Grossi family. Previously, they were one of those families who are always having big dinners on Sunday with tons of relatives. The kids always had numerous cousins to play and get into trouble with. Now the house became a crypt, a mausoleum. Perhaps this, along with the fact that Jeffrey was a little smaller than me, compact, like a pre-Columbian wrestler, appealed to an instinct in me that was protective and made me want to enfold him in my arms and shield him from the pain and trauma of the world.

I took him upstairs to meet my roommate Tom, who clearly found him captivating right away, and then Jeffrey and I went out to dinner. We were having a lovely time. I had so many butterflies in my stomach I couldn't eat. Conversation was flowing easily. I learned he was working for Air France during the day and studying writing at night, and I talked about *States of Independence*, the piece I was preparing for the American Music Theater Festival with Tina Landau. But in a way, none of that mattered, something larger and overwhelming was happening. I kept wanting to reach across the table and kiss him. Then there was a moment when a smile seemed to disintegrate on his face as if it were melting, a terrible shadow seemed to suddenly hover, and he looked down. "What?" I asked. "There's something I have to tell you," he said. "What?" I asked, suddenly deeply concerned. "I'm HIV positive."

A long silence. I just looked at him and took a deep breath. A few nights before this, Mary Guettel had taken me to see Paul Rudnick's play *Jeffrey*. There is a line in the play, "Just think of AIDS as the guest that won't leave. The one we all hate. But you have to remember. It's still our party." Here we were, Jeffrey and I, having dinner, and that line popped into my head. I told him, "It's okay." And I thought, "This is my chance to show up for someone else. I'm going to love this guy right out of this world."

On our second date, we went to see Louis Malle's film *Damage*, based on Josephine Hart's novel, which I remember nothing of except the touching of our elbows, each collision an electrical shock, and that Jeremy Irons starred in it. Then we went to a restaurant near his apartment. I got upset at one point, because sauce from the spaghetti splashed and stained my shirt and I was embarrassed to have this oil stain glaring out like an eye, making me feel like a total slob. I went to the bathroom to stare at it, but there was nothing I could do that wouldn't have made it bigger and more noticeable. I felt so bad I almost wanted to excuse myself and go home, but something else was lurking, and I didn't want to miss it. Then we went to his apartment. We were standing in his tiny bedroom between the dresser with the TV on it and the bed, when I grabbed him as he was in midsentence and kissed him. Kissing him was like falling into a bed of loose feathers. We made love and slept together. Jeffrey's skin was the softest skin I have ever touched, almost like suede. I was thirty-six, eight years older than him.

The next morning, after we had breakfast at a little diner on the Upper East Side near his apartment, a part of town I will never understand, I was in a cab going back to the Upper West Side, feeling a strange combination of love and fear. I was thinking of how I would have to be cautious—no swallowing, no open wounds, no blood, well, nothing that could kill me, which were all new thoughts, because I had never slept with someone who was admittedly HIV positive.

On our first Valentine's Day, I showed up at Jeffrey's house with enough lilacs to fill a stable. We slow danced in the dark, intoxicated by the lovely fragrance. One day much later in our relationship, it was just before Christmas, and after a particularly bad bout with pneumonia, I went out while he was sleeping and bought about ten dozen yellow roses from a flower seller who was selling them at an insanely cheap price.

I was on my way to see the new movie from New Zealand, *Heavenly Creatures*, the one that introduced Kate Winslet, but I went back home and filled the whole room with the roses while he slept, even weaving some of them into the wreaths and greenery already festooning the room, so it would be all he saw when he woke up.

From the beginning, my relationship with Jeffrey had the parentheses of limited time around it. Each moment felt like a gift, criminal to squander. If he entered a room I was in, I felt enveloped by an almost preternatural vapor, leaping up to greet him as if it were the last time I'd see him. If I entered first, he would stare at me with his big, dark, pre-Columbian eyes and throw his arms around me, smiling, as if I were necessary air and water. There was a strange quietness to it all. We often whispered on the phone, though no one was listening. We seemed to glide down the street with each other as if feathers were guiding us. It is perhaps the reason I am prone to using clichés when it comes to Jeffrey like "He was my angel." He took me to a version of myself I never knew existed. I was Ricky before Jeffrey, and now I am Ricky after Jeffrey. Everyone who knows and loves me now, in a way, is loving both of us. Whatever Kevin may think, Jeffrey taught me how to love him the way I do.

Who was Jeffrey when I met him? He was working with his friend Fabrice at Air France in their office on Fifty-Seventh Street, taking reservations. It was uninteresting, but he never complained. Besides studying acting at the American Academy of Dramatic Arts with Dan after high school, he was in a directing class when we met. I went to see a one-act he directed about basketball that was not particularly memorable or well directed.

There are often markers, indicators that interrupt whether I think I am going to be able to love someone or not. Stupid things: they like a movie I hate, their taste, their shoes! Jeffrey told me toward the beginning his favorite singer was Shirley Bassey, a singer I had mixed to bad feelings about. She reminded me of the nightclubs my parents would go to in the borscht belt, hotels we visited when I was little where you could always hear singers like Jerry Vale wafting through the halls. I laughed when he told me. A loud caterwaul of "Gold-finggggguh" battered through my mind and I worried for a moment if our opposing aesthetics might be insurmountable, but the concern passed as quickly as a rain cloud. I even came to appreciate her.

He was taking a writing class and would write essays cramped with all the new words he was learning that felt sophomoric and self-conscious, but in his journals, which I discovered after he died, he was clear-eyed and deeply felt. One of Jeffrey's closest friends was Jim, a squat, older Italian gentleman who, it was clear, was in love with Jeffrey and had been for a while. They met at the Townhouse, a bar on the East Side where older men seek younger men and often become their "sugar daddies." Jim took Jeffrey on cruises to places like Sitges, in Spain, and lavished him with beautiful clothes. They remained friends after Jeffrey and I met, though the cruises stopped. I went out with him a few times after Jeffrey died, and we comforted each other in our grief.

Jeffrey's best friend, Ian, a colorful and slightly obscene charac-ter, had already moved to Paris. At one point, Ian sent his semen in a condom to Allen Ginsberg because he wanted to meet him. It worked. Edmund White begins his novel *The Farewell Symphony* with a story about a man having a funeral for his friend back in America by placing their photo on an existent grave in a Parisian cemetery. It is the true story of Ian, after Jeffrey died, placing Jeffrey's photo on the grave of Edmund White's lover.

I'm not sure how much Jeffrey and I had in common; I sometimes felt it was nothing, and I bemoaned it. The silences between us for lack of things to talk about would scare me. But the moment I saw him walk across the room with Dan, I felt an unfamiliar yet blinding light go off in me and I had to be with him.

Jeffrey delighted in me. He was open to everything I wanted to share with him, the foreign films (it was the season of the incredible

"Sang-Froid" film festival at Lincoln Center. Our favorite double bill
was François Truffaut's *Mississippi Mermaid* and Yves Allégret's *Une si
jolie petite plage*), the poetry, the classical music, the plays, the operas. I
took him to see Benjamin Britten's *Death in Venice* at the Metropolitan
Opera during a snowstorm so violent the house was half-full. In those
days, I still had to pay for tickets, and we were way up in the family
circle, the least expensive seats. But he seemed rapt and grateful. It being Britten's last opera, it is neither an easy nor an ingratiating score,
yet Jeffrey seemed to hear it as if he had been listening to music like it
all his life. He was beaming, starstruck like a child, never once seeming restless or bored. He responded similarly the night I took him to
see our friend Lauren Flanagan sing opposite Luciano Pavarotti in
Verdi's *I Lombardi*. At one of Hal and Judy Prince's family Christmas
parties, when everyone gathered to sing Christmas carols around the
piano while Jason Robert Brown played, Elaine Stritch shot herself in
the belly with insulin right in front of us, Lauren Bacall introduced
herself to us as Betty, Stephen Sondheim and I circled each other
warily, and Carol Burnett nudged Jeffrey over on the arm of the chair
with her behind, putting her arm around him, so she could sit next to
him. They hadn't even spoken. It was simply the warmth and familiarity hanging in the air. I thought he was going to faint.

Conversely, the world hurt us in the same way. He had been
sick, very sick, gasping for air for a month. We barely left the apartment. Finally, our first date out of the house we went to see Terrence
McNally's play *Love! Valour! Compassion!*, which we had heard so many
great things about, and it was somehow the worst possible thing in the
world for us to see. Every note it struck that night, in our fragile states,
was false. It had absolutely nothing to say to us. Who were those men?
We couldn't relate to a single person in it. But even the nightmare of
it was a kind of ecstasy; it was a vitality, an urgency that made everything feel as if it were in Technicolor.

It was always like that, until the end. Everything had this halo,
this fine gray mist of impermanence around it. Everything was sacred, momentous. I had never experienced anything like it. Life was
vital and I was so happy, for a time.

On our first Christmas together, Jeffrey and I decided we would both pick out all the things we wanted for presents, no price concerns whatsoever, as if we had all the money in the world. We went to Barneys, on Madison Avenue, had lunch at Freds, the elegant restaurant on the seventh floor, and then showed each other all the unbelievably expensive items we had chosen. We went to Bergdorf's, where we ate little sandwiches like dowagers in their fabulous café and did the same thing. We had no money, so this was a fun way of almost buying and receiving presents. I mean, I did buy him a brocade vest he eyed longingly in a little boutique in the Village and a sunflower-gold cashmere sweater I couldn't resist because it was his favorite color (he was Catholic and was used to a million presents under the tree). We would try on the clothes, model them for each other while luxuriating in them, engage with the salespeople right up to the moment of purchase, and then renege. It was a little like the shoplifting expedition in *Breakfast at Tiffany's*. It had that kind of energy, excitement, and naughtiness, because the salespeople usually looked as if they wanted to murder us after wasting all their time.

In Newark, Delaware, we spent another Christmas with Jeffrey's sister, Paula, and her two kids, Trisha and Rocco. At thirty-eight, I had finally got my license. Jeffrey's father gave us a car that we parked in a lot on West End Avenue and Sixtieth Street, so I drove us to Delaware, and that in itself, the new agency of being able to drive, was miraculous. Little things, like pee breaks and rest stops, were thrilling. Paula had married a criminal and an addict who was unfortunately the father of Trisha and Rocco, so he was away in prison somewhere. Paula had lupus and was on disability and could work only intermittently, so when I got there, I did some stuff around the house, mostly hanging pictures and rearranging furniture. It was snowing when Jeffrey and I took Trisha and Rocco out for pizza on Christmas Eve. I had this deep feeling of fulfillment that I was useful and part of a family. I loved Jeffrey, and we were taking his niece and nephew out for dinner, and everyone was so happy. That night, Paula gave us her bed, which was a water bed, good for her compromised muscles and joints and great to have sex in, yielding to the body in any and every position. I couldn't wait for the morning, like a little kid. I had never had Christmas with a lover and what felt like my in-laws. I was a "man." I could drive, hang pictures, move furniture, and buy pizza for everybody, and we had beautiful gifts to give. The gift I was maybe the most excited to see opened was a gorgeous red cocktail dress we bought Paula at Banana Republic, which fit her like a glove and made her look gorgeous. Paula was an exotic beauty. She looked like a cross between Sonia Braga and Salma Hayek. I spent two more Christmases with Jeffrey and his family. They could be hilarious, like when Jeffrey wanted to go see some relatives on his father's side of the family, the DelleDonnes. They had a huge pink-foil Christmas tree with all pink lights, which matched their pink-and-silver metallic wallpaper. It was so tacky you were wide-eyed at the sheer gumption of it. Gina DelleDonne was the cousin Jeffrey was closest to. She was warm and friendly and weighed upwards of four hundred pounds, so when she pulled you into her bosom, you felt the earth was enfolding you. Barbara, Jeffrey's aunt, was straight out of central casting for *Goodfellas*, as exaggeratedly thin as Gina was huge, and should have played Joe Pesci's mother. Come to think of it, she sort of looked like Martin Scorsese's mother, who *played* Joe Pesci's mother! Her hair was basically a sculpture of an upside-down tornado atop her head, a construction she held erect with bobby pins and cans and cans of Ozon hair spray.

It was hard to watch what would happen to Rocco and Trisha after they had finished opening all their gifts, which were numerous, because everyone was trying to compensate for their fatherless existence and the possible imminence of their mother's death from the lupus that made her weaker and weaker. They would go into what looked like sugar shock, a place beyond depression in the realms of coma or spell; you wanted to look away, lest you catch it. This combined with their knowing their uncle was terminally ill made for a lethal brew.

When Jeffrey decided he wanted to stop taking AZT about two and a half years into our relationship and heal himself holistically, our lives became a real adventure in, well, I want to say quackery, but what difference does it make, *he* felt more empowered, as if he had more

My mother, Eve Gordon (née
Samberg) (Photograph by my father, Sam)

My sister Susan in Long Beach
(Photograph by my sister Sheila)

My sister Sheila and me at
221 Lincoln Avenue
(Photograph by my father, Sam)

My father, Sam Gordon (née
Goldenberg), and me on the porch
at 221 Lincoln Avenue
(Photograph by my mother, Eve)

Lorraine, Maggie, and
Bobby Shapiro, with me in 1964
(Photograph by my sister Sheila)

Uncle Sid, my "guardian angel,"
and Jeffrey Samberg
(Photograph by my father, Sam)

Joni Goldenberg, Mark Teitelbaum,
and Irving Goldenberg
(Photograph by my father, Sam)

The Goldenbergs, Aunt Blanche,
Mama Yetta, Aunt Sylvia, and Uncle
Freddie (Photograph by my father, Sam)

Peter Randsman and Arthur Levy
(Photograph by me)

Me and Jeffrey Michael Grossi
(Photograph by Jeffrey's mother,
Yvonne Nass)

Tom Piechowski, Mary O'Connor,
Maggie Shapiro, and Brian Frank
(Photograph by me)

Me, Kevin Doyle, and Sinead Foyle's
dog, Bella (Photograph by Sinead Foyle)

Joni Mitchell's letter (Photograph by me)

Me at Carnegie Mellon University,
1975 (Photograph by Susan Klein)

With Kit Grover
(Photograph by Jim Mahady)

"Sondheim" (Jack Rosen Photos LLC)

Adam Guettel at Lincoln Center in the American Songbook Series, March 13, 2000, singing "We Will Always Walk Together" (Richard Termine / The New York Times / Redux)

John O'Shaughnessy (Long Beach High School yearbook photograph, 1973)

With Tony Kushner
(Photograph by Jacqueline Kim)

With Angelina Réaux and
Jim Mahady
(Photograph by Tom Piechowski)

With Diane Sutherland
(née Fratantoni) at the CMU Gala
(Courtesy of Carnegie Mellon University)

Me and Tina Landau. We wrote "States of Independence," "Dream True," and "Stonewall: Night Variations" together.
(Photograph courtesy of the Wright State University public relations office)

Dream True, Vineyard Theater, 1999. Clockwise from bottom left: Jase Blankfort, Amy Hohn, Alex Bowen, and Jessica Molaskey
(Photograph by Carol Rosegg)

Kevin and Lucy (Photograph by me)

Nancy Rhodes and I created *Only Heaven* together for
Encompass Opera. The piece uses about thirty-five poems
by Langston Hughes. One of Hughes's biggest fans, a man
named Kenneth P. Neilson, came to every show and gave
us his painting of Hughes (pictured) to display in the lobby.

(Photograph by Roger Cunningham)

Encompass New Opera Theater presents *Only Heaven* at the
Connelly Theater, January 2001. Clockwise from far left:
Michael Lofton, Monique Rodriquez, Whitney V. Hunter,
Monique McDonald, Keith Byron Kirk, and Sherry Boone

(Photograph by Gerry Goodstein)

Poster for *My Life with Albertine*
(Courtesy of Playwrights Horizons, 2003)

Chad Kimball, Brent Carver, and Kelli O'Hara in
My Life with Albertine, which I wrote with Richard
Nelson, based on the work of Marcel Proust
(Photograph by Joan Marcus)

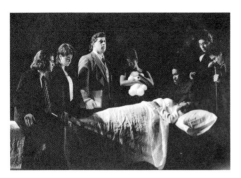

The Tibetan Book of the Dead, with a libretto by Jean Claude Van Itallie, a Houston Grand Opera production, which premiered at the Wortham Opera Theatre at Rice University on May 31, 1996, performed by Jonita Lattimore, Frank Hernandez, Eric Owens, Nicole Heaston, John McVeigh, Jill Grove, Gabriel Gonzales, and Beth Clayton
(Photograph used with permission of Houston Grand Opera)

Melvin Chen, Elizabeth Futral, and Todd Palmer in my *Orpheus and Euridice* for Lincoln Center's Great Performances series at the Rose Theater in 2005
(Photograph by Nan Melville)

Me and Michael Korie, the librettist of *The Grapes of Wrath*
(Photograph by Greg Downer)

Poster for *The Grapes of Wrath* at the Ordway Theater for Minnesota Opera in 2007 (Used with permission of the Minnesota Opera Archives)

Deanne Meek, Rosalind Elias, Roger Honeywell, Peter
Halverson, Robert Orth, Jesse Blumberg, Kelly Kaduce, Brian
Leerhuber, Maeve Moynihan, and Josh Kohl in *The Grapes of
Wrath*, at the Ordway Theater for Minnesota Opera in 2007
(Photograph by Michal Daniel)

Jesse Blumberg with the violist Ethan Pernela, in *Green Sneakers*,
for baritone, string quartet, empty chair, and piano,
commissioned by Bravo! Vail Valley Music Festival in 2008
(Photograph by Michael O'Brien, courtesy of the Hawaii Performing Arts Festival)

Sycamore Trees at the Signature Theater in
Arlington, Virginia: Farah Alvin, Mark Kudisch,
Judy Kuhn, Jessica Molaskey, Matthew Risch,
Diane Sutherland, and Tony Yazbeck
(Photograph by Scott Suchman)

Poster for *Sycamore Trees* at the
Signature Theater in Arlington,
Virginia, in 2010 (Courtesy of Signature
Theater, design by Design Army)

Frederica von Stade in *A Coffin in
Egypt*, with a libretto by Leonard
Foglia, based on Horton Foote's play
(Photograph by Lynn Lane)

With Mark Campbell, the librettist
for *Rappahannock County* (Courtesy
of Virginia Arts Festival, photograph by
Rachel Greenberg)

Kevin Moreno, Matthew Tuell, Aundi Moore, Mark Walters, and Faith Sherman in *Rappahannock County*, with a libretto by Mark Campbell, co-commissioned by Texas Performing Arts, the Virginia Arts Festival, Virginia Opera, and the Modlin Center for the Arts at the University of Richmond (Photograph © David Polston)

Daniel Brevik, Tobias Greenhalgh, Stephanie Blythe, Elizabeth Futral, and Theo Lebow in *27*, with a libretto by Royce Vavrek, commissioned by Opera Theater of St. Louis and premiered in the spring of 2014 (Photograph by Ken Howard)

Lauren Snouffer and Daniel Belcher in *The House Without a Christmas Tree*, with a libretto by Royce Vavrek, based on Gail Rock's book, commissioned by Houston Grand Opera and premiered in December 2017
(Photograph by Lynn Lane)

Me and Royce Vavrek, the librettist of *27* and *The House Without a Christmas Tree*
(Photograph by Bruce-Michael Gelbert)

Elizabeth Zharoff, Liz Pojanowski, and Jennifer Zetlan in the world premiere of *Morning Star*, with a libretto by William Hoffman, based on Sylvia Regan's play, at Cincinnati Opera in 2015
(Photograph by Philip Groshong)

With William Hoffman, the librettist of *Morning Star*
(Phil Groshong / Cincinnati Opera)

Larry Edelson; Frank Bidart, the
poet and librettist of *Ellen West*; and
me at Opera Saratoga in July 2019
(Photograph by Kevin Doyle)

Nathan Gunn and Jennifer Zetlan in
Ellen West, at the Prototype Festival,
January 2020, commissioned by Beth
Morrison Projects and Opera Saratoga
(Photograph by Maria Baranova)

Rachel Blaustein and Anthony Ciaramitaro in *The Garden of the
Finzi-Continis*, with a libretto by Michael Korie, based on the novel by
Giorgio Bassani and premiered at the National Yiddish Theater
Folksbiene at the Museum of Jewish History on January 27, 2022, in a
coproduction with the New York City Opera (Photograph by Steven Pisano)

Me and Lynn Nottage, the librettist
of *Intimate Apparel*
(Photograph by Chasi Annexy)

Errin Duane Brooks, Tesia Kwartung,
Anna Laurenzo, Jasmine Mohammed,
Krysty Swann, Indra Thomas, and
Jorell Williams in *Intimate Apparel*,
commissioned by the Metropolitan
Opera and the Lincoln Center Theater,
with a libretto by Lynn Nottage.
Premiered at the Lincoln Center
Theater in January 2002
(Photograph by Sara Krulwich and T Charles
Erickson, courtesy of Lincoln Center Theater)

Kearstin Piper Brown and Justin
Austin in *Intimate Apparel*
(Photograph by Sara Krulwich and
T Charles Erickson, courtesy of
Lincoln Center Theater)

agency over his life, and that was all that mattered. I had gotten my license so I could chauffeur him around from appointment to appointment. For instance, every Thursday, we would go to some place in Connecticut where they would have him sit with his feet in a basin of water that looked as if it were boiling as they pumped tons of electrical current into it.

The people who did this had a child who suffered from a severe seizure disorder, so he was always lying on a blanket on the floor, uncommunicative and silent, occasionally thrashing around unmercifully. The trips up the Merritt Parkway were beautiful, even if I knew there was no way this was doing anything to prolong Jeffrey's life. He was always drinking water with colloidal silver in it, taking tinctures and drops, and then he heard about an elixir. This elixir was supposed to be *it*, the key, the secret ingredient to saving the lives of people dying from AIDS—or anything.

It cost a lot of money, and I believe it was from Brazil, and when it arrived, it had an air of the mysterious and the miraculous all around it. Something quite mystical happened the first time Jeffrey used it, which we took as a sign. A few years before, I had painted all my furniture. The impetus was discovering that store on Madison Avenue, MacKenzie-Childs, where the furniture is all whimsically painted with stripes and gold, animals and flowers, as if every day were a tea party with Alice in Wonderland (I wanted everything in it), combined with a dream I had, in which the hideous Florida furniture my brother-in-law's mother sent me when she closed up and sold her house in Palm Beach was suddenly painted many colors and gorgeous.

I went crazy and began a project that took months and most probably shortened my life given the amount of polyurethane I inhaled. I was literally high enough to stagger from the fumes. I sanded down everything and painted it all with white primer; then I would draw little designs onto it and paint everything with all the colors I love, oranges, yellows, pinks, blues, purples, and greens. Then I would apply coat after coat of polyurethane, which brightened the colors but also made them recede slightly under an amber glow.

I re-covered chairs with beautiful brocades and painted desks, bookshelves, TV tables. When I was done, my apartment looked like somewhere between Barnum and Bailey's Circus and Pee-wee's Playhouse. So naturally, I felt protective of this furniture, particularly the dining room table, which was huge and took the longest, weeks, to paint. The very first time Jeffrey went to use the magic elixir, a big globule of it dripped onto the table, my eyes nearly shot out of my head, but before I could get upset, because there was no way you could remove this viscous deep purple goop from anything, it formed the Hebrew sign of life, a perfect, undeniable *chai*, as if Moses had painted it.

And it stayed there until Jeffrey died, and then completely disappeared. I don't know what it meant, but it sure was spooky and interesting. The truth is, years later, I finally figured out what that elixir must have been. It was before everyone started talking about the acai berry, before it was westernized and became everybody's favorite smoothie ingredient, so I feel 99 percent sure it was just a potion made up of crushed acai berries, which it looked like and smelled like. I love that stuff because it makes me feel speedy. But it didn't seem to do anything for Jeffrey.

Nothing Jeffrey did held back the inevitable. There were awful periods when he could eat only fettuccine Alfredo because he had so many painful sores in his mouth. There was the excruciating cytomegalovirus in his eyes and ears, for which I'd have to take him once a week for treatment, needles straight into his eyeballs. Each time I almost fainted, but he was always such a brave little soldier.

I took him for ear candling, hoping it would relieve the pressure in the ears, but it didn't. They stick a cone of some kind of paper in your ear and light it on fire, which causes heat to pull so much wax into the cone you can't believe a head could hold so much wax. He spent tons of money every week on high colonics because he was told that having a clean gut would make him better. It didn't.

I would create baths for him of warm sheep's milk to draw the parasites out because that was supposed to extend his life, and you would see funky-looking yellow things swimming around in the milk, but it did nothing. I cooked macrobiotically, we cut out dairy and sugar and white flour, and we filtered our water, but, on July 3, 1996, I had lunch with Duncan Hannah at Cafe Mozart, and I don't even remember why, but when I got home, we had to rush Jeffrey to the hospital.

I was having unbearable abdominal pain from a condition I finally had surgery to correct in 2016, and I was doubled over in agony, but we somehow got him to the emergency room at Mount Sinai. After hours of him being on a gurney in the hallway without a room, I couldn't take it anymore and called his mother, Yvonne, in Delaware, begging her to come and help. She arrived around midnight; I went home and went to sleep. When I called Jeffrey in the morning, when I was finally feeling better, I was trying to get some exercise, but he cried out frantically, "Where are you? Please come. The nurses won't change me."

His mother had left around four in the morning, after they got him checked into a room. I ran over to the hospital. I opened the door to his room, his voice was filled with shame, and he sounded like a child. He was lying in his own mess. I changed his shit-filled sheets and underclothes, resentfully, which I regret, but a lot of stuff was coming at me at once. Why didn't the nurses do this? How could they have left him like this?

One day, about three weeks before he died, the doctor in the hospital decided he needed some of Jeffrey's bone marrow, and while I held Jeffrey, he shoved what looked like an ice pick into Jeffrey's hip bone, which made him shake and scream. The doctor did it twice. What they could possibly have found out from that torture that would have made him live any longer, I will never know. They might as well have pulled out his fingernails with pliers.

My sister Sheila came to New York from Florida to help me get Jeffrey home from the hospital. She had brought him a beautiful watercolor of a house in a beatific setting with all kinds of lovely greenery and flowers, and she said, "Jeffrey, I think this is where you are going." She asked him how he was doing, and he said, "Sheila, I am ready to call it a life." In fact, he had just won the lottery for the experimental cocktail that ended up being really effective for treating the virus and extending lives, but by then he was so sick, so thin, so far gone, he assumed and, I guess, I concurred that a whole new drug regime would just kill him quicker.

We took him home early in the morning. Sheila called a cab and had it waiting in front of the hospital. It had just rained, but now the sun was out, making everything, the grass, the trees, the forsythia, and the wisteria in Central Park across the street, glisten, and a mist rising off the ground made the park look like Valhalla. We wheeled Jeffrey's wheelchair outside and down the ramp. Jeffrey looked around at everything as if he were saying goodbye to the world, craning his head left and right like an egret, tears filling his eyes. It is hard for me to think about that moment without becoming hysterical, this baby bird craning its neck moments before the talons of a raptor haul off and tear it away.

It is one of the most indelible images etched in my mind. It smelled as if the world had just been baptized. For the last few weeks, there was a problem with his insurance, so every day I would have to go to the pharmacy where they would give me only a one-day supply. By this point I started sleeping on the couch in the living room because there was a pretty loud pump sending supplementary nutrition through his veins at night and it sounded like a chugging train engine to me.

One night he called me into our room. His right ear was really hurting him, and he was in enormous distress and agitated. He asked if we could go to the doctor the next day. I got on top of him, and I looked into his eyes, and said, "Jeffrey, there are no more doctor visits, no more hospitals." He was silent for a few seconds. He knew immediately what I was saying. He asked, almost with relief in his eyes, "Do you mean my body is failing?"

And I said, "Yes. The doctor told me to just keep you comfortable and out of pain." I gave him a Vicodin. The next morning, he was calling friends and relatives to tell them the news with the same glee you might have upon getting accepted into Yale. "I'm dying," he screamed, as if it were a good thing. He loved at least knowing once and for all the direction everything was going in.

He was terribly excited to eat whatever he wanted the next morning, after the diet of brown rice, fish, and greens, and requested a
cinnamon roll from Cinnabon and coffee. The next day I had to go to
the East Side to pick up fentanyl patches from one of the doctors, and
Jeffrey asked me if I would consider going down to Little Italy and
picking up his favorite food, chicken Parmesan and pasta, from An-
gelo's on Mulberry Street for what he thought would be his last meal.
I did, but when I got home, I discovered they had left out his favorite
thing of all, the salad dressing.

I cried in a state of utter exasperation, and he made me call the
restaurant demanding they come uptown and deliver the salad dressing, grabbing the phone out of my hand, tearfully explaining the circumstances, "This is my last meal," but they wouldn't; it was too far
uptown. His mother did the best she could with the dressing, but his
disappointment was deep, and he sulked the rest of the day, while I
mumbled about how many miles I had traveled on this godforsaken
day for absolutely nothing.

Jeffrey started presiding over his death, inviting all his friends and
loved ones over to sit around his bed to tell inspirational stories, read
poems, and sing. He was very particular. One day, he screamed at
his friend Dan, who for some reason was talking about moisturizer.
"Dan, I won't need moisturizer where I'm going." We spent as much
time as we could meditating, and based on a ritual I learned from *The
Tibetan Book of Living and Dying*, which I was reading at the time, I
would visualize Jesus over his bed on a huge crucifix and the Virgin
Mary sitting on the edge of the bed, both in layers and layers of what
looked like cheesecloth.

One day I was giving him a bath, rubbing his little bones by now
protruding like razors from his ninety-pound body, and he said, "Do
you notice I'm not crying anymore? That's because I'm detaching.
The only one I'm going to have trouble detaching from is you." And
then we both cried. By then, the doctors were just inviting anyone
who was the caretaker for an AIDS patient to murder them when it
was time. We were all basically assigned euthanasia, and it was up to
us to decide when to do it. Their entreaties to "keep him comfortable"

were definitely code for "help him drift out of his ruined body into wherever he is going next," and I did.

His death was somehow so traumatic that I cried for five years straight, eventually having to face that my grief was no longer about Jeffrey or even AIDS. It cracked something open in me where there was nothing but endless howling pain. I wrote a monologue for *Sycamore Trees*, a musical I wrote about my family, for the main character, Andrew, or me, called "The Last Night of His Life." It is a completely accurate representation of what happened, written in the white heat of almost immediate grief. I called Jeffrey "David" in the show:

> Andrew: (*turning toward the audience reluctantly, but knowing he has to complete the story*) When grief is awakened, it empties out the hallway, decimates all the obstructions, so that suddenly, you are mourning everyone, and everything, and it is like a faucet you can never turn off. (*Pause.*) His ashes are buried beneath a tree, in a children's schoolyard, a Montessori school. Birds collect there, and children play so feverishly around it, it's almost as if he calls from inside it, beckoning with birdseed and lollipops.
>
> There is a plaque there. It says what he wanted it to say, "Think of Others," as well as his name, which he did not want it to say. "Think of Others." It is what he thought the Buddhist monk had said, standing over our bed, ringing the Tibetan Bells, a blessing, and playing with the beads of his Mala, though I am quite sure those were not the exact words he had spoken . . .
>
> It was August 1, 1996. At 7:30 that morning, David left his body. The night before he died, his mother and I slept with him, flanking him on either side. He had one accident that night, so the next morning, after he died, it was his pee-filled clothing that tortured me, tormented me, but also, felt most alive. I never thought I would bury my face in pee, to try to bring someone back to life. His mother's birthday was on the day before he died, and David had asked me to buy her

a present. I bought her two alabaster wall angels at a small
store in the Village. On the back of one, he wrote, "May
our spirits rejoice together, and dance. Happy Birthday,
Mommy, Love, David."

That morning, he screamed. "Goody" when he awoke . . .
"A birthday!" and we sat on his bed opening the presents.
I took her to see *Show Boat*, while his father visited him.
When we came home his condition had worsened drasti-
cally. While he coughed miserably and breathed with great
labor, I lay in bed holding him, singing "Make Believe," and
"Ol' Man River," and "Can't Help Lovin' Dat Man." He
clutched tightly my arms as if those songs were going to keep
him alive. Jerome Kern would have been happy to see how
necessary his songs were at that moment. His father paced
the room wringing his hands and crying, like King Lear.
Then he left for the long drive back to Rehoboth Beach, not
knowing what the next morning would bring.

David didn't want to come to the dinner table and eat
with his mother and me. I gave him more painkillers than
usual that night (he had very painful cytomegalovirus in his
ears) and more sleep medication. Maybe I killed him, I don't
know, and I never will. At around 4:00 a.m., after he careened
toward the porta-potty and ended up missing it entirely, we
finally got him down on the bed, relaxed. He turned his
face toward me, like he needed to hear something. I read the
"Healing into Death" chapter from Stephen Levine's *Healing into Life and Death* straight into his good ear, which was
touching my mouth. I felt like I was making a deposit into a
cloud chamber where echoes were eternal.

In the morning he asked his mother to leave the room.
She had gone to the bathroom and was on her way back
to bed when he startled us both by saying, "What are you
doing here?" He wanted to be alone with me, I guess. He
seemed completely lucid. We held each other and drifted
into sleep, until he woke me with a strange and frighten-

ing gasping, evenly spaced and continuous. I tried to give him his prednisone, which usually, miraculously removed all symptoms quickly. He wouldn't swallow the pill, so I called to his mother to come and help me. She came to the door and said, "He's going."

By now he was sitting on my lap facing me and I was propped up against the pillows. I began to sing the aria from the opera I wrote for him, *The Tibetan Book of the Dead*. "My Friend now is the moment of death. The time has come for you to start out, you are going home, you are going home, you are going home." His mouth opened to a wide O. He leaned in until our faces were touching, and our mouths were parallel. One tear fell from his left eye, and he looked as if he were about to shout for joy, and then he was gone. For a while, the only voice that came out of me was his. He had breathed himself into me and I became both of us.

In the winter of 1995, seven months before Jeffrey died, I noticed his plants had a lot of dead leaves on them. I decided to surprise him by pruning them. Later in the day, he was meditating, and suddenly I heard a shriek from his room, "What did you do to my plants?" to which I replied, "What? I just removed all the dead leaves."

"But I was meditating on impermanence," he screamed.

On the last Christmas, which was obviously the last one, Jeffrey's T cells were so low he almost always had fevers. We went to his doctor, a prominent AIDS specialist, Dr. Paul Bellman, one day, one of the times when he couldn't breathe. There was, by this point, never any good news. When we left the office, we got into a cab where the driver was smoking. I asked him to put his cigarette out, he could hear Jeffrey obviously struggling to breathe, but he wouldn't, so I punched him hard in the face, something I have never done in my life, ushered Jeffrey out of the cab, kicked the car, and if it weren't rush hour and bumper-to-bumper traffic, I would have got us killed.

Before we left to drive to Paula's in Delaware, I bought Jeffrey as tall a Christmas tree as I could find on Columbus Avenue, and all of our friends came over and decorated it while he watched, squealing with delight, from his bed.

We got up early on Christmas morning for a ritual Jeffrey asked all of his loved ones to be part of. He wrote a prayer letter:

Jeffrey Grossi
114 W. 70th Street
Apt. 8A
New York, NY 10023

15 December 1995

Dear One,

I believe that the power of prayer is the most effective healing tool that has ever existed. This has been demonstrated from the beginning of time and recorded in literary works such as the bible and other ancient texts. Jesus was the master when it came to healing. His healing work has been recorded more than any other healer I know. I have come to study Jesus and his life, to research how he healed and where that power came from. My conclusion is very simple: prayer, faith and belief. If you don't have any spiritual practice or religion then a positive thought of a specific intention is just as good. I do not wish to turn anyone off by quoting the New Testament, but I look to Jesus as a Buddha and a teacher. My belief is that God and the power of God is within me. Jesus had said, *I am in my Father, and ye in me, and I in you* (John 14:20). I take great comfort in knowing that I need not look far and wide, and hope that God is listening; for he is as close to me as my heart.

This letter comes to you as a prayer request. I am in need of prayers. I would also ask that you inform your friends and family because many voices having the same intention and praying at approximately the same time would be extremely effective.

I am very grateful this year because by the grace of God I was given another year of life. I see life as the most valuable gift ever created. A gift we all share for we are made from the same source and the same substance. I feel more alive today than I have ever felt. The only challenge is a severely damaged immune system destroyed by the inability to love—to love myself and others. I have learned a very difficult lesson, I have learned humility and the importance of impermanence.

And the prayer of faith shall save the sick, and the Lord shall raise him up (James 5:15). My request is that a prayer be said on the morning of **24 December 1995, upon waking**. I have chosen this time because the universal spiritual energy forming in the air will effectively and greatly support our goal. The intention is that I may heal and become whole, that my immune system be restored back to perfection as God intended it to be. For there are no limitations in life, only those that man creates. Jesus said, *And all things, whatsoever ye shall ask in prayer,* believing, *ye shall receive* (Matthew 21:22).

As the holiday season approaches, I pray that love will dominate our season and take hold of our beings, making us whole and complete, giving us peace within ourselves—as God intended.

Happy Holidays,

Jeffrey

Whether it worked or not, it felt extraordinary to be part of this moment in the last Christmas in the last year of Jeffrey's life, praying for him with what you knew would be so many people. Jeffrey was beloved.

Jeffrey's mother, Yvonne, cried at Christmas dinner, saying, "I know this is our last Christmas together." In normal circumstances, this might have seemed a morbid thing to say, but these weren't normal circumstances. Jeffrey cried, too.

It was Mary O'Connor along with my friend Jim Mahady whom I called the morning Jeffrey died, begging them to come over right away. At one point that morning, after my friend Gary, a Jesuit priest, said a Mass, Jeffrey's wishes, over his body, Mary, Jim, Yvonne, and I cradling his body in our bed, I became so hysterical in the kitchen Mary quietly but desperately entreated me to try to be strong for Yvonne, who was sitting at the dining room table staring straight ahead looking shell-shocked. Two things had set it off. We didn't know to shut Jeffrey's eyes, and when Gary threw the holy water, it went into Jeffrey's eyes making them look even glassier, deader. I felt we had hurt him, and there wasn't anything he could do about it. Then the undertakers, once they had zipped his body into the body bag and rolled him out on the gurney, had to come back. The elevator had broken down. Mary had to take them down herself in the freight elevator. She was afraid of how unhinged I was, and protective of Yvonne.

We had a memorial service at Gary Seibert's church on the Upper East Side. He did a service, with a homily based on Beckett. My friends Angelina Réaux, Patricia Schuman, Camellia Johnson, Melanie Helton, and Jim Mahady sang. It was a tense evening because Jeffrey's father, Frannie, having driven back to Rehoboth the night before Jeffrey died, felt we had gotten rid of him to keep him from being present for his death (which was untrue) and was threatening to kill Yvonne. So, we had to have a line of police in the back patrolling and making sure no one entered with a gun.

There was a celebration of his life at my apartment afterward. Everyone had brought the most beautiful flowers, lilies, orchids, freesias, hydrangeas, and the next day I felt as if they were choking me to death. I had already gotten rid of the porta-potty and the walker, but what was I going to do with all these flowers, which converted my apartment into a grotesquely fragrant funeral parlor?

I called my friend Theresa practically screaming with grief into the phone: "What am I going to do with the flowers, all these flowers, they are making me so sad?" She said, with all the love, compassion, and gentleness she could muster, because she was now crying along with me, "Honey, get a big garbage bag, and throw them all out." It felt so naughty to throw away what must have been a thousand dollars' worth of flowers, but I did it.

Then I went to the corner florist and gave them about thirty vases.

When Paula's lupus got worse and she could no longer drive, Frannie, who ran a construction business, built her a house near him in Rehoboth Beach where he could look after her. In 2007, eleven years after Jeffrey died, a week before my opera *The Grapes of Wrath* opened in Minnesota, Paula was murdered. The circumstances are shady, but sensing danger when two men burst into her house, Paula went to pick up the phone from her wheelchair, and she was shot dead.

Soon after, Frannie, having lost all his children, died. Thus ended the tragedy of that generation of Grossis, Frannie, Gary, Paula, and Jeffrey, the house of Atreus. Yvonne still came to *The Grapes of Wrath* because she needed to do something happy for herself. Not that the opera was particularly happy, it decidedly wasn't, but being there with her friend Kathy, and seeing me, as by now I was both myself *and* Jeffrey, as far as she was concerned, was undoubtedly comforting.

Jeffrey refused to leave the world until he felt Yvonne was set up spiritually. He was convinced she wouldn't make it if she didn't have a practice. He got her to start meditating. She meditates at an altar every day, adorned by photos of her beloved dead.

Still Here |

A year before Jeffrey died, I took him to see an exquisite production of Rodgers and Hammerstein's *Carousel* at the Lincoln Center Theater, replete with the entire onstage construction of a working carousel during the opening waltz. Audra McDonald played Carrie Pipperidge, and when she opened her mouth to sing, you knew you were in the presence of one of the great voices, like Lorraine Hunt or Leontyne Price. It was an astoundingly beautiful sound that went straight through you like a golden arrow. When the show was over, Jeffrey and I got about as far as the Henry Moore sculpture on the plaza and collapsed in each other's arms sobbing. The grief of what lay behind and what we knew was to come overwhelmed us.

My friend Arthur Levy, who, it turned out, was Audra's voice teacher, told me she was a fan of mine. She had heard the songs I wrote for Harolyn Blackwell in *Genius Child* and wanted to sing some of my songs, which was thrilling news for both Jeffrey and me.

Audra was in Toronto, with the show *Ragtime*, but I got in touch and started sending her songs. I would call people and sing them things I was writing or had written over the phone. Adam did it too. The first time I heard "Come to Jesus," from *Saturn Returns*, and "Love to Me," from *The Light in the Piazza*, was by Adam singing them to me over the phone. I called Audra one day, after I wrote "Poor Girl's Ruination/The Dream Keeper" for her, my mash-up of two Langston Hughes poems. I wrote it because I thought it would be a great opportunity for her to play two completely different characters in one song, one bitter and defensive and one broken and wistful. I sang it to her over the phone, and she said, "How do you do that?!"

After Jeffrey died, I wanted to do something to honor him on his birthday—the first one since his death. I planned a big concert, an AIDS benefit, with Broadway Cares/Equity Fights AIDS. The concert was called "Jeffrey's Birthday," which was a thrill to see in bright yellow neon letters outside Symphony Space on the Upper West Side. I put together a script out of Jeffrey's journals and poems and set up songs and piano pieces. Cherry Jones, the actress I knew from Carnegie Mellon, and the actor Martin Moran were the readers. When Cherry was nominated for a Tony Award for her role in *The Heiress* on Broadway, Jeffrey wrote in his journal, "Cherry Jones is a MAJOR STAR TODAY!" I had her read that entry.

I asked Audra (we still hadn't met in person) if she would come down from Canada and sing in the concert. She said yes right away. We agreed she would sing three of my newer Hughes settings, "Dream Variations," "Song for a Dark Girl," and "Daybreak in Alabama." Audra is such a high-charisma individual it's as if the lights flicker and the fuses blow when she walks into a room. She is an explosion of everything good. The day of the concert, when she arrived at my apartment, she was so beautiful I wanted to weep. And then we went through the songs.

When I do master classes, I always tell young singers about that day and about why Audra is a star. She hadn't just learned the songs flawlessly; she had digested them, examined them, knew every nuance of them, made them her own, and sang them as if she had written them, as if she were ready to film and record them. I hadn't a single note except to scream "Oh my God" and "Thank you" a thousand times like a blithering idiot.

When she left, my sister Sheila and I were speechless, as if a train had hit us. And that night, at the concert for Jeffrey, she tore down the house. Bob Hurwitz, the president of Nonesuch Records, was in the audience because they had already signed her exclusively and were planning her first recording. He heard those three songs that night and wanted them to be on the album. So it was decided that the album would be all new music.

At the end of that concert, I got up from the piano and sang "We Will Always Walk Together," a song I had written for Jeffrey while he was in the hospital. Tina Landau was in the audience and told me afterward that she had just booked a residency at Duke University to create a piece. She asked if I would come with her, because she wanted to create an entire musical around the song.

We went down to Durham and created *Dream True*, a musical about two boys, Peppy and Verne, inseparable friends, and their single mothers, Sarah and Dray, both widowed, living on adjoining ranches in the isolated wilds of Wyoming. Sarah, fearing Peppy will end up like his father, who committed suicide when the wilds and isolation of Wyoming drove him mad, decides Peppy needs to be educated in the East and sends him to his uncle in New Haven. The piece is about the upheaval that happens when the boys are separated, the gulfs, the chasms in each of them the absence of the other causes, and the myriad ways the trauma affects each of their lives.

At Yale, Peppy becomes Peter, a preppy, meets Madge, gets married, and moves to New York City. A successful architect, he sees his career begin to plummet when, in his intentness to re-create the space of his childhood and his longing for Verne in his buildings, they become almost nothing but air. One evening he is out walking, and he bumps into a man who looks familiar. That night he dreams about the stranger. It is a "True Dream," something he and Vernon discovered together when they were boys as a way of being together in their dreams. In the dream, the stranger is Verne.

The next night, he waits for the stranger in the same spot where he bumped into him. They recognize each other, and Peter and Vernon reunite ecstatically. But the intensity of their bond becomes untenable for both of them. Vernon, now gay, is in love with Peter and wants to be with him. Peter, who is not gay, nevertheless knows he loves Vernon more than anyone else in the world, and his confusion eats away at his relationship with Madge. Peter loses his temper with his uncle, who clearly has a suspect interest in his nephew, and becomes so violent his uncle has him committed to a sanitarium.

Only there does he finally find peace, because every night in their "True Dreams" he and Vernon return to Wyoming, the scene of their idyllic childhood. In one of these dreams, Vernon tells Peter he has tested positive for AIDS, which puts Peter in a state of almost unbearable agitation. The next night, in a "True Dream," Peter is reliving a scene from his childhood where Vernon got lost in the snow and Peter had to find him and save him before he died of frostbite. He finds him in a bank of snow, but it is not a bank of snow, it is Vernon, wrapped in white sheets on a white bed, where he sits up and sings "We Will Always Walk Together," which I wrote for Jeffrey in the last two weeks of his life, letting Peter know his death is imminent but their friendship is eternal.

Susan and I were going with my father to his "fishing hole," the concrete pier in Boynton Beach where he would go every night to quell his loneliness. People went there to fish, drink beer, and kibitz, and he knew them all. Susan was in the back, I was driving, and he was riding shotgun. He and my mother had come to New York to see *Dream True*, but he never said anything about it. "Don't ever let anyone tell you, Rick, that you didn't write a good show," and then he proceeded to tell Susan and me about his lifelong friendship with Frankie Huber, whom my father knew since they were little boys. He needed to tell us how much he loved Frankie. It seemed he was about to weep. And I think I realized that my father might not have loved anyone in his life as much as Frankie. Frankie would visit us on Sundays when I was growing up in Island Park, and it is almost as if my dad were Frankie's older brother. He became a different person around Frankie, gentle, bringing his voice down, well-tempered.

How would I know in what way my father and Frankie loved each other? We are all so mysterious. Whatever we got at in *Dream True*, we seemed, for my father, to get at the endurance of friendship and it moved him. It felt as though my father were giving Susan and me a gift. It broke my heart because you could tell in the late evening of his life my father wanted us to know him better, to finally love him, and it wasn't hard that night, or ever again.

After the success of Audra McDonald's first album, *Way Back to Paradise*, Bob Hurwitz invited me to his office. I was scared it was going to be one of his invitations where he plays you music by all the other composers Nonesuch represents, like John Adams, and it is utterly withering. But it wasn't that day. He said, "We want to do a Ricky project. Let's do an album of your songs using all the Nonesuch singers, Audra, Dawn Upshaw, Terry McCarthy . . ." I was overjoyed! To that trio of incredible women, we added Darius de Haas, Judy Blazer, Adam Guettel, and Chris Pedro Trakas. I played piano, along with Ted Sperling, Grant Gershon, and Todd Ellison. Bob saw a video of me being interviewed underneath a huge Duncan Hannah painting of two boys standing on their hands that hangs in my living room, and said, "Let's use that for the cover."

It was the same video where Daisy Prince interviewed a bunch of us composers about what we ate for breakfast, though Daisy edited out Adam's "pussy" answer. Bob also came up with the title for the album, *Bright Eyed Joy*, which is from the Langston Hughes poem "Joy," one of the songs on the album. To me, there is, on that album, a moment that expresses everything about what was productive and meaningful about my friendship with Adam. At 10:00 one morning, we went into the studio. I played and he sang "Souvenir" so simply and sweetly it was overwhelming.

Way Back to Paradise got a lot of attention, much of it good but a lot of it mean and bitchy as well from critics who found it stuffy and boring and didn't like anything "artsy" or new, but in particular, and this is a big particular, there were a lot of comparisons. We, meaning the five songwriters on the CD, were falsely designated as a coterie, and were constantly being compared with each other, and, though the review was quite positive, Stephen Holden in the *Times* called Adam the only genius on the album, eliminating the worth of everyone else's work with a swipe of his entitled hand.

I was home visiting my family, and when I read it, it felt as if someone had thrown a boulder at my chest. And for the rest of the time with my family, I could barely speak. I had to feign happiness and hide abjectness. One of the reasons I have to be on antidepressants is that if something like that sets me off, as it did then, the pain that arises in me paralyzes me. I am overtaken by a blackness that threatens to subsume me, and it can ruin weeks at a time, or in some cases, months, and in one or two cases, years.

I was determined to prove Stephen Holden wrong. In March 2001, I was the first living composer to be presented as part of the American Songbook series at Lincoln Center. We called the concert "Bright Eyed Joy," after the new album. To show my affinity for words, at the opening of the show I had Cherry Jones come out and recite "Souvenir," the Millay poem, while Lorraine Hunt Lieberson sat on a stool and watched, so the concert began with a poem.

Then I played and Lorraine stood and sang my setting of it while Cherry listened. This happened throughout the concert, with Lorraine again singing my Jane Kenyon settings, "Otherwise" and "Let Evening Come," after Cherry speaking them. A large selection of my works, songs, and excerpts from theater pieces were spread out over a two-act evening. Ted Sperling was the musical director, and Ted, Grant Gershon, and I took turns playing the piano, along with a ten-instrument orchestra. Kristin Chenoweth, Billy Porter, Brian d'Arcy James, Adam Guettel, Judy Blazer, Camellia Johnson, Monique McDonald, and Chris Pedro Trakas were the singers.

The next morning, I met Colin Graham, who directed spectacularly John Corigliano and Bill Hoffman's *Ghosts of Versailles* at the Met, for breakfast. Something funny happened on my way to meet him at the Empire Hotel. I saw a review of our concert from *The New York Times* blowing around on the sidewalk between Sixty-Ninth and Seventieth Streets on Columbus Avenue. It was as if God had torn it out of the paper for me to see! There was a great quotation in it: "If the music of Ricky Ian Gordon had to be defined by a single quality, it would be the bursting effervescence infusing songs that blithely blur the lines between art song and the high-end Broadway music of Leonard Bernstein and Stephen Sondheim . . . It's caviar for a world gorging on pizza." It was the best review I had ever received.

I ran into Ned Rorem at a New York Festival of Song concert; he had seen that review and said I was never allowed to complain about *The New York Times* again. Colin couldn't even talk about Adam's tremulous and utterly vulnerable rendition of "We Will Always Walk Together" at the concert without crying. All the friends we had both lost, and his delicate health, this once robust muscleman who

loved his leather jackets and his motorcycle, which was beginning to
fail, made the song almost too much to bear. It was a melancholy and
wistful breakfast, the last time I would ever see him.

Soon after, we did *Bright Eyed Joy* at the Guggenheim Museum,
this time with Audra, Terry McCarthy, Darius de Haas, and Lewis
Cleale. It was part of Mary Sharp Cronson's Works & Process series.
Richard Nelson interviewed me beforehand because we were preparing our *My Life with Albertine* for Playwrights Horizons. An excerpt of
the review in *The New York Times* read, "He writes extremely singer-
friendly music that conveys the happy-sad mood swings of an open-
hearted child . . . [T]he music bubbled and cascaded like a mountain
brook after a spring rain. Over and over, one had the image of a boy
skipping ecstatically through fields and woods on a crisp April morning." I felt as if a spell had lifted.

A year after Jeffrey died, I was walking with Duncan Hannah down
Fifth Avenue when I saw something glitter on the sidewalk as I walked
past it and a voice whispered clearly in my head, "That is meant for
you." It was a clear plastic cube, a two-sided key chain. Inside, a message was inscribed over a light blue sky with a white dove flying away,
in darker blue lettering: "I am with you always."

A few weeks later, as I was walking home after performing at Joe's
Pub at 3:30 in the morning, a white dove flew out of the sky, circled
my head, and fluttered its wings in my face wildly. It would not let me
go into my building. If I tried to, it dashed itself against the glass of
the door. I had to go out and take a walk with it.

At the grief rehab where my generous friend David Brunetti paid
for me to go, where I could focus solely on grief since it was all I
could focus on anyway, I was out walking one day, when two horses
spotted me from far across a field, slowly walked toward me, and put
their heads on my shoulders, flanking me. I feel it now, the weight, the
warmth, the dampness of their wild hot breath.

In Sag Harbor, after Jeffrey's funeral, before I had to abort the weekend because being around people was unbearable, a dog heard me weeping and followed me around all day.

In the morning of the day we were going to bury Jeffrey's ashes, his mother called, asking if she could have one of his T-shirts. I had put them all into a huge black plastic bag to donate to Housing Works. I reached in and pulled one out. In bright yellow and blue letters, it said, "Still Here."

PART VI

SELECTED WORKS, PART ONE

My Process

Out of the various threads of my life, topics I have irrepressibly been drawn to, and in honor and tribute to all the artists who have excited and influenced me, I have tried to create a body of work that might be meaningful and beautiful, that might stand the test of time. The need to connect, to be heard, to be understood, is always the engine.

I have to start writing first thing in the morning. That is when I am as yet unpolluted by my own self-doubt and undistracted by the world. I have no formula for how long I write. I remember hearing somewhere that Jerome Robbins said, if you do a little bit of work every day, it accrues. That makes sense to me. Sometimes I work for an hour, sometimes three, sometimes eight. It is all about how long the inspiration or the energy lasts. I always wish I had more stamina, more engagement, and more concerted concentration, but I work with what I have.

Aaron Copland was known to have said you should leave your worktable while you are still excited about what you're doing so you are looking forward to coming back to it. When I set words to music, like poems, I have found that in any instance when I actually memorized the poem before I set it, the setting had a depth to it that came from the poem having lived in me, marinated for a while.

I always have to make peace with the fact that I hate everything I write at first, but I can't throw it out, because usually, as I add to it, I begin to like it, and as it becomes like tumbleweed growing as it rolls, it becomes the piece. Most often, the first idea is the right or correct one. I only trust that from experience.

I have to take long walks and listen to recordings of poetry, podcasts, everyone's new operas, symphonies, and lectures to get ideas, and I have to watch foreign movies over and over again. I have to keep the flame alive. It is bad for me, in general, to read about other composers and their processes, because I compare myself with everyone and come up short.

Stravinsky exercised in the morning when he got up. I try to do a little exercise each day because the better I feel about myself, the more prone I am to write. Liking myself is always an advantage. But it is elusive. It hinges on how thin I feel, which falls under how attractive I feel, how talented I feel, how praised or derided I have been; so consequently, liking myself is a welcome guest that comes and goes, and I often have to take many steps to make it happen. Anger is a great motivator; another is jealousy.

I work in order to at least try to prove myself equal to all I love and admire. Right now, as I write this, it all feels so shallow. All I can think of is Shostakovich writing under the constraints of Stalin and having to say in notes what he couldn't in words. Writing his incredible Seventh Symphony, *Leningrad*, when the Germans, instead of just invading and seizing the city, surrounded it and starved its inhabitants to death.

I recently listened to a podcast where a conductor cleverly analyzes music, interviews people, and tells rousing stories surrounding the premieres of pieces. *Leningrad*, he reports, was so stressful for the bedraggled, impoverished, and hungry players that twenty-five of them died when they were finished playing the premiere. When the music was piped out into the city, the Germans were so stirred by its astounding power they knew instinctively they were going to lose the war. I don't wish for a world that miserable, but, oh, for a time when music mattered that much, when music could stir the hearts of men, when concert halls filled with eager listeners without cell phones who couldn't wait for what the composer had to say because it was the only place they were hearing music, who booed loudly or cheered wildly, for whom music was a vital and singular conversation.

Music matters so much to me, but not necessarily to the world. You go to an opera at the Met, and half the patrons flee the hall at the end rather than applaud the singers who have just sung their guts out for them for four hours. After *Intimate Apparel*, one night I confronted a man running out before the curtain call. "You don't have time to acknowledge the performers or the performance you just sat through?" I asked. He was indignant and pushed past me.

"Nowadays the world is lit by lightning!" Tom says, at the end of Tennessee Williams's *Glass Menagerie*, before he tells Laura to blow out the candles. Oh, that it were. Nowadays the world is lit by the glow of cell phone screens, and everyone has become Alice, entering Wonderland through the blue light of eternity and getting permanently lost.

I have always liked the idea of the artists who wrote during the day so they could drink and see friends at night. Wasn't that Schubert's story? I am like that, only without the drinking now. When night falls, I am done working, and I hate the moment in rehearsals when your nights get eaten up *as well as* your days. I bitterly resent having my nights stolen. Nights are for fun.

Below are some of my carelessly *not* numbered opuses. They exist in spite of myself. They are by no means everything I have written. I have written dozens of songs and song cycles, many of them are published and recorded, but I decided to describe the evolution of some of my larger pieces because whereas the geneses of the songs are published in the songbooks, the more complicated stories of the works for the theater are not.

Before I begin, a word on Peter Randsman and my becoming a successful opera composer (well, neither starving nor dead). It is in many ways due to our rabid, feral shared obsession with opera that I do what I do. I don't need to mention him on every page for you to know and understand the intensity of our relationship on this subject. I rarely put anything out into the world without his hearing it, and it is only after his hearing it and approving, which he *always* does because he cannot believe I did this with my life, that I send it out into the battlefield for either triumph or slaughter, or some of each. No one cries more or bravos more in the presence of my work, and it is necessary oxygen for my continuance in this field.

Orpheus and Euridice 𝄢

(Premiere, October 5, 2005, New York's Rose Theater, part of the Lincoln Center for the Performing Arts American Songbook and New Visions series)

In 1994, Todd Palmer, the clarinetist, commissioned me to write a short companion piece to Franz Schubert's "Shepherd on the Rock," which he was performing frequently at that time with Kathleen Battle. Though the timing was not ideal, I didn't feel I could turn it down, because among other things Jeffrey's condition was worsening and we needed the money. At that point, Broadway Cares/Equity Fights AIDS was giving us money for groceries and someone to clean our apartment.

I wavered wildly about whether to write my own text or choose one. I jerked Todd around with various ideas and fruitless meetings, and finally, overwhelmed, I told him, to his disappointment, I didn't believe I was up to delivering what he had asked for. The next day, at 4:00 a.m., I awoke from a strange dream that was more like a vision wherein Todd was Orpheus, wearing a French sailor shirt, and his clarinet substituted for Orpheus's lyre. I went to the dining room table and wrote, "Orpheus played his pipe, music, like a cool blue stripe circling the heavens."

Sensing a bizarre energy, at 5:00 a.m. Jeffrey awoke, and I read him the already-completed text. I was sweating and wrung out. I called Todd at 8:00 a.m. to tell him that instead of a ten-minute piece I was writing him an evening-length work for the musical theater. I assume he was disappointed because it was not what he had in mind, but once we started working on it, and he grasped the scope of it, I could see he was excited.

There's a notion that a myth lives inside you subconsciously, and when your own story becomes too difficult to tell, the myth transposes itself onto you. I needed to tell the story of what was happening to Jeffrey and me at that moment. It wasn't just the Greek myth but Marcel Camus's film *Black Orpheus* that influenced me because of the freedom with which it *reinterprets* the myth.

In two acts, my *Orpheus and Euridice* is about the birth of love in act 1, culminating in a song Orpheus writes for Euridice called "I Am Part of Something Now." Act 2 is about the birth of art through suffering. Euridice is taken ill with a mysterious virus that robs her from Orpheus in small increments, as AIDS was doing to Jeffrey and me. In a section called "Death," there is a line I couldn't write until Jeffrey was gone:

> *When it came, her death, he struggled hard and long.*
> *All throughout her suffering, she'd act so strong.*
> *Ashamed, he somehow felt his own survival wrong.*

On October 31, 2001, the first version of *Orpheus and Euridice* premiered at Cooper Union as the city still smoldered from September 11. As I watched the piece, I felt it wasn't finished yet, that a concert venue wasn't its ideal form. I kept thinking about a collaboration I saw between the choreographer Trisha Brown and the baritone Simon Keenlyside, wherein Schubert's *Winterreise* was elegantly choreographed with Simon actually moving, so the song cycle was relieved of the usual singer in the crook of the piano format and became riveting theater. The performance felt refreshingly new to me. I asked Jane Moss if I could expand and reenvision my *Orpheus and Euridice* that way for Lincoln Center, and she said yes.

Lincoln Center left me with the task of finding a choreographer. I approached Christopher Wheeldon, whose work I was a fan of, but he was too busy. Someone suggested Doug Varone to me. He was animated and stimulating on the phone and sent videos of his work, which felt modern to me, muscular, energetic, and "on" the music in the way I love dance to be. After I played him the piece, he enthusiastically agreed to do it. Lincoln Center gave us everything we wanted and needed.

Before the premiere in October 2005, they sponsored a workshop. Doug's company, along with Todd Palmer, the soprano Elizabeth Futral, and the pianist Melvin Chen, went into a rehearsal room for a week to explore how the piece might move. All three musicians were going to be required to dance. Todd, having been a figure skater, moved beautifully, Elizabeth, a swan, was the epitome of grace, and Melvin, with his lithe, almost crane-like frame, moved sexily, with authority and confidence. Doug filmed the week to see what he might want to use later. For the production, he decided he wanted everything on the stage to dance, including the grand piano, so a special floor was installed, and the white piano on wheels whirled about the stage like a member of the company. As for Todd, I have never seen an instrumentalist enact such miracles. Along with dancing, flying, moving, and acting beautifully, he played the piece from memory. Allen Moyer designed a lovely box made out of scrim, the gauzy fabric that is opaque until it is lit from behind, to house the piece at the Rose Theater, making it look ghostly and evanescent, Robert Wierzel lit it with fittingly dreamy colors, and Jane Greenwood's costumes made it all look like something between a painting by Fragonard and the opening of Shakespeare's *Macbeth*.

Watching it come to life was one of the most extraordinary moments of my life. After we opened, Peter G. Davis, writing in *New York* magazine, said:

What began as a modest request from clarinetist Todd Palmer for a companion to Schubert's ballad *The Shepherd on the Rock* eventually developed into a 70-minute theater piece that, like the Schubert song, calls for soprano, clarinet, and piano but also adds a troupe of dancers. The soprano doubles as Euridice and a narrator, Orpheus exchanges his lyre for a clarinet with no loss of musical eloquence, and eight dancers represent the Furies, blessed spirits, and, in the end, a moved audience of wondering humanity. Both Gordon's text and music are couched in an accessible idiom of disarming lyrical directness, a cleverly disguised *faux* naïveté that always resolves dissonant situations with grace and a sure sense of dramatic effect—the mark of a born theater composer.

We won an Obie Award.

The opera, one of my most successful chamber pieces, has been performed in swimming pools, cemeteries, abandoned factories, and art museums.

Inauspicious Beginnings and *The Grapes of Wrath* |▤

The night that Dale Johnson and Floyd Anderson, the artistic director and the artists relations and planning director of Minnesota Opera, came to New York to talk to me about writing an opera based on
The Grapes of Wrath, I needed to look my best, and I had to make up a
story in order to be home by ten, because I had hired a Black hustler
to come over for my very first paid sex experience and that excited me
more than writing an opera based on the Steinbeck classic—which
only made me want to vomit and scream "I can't" into the heavens and
beg God to kill me before I had to do it.

I lied twice. The second lie was that I told them I had to reread the
book, when I had never read it.

When my buzzer rang at ten, I began to get nervous, sweaty nervous. He walked in, and he was not my type at all. As we've already
established, I have father issues. This guy looked like one in his photo,
but in real life he was very delicate and somewhat effeminate, and I
was turned off right away, or at least my fantasy was dashed. He was
pretty, not rugged handsome, the way he looked in his particularly
"straight acting" photo for someone who was quite the contrary. But
he was nice and experienced and could see what was going on immediately. We had a lovely chat, and he left without even making me pay,
which to this day I find amazing. So, it was sex "on spec." Now, that's
a good businessman. He even told me, "Yaw so cute. Wher' you been
hiding yo'self?" Thinking about it now, I'm surprised we didn't go out
for herb tea.

Dale and Floyd approached me for this project because, when I decided I wanted to write operas, I sent out a CD of sixteen of my songs
with various friends singing them. Apparently, because of Lauren

Flanigan singing my setting of Emily Dickinson's poem "Will There Really Be a 'Morning'?," along with the director Eric Simonson, who had been in Frank Galati's play version of the novel on Broadway and who suggested the idea for an opera, they felt my language was right for the piece and I should be the composer.

There are times in my life when I knew from how a book shook and awakened me that I would never be the same again. Dostoevsky's *Brothers Karamazov* was one, Camus's *Plague*, Shusaku Endo's *Deep River*, Evelyn Waugh's *Brideshead Revisited*, F. Scott Fitzgerald's *Tender Is the Night*, Willa Cather's *My Ántonia*, and Proust's *Swann's Way*. When I was finished reading *The Grapes of Wrath*, I knew I had to say yes to making an opera out of it, because it was bigger than me. It felt like fate.

The two commissioning companies were Minnesota, where it would premiere, and Utah. I had to find a librettist to write it with me. Utah wanted me to use a local poet, and they had her send me some of her ideas. She was talented, and they weren't bad, but I knew I needed a seasoned theater writer. *The Grapes of Wrath* is a huge book, and I wanted to make sure whoever wrote the libretto had a good handle on dramaturgy, theatricality, beats, and spacing. If it got bogged down in poetic language, it could end up being ponderous, or intellectual, which I didn't want.

I asked Michael Korie to collaborate with me. We were working on a musical of Sarah Schulman's novel *Shimmer*, but it wasn't going well. Musicals are difficult beasts to tackle. Getting the proportions correct, the balance between the book and the songs, is perilous. After a difficult workshop, it was clear we needed to disband. I learned through that experience, though, that Michael was able to take whole chapters and lyricize them in a way that felt dramatically viable and utterly singable.

His sense of structure and his mastery of language were so strong I could look at the page and hear the music in my head. Michael lives around the block from me, and I ran into him in the corner bodega. "How would you feel about doing an opera of Steinbeck's *The Grapes of Wrath*?" I asked, and he answered, "Are you kidding?" as if I had asked him how he'd feel about planting a bomb in a bank. I said, "Why don't you just reread it?" Assuming, unlike me, he had probably already read it. When he was done, he said yes, because, for one thing, he saw a clear three-act biblical structure, Exodus, Canaan, and Flood, and could see how he would dramatize it.

The Utah team balked, worried that Michael was perhaps too urbane and New York Jewish (they did not say that, but I'm sure they were thinking it) for such a folksy American book. Michael worked on act 1 over the summer at the MacDowell Colony, an artists' retreat in New Hampshire, with September as his deadline.

Before he left, we discussed a few things. One was Steinbeck's construction of the novel. Chapters alternate between the story of the Joads and other families like them, their exodus from barren land and ruined lives toward a promised land that doesn't exist, and the interstitial chapters illustrating a country that could allow this to happen to people, through greed, corruption, antipathy toward the poor, and passing the buck, basically, the government's complete disregard for them.

Think children shot by assault weapons when they go to school and the politicians who crow they are pro-life doing nothing. Think self-obsessed despots with ambitions that overshadow any morality they might ever have had. Think migrant children separated from their parents and caged at the border. Think Putin and Ukraine right now.

Neither the John Ford movie nor the Frank Galati play adaptation attempted to dramatize those chapters, so, we decided, with the huge chorus we were given to work with, there would be those "in between" chapters, in the voice of Steinbeck. I wanted it to feel like a "ballad" opera, or a musical, with set pieces, choruses, arias, duets, trios, and dances that all felt like songs, because the book felt to me so much like the people's novel, simple enough for anyone to understand and enter, and I didn't want to write something so complex it would alienate the people it was meant for. Opera is considered elitist in this country. Ironically, this is an opera about people who could never afford to see one. I wanted to see if we could somehow transcend these barriers.

That September in 2003, when the folks from Minnesota and

Utah and I reconvened at Michael's apartment, Michael had a bound sample of act 1 for each of us. It was gorgeously illustrated, something Michael, with his impeccable and discerning eye, is brilliant at. It looked like a work of art. We were stunned just staring at it. On page 1, following a list of characters with an accompanying photo Michael had dug up from one archive or another, perfectly evocative of what they should look like, was an image of a beautiful green cornfield in the rain.

The first chapter of the book is all about the end of rain, the conditions that created the drought, the stripping of the prairies out of greed, and then the disastrous Dust Bowl because there was nothing to hold the dirt down.

PROLOGUE—AN OPEN FIELD

The curtain rises to the sound of soft rain. The stage is filled with a growing field of green corn in the morning mist, dozens of stalks each shoulder height to a man. It is a bucolic vision of the past. A woman appears standing among the stalks, then a man, Oklahoma tenant sharecroppers of the early 1930s. More and more appear remembering how it was before the rain stopped.

WOMAN TWO

The last time there was rain
I smelt it in the air,
and filled a pail to wash my hair.

WOMAN ONE

My kids was in the yard.
I made 'em play inside.
My smallest one, the boy—he cried.

MAN ONE

The last time there was rain
the rich red earth was soaked,
'n up them baby corn shoots poked.

MAN TWO

The spill-off from the ditch
made gullies in the ground,
and birds which ate the bugs
made such a pretty sound.

The rain stops. The sun comes out.

ALL

When the last rain came
and the sky turned blue
it was gone for good,
only no one knew.

We enjoyed the shade
with a cherry fizz
when it's warm, like Oklahoma is . . .

In the course of the number, the rains stop, the corn turns brown, there is a dust storm, and by the end there is no corn, just a stage full of croppers staring hollow-eyed, straight ahead. They sing,

At last the wind died down
when everything was ruined,
like bein' on the moon . . . marooned.

After reading through the prologue, we were confidently wide-eyed and dazzled, gobsmacked. Michael had found a way to keep the simplicity of the text, but animate it by giving it to the characters. Whereas in the book the people are often inarticulate, muttering one-word answers like "yup," Michael gave the characters the eloquence and the elegance that Steinbeck gave the prose. I was so inspired I went home that day and began "The Last Time There Was Rain," and within a week it was done.

I had to change the way I wrote for *The Grapes of Wrath*. Until then, I wrote with a pencil and paper at the piano. I could usually play and sing my entire score from cover to cover. But this opera was a whole new thing with necessities of its own, and I knew my little pencil and paper thing wouldn't be enough.

I had always skirted the margins where computer technology was concerned. But I knew with *Grapes* I needed to learn Finale, one of the complicated music writing software programs. I could see, by what Michael was doing with the libretto, there was so much simultaneity on the page I felt I had to hear what I was doing at all times because the potential for collision, or unintended dissonance, was huge.

Teaching myself Finale with what I feel has always been a learning disability meant many times I punched my desk, my computer, screamed, and raised my fists against God. I am not new to this kind of behavior. There was a period in my life when I was coaching singers and playing auditions, and the profusion of desperate messages on my phone machine every day drove me so crazy I tore it out of the wall and threw it out the window. Luckily, I threw it into the courtyard behind my building, or I might be writing this from prison, because the velocity I threw that thing with would have easily decapitated someone.

This was pre-sobriety, so I might have been hungover. Eventually, Finale became intuitive and second nature to me. My files were rich with mock orchestrations, huge choral sounds, and soloists soaring on top. I began playing my operas for people by having them sit in front of my computer and watch the music scroll by while I sang all the parts, because the sounds were generated by using samples of either real solo instruments or whole sections, strings, brass, woodwinds, even percussion, and I could give a pretty good sense of what the opera would sound like later when it was orchestrated.

When I gave presentations, I would hook my computer up to the technology in any auditorium, the sound came through the sound system, a movie screen became my computer screen with the music scrolling by, like "follow the bouncing ball," and I sang along on a mic. It was liberating to get up from the piano. Occasionally, I still presented from the piano, but I usually needed more than two hands, because I used two grand staves, meaning two pianos instead of one, so I had to get someone to play with me. Basically, my music got bigger and fatter.

Even now, when I orchestrate something like *Green Sneakers*, which is just string quartet and piano, or *Ellen West*, which is the same configuration but with an added bass, or *A Coffin in Egypt* and *The House Without a Christmas Tree*, which are both chamber orchestrations, though you have to spend enormous amounts of time getting all the markings, the precise tempi and dynamics you want, in the music, because the computer is only responding to the precise information you are feeding it, you can give everyone involved, and anyone you want to interest, a *really* good idea of what the final product will be. The files are terrific learning tools as well, because singers can hear what will be under their vocal lines and conductors can get a sense of the piece as a whole. *The Grapes of Wrath* was epic, so I had to think epically.

Magical things happen when you are collaborating, coincidences where you are finishing each other's sentences. If a collaboration is working, it can happen a lot.

Toward the end of act 1, there is a moment when the Joads' pregnant daughter, Rosasharn, and her husband, Connie Rivers, are sitting on a highway overpass with their legs dangling. In the first draft of the libretto, it was just a moment for Connie to be excited about the Lincoln Zephyrs, his favorite automobile, whizzing by. Having no experience with highways, Connie has only seen the Lincoln Zephyr in photos, and he is awestruck. I loved what Michael had done, but I thought it wasn't enough. I knew the moment needed to evolve into a love duet. It comes at a pivotal moment, the eleven o'clock moment of the act, when all the themes are burbling and waiting to explode. We needed to see who these two people, the lovers, are to each other. We needed a demonstration of love and a "love" theme.

I had yet to declare and shape Rosasharn's theme, and her pregnancy represents all the hopes and dreams of mankind, the nascent, the unborn. She is Mary Magdalene. What is she awed by? Michael agreed, even grateful I brought it up. He came back the next day with

"One Star," a lyric of such crystalline tenderness and beauty it was clear Michael had been struck by lightning.

While Connie sees the Lincoln Zephyrs, Rosasharn sees one star up in the sky, the glittering receptacle of all she hopes for, the star of Bethlehem:

> *Sometimes, when faith ain't quite enough,*
> *Nights when the moon don't shine,*
> *When you can't see your nose*
> *Through a maze of shadows,*
> *Heaven hangs out a sign.*
> *One star, one star, one small star . . .*
> *That's mine.*

I went into a trance writing this duet, and Michael seemed genuinely moved when it was finished. You want to please your collaborator; if you sense even a glimmer of disappointment, you go straight back to the drawing board until it's right, because they *must* like it.

I wrote a prelude to act 3 because I always hope I'm going to have a prelude, an interlude, or an overture, but the story always takes over and there is rarely room. When I write my own libretti, like *Orpheus and Euridice* and *Green Sneakers*, I build them into the structure from the start.

Workshopping is going through a series of steps to get the piece on its feet, see how it works, what it needs, what it doesn't need, and so on. *The Grapes of Wrath* is so big we were never able to workshop more than an act at a time. One helpful thing, though, was Utah insisted in the contract that we do three workshops over three consecutive summers, and two of those would require a full orchestra.

Because of the size of the task, when Bruce Coughlin and I orchestrated the opera, he did half, and I did half. Bruce has been a great friend, a brother really, since we worked on *States of Independence* in the early 1990s. We think similarly, coming at the task from the same angle, so gratefully, the piece can sound seamless. With our added color instruments, banjo, harmonica, guitar, and sax, the only way to know if everything balanced out was to hear it on a stage with the singers, which this opportunity afforded us. Then we could make adjustments, with plenty of time to make them.

If I had my way, I'd mic all my operas. I believe younger audiences, because they have grown up with headphones, come to live performance with ears that are accustomed to amplification. They are not used to having to lean forward in their seats to hear. Not that I object to exposing them to new ways of hearing, but I guess I have to admit I like amplification as well.

When I was growing up, opera was a less cosmetic affair. Opera singers came in all shapes and sizes, and most of the time they were trained to fill huge houses with huge voices. Even in the theater, Ethel Merman didn't need a mic. I don't know if vocal pedagogy has changed, or the style of singing, but many gorgeous voices are not necessarily built for ringing through the four-thousand-seat Metropolitan Opera House, and I am not opposed to their having a little help.

Many of the grander, more heroic operas, which cannot be done if there aren't voices big enough available to sing them, could be more *readily* available if singers with slightly smaller voices just had a little help. And it would be useful for stamina as well as nuance. John Adams requires it in all his operas; it's in the contract. Why? Not to shame singers for not singing loud enough, but because it is part of his aesthetic. He can orchestrate in the big epic way he does, using electronics, and though this requires a sound department to balance it all out, which most opera companies neither have nor can afford, and I sympathize, it is spectacularly exciting when it works.

Also, I like being able to hear every word! I just feel like, hey, folks, it's the twenty-first century, we have amplification, get over it. Let's use it, even judiciously. In this way, I think all opera houses should be set up for sound and sound design, and I hope that is a wave of the future because I actually think it is key to building new audiences. When we did *The Grapes of Wrath* at Carnegie Hall, narrated by Jane Fonda, who began to cry at the first rehearsal when she uttered the words "A young Tom Joad" because her father, Henry, had played him in the classic John Ford movie and she was doing this to honor him, we had mics, and because of it we were able to mix an all-star cast of opera singers with theater singers and create something that I felt was truly eclectic and suited to the piece. The sixty-piece orchestra could play out and sound as epic as we meant it to without overwhelming anyone, and no one had to push to be heard. I was in heaven. I'm not saying that all opera should now be amplified, just that if the composer's aesthetic requires it as part of his vision, it should be by choice, and he or she should not be castigated for it.

Every time a mic is used in an opera house, another critic comes forward to write about how dispiriting it is and what a corruption of the art form it is. How do we know Mozart, Beethoven, and Handel wouldn't have used micing if it had been available to them then? Would Bach really be upset to hear Glenn Gould playing his works on a piano rather than a harpsichord? The piano is a magnificent orchestral instrument, and I believe he would have welcomed all the overtones and colors. The harpsichord and its exigencies made his music hard to play because it has to be completely fingered so the counterpoint is crystalline and clean, so yes, the music is authentic on a harpsichord but, I believe, heightened on a piano, and I think Bach would have loved it. Composers write for what is available to them. The more the better.

In 2008, the economy went belly up. Everyone's endowments were shrinking, and it was no longer feasible to do an opera as big as ours, so each time it was done, it was different, smaller in some way. Luckily, it was recorded live in Minnesota, even if the guys recording it only placed mics here and there, and not always where people were singing, but we take what we can get. *The Grapes of Wrath* also came just before everyone started filming and streaming their operas, so that too is heartbreaking.

And for the record, when we did our Carnegie Hall version, there was talk of filming it for PBS, but they wouldn't do it unless we had more than one performance, and MasterVoices, or the Collegiate Chorale, as it was called in 2010, could barely afford one.

I want to tell you a fantasy I have. The room run (the last time you run the entire piece in the rehearsal room before you move onto the stage) for *Grapes* was completely overwhelming, so much so that I remember wishing people could have seen it that way. I have a fantasy of doing *The Grapes of Wrath*, our original version, in a huge rehearsal space for as many people as could fit, no orchestra, just the two pianos we rehearsed with. I want people to see the opera like that someday, surrounded by the story, with the singers so close to the audience their slightest facial expressions are discernible, like a movie.

In 2014, when we were rehearsing *27* in St. Louis, Phyllis Brissenden, a patron of the opera company who left it millions of dollars when she died, came over to me at a party and mischievously started singing "The Last Time There Was Rain," which was surprising and delightful. It was her way of introducing herself to me. Later that night, I was talking to Timothy O'Leary, the general director of the company, and Phyllis, inserting herself into the conversation, said, "Tim, if you produce *The Grapes of Wrath*, I will pay for it."

A year later, the director Jim Robinson, who is also the artistic director of Opera Theatre of St. Louis, where he directed the world premiere of my *27*, heard Michael and I were thinking of creating a smaller version of the opera. Glimmerglass approached us first but seemed to drop the ball, so he got Opera Theatre of St. Louis to commission the new version, and Phyllis underwrote it. It was a great opportunity, because rather than our having to scramble around figuring out what we could cut to come in on time, Michael and I got to rethink the piece entirely and ten years after the premiere really see it differently.

We made it two acts instead of three. Letting go of things we loved broke our hearts, but we were ready to see what a new, smaller version would look like. Jim, along with Allen Moyer, the original set designer in Minnesota, came up with a brilliant concept. It would be staged in a soup kitchen during the Depression.

The set looked incredibly authentic, like an American Legion, a town hall, or a VFW. The preshow, while audiences were assembling in the theater, was people entering onstage from the pouring rain in James Schuette's wonderfully depressing costumes, moodily lit by

Christopher Akerlind to look like an Edward Hopper painting, slowly lining up for soup and taking their seats at the enormous room-length tables while huge vats were rolled around and soup was served.

It looked so real, like a documentary about the Depression happening on the stage. When the lights dimmed, Bob Orth, who played Uncle John, the Joad whom Ma eventually charges with the task of burying Rosasharn's dead baby, goes over to an old upright piano that looks as if it has been in the hall since it was built and begins picking out the first few notes of "The Last Time There Was Rain," as if a rehearsal were starting. The orchestra creeps in with the solo trumpet and strings, and everyone becomes the sharecroppers singing about their ruined land and lives.

It was chilling. At the end, when the words "At last the wind died down / when everything was ruined, / like bein' on the moon . . . marooned" were sung by the dead-in-the-eyes bewildered croppers, including the Joads, they all, at the same time, blew into their metal soup bowls, which, instead of soup, were filled with dust, and the whole stage became the Dust Bowl. It was a moment of incredibly inspired stage magic.

Writing an opera is like constructing a building. You create brick by brick, fit them together and constantly shift them until the scale is right. Each time you create a new motif, you keep a list of them on the side and sew the opera together with various iterations of them. Following my instincts, I first found all the moments in the libretto that had the most heat for me, the ones I could just look at on the page and know what to do.

At the beginning of writing a piece, you have to get past the panic about the immensity of the task that awaits you and just start accruing notes. Little by little, the more you have, you slowly begin to feel assured you can do it, and you feel better, even empowered.

After I wrote "The Last Time There Was Rain," I gravitated to the scene in Uncle John's cabin, where Ma sits in front of the woodstove with a box of the Joad family belongings, mementos, heirlooms—in short, treasures—and decides which things they will have room for on the truck and which ones they won't. Those she decides they won't, she throws into the fire. Michael titled the scene "Empty Room," and the aria is called "Us." Here is an excerpt: .

MA

> *This dead land—is us.*
> *All its hardship—is us.*
> *And the flood years.*
> *And the drought years.*
>
> *And the dust years—all us.*
> *When the owner threw us off—is us.*
> *When the tractor hit the house—is us.*
> *The table that we sold.*
> *The cupboard and the chairs.*
> *The tubs and tanks, the piggybanks.*
>
> *This corncob pipe, Lord knows, I used to cuss.*
> *A postcard from a fair.*
> *A Pilgrim's Progress book.*
> *Feathers for a hat I didn't wear.*
> *A child's lock of hair . . . that's us.*

This was the first aria I wrote. Everything about it, including the way Michael illustrated the two pages of the scene with a photograph of the insides of an empty cropper's cabin, roiled my insides. I knew what could immediately become music. Once I had "Us" and "The Last Time There Was Rain," I had the first bricks, meaning, I already had a plethora of usable motifs.

Next, I set Tom Joad's wonderfully jocular "I Keep My Nose Clean," which he sings when he says goodbye to the guard at McAlester prison, where he is out on parole after four years of a seven-year sentence for stabbing a man in self-defense. Next, Casy, the deposed preacher, drunkenly strums a sleazy plaint on his ukulele, "A Naked Tree A-wastin' in the Sun," when Tom comes upon him.

I was building the house character by character, motif by motif, and the score slowly came together over years. After urging Michael to expand Connie Rivers's "Zephyr" moment into "One Star," I felt I was on my way, no longer alone but co-creating. Me and God were doing our thing.

Deanne Meek, the great mezzo-soprano who was singing Ma Joad, was incredibly exacting and would not make a move on the stage if it didn't feel real to her, authentic. There was a lyric in "Us" when Ma Joad, finding a vase in the box among the family's possessions, sings at the end of a verse, "Oh, look, Here's a vase, that's us."

Every time she came to it, rehearsal would grind to a halt, and we'd have to have a lengthy discussion where she'd squint her eyes and look at us with utter confusion as if we had handed her a turd. "A vase?" she'd say. It made perfect sense to me, but she simply could not make it work.

Of course, Michael and I pegged her as "a pain in the ass," but finally, one night, after rehearsal, Michael went home and wrote, "A child's lock o' hair, that's us." She could barely get it out the next day, her voice breaking the first time she sang it, and we never had that discussion again.

At our very first rehearsal, Eric Simonson, our director, whose young wife had just died from cancer, leaving him alone with their little boy, gave an extremely stirring and inspiring speech, imbuing everyone in the room with the need for truth and authenticity. It was as if he put a magic spell over the proceedings, and everyone was desperate to make the opera real and meaningful. We were doing it for Eric, to lift him on our angel wings and hold him aloft for the entire process.

Eric and Doug Varone, our choreographer, watched rehearsals together, one eliciting the performances and the other making it move. There is a moment when what you have written suddenly has a life of its own. It begins to belong to the world more than to you, with the capacity to get its own needs met, almost as if it thanks you for birthing it, then nudges you away. The day the truck was assembled, it was wheeled onto the stage, and when the Joads got on it, setting out, full of hope, for California, singing "The Plenty Road," the hair on the back of my neck stood up. "The Joads are here!" I thought. "This is real!"

One scene, born independent of Steinbeck's novel, bears recounting because it was a risk and it paid off. In the book, Steinbeck has Noah, the oldest Joad son, born "slow" from Pa's having to pull him out at birth, walk down the river on his own and disappear. We never hear from him again. Michael concocted a way to fill out his story to end act 2, in a brilliant stroke of theatrical genius.

"Hooverville" is the nadir for the Joads, a squalid camp of lean-tos and tarp tents. No one has enough food or water, they are filthy, and everyone is at the end of their rope. Noah tries to help put up the tent, but Al Joad blows up at him:

> *Leave the tent be, pea brain!*
> *Ya'll tangle them ropes an' strangle y'self!*
> *Honestly, sometimes! . . .*
> *You're my big brother, Noah, an' I love you . . .*
> *but you're dead weight.*
> *Extra freight. Ballast on a sinkin' ship*
> *I hate to say't.*

Noah asks,
> *What's ballast?*

Al replies,
> *What weigh us down and don' earn a cent.*
> *No wonder we can't make a dent in California;*
> *two kids, one numbskull, and one pregnant gal.*
> *They see us coming 'n' WHAM!*
> *Up goes that wall.*

A fight breaks out in Hooverville and Tom is badly cut. Ma, exasperated, barks at Noah,

Be a help! Take this bucket down to the creek and fetch some water.
For once, just once in your life, Noah, think how to help yer fambly!

Noah is at the creek in the dark. The only story he knows is the story of his namesake, saving all the animals in the ark when the rains came. Ecstatically, he comes up with a plan for saving his family: He'll be one less mouth to feed. Instead of filling the bucket with water, he remembers "ballast," the word Al taught him, fills it with stones, and drowns himself. As he is dying, he remembers Ma, singing to him as a baby:

Dream beautiful,
freely as a herd of horses runnin' wild.
No innocence.
as the dream of a simple child.

Noah's bucket slowly falls out of his hand, floating to the bottom as Hooverville burns to the ground.

One week, Doug disappeared into a rehearsal room with the entire chorus, and no one was allowed in to see what they were working on until they were ready.

Rosasharn gives birth to a stillborn baby, and Ma begs Uncle John to bury it. He refuses, because it reminds him of when his own wife and child died in childbirth. Ma pleads with him,

My girl is lying at death's door!
IF she makes it,
it won't do her no good to see it!

Ma hands him a shovel. When she goes inside, he slams the shovel down, screaming, "No! This child ain't goin' in the ground!"

And putting the baby in a plum crate, he sends it down the river, wailing, "Go down, little dead Moses, show 'em what they done! Go down and ROT!"

When Doug emerged, he had choreographed the entire chorus into a magnificent, shattering representation of the river, rippling like waves, rushing like currents, rising and falling like the tide, rushing the baby downstream. Onstage, with Wendall Harrington's projected film of a rushing river, it was almost unbearably powerful.

Eric had everyone leave the room when he staged the end: Rosasharn suckling a starving Black man with the milk meant for her dead baby. He knew Kelly Kaduce, our Rosasharn, was going to need space to do it a few times and get the tears out, and tears there were, aplenty, but she was sublime, staring into the sunlight through the slats in the barn.

She looked up and across the barn, and her lips came together and smiled mysteriously.

On opening night, February 10, 2007, at the Ordway Center for the Performing Arts in St. Paul, it was forty-eight below zero. It hurt to be outside and was even deadly. There was a big sit-down dinner at 5:00 p.m. in a beautiful bank lobby for the creators, the patrons, the critics, and the VIPs who were there from around the world. Needless to say, I was not hungry. I knew that the course of the evening was going to determine my fate for a while, and I was so nervous I could have vomited right there at the table. The evening was spectacular. We got ovation after ovation, and I felt as if I had taken good LSD. This was a "good" trip! My friends Ted and Mary Jo Shen had flown a bunch of my friends in from New York to be there, Diane and Brian Sutherland, Jim Mahady and Jeff Richardson, Don and Leslie Katz, Joseph Thalken, and Laurie and Oskar Eustis. Elizabeth Futral flew in on her own, as did Jake Heggie.

The next morning the company threw a huge brunch for all the visitors, and slowly the reviews started coming in. In general, they were great! Jane Moss called to ask me if I had seen *Musical America* yet. "No," I said, worried she was calling to tell me to brace myself, but their review had called it "the great American opera." Perhaps the review I was most excited about was Alex Ross in *The New Yorker*, because, well, it's Alex Ross and *The New Yorker*. For about two weeks I got calls every day from the fact-checker at the magazine asking me if this and that were correct, and finally I said, "Look, is this review good? Because I am certainly giving you a hell of a lot of my time." To which he replied, "If it wasn't good, I wouldn't be calling you." Kevin and I went on vacation in Ireland, and I checked the internet in the hotel one morning.

The review was great.

But, you know, not *everyone* liked it.

Green Sneakers ▐▬

In 1996, Jeffrey came to Houston for the world premiere of *The Tibetan Book of the Dead*, the opera I wrote for him to help him die. Our friend Tom helped him pack the day before, weaving his clothes, medicines, and toiletries into a remarkable latticework evoking Jeffrey's excitement and the tender protectiveness he naturally elicited.

David Gockley, the artistic director of Houston Grand Opera, took me to pick him up at the airport. I was shocked by how much weight he had lost in two weeks. We needed a cart to get him to the exit.

Immediately, everything in Houston made him sick; we went to a Mexican restaurant, and he trembled, his teeth chattering from the air-conditioning, the heat outside was oppressive, and the humidity smothering. I wore moisturizer to bed the first night, and when I got up in the middle of the night, there was a note on the mirror: "Please don't moisturize with scented cream." The slightest fragrance could be deadly, and after weeks away I had forgotten, casually enacting my nightly ritual. He needed new sneakers. In the department store he started coughing so hard passing through the cologne department I thought he would die. We quickly bought the sneakers, and I rushed him back to my apartment. He was gasping for air. When I called the opera company to tell them what was happening, I couldn't speak; no words came out. Then I started crying so hard Jeffrey had to comfort *me*. We had to send him home the next morning. I wrapped him in a light blue-black blanket like he was an Easter egg for the flight home. Not until it opened in Philadelphia could he see it, a blue dust mask covering his face. After Jeffrey died, I stared out from our bed in shock, focusing on those sneakers in the closet, and wrote about that time in a set of poems called *Green Sneakers*.

In 2006, when Jake Heggie and I were doing joint concerts of our music, a tour that included Carnegie's Weill Recital Hall, the Ravinia Festival, the Library of Congress, and Hertz Hall in Berkeley, California, I met the flutist Eugenia Zukerman, who played with us. She invited me to be the 2008 composer in residence at Bravo! Vail Valley Music Festival in Vail, Colorado, requesting a ten-to-twenty-minute piece for the Miami String Quartet, who would also be there that summer.

Because it was a co-commission with Utah Opera, after *The Grapes of Wrath* premiered in Minnesota, it was scheduled to go next to Salt Lake City. Before we opened, meditating in my room one morning, I remembered the *Green Sneakers* poems and saw the whole piece in my head. Once you see it, you have to write it.

I worried about what I was going to tell Genie, because I knew it wasn't going to be ten to twenty minutes. I called Jake. He said, "Don't worry, just write the piece, and read her the poems later." That year, I went to Ucross, my favorite arts colony, in Wyoming, to compose the music. It was excruciating. I would wake up in the middle of the night sweaty and terrified. The poems, written in a fever, are so bald-faced, plainspoken, and unfettered I knew any falseness in the music would stick out like a sore thumb. I had to get it right.

Finally, when I was finished, I called Genie, told her the situation, and read her the poems. Without flinching, she not only assented but assigned me my own theater to do it in.

I knew whom I wanted to premiere the piece along with the Miami String Quartet. Jesse Blumberg was the baritone who'd played Rosasharn's erstwhile husband, Connie, in *The Grapes of Wrath*, and I loved his performance in the piece. Jesse is the kind of performer who is so real, so honest on the stage, he looks as if it were happening for him, and your eye is drawn to him because of his ease and naturalness. I knew Jesse was straight; in fact he was married at the time to Rita Donahue, who was one of the beautiful stars of the Mark Morris Dance Group. But I knew it would help me if I knew I was writing it for him. If I am excited by the artists who are going to perform my piece, it makes the writing easier. I sent Jesse the poems, asking him to respond honestly: Did he feel he could be convincing singing these texts? He wrote back right away and said he'd be honored.

Something happened the day before the premiere that was very unsettling. The critic from *The Denver Post* and *Opera Today*, Wes Blomster, came to the dress rehearsal and completely unraveled. I had to hold him while he shook and sobbed. This piece is a direct container for a palpable grief.

The next day we opened. In the lobby, afterward, the whole audience stayed, and everyone shared with remarkable honesty their stories of grief and loss. Wes wrote, "Gordon Creates Masterpiece with 'Green Sneakers.'"

PART VII

LARGER THAN LIFE: OBSESSIONS

John O'Shaughnessy 𝄆

There is indeed in every artist a wanton and treacherous proneness
to side with beauty.

—from Myfanwy Piper's libretto for Benjamin Britten's adaptation of
Thomas Mann's *Death in Venice*

The high school musical that year was *Fiddler on the Roof.* I was a
sophomore. I was determined to get a role in it, after the scarring
heartbreak of the year before when I lost the role of Patrick Dennis in
Mame to Barry Rosenfeld. I belted "Misty," accompanying myself at
the piano, which worked to get me cast as Louis in *The King and I* at
Camp Lenape when I was eight, so I thought it would bring me luck. I
was cast as Perchik, the young revolutionary who steals Hodel's heart.
The show was directed by the high school science teacher, Arlene
Newman, who had a very low voice and was at least as masculine as
my father or Arnold Schwarzenegger. She cast Fradi Sadow as Tevye.
Fradi was also a teacher, and she and Arlene lived together. Fradi was
also quite masculine, with a sturdy Buster Brown bowl cut, and consequently completely believable as Tevye, maybe even more so than
Zero Mostel or Topol. Arlene was always telling me to be less light in
my loafers, but it was a lot to compete with Fradi, who made *everyone*
onstage seem light in their loafers.

There was an absolutely stunning girl in the show named Gloria
Fusillo. She was Miss West Hempstead, the head of the cheerleading
team, and everything else it is possible to be as the glittering female
star of a high school that was a quarter of a mile long. I could tell
she liked me, and I loved looking at her, plus, I was flattered by her

attention, so I asked her out. We went on a double date to Enrico and Paglieri's for spaghetti. You would expect to see Gloria laughing in an olive oil or wine commercial, stomping on grapes in a huge wooden vat. She was a raven-haired, olive-skinned Italian, warm and intelligent, with a smoky voice and a glittering smile. We made out that night in the backseat on the way to take her home. I put my tongue in her mouth like putting a toe in the water, to feel the temperature. I knew instinctively a kiss was supposed to be accompanied by desire, and desire was missing for me. By now, I knew I was gay, but I didn't want to be. I wanted to be successful at being with girls. It felt like the only way to be happy and respectable in the world. It was difficult because Gloria radiated integrity, and I knew it would be awful to hurt her, so I decided to keep seeing her.

My friend Peter had moved over the bridge to Long Beach. All of our trips to the opera paid off. It turns out Peter had a voice, an extraordinary one, shockingly beyond his years. We sort of discovered it together.

We were constantly fooling around at the piano, me playing and both of us singing. One day, we were at my house, and I was playing through the score Uncle Sid had given me of *Porgy and Bess*. Peter started singing "Bess, You Is My Woman Now," imitating Lawrence Tibbett, the Porgy on my recording, the one where Helen Jepson was Bess. This would never happen now and could only happen in a recording then because Lawrence Tibbett and Helen Jepson were both white as snow. It turned out Peter, who thought he was just fooling around, had an incredible and enormous voice, completely anomalous with his age and physical appearance.

My mother was washing dishes. She walked out of the kitchen astonished, a dish towel in her hands, and said, "You've got it, baby." With a look of complete disbelief on her face, she said, "Peter, you have a real voice. That is a real voice, sweetheart. Do it again." From then on, Peter was the singer, and I, the pianist. At this point, Peter's graduation from "different" to "special" was cemented, as was mine, and we were never taunted by Sheila's friends again. We were no longer just "fags"; we had somehow become "exotics."

Like our friend Richie, Peter got a nose job, a necessity, he thought, in preparation for what he felt sure was his rising star in the American musical theater. But first, he was the star of all of his high school musicals. This year it was *Brigadoon*. Peter played Tommy Albright, the American on a hunting trip in Scotland who becomes lost in the woodlands with his friend Jeff Douglas. They happen upon Brigadoon, a miraculously blessed village that rises out of the mists every hundred years for only a day.

I took Gloria and we also went with another friend of mine from West Hempstead, Charlie Buttacavoli, who could have been comfortably cast in *The Sopranos*, and he and Gloria perfectly represented the Italian contingent of West Hempstead High School. Peter had a crush on Charlie. Charlie was straight, though also enamored of boys like Peter and me who were cultured and colorful.

The lights dimmed, and we sat up to watch the show. It was always a little hard for me to watch Peter because of how intimately I knew him. His singing voice was deep and masculine, huge, but he was physically diminutive, and the two didn't completely gel, so he affected a persona on the stage that he felt was congruent with his voice, "manly," and probably was, but I knew him too well to be completely comfortable with it. It was as if he were wearing clothes I didn't recognize, and I wanted my old friend back. Everyone else, however, bought it hook, line, and sinker, and he definitely had his moment of stardom in Long Island. One of the other stars of the show that night, John O'Shaughnessy, played the jealous Harry Beaton, who announces he is leaving Brigadoon to make everything disappear, since the girl he loves, Jean, is marrying another man. If anyone leaves, it kills the dream of Brigadoon and it's over. He is accidentally shot and killed on his way out of town, and there is a heartbreaking, tragic funeral dance for him.

I had never met or even heard of him. Peter didn't talk much about the show when he was in rehearsals. How could he not have mentioned John O'Shaughnessy, this epitome of beauty? Still caught in the flush of late boyhood, John was the handsomest man I had ever seen. He had a square jaw and a massive, almost cliché-like smile, like a Leyendecker illustration from the 1940s. The blood in his cheeks seemed to rise from his feet because it too wanted to be where the beauty was. He sang with a sweet Irish tenor, tremulous and untrained but heartbreaking; you could tell he had hurt in him, which I came to find out had a lot to do with his brutal, unpredictable alcoholic father, John Sr., a sort of James Tyrone type from *Long Day's Journey into Night*, whose speech was always slurred and whom I found terrifying. His spindly mother, Lillian, radiated absolutely nothing one could call maternal or warm and was the antithesis of my Jewish mother. She always looked perplexed, as if she were incorrectly cast into a human body and was looking for another container to house her, or like a cat surreptitiously looking for a litter box.

John, the oldest in his family, emanated strength, heroism, and vulnerability all at once. He had enormously wide shoulders, like a swimmer. I remember only one of his siblings, Lillian, his sister, who was as *Vogue* model magnificent as he was, shockingly so. She looked as if Christie Brinkley were crossed with a swan. I literally gasped when I met her.

Onstage, John seemed curiously incapable, given his age, of a false move. He had none of the physical awkwardness young actors have in high school shows, hands and arms that go awry, an inability to walk across the stage, awkward double takes. For him, this seemed to be happening. He looked, sounded, and acted the part, and whenever he was onstage, you were there. When Harry Beaton is killed in the show, I was crestfallen. I was holding Gloria's hand, but I was so confused by the end of the show I was crying. I was out on a date with the most beautiful girl in the world, whom I was lucky to have on my arm, but beside myself about who I was, what I wanted, and what to do. I just wanted to hold Harry Beaton, comfort him. His tragedy was all I could think of.

There was a cast party afterward. I don't remember what I did with Gloria or Charlie. Clearly, I ditched them because they disappeared from my consciousness altogether. I was on a mission to find Harry Beaton, and that was all I could think about.

John O'Shaughnessy was wearing a London Fog raincoat he never took off that night, as if it were the only garment in his wardrobe he was proud of, so he looked like a spy in a British war film or a Graham

Greene novel. He had very white shiny and formidable movie star teeth, floppy hair coarsened by the sea air, not blond but full of sparkling light-catching highlights, as if that were where the sun wanted to be. He laughed through his nose and spoke high like an Irish tenor.

I went over and began talking to him with the plain objective that he had to be in my life or I would have to kill myself. I began by telling him how affectingly gripping I thought his performance was, how absorbing and moving. He was disarmingly guileless, truly appreciative, warm, self-deprecating, and humble. Whatever else we said, this remains as the aura-surrounded moment in my life when I first fell in love. By the end of the encounter, we had exchanged numbers and were new friends.

Soon after, in a stairwell at school, I broke up with Gloria. I didn't say why. I probably said one of those dumb things people say at that age that they have heard in movies but have no idea what they mean: "I'm not ready for a commitment." It felt awful because I could see confoundment in her face, and I simply could not tell the truth. Thinking about it now, what was she doing with me anyway? She could have had any guy she wanted in the entire school, but of course, like most human beings, she had to pick the unavailable one. All I knew was, I had to be around John, whom I already felt as though I loved more than *anyone* in the world, anyone I had ever *met*, and anyone who ever *would* be in the world. Gloria was the last girl I would ever hurt that way, by pretending I was straight.

John called me first, assuaging my fear about how to approach calling him! I don't remember ever being so purely happy to receive a phone call, to hear a voice, his friendly, melodious voice. We made a date. I don't remember what we did together. It was the curtain rising into a world I had never known.

John and I started hanging out all the time. We were inseparable. He lived on West Olive Street in Long Beach, which was over the bridge from Island Park. I don't think his parents liked me because I was Jewish. Running was John's main mode of transportation. He would run from his house all the way to Harbor Isle, and then, when he left, he would run home, like a racehorse. For this reason, his legs were very muscular, and I had never seen such developed calves. He always had the slight smell of sweat on him but not the sweat of someone who was unclean, the sweet sweat of an athlete, of exertion. He also had a bike and used that a lot too. I started running with him, and we would run all around Harbor Isle, which was maybe a five-mile course. I became someone I had never been.

The world, because I was feeling these things for the first time, became entirely different. There was a new kind of happiness and a new kind of unhappiness. It was black and white; I was happy when I was with John and unhappy when I wasn't. I found courage with John, stamina, and masculinity. Shortly before we met, in an effort to be and look stronger than the thugs who beat me up all the time, I had begun exercising on my own, but I suddenly had a need to keep up with John, because doing whatever he did meant being with him. My looks started to change dramatically. I got handsome, and I was living in my body in a whole new way. I started looking like a man with flushed cheeks, like John, and I'm sure I was incandescent, burning, gleaming, phosphorescent with love for the first time in my life.

I asked for a bike so I could ride with John. My parents bought me a beautiful white Peugeot, and I rode it everywhere. John and I would ride all the way to West Hempstead, where my high school was, ten miles and back, a four-hour excursion at least. Sleep became unimportant and unnecessary, a thief stealing time away from my time with John. The world smelled differently with John, as if it had just rained, as if everything were screaming, "Life!"

We would swim off the dock from the boatyard, one time so far that the threading disintegrated in my bathing suit and I had to hold my bathing suit together on the walk home. We had been swimming by the Long Island Lighting Company, which was practically in Oceanside, the next town over. The water was warmer and probably filled with deadly chemicals, so perhaps that is what dissolved my bathing suit. We would swim at night, in the ocean and behind the boatyard. This was before *Jaws* scared everybody out of swimming at night, or swimming, period.

We would take flashlights and swim to the bottom around the docks with snorkels, looking for blue-claw crabs. They would freeze in the light, and we'd catch them and put them in buckets. We never ate them or gave them to people who did; we just threw them back. I just remember doing it with John and what it felt like to love someone so much. Every moment I spent with him was important, memorable, parenthetical; I had never felt so radiant, so alive. Sometimes Peter, who had a penchant for torturing poor defenseless creatures, liked to poke at the crabs in the bucket, screaming and laughing like a girl when they would leap at him with their enormous claws, but he never killed one. You'd think Peter would have been jealous or felt replaced by John, but he seemed more fascinated than anything by the intensity of what was happening. Even he seemed bowled over by the mutual tenderness he saw blossoming.

No one mattered more to me than John, not my mother, not my sisters; I don't remember any other friends mattering at that time, only him. He slept over a lot, but if he went home, I would end up walking him home all the way to Long Beach while we wheeled our bicycles, but then we'd get to his house and somehow couldn't bear to part, so he'd turn right around and walk me home. We would do this over and over again night after night until it got light out because we couldn't bear to part from each other. The whole cycle of it, the quiet that would descend at four in the morning, *l'heure bleue*, the slow beginning of chirping as light began to fill the sky, and the air still cooled by the darkness, felt sanctified, holy. I was with John, and the world glittered like silver and gold.

I don't even know what we talked about for all of those hours on end. Nowadays I spend so much time alone and silent I can't imagine having that much to say.

I remember once I said the word "blow job" in the pink-and-yellow kitchen at the boatyard and he didn't know what it meant. He was *that* innocent. I didn't tell him the unfortunate circumstance under which I had to learn the meaning of that word, but I told him what it meant, and maybe with some heightened sense of excitement and even hope that it was something I might like to try on him someday. But the idea of ever pushing what was happening between us to that seemed implausible.

He seemed to have as much love and trust for me as I had for him.

Nothing about me, nothing I said or did, ever made him recoil. He seemed perfectly willing to accept whatever I gave him. I was good at making him laugh, which is good because his laughter lives inside me like a precious relic. Maybe this kind of friendship can only happen when you are young.

Eventually our circle opened up somewhat. I became friends with a bunch of intellectuals, honor society types. One of these friends was Susan Kushner. Everything about her and her family was different from mine. They had to be Jewish because this was Harbor Isle and almost everyone was Jewish, but there was absolutely nothing about them that was Jewish. They didn't go to synagogue or observe even the most important holidays. They emanated a cool intelligence and actually were rather cool altogether. Susan's mother was sort of masculine with a short haircut, no makeup, no cleavage, and didn't seem to care in the least what she looked like, the antithesis of my mother.

Susan's mother was committed entirely to utilitarian style, no makeup, a house and clothes for which I remember only beige, brown, olive green, and maybe here and there a touch of rust. Susan's father was quite overweight; I remember his short-sleeve white shirt tucked into gray wool pants that were pulled up too high and hugged a formidable potbelly. Susan's mother would feed him cottage cheese on melba toast in the morning because he was always on a diet, though I don't remember him ever losing a single pound. She had an older brother who just seemed invisible to me, partially because I think he was for Susan. She *never* talked about him, waving the whole notion of him off with her hand. I guess that emphasizes their non-Jewishness as well; the son did not appear to be the most important child.

Susan became a confidante, as well as someone who thoroughly appreciated anything I brought to the table for contemplation. I would read her poetry, and we would listen to music and watch foreign movies together. She would cry around me, getting all bound up, and do funny things with her hands, picking at her face and throwing around her long hair, which was long not out of vanity but out of choice because her hair and clothes existed to hide her face and body. Like me, she was neurotic, had emotional problems, and suffered from depression, so we became really close.

I could talk to her about John. No one else knew how much I loved him, but she did. She never rolled her eyes, judged me, or tired of my repetitive paeans to John. She had a deeply endearing way of saying goodbye. She would throw her arms wide open and say, "Give me a hug!" with a giggle and her eyes all scrunched up in delight, as if you had a surprise gift you would give her when she opened them. She made me feel loved. She had about her the isolated air of one of those southern writers, Carson McCullers, Flannery O'Connor, or Harper Lee. Susan, John, and I became like the movie *Jules and Jim*, a triangle. She loved me, but I think she loved him too because I loved him so much.

We would get drunk, and sometimes John and I would sleep over at Susan's, all three of us in her little twin bed. Nothing sexual would happen, though it was certainly in the air. It's amazing her parents never said anything; I mean, we could have been having a ménage à trois up there. Sometimes a small part of me, an elbow or a knee, would be touching John, even the tip of a finger, or I would purposely allow my hand to lazily fall on his hair, and I would stay up all night to enjoy the heat it generated in me. Usually, Susan was in the middle, but if I was, I'd make believe I was sleeping and turn my face toward his with the fantasy of his lips touching mine. I wouldn't let myself sleep and waste these miraculous moments of proximity.

I was definitely like no one else he had ever met; of that I am pretty sure. I took them to see Stephen Sondheim's *A Little Night Music*. That was one of the six times I saw it. We stood in the back. I took them to see Ingmar Bergman's *Cries and Whispers*. I was undeniably their arts and culture minister. I loved preparing them for what they were about to see, adapting both a history teacher and a ringleader kind of pose.

John was funny about food and gave off a sympathy-inducing poverty. He loved fast food, McDonald's. I took him one night to the city to eat Italian food at Mamma Leone's. I swear, I don't think he had ever eaten Italian food! He approached it as I might approach chocolate-covered grasshoppers. I loved feeling as if I were opening his world up. I think he liked it but not as much as McDonald's, which he bought to eat on the train ride home with a look of "finally, I can eat dinner!" on his face.

Cries and Whispers is the only time I remember taking him to a movie. Mostly we would hang out, run, swim, ride our bikes, walk each other home, and talk relentlessly. John would sleep over all the time, on the floor, and I would stare at him, fantasize about him, but with him it didn't feel like objectification, because it had around it the halo of true love. I would have done anything for him. I even felt protective of him.

One night his scary father pulled up to the boatyard drunk, looking for John as if he intended to kill him. He struggled to be cordial, not so much looking *at* me as looking *through* me, as if I were merely an obstruction, or worse, a toxic pollutant in his son's life. John, who could easily have been cast as the Hitler youth rousing the SS into action with his dazzling Aryan looks singing "Tomorrow Belongs to Me" in *Cabaret*, was anomalous enough, but his father seemed terrifically out of place driving around Harbor Isle, this bastion of Jewish life, like Goering.

His father sensed something in me he distrusted, not necessarily my love for his son, though that certainly could have been it, but perhaps my protectiveness and my ability to change his son into something he didn't want him to be. He was most probably invested in John's remaining unsophisticated and afraid of him. I think his father demanded subservience, and with me John had a whole new independent life, one his father had no hand in, which was beyond his understanding. Believe me, John's father did not attend Broadway shows and foreign films. If there was joy in John's house, or a sense of community, if it ever felt like a family, I never once heard him mention it. His house seemed to be one thing, a place to escape from. His father seemed to loathe me for offering that escape. Sometimes, I think about John's wedding, or I think, was there a wedding? Who went? Because by then, the bright light of our friendship had dimmed. But were his parents there? I can't imagine celebration within the confines of his unhappy home.

One afternoon, John and I were sitting in my room. I was on the bed and John was on the floor. I don't remember what we were talking about, but there was a lull in the conversation. We could even be quiet together; we were that comfortable with each other. But this was a strange and pregnant silence where all the particles became nuclear, charged. Suddenly John put his hand on mine. It might have lasted ten seconds, maybe twenty. "Suddenly" isn't the right word, because there was nothing remotely sudden about it. Our eyes were not on each other but on our hands. It was a moment of such extreme, inexplicable tenderness out of time, out of place. There was John's hand, covering my hand. I remember it as one of the most beatific and vivid moments of my life. Still. What did it mean? I mull it over and over again in my head, thinking, maybe it was a missed opportunity, and if I were a little more aggressive, I could have kissed him. What was he saying with that gesture? Whatever it was, I will never know. He probably doesn't even remember it. He might even if he read this deny it ever happened, but it did.

It reminds me of that moment in Michael Cunningham's *The Hours* when Richard kisses Mrs. Dalloway. She is so busy wondering what this extraordinary moment, this kiss from someone she loves so much, will portend that she misses the kiss. It is sort of the tragedy of life, isn't it? In wondering what this or that portends, we stop paying attention, stop living, miss the moment, so that all there is to remember is the disappointment for what didn't happen, having missed what did. Even then, I knew to pay attention, put parentheses around that moment, a breathtakingly strange, unusually tender show of intimacy. Because of it or including it, I cannot imagine anything but loving John forever, my first love, John O'Shaughnessy, for whatever it was. I see him, hear him, and smell him as I write this. I bless him.

My family took him in, and my mother treated him as a son, though I'm sure she was bemused and mystified because he was so completely different from any friend I had ever brought home. My sister Sheila, who was away for the entire episode and doesn't even remember meeting him, says maybe my mother loved him too; she says mothers are not immune to the crushes their children have. She might have even suspected in seeing the depth of my feelings my sexuality, because I changed completely when John came into my life, but she never said anything, ever. She just plied him with Jewish food as she did every-

one else. There was a girl in that production of *Brigadoon*. She played
Jean MacLaren, the Jean of "I'll Go Home with Bonnie Jean" and
"Jeanie's Packing Up." She was pretty, a pretty little Irish lass named
Joyce Ward. She had a fluttery, birdlike light soprano voice, thin lips,
and a toothy smile and actually even looked like his sister, as well as
the embodiment of Ireland. Joyce was wary of me, because she had her
eye on John too, and he and I were so wrapped up in each other that I
threatened that. One time Joyce and her friend, another singer, Melody Breyer, who played the wild harridan of Brigadoon, Meg Brockie,
were over at the boatyard. They were like mean girls when they were
together, perhaps incited by the obvious intimacy and almost impenetrable exclusivity and secretiveness of my relationship with John.
Those two would sometimes just show up unannounced with a look
on their faces as if they were up to no good, a bad seed glare in their
eyes. We would all get drunk, which only exacerbated their meanness.

    One night, John and Joyce ended up in my parents' bed with the
door closed. That was the beginning of the end of my friendship
with John. I felt doomed, sad, and jealous. I knew. He wasn't mine
anymore. Joyce had won. There wasn't room in the picture for both
of us. But maybe these things, secret relationships, have a built-in du-
ration. They die when they are exposed to too many outside sources.
Around this time my white Peugeot was stolen, and I grieved for it
the way I was already grieving for John. It was as if the hundred years
were up, and Brigadoon was over. Harry Beaton was gone, and it all
ended. The depressing haze settled over the moor; the heather disappeared. John went away to college; he was a year older than me.

    We were barely in touch, but one day he called and said he had
a roommate he thought I should know. Clearly the roommate was
gay. We started talking on the phone all the time, having very sweet
conversations, and I was excited to meet him. He would gossip about
John, saying that John had the dirtiest underwear in the world and was
a slob. He gave me an indelible description of what it looked like under John's bed. He said it was a catastrophe under there, a Sodom and
Gomorrah all at once. He was funny. This was interesting to me and
new information because I never even thought of John as going to the

bathroom. I never remember him excusing himself to go pee or shit, and we never talked about it, though that makes sense because those were things I *never* talked about and *never* wanted to know. So, this new information about John's underwear was as funny as was the act of gossiping about him and giggling about him with someone whom I might end up loving more than him because at this point I was falling in love over the phone and very excited. I think his name was Charlie. I finally met him one day on the beach in Long Beach. I was crestfallen, overwhelmingly so. He had white pasty skin, even clammy, as if he hadn't a single red blood cell, and his hair looked like a nest of pubic hair on his head. He almost looked like a Hasid without the outfit, though I don't think he was Jewish. He was so unattractive and the whole thing was so disappointing that I think it put an end to the entire John story. My feelings changed, and my first love began to die.

Many years later, in 1997, after Jeffrey died, I found John again. Maybe I thought we could tesseract back to high school, I don't know. Maybe I wanted to be rescued from the unbearable pain I was in. I wanted to feel something as tender as first love again. I found out where he lived in California. I had heard through Melody that he and Joyce (yes, they had married in the late 1970s) had recently lost a child, a little boy, to sudden infant death syndrome. I thought we could commiserate in our grief. We did, and it was certainly tender, but nothing hooked. It didn't reinstate anything. We were old friends, but the halo of that time long ago was not reinvigorated. There have been times when I was working close enough to where they live, in California, a new opera in Long Beach, a concert of my music at Disney Concert Hall, and I let them know, but they made no effort to come. Weren't they curious?

It is 2020, and I am sequestered in the country, in Sullivan County, New York, with my partner, Kevin. Recently, when we had started socially isolating during this time, something interesting happened inside me. I was using Zoom all the time for my AA meetings and for teaching classes, and I grew to have a whole new relationship with myself. I liked the way I looked. I would watch myself on Zoom and think, "I'm handsome!" I was feeling strangely and uncharacteristically confident, and I had an inexplicable urge to see John again. I wanted to

Zoom with him, see what he looked like, see what it felt like to talk to him, see his face again, and for him to see mine. I thought seeing him now, at this age, would put the past in the past and create a present that perhaps something could grow out of.

There is something about this pandemic, and I have heard this from others as well, that makes you want to revisit your past. Maybe it is the cloud of possible death. I have been visiting my past including my early childhood a lot during this time. Even in dreams, I have had visits from my mother and father and from Jeffrey. My two dead sisters, Lorraine and Susan, have appeared as well. I have been writing about these dreams, these celestial visits. It has been very comforting. I found John's son Conor on Facebook, and through him I got John's phone number. I thought for sure he would love me again and want to be my friend.

We had a long talk about who we were to each other at that time and what we were both doing now. After we spoke, I sent him a text: "It was really nice talking to you, John. I didn't want anything to happen to either of us before I was able to say how much I loved you and valued the incredibly tender time in which our friendship took place." He wrote back, "Thanks Ricky. Yeah, that was a magical time in my life I will always treasure. You were my best friend at a time when I needed a best friend. So happy to hear that you are happy, healthy and successful. We'll stay in touch from now on." I wrote back, "That makes me happy, John. I think I needed to hear that. Because of the age we were and that particular time in life, you were the best friend I needed as well. You have too big a home in my heart, and in the importance of my own evolution, to ever let go of. I will always love you." He replied, "I love you too Ricky. And I'm so glad that you are happy. So many people are not."

I got all excited. Seeing the words "I love you" made me want to rekindle what we had. I decided to familiarize him with me as I am now. I sent him a link to the video of the commencement speech I did at the University of Michigan that I felt really expressed many essential things about me now and went viral, but I didn't hear back. I sent pictures of me with my dog Lucy and my partner, Kevin (Kevin and

I are married, but I cannot *bear* the word husband!), pictures of the lake in my backyard. I wrote to him on my birthday, and his. I wanted him to engage. He wasn't interested in Zooming, but I thought we could send photos to each other. I even imagined he might like to finally hear some of the music I have become known for. He wasn't completely unresponsive, but it was extremely selective and didn't betray any exploding excitement to be in touch again, as mine was. It flickered and then went out. I wrote, "Reviving our friendship seems to have been a failed mission, but I'm glad I found you." and he replied, with what felt like an almost disarming and chilly detachment, "Dear Ricky, long distance relationships are hard. Reviving relationships over long distance after 45 years is harder. I'm glad that you are healthy, happy, and doing so well in your career. Right now, I'm still working from home. Don't go out except to get food. Kinda like a monk. But then I was never a social animal. Stay safe. John."

One night a couple of years ago, Joyce called me drunk and raucous at about two or three in the morning. She was in New York City with her daughter Brigid. They wanted to see me. They were yelling back and forth with each other like fishwives. I had to leave the next day to go to St. Louis for my new opera, 27, but I agreed to meet them at a diner at 8:00 a.m. for breakfast, which she winced at but said yes, nevertheless.

I waited for an hour that morning before I ordered myself breakfast and never heard from Joyce again.

There is a moment in my life when someone touched my hand, and like Proust's Marcel, savoring the madeleine dipped in lime blossom tea, time stopped, redefining itself. Love was carved into the granite of my iconography, and mythology was made, which became perhaps the most important moment of sense memory I would ever have. In each of my obsessions, there was either a duplicate or a wished-for duplicate of that moment. The details would be changed, but the feelings were the same, evidence; I had made someone love me; proven my specialness to them. Always, at the other end of this rainbow would lie the possibility of kissing, of sex, or at least, a hand touching mine. I had made myself indispensable to them.

If I Knew Then What I Know Now . . .
Stephen Sondheim

I said to Mary Guettel, "Well, if I am going to alienate one composer, it might as well be America's *premier* composer."

⌖

I got off on the wrong foot with Stephen Sondheim right from the start, and I never quite got back on the right one.

When he died suddenly, on November 26, 2021, I felt something between nothing and relief. My friend Michael Klein texted everyone in my writing group: "devastating news for so many people. Stephen Sondheim died. suddenly apparently. [three crying emojis] We won't be hearing from that kind anymore and not very soon again I think."

At first, I felt irritation. There's Michael, with an announcement and a pronouncement all at once . . . as if he knows everyone and everything out there and the last word has been spoken.

I had been hoping on some level he wouldn't be around when I published my book. Did I kill him? I was trying to grapple with something so large happening, when all of the sudden Facebook became extremely crowded with everyone's reminiscences, photos of notes he sent them, his famous typed notes with his gorgeous signature, or photos of them with him . . . his kind smile, their arms around one another, everyone greedily claiming their memories of him, their connections with him, their feelings about him, five minutes after they had found out. It felt like me me me instead of him him him.

But how should it have been? Who am I to say how anyone should deal with anything, but it still felt like a preponderance, a wave of self-importance. My relationship with him, since the very first time we met, was so fraught I thought the news would make me happy. It didn't. I felt strange and oddly sick all night. Suddenly, in all the photos of him everyone was posting, I saw tenderness, vulnerability, instead of meanness and his ability to hurt me.

I woke up this morning to Yvonne De Carlo in my head, singing "I'm Still Here," as she first sang it in *Follies*. I know all the words, as I do to hundreds of his songs. I thought of my little carriage house in Pittsburgh, when I was at CMU, where I played the record of *Pacific Overtures* obsessively, because that was the year it came out. Stephen Sondheim came flooding back to me.

I won't censor my story below, but respect had to be paid. He is beyond an influence at this point; he is part of my DNA. Way inside the archives division of my heart, there is a box marked "fear," with equal amounts derision and looming love like an asteroid threatening to destroy the earth, and he sits in there, vibrating like a sentry, imposingly large as my father. Stephen Sondheim.

Why is there so much bitterness mixed up in my feelings?

I was commissioned in 2010 to write something for the Bucks County Choral Society. On the weekend of the premiere, during a reception at some museum, I was shown a terrific photograph by a photographer named Jack Rosen, of Steve, who grew up in Bucks County, floating in a boat half-naked by himself down the river. I admired it so much that at the end of my stay there his son Rick generously gave me a beautiful print of it.

Back in New York, I took a photo of the photo and sent it to Steve with a note recounting my experience in his hometown and asking him if he would consider signing the photo for me. He sent me back a note. "Dear Ricky, I would gladly sign it for you, but it is not me."

I was so confounded. How could it be in a museum with the title *Sondheim*, photo by Jack Rosen, and not be him? But it wasn't, because I wrote back, and he was quite insistent about it. It all seemed so perfect. I, of all people, sending him a photo of himself to sign that wasn't him. Of course, if you simply blow up the face in the photo, you see it looks nothing like him, but that is how legends are born, and who am I to steal their thunder? Also, given my relationship with Sondheim, it might actually be him.

So Stephen Sondheim is gone, and this artist whom I admired, well, I can't say *more* than any other artist, though that feels like what I *should* write, but up there with my top five, lives inside me, not in a glow, not in the yellow light I painted him in after his first heart attack, but in a strobe, an eddy I have struggled to swim away from for forty years or so.

I was not a composer. I didn't really know what I was. I mean, I had written some absolutely terrible songs in seventh grade, "Black Thorn to Hell," "Go Do What You Feel, Babe," and in protest against the war in Vietnam, for which I wore a black armband to school every day, the highly impassioned "Oh, I Wish I Was a Dove," but I never actually assumed the mantle of composer.

Out of my multiple obsessions—Joni Mitchell, opera, speed, existential literature, suicidal poets, foreign films, modern art—probably the most enduring was music. I lived less than an hour from the city, and I would go every Saturday to the New York Public Library for the Performing Arts at Lincoln Center. I would leave the library with huge piles of scores and records by composers I never heard of who wrote music in the twentieth century and excitedly peruse them on the train on the way home, dying with anticipation to hear what I had gotten. If I liked them, I devoured their entire published and recorded body of work. As a pianist, I would explore the chords, the construction of their music with my fingers, endlessly playing through their work to see what they were doing.

We lived a town away from the Boosey & Hawkes factory, one of the most august publishers for classical music in the world. A little man, friendly and almost protective of me, would see me walk in and sell me piles of scores he had put aside for me for almost nothing, because they had a bent page or a smudged cover and couldn't be sold. Ned Rorem, Béla Bartók, Nicholas Maw, who couldn't believe how much of his music I knew when I met him, Benjamin Britten, Igor Stravinsky—I studied their scores, and their music became the soundtrack of my life. Whatever was happening outside my room, the volatility in my house, the danger on the streets, in the realm of great music I felt not only humanized but ennobled, relieved of the world, of gym class, where I was the pariah who moved like a spastic and got picked last for every team.

One day, Peter, who had moved to Long Beach, where his high school took them to lots of Broadway shows, had seen a show called *Company*. He was over the moon about it and invited me to come over and hear the record. I cannot say that before I heard that show, I had any interest in musicals. The music was often disappointing to me: predictable. It was never spicy or surprising enough. I mean, I remember being little and *dying* for Ann-Margret singing "Bye Bye Birdy" against that blue backdrop, her Technicolor red hair blowing in the wind, and Julie Andrews whirling around on the mountains of Austria in *The Sound of Music*. But the music didn't catch me, obsess me. I didn't have to have the albums. I liked passages in some shows, I loved "The Dream" in *Fiddler on the Roof*, or "The Carousel Waltz," or "March of the Siamese Children" and "Something Wonderful" in *The King and I*. *West Side Story* was a whole other story, but I was too little to associate it with a form, being one when it premiered, I didn't think of it as a musical, it was just my sister's record and I loved it.

Company astounded me. It was not only unlike any musical I had ever heard; it was unlike *anything* I had ever heard. Even now, I think, where did Stephen Sondheim come from? I mean, no one was writing like that, had ever written like that for the musical theater. Like Beethoven, he was building from rhythmic ideas, cells. His scores were organized, intelligent, contrapuntal, and motivic. He was not just writing accompaniments and vamps, the usual lexicon for so much musical theater. Nothing felt randomly put together. From the first repeated notes like buzzers or a telephone ringer, the organized mayhem growing out of the name Bobby, the rhythmic vitality and complicated, often dissonant harmonies like modern music, the wise and searing, even kaleidoscopic probing, poetic, introspective, and foreign movie-ish lyrics, the broken relationships, unmoored alcoholics, no easy solutions, to the unbelievably sophisticated ensemble writing in songs like "Poor Baby," I was stunned, riveted. I couldn't get enough of it. My mother bought me the score. I played through it over and over until I could sing and play every note. I practiced "Another Hundred People," as complex as one of Albéniz's *Iberia* pieces, the way I practiced Chopin. I had played so much twentieth-century music, but this new composer, Stephen Sondheim, seemed to combine everything I loved about everything! I was beside myself. I guess you could say he was my new Joni Mitchell, except I had no desire to make him a dress.

A friend from high school, Shelly Stangler, who played Tevye's wife in *Fiddler on the Roof* when I played Perchik, the young revolutionary, was the high school star because she was the loudest belter. She took me to see Stephen Sondheim's *Follies*. She didn't like it, but I was transfixed, mesmerized, and it entered me in the strangest way. While I was watching it, I don't believe I really understood it, because it was so far from what I expected; it wasn't even a musical! What was it? It was so sad, and afterward I was haunted by it. I kept thinking of Alexis Smith, icy and growling, in that slinky skintight red sequined dress, eviscerating her husband, and Dorothy Collins, dressed like a faded movie star, with her out-of-date Alice blue gown and platinum bob, singing about losing her mind. Here, I thought I was going to see a musical about the Follies, with all kinds of vaudeville pastiches, and instead, as in *Company*, I got something along the lines of all the foreign movies I lived for: introspective, probing, and mysterious. What was onstage were ghosts, broken marriages, disappointments, thwarted dreams, self-loathing, nervous breakdowns. It was one of the most pessimistic and bitter things I had ever seen, but the packaging was bright, shiny, splashy, and spectacular. It was an evening full of antithesis and ambivalence, but *entertaining*! It was exhilarating. How the hell did they do that?

In 1973, I saw *A Little Night Music* six times, standing in the back of the theater, and I made everyone I knew in the world see it, with the same tenacity that I made everybody see Bergman's *Cries and Whispers*, which, believe me, many of them did not appreciate! That was almost too good to be true, Sondheim and Bergman, it was like the stars had aligned for me alone! Sondheim took Bergman's great *Smiles of a Summer Night*, one of his only comedies and inarguably the only successful one, and turned it into a delicious soufflé of a musical. Every number was a variation of a waltz rhythm in three. It was, to me, as elegant and wise as the film it was adapted from, if not better. I could play and sing every note of Sondheim's scores. I was that kid who was invited to the party because I could play anything, no matter how hard, and incite everyone into singing all night. I loved to have everyone gathered around me at the piano. It felt like the same kind of love my mother gave me growing up when I played all the old songs or the latest Broadway hits, like "If He Walked into My Life," from *Mame*, or "As Long as He Needs Me," from *Oliver!*, or "What Kind of Fool Am I," from *Stop the World—I Want to Get Off*, while she sang with her hands on my shoulders. Whenever anyone wrote something about Sondheim, I read it as if my life depended on it, for instance, Craig Zadan's book *Sondheim & Co.*, which I devoured the moment it came out. There was the Sondheim tribute album with all those great songs like "We're Gonna Be All Right" from *Do I Hear a Waltz?*, and "Silly People," a song that was cut from *A Little Night Music*, but I was particularly captivated by "Pleasant Little Kingdom," a skittery and nervous little song that was cut from *Follies*, and still am. For some reason, that and "Every Day a Little Death" from *A Little Night Music* are my two favorite songs of Steve's. They break my heart. When the pianist Tony de Mare invited me to be part of his massive *Liaisons* project, commissioning various composers to write piano pieces based on Sondheim songs, I was the first to accept and the first to write one, because I wanted to claim "Every Day a Little Death" before anyone else did.

When Sondheim was being honored by the Poetry Society of America in 1992, the poet Robert Creeley was put in charge of the event. We knew each other because I had set some of his poems to music and we corresponded frequently, so because he knew nothing whatsoever about Stephen Sondheim, he asked me to write an essay about Steve as a *poet* for the booklet, and I did, focusing on the exquisite and delicately devastating lyric of "Every Day a Little Death":

Every day a little death
In the parlor, in the bed

In the curtains, in the silver
In the buttons, in the bread.

Every day a little sting
In the heart and in the head
Every move and every breath
And you hardly feel a thing
Brings a perfect little death

In the summer of 1976, America's bicentennial, *Pacific Overtures* is playing, and I'm obsessed with it. Recognizing some of Sondheim's influences makes it even richer; I recognize elements from the great Japanese film director Kenji Mizoguchi's masterpiece, *Ugetsu*, and I am transported straight back to my childhood when the huge ship unfolds onstage like origami!

I get a job for my summer vacation. There is a new Italian restaurant in Greenwich Village called Alfredo's Settebello on Seventh Avenue, where I am a waiter during the day and the pianist at cocktail hour. My boss is Alfredo Viazzi, famous for bringing northern Italian cuisine, things like pesto and white sauces instead of red, to America. He is married to Jane White, who makes me play her Chopin's "Raindrop" prelude every night after I have gotten her a Campari and soda. I put it together upon hearing her very distinctive voice that she was the madam in *Klute*, starring Jane Fonda, and Queen Aggravain in the musical *Once upon a Mattress*, starring Carol Burnett, and I worship her accordingly. Someone tells me that "she is a Black woman masquerading as white," which due to her imperious carriage and the way she enunciates only adds to her allure.

I live with my parents at the boatyard, and I commute to and from work. My mother is trying to lose weight that summer using "diet drops," which are unbelievably powerful, like crystal meth, and she is unknowingly sharing them with me. Whenever she takes her shower, I add a few to my coffee. So, I often refer to the summer of 1976 as my health and beauty summer because when I am not at Alfredo's Settebello, I am jogging around Harbor Isle, starving myself, doing countless push-ups and sit-ups, and hennaing my hair. My friend from CMU Cheryl Utsunomiya, who is now Kim Miyore, having changed her name after being cast as Yoko Ono in a movie about John and Yoko, lands a job in *Pacific Overtures* right out of college. Kim and I became close friends, having both had our hearts broken by Donn Simione.

One day Kim drops by the restaurant during cocktail hour to tell me she is taking me to a cast party at Stephen Sondheim's house. I am overwhelmed with gratitude, and I can barely get through the rest of the night. When she leaves, I play only Sondheim for the rest of the evening, starting with "You Must Meet My Wife," from *A Little Night Music*.

The day of the party I decide on a skintight maroon cotton turtleneck and jeans, which I think make me look sexy. I know I am in for a star-studded evening; maybe I will even have sex with someone famous! When I arrive, Sondheim answers the door! I am in an instant state of shock. He is almost handsome, in a bedraggled, gravity-ravaged sort of way, but I am instantly drawn to him. I see Angela Lansbury, Hal Prince, Joel Grey, and Anthony Perkins, a.k.a. Norman Bates from *Psycho*, across the room, and I think, I need alcohol!

I love the story of Jane Bowles, wearing a sundress and espadrilles, taking a train from Santa Fe to New York with little thought of what the weather in the East might be. The train has to stop in Philadelphia because of a huge blizzard. Disembarking from the train in her summer garb, she approaches a police officer and asks, "Excuse me, Officer, can you direct me to the nearest cocktail center?" I ask the bartender to just fill a glass with scotch, I guzzle two such glasses, and within the hour I am half-walking, half-careening, and Stephen Sondheim is taking us on a tour of his house.

By now, we are in his famed game room and my head starts to spin. I have to excuse myself to go vomit so violently Kim has to peel me up off the floor of the bathroom, get me into a cab to Penn Station, accompany me home to Island Park, and sleep over at the boatyard because we get home so late. This aborted ending to a wildly looked-forward-to event is not uncommon in my life as a drunk. In college, my friend Helen Dungan and I spent weeks preparing for a costume party at Halloween where we would be F. Scott Fitzgerald and Zelda. We did indeed look great, but about fifteen minutes into the party, Helen, like Kim, had to peel me off the floor where I was wrapped around the toilet bowl and get me home. The next morning, on the undulating dock with Kim, I felt awful, ugly, hungover, and guilty that Kim, who was being such a good sport about it, was at my house and I had dragged her into this. The shrill summer sunlight was hurting my eyes as gulls darted in and out of the water like projectiles.

Fast-forward.

I am twenty-five, living in New York City, and Stephen Sondheim has a new show, *Merrily We Roll Along*. Excitedly, I buy a ticket to the first preview, which I think is the first show, knowing nothing about how a Broadway show is created. The overture is big and brassy, an unfamiliar sound for Sondheim, but exciting, heralding great things. The show begins. All the characters are dressed in sweatshirts with the names of their characters printed on them in big letters. Everyone has lockers in what looks like a high school locker room. They are all young, but they are playing old, jaded cynics at the top of the show, which they are not necessarily equipped to do, and it feels forced and awkward. Then it moves backward in time, and they get younger, which they are better at, but something feels really off about the evening. It is hard to follow, and people are leaving in droves. I have to admit I am so confused I tune out, and when it is over, I, too, leave the theater totally mystified. I dismiss it, but I am too young to have a community I can go out and trumpet my disapproval to. I just think, wow, Stephen Sondheim, my idol, has a new show and I don't like it. From the word on the street, apparently, the show is not getting better, and the reviews aren't great, but I only say that in hindsight because I was not yet someone in the throes of the nightmare called "caring about reviews or even reading them." That only started happening when I myself was one of the dreaded reviewed. Then the original cast recording comes out and I am astonished, stunned, beside myself with love. How did I not hear this in the theater? I don't even remember this! It's as if what I saw onstage that night deafened me to the beauty and the genius of the score.

I am cleaning houses for a living and running lunches to offices for fast-food restaurants. I have the work life of an addict with low self-esteem, unmoored and rudderless, ending up where I end up, which feels like nowhere. I get a job with a temp agency called Lend-a-Hand. They send you to clean people's homes with a tacit agreement that something else might occur. For that reason, people refer to it as Lend-a-Boy.

I have a client whose house is filthy, uncleanable, but all he wants to do is suck my toes and jerk off. He is plump and pasty, a sort of low-rent Truman Capote, but he pays me double, so I am game. Occasionally, I even grab his dick for him, which is like a clotted little blood sausage. He takes me out for dinner and invites me to Guadalajara.

I have another client, in Queens, who doesn't believe in kitty litter boxes, so there is cat shit and the stink of pee all over the carpet. Another client has a string of Xerox copy shops, and after sleeping with him once, I start cleaning his apartment and working in his shop on University Place. I arrive at his apartment speeding, and he keeps a bowl of cocaine on the piano, so I have a grand old time cleaning his place. He has a piano with several keys missing, and one day, high as I can possibly be, instead of cleaning, I write a song called "The Matter of Minutes" to a lyric my friend Tom Piechowski gave me that I was keeping in my pocket for just this moment: "Time is an illusion, false and true and fact. The matter of a minute keeps the universe intact." It has a zany and difficult accompaniment in jangly, uneven time signatures based on the keys that aren't there. This is how I write during this period, intermittently, always high, and in between all the stupid jobs that reflect my derision for myself, like waiting tables on the graveyard shift at an all-night diner on the Lower East Side called 103 Second. One morning, walking home from work up Fifth Avenue, the speed having worn off, I literally fall asleep while I am walking near St. Patrick's Cathedral. I wake up mid-step on a curb and realize I could have died.

During this period, I need a source for speed. Conveniently, I find Dr. Armand Villanueva right on my block. All he wants to do is feel my penis and testicles for a little while, and then he gives me a prescription. I just look around his office as if he were giving me a pedicure while he "examines" me.

At one point I am taking so much speed my heart becomes arrhythmic. He still feels my penis and balls, but this time he sends me for an EKG before giving me the prescription. One day I come home from work and there are ambulances and police cars with their lights spinning by his office door. He has been bludgeoned to death.

One of my jobs is cleaning an office for a company called Score Productions, which creates music and jingles for commercials. My friend Arthur works there during the day, and he gets me the job, knowing how desperate I am. It is directly across the street from Sondheim's house on Forty-Ninth Street. I have to get there around 6:00 a.m. and be gone by 8:30, before anyone arrives. I turn on *The Today Show* while I am cleaning. Jane Pauley and Tom Brokaw are the hosts, and Bryant Gumbel is the sportscaster. One day, Bryant Gumbel is interviewing Anita O'Day with considerable hauteur, and addressing her ignobility quite condescendingly, he asks her something along the lines of "Anita, you've been a jazz singer, a heroin addict, a prostitute, a grave digger, a chorus girl, a common thief, a circus clown . . . what do you have to say for yourself?" And she answers with clipped contempt, "That's what went down, Bryant." I squeal with delight.

I loathe myself at that job and buy huge bags of caramels or family-size five-pound chocolate bars when I leave to eat on the crosstown bus, so I feel psychotic by the time I get home and have a bulimic episode. I stand in front of Sondheim's house gawking and looming every day as well, but I never catch a glimpse of him. One day, I find a vial in the snow directly in front of his house. I assume it's his. I take it home and snort its contents, which should indicate my state of mind in those days. Luckily, the vial wasn't filled with anthrax but with very good cocaine, and my whole head goes numb.

One day I write Sondheim a letter. I recount in vivid detail my calamitous attendance at his *Pacific Overtures* party; I laud him for his magnificent score of *Merrily We Roll Along* and tell him I clean an office across the street from him every day and stalk his home. I tell him he is talented and to keep up the good work. I don't tell him about the cocaine just in case he wants it back. He writes back immediately, sorry about my hilarious misfortunes at his party, gives me his number, and invites me over for drinks. A second chance! This time I won't fuck it up.

On the day of the visit, I pick a new olive-green suit I bought at a funky expensive clothing store on Seventy-Second Street called Stone Free. I want to look just right. I am thinking business attire, official, adult, because, well, I don't want to end up in bed, or in some highly equipped S&M dungeon he supposedly had in his basement that I have heard rumors of, though it has never been authenticated. I try to look handsome but with an official vibe.

I stop for a beer at a bar on Second Avenue near his house because I am nervous and need some loosening up. When I get there, after a small wait in the living room I half remember filled with all those celebrities before I got sick in 1976, he ushers me upstairs to an outdoor terrace. I imagine Katharine Hepburn next door when she famously marched over to his house one night and admonished him for making too much noise. I start drinking wine. He is drinking kirs and smoking pot. We are having a lovely time. I think about smoking pot with him, but for once in my life I listen to my inner logic and think better of it, lest I have a reoccurrence of my bad acid trip and freak out. I feel comfortable thanks to liquid courage, and the conversation is flowing amazingly well. I am fulfilling a deep fantasy conversing with my hero; only a meeting with Stravinsky, I tell him, would be equivalent.

We have both seen the recent opera *Satyagraha* by Philip Glass at BAM and liked it very much, so that is a big topic.

Finally, feeling capacious, and lubricated, I ask, almost salaciously, "So what ever happened with *Merrily We Roll Along*?" I was fishing for gossip. I thought our bright and breezy conversation, our insouciance, entitled me to the insider's view. "When did you see it?" he asks. I catch a glimpse of something scary and dangerous behind his eyes. I try to ignore it. "The first preview," I say, though even as I am saying it, it feels wrong coming out of my mouth.

An arctic chill blows across the terrace like the Ghost of Christmas Past, his face drops, his movements become anxious and clipped, hands playing awkwardly with his pockets, and he abruptly storms off the terrace. "Whoa. What just happened?" I think. I wait a long while in a state of hyper-anxious vigilance, but he doesn't come back. Did he have to go to the bathroom? I don't know what to do. I walk off the terrace into his library. I am thinking, "Is this really happening? Is Stephen Sondheim mad at me? Have I done something wrong?" He rushes in like a tsunami, and amid a mass of angry half sentences I can't decipher because I am scared, devastated, and completely freaked out that Stephen Sondheim is yelling at me, looking as if he wants to kill me, I hear him say, "People like you are why I am leaving the theater!" Suddenly I gather myself, accessing my inner seething-from-birth rage: "What?" And grasping deep inside for some line of defense, I scream, "People like me see everything you write six times! Six times! If you don't write for people like me, I don't know who the hell you think you're writing for!" But I didn't have a leg to stand on. I had not gone back to *Merrily*. I had no idea how it progressed. I didn't know the rules! I follow him as he darts around getting ready to leave his own house, which he suddenly has to do, and it is 100 percent clear the party is over and has ended very badly.

We are leaving his house, and I have fucked up this evening ten times worse than I fucked up the first one. We are outside, in front of his house now, screaming at each other, which passersby seem to be cataloging—"There's Stephen Sondheim having a fight"—and I am sick, very sick inside. I can't rescue the evening. It is an unmitigated disaster. There is a limo in front of his house, and I say, most probably snottily, because by this point he is now my father, and we are playing out a hysterical primal scenario, "Well, there's your limo." I feel as if I were out of my body and blowing up like a balloon. "It isn't my limo!" he spits back. "And it's presumptuous of you to assume it is!" I am amazed by my ability to keep digging the hole a little deeper. I don't know what to do. Awkwardly, following some code that seems ridiculous now, I lean in to shake his hand, fumbling an apology, and careen off into the evening, trembling.

At another point in my life, 1987, to be precise, the playwright John Guare was extremely tough and critical with me about something I wrote, cruel even. He was writing a show with Leonard Bernstein and Jerome Robbins based on Bertolt Brecht's *Measures Taken*, and my friend Stephen Bogardus was auditioning for it. I played for him, and he sang a song of mine from what ended up being *Sycamore Trees*. John was quite effusive about the song, so I decided to take advantage of the moment and sent him something else from the show, which he hated. Though I was devastated when I hung up the phone, I made him a painting and sent him an ebullient, almost obsequious note of thanks. Soon after, we were at a party at Leonard Bernstein's after Lenny had conducted a thrilling performance of Mahler's Second Symphony with the New York Philharmonic and Christa Ludwig as the soloist. John Guare and I were standing at the bar, and he confronted me. He didn't understand the motivation behind such a detailed and ceremonial gesture of gratitude when he was so clearly *mean to me*. Neither did I. Looking back, I see, I needed therapy, and I needed to get clean and sober.

My friend Tom Piechowski lived across from Roosevelt Hospital with his friend Lorraine Matovina, whom he had grown up with in Cleveland. Tom and Brian Frank lived with me when I first moved to the city, in 1977, but in a fit of pique I kicked them both out because all we did was party, and I was terrified I wouldn't do anything with my life. Tom had written the lyric for the song "The Matter of Minutes" and was my frequent writing partner. Lorraine was a cyto-technologist at Montefiore Hospital and had been madly in love with

Tom from the first moment she met him in Cleveland even though he was gay, so she always seemed to be suffering from a low-grade depression, and drinking too much, but we were all drinking too much. Tom was brilliant, handsome, charming, and tragic, so central casting couldn't have supplied a better candidate for her fixation. He modeled himself after Lord Sebastian Flyte in Evelyn Waugh's *Brideshead Revisited*, which should tell you everything you need to know.

I prayed they were home. I really needed friends at that moment. I stumbled in miserable but also excited because I had such a horrible yet dramatic and life-changing saga to tell. We sat around a little table in the living room, drinking and getting high, while I recounted every moment from the ecstatic to the miserable of this disastrous evening. I was traumatized, but they were fascinated, hanging on every word with an almost unseemly relish, so all was not lost. In youth, a catastrophe, if you make it through, no matter how excruciating, is at least fodder for your catalog of horrors.

The next show Sondheim writes is *Sunday in the Park with George*, a huge departure for him because he is working with the playwright and director James Lapine and *not* Hal Prince, the great producer and director, his usual partner in crime. The change elicits a whole other kind of work from him. Lapine's work is more experimental and conceptual. It doesn't attempt to dazzle, no razzmatazz, more blink and flicker, in an almost ephemeral way. His style was perfect for Sondheim in this piece about the painter Georges Seurat, as if they both became the subject matter. Sondheim mirrors Seurat's pointillist style of painting with his score to stunning effect. There is a sequence called "Color and Light"; we see Seurat dabbing the canvas with his brush to the same rhythm as Dot, his irreverent paramour, powdering her face, and we get the whole story of their relationship, the impossibility and tragedy of it, as well as his philosophy of color and paint, a moment unparalleled in the musical theater. For me, it is the most ravishing and unbelievably moving musical I have ever seen.

By now, because what happened between us sits inside me like a dead fetus, I have tried in countless desperate letters to apologize for my indiscretion, but I only get back terse and pointed little notes from him, all starting with "Dear Ricky" and signed, but otherwise as cold and smoking as dry ice. I have a pile of them, stinging keepsakes. At this point I still believe he is somehow wrong and crazy for blowing up at me. I still don't get it.

It is the summer of 1984. I am in Monaco for the Grand Prix, conducting Terri Klausner's nightclub act at the Casino de Monte-Carlo. All the players call me "Chef d'orchestre." Every night I wear my fabulous Armani tuxedo, a birthday present from my roommate, Daniel Glynn.

Terri Klausner made her name as the matinee *Evita* in Los Angeles and New York, when Patti LuPone played nights. She went on to star in other Broadway shows including *Sophisticated Ladies*, a very entertaining compendium of songs by Duke Ellington, in which she tore down the house every night singing "Hit Me with a Hot Note and Watch Me Bounce." She asked me to be her music director after I was recommended to her for another project by her voice teacher Lehman Bick, an esteemed pedagogue for many Broadway stars.

The composer of the scores for the shows *Damn Yankees* and *The Pajama Game*, Richard Adler, heard Terri in a nightclub and was bowled over by her. He asked her to record some unpublished songs of his, and she needed a pianist and an arranger, so she hired me. He had a fabulous town house on the East Side where, when you entered, you were greeted by an amazing collection of colorful and twisted faces on pottery by Picasso. His dashing son Christopher was always running up and down the stairs with seemingly endless creative projects, which never happened, because he was one of the first promising and gifted young men to die of AIDS. I made a faux pas my first time meeting Richard—maybe there is a pattern here—telling him my favorite song of his was "A New Town Is a Blue Town," from *The Pajama Game*. He scowled at me, saying it was the worst song in the show. I later learned that the composer and lyricist of *Guys and Dolls* and *The Most Happy Fella*, Frank Loesser, was the ghostwriter on *The Pajama Game* and had most probably written "A New Town Is a Blue Town," because it was clearly in his style and not Richard Adler's, so I understand why he took an instant dislike to me. For the record,

I now know from personal experience telling someone your favorite anything from their body of work is like sweeping away with one brisk gesture everything else they have ever done and feels more like a jab from a bayonet than a compliment.

In Monaco, we open with "Maniac" from the hit movie *Flashdance*. Four fantastic male dancer/singer/actors do flips around Terri as she comes out (two of them were dead from AIDS within the year). It is perhaps the most anomalous act of my career, and I spend the entire summer drunk and trying to compensate by listening to W. H. Auden read his poetry on an endless tape loop—"There is no love; / There are only the various envies, all of them sad"*—but it is an unbelievably fun time. All of us walk up the steps into Beausoleil, France, every night to eat and drink at a place called Le Select, where the chef, Bernard, and his wife, Dani, take a liking to us and create the most sumptuous feasts for us, plying us with endless bottles of wine. One day they have us out to their terraced farm in southern France, and as we sit on blankets overlooking a spectacular vista, Bernard takes out individual little country breads he has made for us that morning and stuffs each one with a delectable salade Niçoise using ingredients they have grown right there on these terraces. We get drunk and I perform an Isadora Duncan–like ode to the sun up and down the countryside for everyone's entertainment. I don't believe I ever performed sober once that whole summer.

One day I am swimming at the beach club, the one Hitler coopted for his headquarters during World War II, and I hear Stephen Sondheim has had a heart attack. I am forlorn. I must get back into his good graces before he dies! When I get back to New York, I make him a painting called *Stephen Sondheim in Yellow Healing Light*. He is rising out of the water like Jesus Christ with fish swimming all around him, influenced by a drawing my friend Wendy Storch did for me at CMU called *St. R and the Fishes*. There is a storm. The sea is roiling, a sailboat is tipping, and seagulls are diving. I take it to his wing at

* From "In Praise of Limestone."

the hospital, but he is not in the room, so I ask the head nurse to give it to him. I write a letter accompanying it about how he is always in my dreams, having become a stand-in for all the men in my life. It is unbearably painful having him as an enemy, I tell him, and I will do anything in my power to rectify the situation. I never hear from him.

About a month later, I write, asking him if he ever received the painting. "No," he replies, quite tersely, maybe even terser than his previous ten or so iceberg notes. I do the whole painting all over again even better, try to re-create the letter, and send it again. I assume the head nurse swiped the first one. This time he writes thanking me, telling me he likes the painting very much, and he knows what it must have cost me to write what I wrote in the letter. I am overjoyed, feeling as if I can finally put all this behind me.

Fast-forward again.

In 1992, *Home Fires*, a brilliant, copiously researched book about my family by Donald Katz, my friend and running partner, is published. The "Sondheim Story," as it is now dubbed, is in the book, though recounted in the same way I have been telling it, as if somehow he were wrong for blowing his cool with such an innocent young fan. This is not Don's fault; it is still the lens through which I see the story when Don interviews me. Mary Guettel, Richard Rodgers's daughter, a very close friend of Sondheim's, and one of the inspirations for *Merrily We Roll Along*, reads the book and, thinking the story about Steve is charming, says I must send it to him with the parts about him highlighted. "Oh, he'll love it!" she says. Mary is mischievous, like Till Eulenspiegel. He is not amused. Don Katz receives a fairly unpleasant letter. Mr. Sondheim, wordsmith that he is, can be excoriating. You do not want Stephen Sondheim to be mad at you.

Along the way, I win the Stephen Sondheim Award in the early 1990s, the Richard Rodgers Award, for which Steve is one of the judges, in 1999, and the Constance Klinsky Award, which Steve presents

me with at the Second Stage Theater in 2000. We are often in the
same room together, cordial, but it always feels awkward.

Fast-forward again, for the last time.

It is 2003. I have written a new musical, *My Life with Albertine*,
with Richard Nelson for Playwrights Horizons based on the Albertine sections of Marcel Proust's monumental seven-volume *In Search
of Lost Time*. Fascinated by Proust, I have taken any number of steps
toward reading him, though sporadically, because he intimidates me.
I actually *married* Agneta Lindelöf, a Swedish judge, because she read
Proust in French, which is another story altogether (I was dead drunk
when I proposed, and she was dead drunk when she accepted. I asked
her to come to America and be my writing partner, but all we did
was drink. She moved back to Sweden, annulled our wedding, and
died of alcoholism). I carefully perfume the score with everything I
love about French music and that period. At one point I am in Dayton, Ohio, for a production of *Only Heaven*, my mash-up of poems
by Langston Hughes. I write *Albertine* in the early mornings before
I go to work, and there is a white church outside my window with
sonorous chimes every hour, making me feel as if I were in Combray,
the mythical village of Proust's book. Kelli O'Hara, an exquisite glittering star I first discovered in the Broadway musical *Sweet Smell of
Success*, which, contrary to most critics, Kevin and I loved, is Albertine. She has the unusual combination of being stunningly beautiful
and unpredictably deep, and I have a crush on her. Brent Carver, the
Tony Award–winning actor who starred in Kander and Ebb's *Kiss of
the Spider Woman*, is Marcel, moody, mysterious, and captivating, and
I am excited about what we have all created, and very proud.

Charlie Prince, Hal and Judy Prince's son, sets me up with Richard,
and we get along like a house on fire. I first met Charlie in 1994, when
I was at work on my first opera, *The Tibetan Book of the Dead*. Charlie,
a practicing Buddhist, begged me to allow him to conduct the opera,
so I did. We became close friends, which meant invitations every year

to the star-studded Prince Christmas party. Sondheim is always an honored guest, but I avoid him and vice versa.

Charlie is conducting *My Life with Albertine*, and Hal, having seen a preview, writes me a fan letter for opening night. He brings Sondheim, who says nothing, but I guess I had it coming.

At our first preview, I ask a friend whose opinion I value and whose friendship I trust to come, because I feel fragile and need the support. He comes with his new boyfriend. They both dislike the show and almost sneer at me after it, making fun of the work and me. It is perhaps the most insensitive act a friend has ever performed toward me. He never comes back to see it and never mentions it again, and this show I am so proud of is, to him, whatever he has seen that first night. He never even buys the recording. I don't speak to him for a long time.

Now I know the first preview is often the first time a show is even on its feet, with costumes, lighting, and a set. It is the beginning of sorting out a plethora of problems. Between a first preview and its opening night, a show is often rewritten, songs are cut, new ones tried, things are reordered, costumes changed, choreography changed, sometimes even the set. There is a famous story about Tony Kushner, before the first revival of *Angels in America*, in New York City, demanding that the set be scrapped. It is no better than a dress rehearsal, and rarely even that. I have heard that *Merrily*, when it opened, looked nothing like what I saw that night, when I formed my fast opinion, which I did not form maliciously, I just didn't know better. Frankly, knowing what I know now, I am shocked that tickets are even sold to previews. But what Sondheim felt, and he was right, was that there are those who go to the first preview to "report its flaws," in a catty way, to doom it. This was before the internet. Now there is absolutely nothing one can do about the public crowing of everyone who feels their opinion about something in utero will give them cachet.

I know what it is like now, to be dismissed. I know what it feels like to take a drubbing from the critics with absolutely no recourse. I know now what it feels like to work long and hard on something torn straight from your gut that, once it is dismissed, disappears, sometimes even while it is still there. On the day you get bad reviews, friends don't call you, neighbors in your building treat you as if you've defecated in the elevator, and people stop coming to your show, or if they come, they bring with them a delight in feeling exactly as the critics felt, a smugness. New York is a tough and mean old town when it wants to be. There are the occasional fans who love to differ, who genuinely get your work, and you cling to their praise like necessary oxygen, but the hurt is so intense, so sickening, nothing can really buffet it.

Knowing all of this, and after years of ingesting so much beautiful, thoughtful, and poetic work brimming with integrity from Stephen Sondheim, I am truly sorry we got off on the wrong foot. He was a great artist, and the world certainly doesn't need me to say it.

In 2012, at Symphony Space, when Tony de Mare finally premiered the piano pieces a bunch of us composers wrote using Steve's songs as our departure points, we were all interviewed on the stage with Steve during the concert. I was wearing one of my favorite red hats. After the concert, there was a celebration at a nearby saloon. Kevin and I were standing at the bar, and we asked Steve, who was standing by himself, to come over and talk to us. He was being playful and only a little bit bullying when he said to me, "I won't talk to you unless you take that hat off!" Which I did. With him being openly lighthearted, hostile, sarcastic, and even loving, all at once, I knew we were good now, and I was proud of my piece that night, which came second, after William Bolcom's. I felt, like Millay's Harp Weaver, I had spun a beautiful piano piece out of Steve's magnificent song "Every Day a Little Death," spun with the gold threads of my heartstrings.

Adam 𝄞

In 1990, I needed extra singers for a choral piece called "Where Do They Go?" I had written for an AIDS benefit, and my friend Tina Landau, along with her friend Jeff Halpern, who was conducting the piece, showed up one day at my apartment with an incredibly disciplined and wonderful group of fine young theater singers. One of them was Theresa McCarthy. Terry's voice had a purity and an innocence that was disarmingly beautiful and sad; with big almond eyes and a wide-open heart, she was arresting looking, like a Modigliani. She learned about eight songs of mine and sang them exquisitely, so she suggested we go down to her friend Adam Guettel's loft in SoHo to record them.

I knew Adam was Richard Rodgers's grandson, and I had heard a story about him when he and Tina attended Yale together. They were doing a production of *A Christmas Carol* at Trinity Rep in Providence, Rhode Island. Jeff Halpern was the music director, and one day he and Adam got into such a fight that Adam punched the wall and broke his hand. Other than that, I knew nothing.

Adam's loft was the size of a city block. You walked through an immense cavernous space to a salon filled with books, Persian rugs, and one of Richard Rodgers's grand pianos. Through there was a fully equipped professional sound studio. Adam was handsome and friendly, wry and funny, and I liked him instantly. He was a wonderful engineer and producer. Terry and I felt comfortable and well taken care of, so genuine beauty poured out onto the tape.

When we were done, Adam, who seemed to like my music, asked me if I would participate in a benefit for the Gay Men's Health Crisis he was about to host at his loft. He wanted to present four composers and asked me if I would be one of them. Flattered, and having no idea what I was getting myself into, I said yes. Before we left, Terry asked Adam to play me some of his music, which I dreaded, because so often in that position I don't like what I am hearing and I have to lie. He played me two songs from *A Christmas Carol* first. There was a moment in one of them where Terry as Belle sings to Scrooge, "I release you with a full heart for the love of him you once were," and I almost burst into tears. It was unusual and strange, with wonderfully weird melismas that Terry navigated exquisitely; in short, it was wholly original! His voice as a composer was immediately rich and apparent. The last thing he played me was a big extended song based on his interpretation of the myth of Icarus, which was nothing short of sensational. He sang it and his voice was stunning. I couldn't believe it. I was trembling inside. He was a real composer, the kind I would have devoured when I was a kid, demanding to hear every note he had written. Eventually, I did.

The first composer that evening was Jack Eric Williams, a phenomenal composer/lyricist who was writing *Mrs. Farmer's Daughter*, a gorgeous musical about Frances Farmer. People knew him as the actor who originated the role of Beadle Bamford in *Sweeney Todd*. We met when the American Music Theater Festival in Philadelphia commissioned a bunch of composers and lyricists to write pieces about the 1939 World's Fair, "The World of Tomorrow," and I wrote "I Love Electro," with the lyricist Bill Solly, a duet about a robot that does *everything* for the modern housewife. Jack Eric and I became good friends and mutual admirers of each other's work. Then something terrible came between us.

In 1982, Ira Weitzman was producing a cabaret series for Playwrights Horizons at the West Bank Cafe, and he asked me to do an evening of my work. I asked Diane Sutherland (née Fratantoni) and Jack Eric to do it with me. Jack had an unearthly tenor voice suffused with southern soul from his New Orleans childhood, and I loved the way he sang my music. Diane was my dear friend from college, my muse, and my favorite performer to make music with. She was playing Morales in *A Chorus Line* on Broadway at that time, so this was an auspicious cast for my cabaret debut. Jack had just returned from a theater company in Minnesota where he played Big Daddy in Tennessee Williams's *Cat on a Hot Tin Roof.* While there, he slipped on the ice and broke his foot.

The actor who played Brick, a handsome guy named Tom Hasselwander, accompanied Jack back to New York to help him get around and live in his extra bedroom. I needed a page turner for the concert, so Jack asked Tom to do it. Tom and I had instant chemistry, a useful thing because having him next to me all night made me sing and play my best to impress him. We decided we would see each other again. One night I went over to Jack's apartment—Angela Lansbury had originally bought the place for her son, and she was letting Jack live there—to see Tom. Jack was in the living room. We chatted about this and that, and then I excused myself and went into Tom's room. Jack seemed totally cool about my visiting Tom.

Tom played me a recording of Stravinsky's *L'histoire du soldat* he had conducted, and soon we were kissing. One thing led to another, our clothes came off, and we were having sex, when, suddenly, the door burst open and Jack, who was at least six feet tall and weighed about four hundred pounds, was towering over us, screaming at the top of his voice, "Get the fuck out of my house!" I was in shock, terrified, fumbling to cover myself while begging Jack to get out of the room so we could get dressed. Tom and I fled to my house, completely shaken up, where he filled me in on a few details I probably should have known. Jack was in love with Tom. Tom had let Jack kiss him in Minneapolis, underestimating the strength of Jack's feelings, and I got caught in the cross fire.

A few days later, I received a letter from Jack. In line at the bank reading it, I almost threw up. It was the nastiest letter I have ever read. Jack was whip-smart and articulate, so his hate-filled, vitriolic diatribe was devastating. It was so dark I wouldn't even show anyone. Before now, there had never been even a moment of tension between us.

I wouldn't talk to Jack for two years. Tom and I didn't last due to the cursed start. Clearly, I had walked into a minefield.

But this night, we were civil to each other again. The hurt was there, but also relief, because we really did love each other at one point. The other composers were Michael John LaChiusa and John Boswell. Adam put me last. His loft was filled with *hundreds* of people! I had just written a song cycle for a beautiful young soprano, Patricia Schuman, who made a name for herself in Peter Brook's *La tragédie de Carmen*.

Pat, half Nicaraguan, half Scottish, was a great beauty, which, combined with the dark, velvety richness of her voice, made her highly charismatic. She was in New York that summer to sing with the Metropolitan Opera in Central Park.

My song cycle *I Was Thinking of You* used poems by May Sarton, Stevie Smith, Frank O'Hara, Susan Klein, my friend from Carnegie Mellon, and a rousing setting of "Who knows if the moon's" by E. E. Cummings. We got a standing ovation, and the first two people to come up to me were Adam's mother, Mary, and Sheldon Harnick, the lyricist.

Mary was a surprisingly attractive older woman with a somewhat pointed, birdlike face she wasn't afraid to bring quite close to yours, a wonderfully crispy voice clearly honed by a lifetime of smoking and drinking, and just enough fragrance, a classic like Van Cleef & Arpels, that she smelled like money. She had a perfect Le Cirque hairdo and wore a simple Chanel suit and Susan Bennis/Warren Edwards shoes. I loved her immediately. Sheldon was like your favorite uncle, warm and disarmingly open, with a proclivity as well for getting so close I wanted to kiss him on the mouth. I was enshrouded in light.

Sheldon wrote the lyrics to every Jew in the world's favorite musical, *Fiddler on the Roof*, which in my world was about as important as the Koran was to Muslims: *Fiddluh*, as it was referred to by the Jews of Long Island, "play something from *Fiddluh*," and everyone knew what it meant.

Where had I been hiding myself, they asked, why didn't they know who I was? I didn't want to tell them that I had been slowly annihilating myself for the last twenty-two years, so I made up a story. About two weeks later, Mary invited me over to her apartment at the Beresford on Central Park West, where Sheldon lived as well, to play her more music. It was astonishing to be surrounded by Jo Mielziner's original set designs for *South Pacific, Oklahoma!, The King and I* (I played Louis at Camp Lenape), and *Carousel,* and to perform on Richard Rodgers's *primary* piano he wrote those shows on! Mary was fun to play for because she kept showing me when she had chills and goose bumps and couldn't have been more doting. She even cried at one point. Then, just when I was about to leave, her husband, Hank, came home and she asked me to play everything all over again, which I was more than happy to do, though I was jealous of the sizable martinis she mixed them both and the cigarettes. Hank was the perfect gentleman, kind, warm, and handsome, with a full head of white hair, blue eyes, burnished skin, a strong handshake, and a look straight into your eyes so deep I almost had the feeling he was flirting with me. Hank *too* seemed to love my music.

Afterward, I was walking on air when I called my parents and recounted in detail what had just occurred, remembering how they left me at Mama Yetta's when I was a little boy so they could go see the movie of *Oklahoma!* the day it opened.

Mary invited me back about a week later to play for Oscar Hammerstein's two sons, Jamie and Bill, and Ted Chapin. I played a bunch of stuff, and after "Father's Song," which I wrote for my musical *Sycamore Trees,* Ted jumped up and asked me if I had any other publishers representing me, or if I had signed any other contracts.

For five years the Rodgers and Hammerstein Organization paid for me to live and write, a huge vote of confidence as well as an enormous relief financially. I imagine I was a huge disappointment to them because I never wrote anything that was commercially viable, but I would go to the offices with wonderful singers all the time to play them new songs, and they at least seemed amused by me, if not mystified.

Soon after I signed with R&H, I wrote a song cycle for the young African American soprano Harolyn Blackwell, whom I met at the Glyndebourne opera festival in England, where she was singing the role of Clara in Trevor Nunn's production of *Porgy and Bess.* I was there because I had written a song cycle for the American soprano

Carol Vaness, who was singing Donna Anna in *Don Giovanni*. Carol threw a party, and Harolyn said to me, with the toothy pixie-like smile she is now famous for, "You're going to write something for me," and I came back to New York City and wrote *Genius Child*, a setting of ten Langston Hughes poems, for her.

The cycle ended up being fortunate for a few reasons: the press was amazing, RCA was already planning a solo album for Harolyn, and because the premiere of *Genius Child* had gone so well at Carnegie Hall, they decided that night to record it! And, when it was about to be released, Kathleen Battle was fired from a production of *The Daughter of the Regiment* at the Met for her notoriously bad behavior. Harolyn was her understudy, and, consequently, she would be taking over the role, so every time the story was reported on the radio, they played our recording to demonstrate Harolyn's bright angelic voice, and it was a great launch for our CD. Harolyn even went on *Charlie Rose* to talk about it. So, in a very short time, I had a publishing contract *and* a recording contract.

One of my first publications through the R&H publishing company Williamson Music was *Genius Child*, and I dedicated it to the Guettel family. Never before had I been so taken in, loved, and supported by a family in my life. I would write to Mary from wherever I was, sending her poems or just filling her in on whatever details of my life I thought might entertain her. When Mary's mother, Dorothy, died, I wrote her a long loving letter of condolence with quotations from a beautiful letter and a poem Anne Sexton wrote to her daughter Linda. Mary, having met my entire family at the book party for *Home Fires*, wrote me back a terse note: "Yeah, but your mother's a peach. Mine was a lemon. Love, Mary."

Adam and I became fast friends, almost inseparable. I was working with the writer/director Frank Galati on a musical theater piece based on the writings of Jean Cocteau. We had worked on one aria, "Song of the Transparent Mirror," an erotic aria based on Cocteau's book *Le livre blanc*, which portrays a man masturbating while watching an erotic act behind two-way glass. He is not seen watching, and the person inside cannot see out. I asked Adam if I could record it at his studio, and he was so generous with his time not only did we record that but we also spent all day recording other songs of mine, with Adam singing beautifully.

Adam had not yet done anything to put him on the map, and there was no discernible competitiveness in the air. As a matter of fact, his mother, Mary, once introduced me at one of her Christmas parties as her "favorite composer" right in front of Adam, and I felt weird, but he was downright magnanimous.

Adam would buy me gifts. One time, he was on his way up to my apartment for lunch, and he stopped at a flea market in SoHo and bought me a magnificent yellow-and-blue velvet Knights of Columbus robe, very grand and regal, which, of course, I wore at lunch that day. He gave me a stereopticon with a handful of spectacular images to view in it, a raw silk vest that had Frank Lloyd Wright's architectural drawings of the Guggenheim Museum silk-screened onto it, and a beautiful framed Italian print of a cathedral in Tuscany he brought back from Italy.

I wore the vest when Mary allowed me and my friend Elizabeth Futral to do a salon at her apartment. I had met Elizabeth when my friend Tom Bogdan told me I needed to hear a young singer he was performing with in Florida, and she looked me up when she came to New York. We loved each other instantly, and I found her heavenly, celestial voice to be a perfect fit for my songs. I knew I needed people to hear her singing my music, so I asked Mary if she would host a salon, and she said yes immediately. We performed for about a hundred people, an hour's worth of my songs, and Mary and Hank catered it. I had just started seeing Jeffrey, and I remember him sitting closer to the piano than anyone else that night, staring at me in a way no one had ever looked at me before. When it was over, Jeffrey said, "They don't even know who you are," a statement so filled with mystery and appreciation that I decided not to ask what he meant. It's funny, because Kevin is constantly screaming, "You don't know who you are!" at me, and it all seems somewhat related.

Adam wrote me a song. We were always talking about what we wanted to be when we grew up, and I would always say I wanted to be "a great artist." So, Adam wrote me a song that was one of his fantastically engineered recording spectaculars called "You're Great!" He premiered it at one of Mary's parties, and I felt truly honored. I wrote him a melancholy piano solo that I played that night as well, and then Mary asked me to sing "My Mother Is a Singer," which I'd written for *Sycamore Trees*. It was a star-studded event and I remember staring straight at Jessica Walter, who was there with her husband, Ron Liebman, while I was singing, and remembering that she scared the shit out of me in Clint Eastwood's terrifying movie *Play Misty for Me*. Adam threw me a birthday party at his loft and said I could ask anyone I wanted to perform and invite whomever I wanted to come, so I called my friends Patricia Schuman, Melanie Helton, Angelina Réaux, and more, and we did a spectacular concert and had a deliriously good party. (A good story: Angelina Réaux was the Beggar Woman in the national tour of *Sweeney Todd*. They were in Washington, D.C., and Angelina's parents were in the audience for the matinee. Angelina had been complaining about the shoes of Merle Louise, the original Beggar Woman, being too big for her, but no one listened. Sweeney had just slit her throat and sent her down the chute, but on her way down her shoes got caught, her legs twisted, and shattered in fifty places. Her parents heard the bloodcurdling screams, and Angela Lansbury, seeing her legs, said, "Get her wig off!" and shoved it on to Angelina's understudy, because "the show must go on." Angelina was in the hospital unable to walk for a year, during which time, on Hal Prince's suggestion, she became an opera singer. Leonard Bernstein heard her sing in a review of his music at the Skylight Opera Theater, which Stephen Wadsworth and Francesca Zambello ran in Milwaukee, and cast her as Mimi in his final recording of *La bohème*, bringing her to Rome to perform it there as well. You can't *not* tell that story.)

In AA they say it is all about attraction, not promotion. We were hanging out all the time and I am not sure what it was that attracted him, but Adam could see how sobriety was benefiting me, and he decided to accompany me to a meeting one day. (I asked Adam for permission to write about this.) There is something deep and tender about sharing such a thing with someone. You are there because you simply want to get better and, by doing so, improve your life. It is humbling. He took to it right away and started counting days. He softened in every possible way quickly, and it was truly moving. Almost immediately, he asked Jeffrey to be his sponsor because Jeffrey was an angel and Adam needed one. A sponsor is another alcoholic who can hold your hand and guide you through the steps they have taken before you.

Jeffrey had a beat-up first edition of the AA big book with so much highlighting and writing in the margins you would think he was copy-editing it. He was a perfect sponsor for Adam because he worked his program with enormous integrity and wasn't particularly codependent when it came to tough love, so Adam had a strong heart and a firm hand looking out for him.

In June 1995, Jeffrey and I went to visit Adam at his lovely red farmhouse in Tinmouth, Vermont. I was in the midst of writing my first opera, *The Tibetan Book of the Dead*. Jeffrey had asked me to help him die as a Buddhist. David Gockley commissioned a new opera from me, but we hadn't arrived at a topic. I told him I was reading an incredible book for Jeffrey called *The Tibetan Book of Living and Dying*, by Sogyal Rinpoche, a simplification of the Tibetan teachings for Westerners to understand, and he said, "Why don't you make an opera out of that?" Nothing like that would have ever occurred to me, but it seemed like a perfect, albeit weird, idea. I went home and called my friend Bill Hoffman and asked him to meet me for lunch. Bill had made a splash as a playwright with the play *As Is* on Broadway and the libretto for John Corigliano's opera, *The Ghosts of Versailles*, at the Metropolitan Opera. I told him about the project, and I asked him if he would collaborate with me, but he said to call his friend the playwright Jean Claude van Itallie, who had already written a play of *The Tibetan Book of the Dead* for La MaMa in 1983. I called Jean Claude after lunch, and the next day the play was FedExed to me. The play, subtitled "Or, How Not to Do It Again," was written in seventeen terse, economical, exhilarating scenes. It illustrated the journey from sickness to death, through the

bardo, and back to life again, brilliantly, with great clarity, and was exactly what I needed. I began setting it to music, and it was strange and
satisfying, perfect really, to be setting the teachings Jeffrey had asked
me to learn, so I was in a constant state of learning, and he was in a
constant state of hearing. There was one moment, "The Moment of
Death," which was the aria Jeffrey wanted playing while he was dying:
"My friend, now is the moment of death. The time has come for you
to start out. You are going home." I made a beautiful recording of it
with an exquisite African American soprano named Theresa Hamm-
Smith, who had starred in my *Only Heaven*, and kept it in a special
spot for when the moment arose.

In Tinmouth, Adam got me the key to a little church nearby his
house with a piano where they let me come and write every day. One
day, I had the irrepressible urge to masturbate right out in the open
in this sweet empty little church. It was so quiet and so holy and the
energy inside me was bursting. It was that feeling where you want to
do something naughty someplace good. The satyr in you screams to be
let loose. I went home with the thought I was never going to tell Jeffrey
and Adam, but I couldn't resist and blurted it out. Adam was worried
the church would burn down.

It was such a sweet time. I did all the cooking. I had taken a macro-
biotic cooking class because Jeffrey believed eating macrobiotically
would extend his life, so I made big pots of lentil soups, fish, tofu, and
tons of kale. I got so skinny I'm sure people thought I was as sick as
Jeffrey. We ate no meat, no dairy, no white flour, and no sugar. Adam
was a good sport about our extremely restricted diet. We would all
go to AA meetings at the Wilson House in East Dorset, Vermont.
Adam's brother Alec came up at one point to visit, and he and I ran
together. Alec is an anomaly for the Guettel family. He strayed away
from anything artistic, doesn't seem to have a neurotic bone in his
body, and is completely kind, uncomplicated, and egoless. He just
wants to make the world a better place. He is also very handsome.

There was a drought, so it was harshly sunny and dry, with crackling reeds and cicadas singing all the time. Everything was green but
tinged with ocher for want of moisture. One morning, Jeffrey left the

house after breakfast to stroll out into the fields and do his chants and affirmations, as well as a little dance he was taught by a medicine man, basically a series of ablutions that he was given by various spiritual teachers that were supposed to keep his mind clear and his heart positive so he could heal. Suddenly the sky turned black, it began thundering and lightning, and Jeffrey came flying through the fields in the pouring rain screaming, "I made it rain! I made it rain!" Adam and I had absolutely no doubt that he had.

Adam sat out in the backyard writing music on music paper clipped to a drawing board on his lap, and I marveled at how different we were in our approach. I need the instrument and my hands to explore ideas until I find them. I'm sure Adam does too, but mostly he was out there in the sun and the wind scribbling with his pencil and paper. There was a beautiful breeze breaking through the heat, and I thought, "This is heaven."

When Jeffrey and I went to see *Floyd Collins*, the show Adam wrote with Tina Landau, something happened. It was happening for a while and continued happening and maybe even started happening before I knew it was happening, but it was excruciating and like a plague that pulled us apart and nearly threatened to destroy me. As a child growing up, I experienced many things, many of them unfortunate, and many of them destructive, but none quite so devastating as jealousy and envy, which I don't remember ever experiencing, being the only boy and the youngest, as a child. Strangely, even all those situations like gym class when over and over I'd be the only one to never shoot a basket, or the last to be picked for the team, I wouldn't look at all the boys who excelled and wish I were them. I just wanted to be elsewhere doing what I wanted to be doing.

When Adam first started writing *Floyd Collins*, it was before Jeffrey came into my life, perhaps the early 1990s, so not much before, but before. He first presented it in his loft as a long monologue for Floyd, and I learned that day the full spectrum of Adam's talent, and I guess you could say I felt subsumed by it. I cried in the cab on the way home. I rode uptown shell-shocked. I felt physically ill. I wondered how we could ever coexist, but I hid the feeling away. It seemed too ugly to reveal. Next, there was a reading of the piece when it was further along and had more characters, and I was buried a little deeper in a previously unknown place in myself, a place so shameful and dreary that heretofore I had been spared from. I thought it would eat me alive. Before I started this chapter, I began to read through old journals. I found what I had written in my journal when I first heard Adam's *Floyd Collins* music and thought, "I should put that in the book!" But then I decided against it, because I felt by including it, I would disappear myself. That day was the first time I saw or heard Brian d'Arcy James, who had been cast for the workshop and who ended up being for all of us a friend and someone we all loved and hired all the time.

Finally, *Floyd Collins* premiered in Philadelphia at the American Music Theater Festival. Tina and I had done our *States of Independence*, which Mary attended and supported, accompanied by her wonderful friend the writer Walter Clemons. In Philadelphia, *Floyd Collins*, for me, was impossibly moving and beautiful, but I was still alive when it was over; I could still feel my hands and my feet. The thing I *don't* remember from Philadelphia was the part of Floyd's crazy sister, Nellie; I remember only the deeply affecting performance of Floyd, played by a fragile and tremulous actor named Jim Morlino, who was one of the singers who ended up singing in my choral piece "Where Do They Go?"

In New York, Theresa McCarthy was cast as Nellie, who was a little "off." Her performance in this role I consider one of the greatest performances I have ever seen. Terry made a physical choice about Nellie that was strange and otherworldly, showing her off-ness in a clear and specific way. Terry as Nellie always took steps that were a little too big, so whenever she walked across the stage, it was as if a game of hopscotch for giants got stuck in her head and she was still playing it, or she was still avoiding cracks in the sidewalk for some unusual and insane reason. She was always circling her head with one hand as if an invisible halo needed shining.

The story of this man, trapped in a cave with no one to save him, and the way it mirrored Jeffrey's fragility and my impotence in the face of it, was overwhelming. Adam had me over to his loft and sang

"Lucky" and "How Glory Goes," but in context, and with Tina Landau's ingenious direction, they murdered me.

We went backstage, and when I saw Terry, I became unhinged. I didn't know what was happening to me. My self-confidence and sense of self were eroding. A crushing feeling that I could be disappeared, destroyed at any moment, and that nothing I wrote would ever mean anything began to eat away at me like maggots. How was I going to live with this pain, and there was still so much responsibility with Jeffrey getting sicker and sicker and every day a potential life-and-death emergency.

It affected Adam too. One day, at his loft, I sang him a simple setting I had done of the Langston Hughes poem "My People," and when I was done, I asked, "Did you like it?" and he showed me a badly bloodied thumb he had torn apart as I played it. It was funny, but sad, too, because something was changing, and it wasn't good. Our feelings of jealousy and our fears of being threatened by each other were destroying our friendship. One day, Adam came over to our apartment. He and Jeffrey were working on the fourth and fifth steps together. I told him I had a new song I was dedicating to him and I wanted him to hear it. He sat on the piano bench next to me, and I played him a duet I had made out of Langston Hughes's poem "Love Song for Lucinda." Instead of feeling flattered or happy, Adam started grilling me in a strange and aggressive way, taking a tone I had never heard from him before, accusing me of being disingenuous. What did he think? That I was co-opting him, making fun of him? Soon, we were pushing and shoving each other, and Jeffrey had to break us up. I stormed out of the house in my pajamas and wouldn't return until Adam was gone, telling Jeffrey I had no intention of ever speaking to Adam again. By this point, I was no longer invited to parties at the Guettel house. I assumed it was because I was a failure, no longer Mary's favorite composer, and most of all competition; there could be only one star composer at the party, and that star was Adam. At one point, the Guettels had planned to lend me one of the Richard Rodgers pianos, but that was over. I took it like a man, I already felt so bad about myself anyway, it was actually easier, less painful to stay away.

Toward the end with Jeffrey, Adam was working on his magnificent song cycle, *Saturn Returns*. I felt responsible for the title because
he was feeling awful one day and I told him he was in his Saturn Return, the moment in your late twenties when Saturn returns to where
it was when you were born and you can no longer escape the ago-
nizing reality of adulthood. He had played me so many of the songs,
including things that never went into it, a fantastic retelling of the
Medusa myth, for example. "Hero and Leander" had different words
at one point in Portuguese. He had written it sitting on a piano bench
improvising with Sonia Braga, probably trying to get her into bed, or,
knowing Adam, succeeding, which I understood, because I often used
the piano bench and my talent toward seduction, but he rewrote it for
the show. He came over weeks before Jeffrey died, and just as he had
played us the entire opening of *Floyd Collins* a few years before, he sang
"Migratory V." It was summer but unseasonably cool.

Jeffrey's mother was living with us at that point because I needed
help. His father was creating a drama that day because he was in de-
nial that Jeffrey was dying and became obsessed with buying us a
La-Z-Boy. "Dad! I'm not even going to live long enough to enjoy it!"
Jeffrey exclaimed, but his dad insisted, as if a La-Z-Boy were the key
to saving his life.

We had gone to visit his father in Rehoboth Beach, Delaware,
and while we were there, Jeffrey had a coughing fit that was so bad
we decided, when we got back to New York, we would invite all our
friends over to say goodbye and then I would kill him. I was helping
him up the stairs, and when I turned around for a second, his father
stood at the bottom of the stairs looking as if he were stranded on a
quickly moving ice floe. I have never seen a man so upset and scared.
We didn't have to kill him when we got home; nature took its course.
When Adam sang "Migratory V" that day, there was so much extreme
sadness swirling in the air I could barely hear it. I just wanted God to
come and take Jeffrey and me upon his great huge wing and deliver us
from our misery. I can't hear that song now.

I did something terrible one day. I made plans to go with Charlie
Prince to see a revival of Ingmar Bergman's *Persona* at Lincoln Cen-

ter. Right before I was supposed to meet Charlie, Jeffrey came down with pneumonia and had to go straight to the hospital. Because these emergencies were continuous, and I was at my wit's end, I put Jeffrey in a cab, making him get himself to the hospital, and went to the movie with Charlie. Sizzling with shame and guilt, I could barely watch the movie, and when it was over, I ran home in tears to apologize three hundred times to Jeffrey, who lovingly forgave me, but I could never forgive myself, and though Bergman is still my favorite director, I never want to see that movie again.

I went down to visit Adam in his loft one day in 1999. We had slightly relaxed our long period of not playing anything for each other and avoiding the topic of work altogether, and he played me some things he was writing for a show called *The Light in the Piazza*. They were very beautiful, suffused with a particular Italian light and the august and restless harmony of late Fauré. They were so beautiful, in fact, they hurt.

The next I heard any of them was when Adam did a concert of his music at Town Hall that May, which was an experience because I don't know how it happened, but I was sitting with a shaking and clearly jonesing Liza Minnelli. I was very aware that day of the crowd, of Adam's lineage, his Exeter and Yale education, his money. How could I possibly compete? Adam had at his fingertips the most expensive equipment available for making music, for recording and mixing, and he knew how to use it all. If a demo was to be made, it was good enough to be released. At this concert, there was an incredible polish to it, though Adam came out to play some of the music from *The Light in the Piazza* at one point, with the cellist Adam Grabois and the violinist Michael Nicholas, and he fell apart at the piano, explaining how his nerves often overtook him if he had to play in public, but it was utterly charming, and then he continued on beautifully.

Kevin and I accompanied our friends Mary Jo and Ted Shen and Diane and Brian Sutherland to see *The Light in the Piazza* in Chicago before it came to New York. It was ravishing, heart wrenchingly so. I loved it and I felt pummeled by it. I felt the possibility of a grinding depression's descent. Celia Keenan-Bolger, who played Clara, the girl stunted mentally by a pony's kick to her head in childhood, was shatterable as crystal, projecting a childlike excitability that was deeply poignant, and Vicki Clark as her mother was funny and devastating. It was one of the most beautiful and moving pieces of musical theater I had ever seen. Soon after that, I was doing a master class at the University of Michigan in Ann Arbor, and the teacher who brought me there said as much but went all the way just before I went onstage, "I think it is the most beautiful piece of theater I have ever seen," withering my confidence for the rest of the day, making it hard to teach and live.

On the opening night of *The Light in the Piazza* in New York, when Adam and the book's writer, Craig Lucas, came out for their bows, they got a roaring and endless extended standing ovation. Overwhelmed with envy, I wanted the earth to swallow me up. I felt as if I were on fire. At the party afterward at Tavern on the Green, Mary Guettel, standing behind me in the food line, said, "Oh God, this must have been a terrible evening for you." I hated that she could see through me like that, hated that she knew, and I felt ashamed of myself, ashamed that I could not just be happy for everyone, ashamed as if I were wearing a placard across myself that spelled MEDIOCRITY, ashamed and terribly jealous that Adam was anointed and I wasn't, and for months and months I walked around as if I were one of Argentina's *desaparecidos*.

Picasso bought a Modigliani simply to paint over it, so I know I am in good company.

Gore Vidal wrote, "When a friend succeeds, a part of me dies."

My Life with Albertine was running at Playwrights Horizons. My friend the extremely talented and wonderfully wacky composer/lyricist Michael John LaChiusa had just left his review of the show on my phone machine, "Honey, you nailed that pussy to the floor!" and I was feeling pretty good about it. I sat with Adam, and he wept copiously at the end. I felt he really heard what I had done. I felt we were equals. I loved his tears as if they were holy water; nobody wanted or needed to win or be the greatest that day, or if they did, it didn't deafen or blind them to what was happening. That show was treated quite ungenerously by the New York press and is one of the *longer* hurts of my life.

Will this book be an act of willful self-destruction, satisfying, even cathartic to write, but a grenade to all I have built?

At the end of my first year of friendship with Adam, he sent me a card that said, "Best new friend this year."

Since Adam's *Light in the Piazza,* I have written the operas *Orpheus and Euridice, The Grapes of Wrath, Green Sneakers, Morning Star, 27, A Coffin in Egypt, The House Without a Christmas Tree, Intimate Apparel, The Garden of the Finzi-Continis,* and *Ellen West,* and I have proven to myself that I can write no matter how shitty I feel about myself, no matter how intense my attacks of jealousy and envy are, no matter how buried in grief I am; I write, I know how to, and I do it every day. I have proved an awful lot to myself *about* myself by persisting through bad bouts of every sort of mental and emotional instability the gods can *possibly* extract from their arsenal and throw at me, so I feel much better now. Otherwise, I never could have written this. And this: I am proud of my body of work.

In 2002, there was a psychic I went to who told me Adam and I had another life together in Italy. One of the reasons I went to see her was that while I was in Dayton, Ohio, working on a new production of *Only Heaven* at the Dayton Art Institute, while writing *My Life with Albertine* in the mornings, something strange and troubling was growing on my back, a lump, and I had no idea what it was. Kevin came to visit me early in our relationship, and I was *terribly* self-conscious about it, but he didn't seem to care. Early love. When I got back to New York, I was showering one night, and it burst. The water in the tub kept getting redder and redder, and I couldn't believe how much blood was pouring out of it. It was like a portal to somewhere else. It happened just before my appointment with the psychic. At one point she got very quiet; then she said, "You have a friend with whom you have an intense relationship, one both productive and fraught. You have a powerful connection. Adam?" She said in another life, during the Renaissance, I had been an instrument builder with a very successful business. I had enormous integrity and was very hardworking, and my work was exquisite. My instruments were works of art. Adam was a competitor, and envious of my business, so he hired someone to stab me in the back while we were walking one day. The assassin came upon me from behind and attacked, so the last thing I saw, while I was dying, was Adam's eyes. That is why this thing grew on my back and then burst before going to her. She said it was important I knew this. She said we had huge karma together and that we recognized each other right away in this lifetime. I have never told him this story. I think he'll probably roll his eyes; I think you will too.

Last night, Kevin and I watched *Truman & Tennessee*, a documentary about Truman Capote and Tennessee Williams. Tennessee Williams said point-blank, "I am jealous of every other writer." God bless him.

Sheila and I went out to California for the publication of Susan's last book, *Knitting Heaven and Earth*. First, we went to Point Reyes National Seashore, which neither of us had ever seen. Its spectacular vistas of sea and cliffs in the fog reminded me of Ireland. Then we drove to Oakland to check into a hotel near Susan's house. Susan had lived alone for so long there were piles everywhere, books, knitting projects, writing projects, and nowhere to sit, much less sleep, for guests.

After her book party and a reading at a restaurant in Berkeley, my mother called me excitedly to tell me that Adam Guettel had won a Tony Award for *The Light in the Piazza*. It was unlike her, because she didn't tell me as if she wanted to make me happy; she told me as if she were implying, "Why don't you have a Tony Award yet?"

David Gockley invited Speight Jenkins, the general director of Seattle Opera, to Houston to hear *The Tibetan Book of the Dead*. It was a strange and surreal time.

After the fiasco of Jeffrey's coming for the premiere, getting sick and nearly dying, leaving before he could see it when it was written for him, and my calling the company in a state of such hysteria I went mute, my sisters Sheila and Susan, sensing my distress, like saviors, just showed up on my doorstep. Susan had visited Jeffrey in New York and smudged him with sage. I read her "Sleep," the poem I wrote for Jeffrey's birthday, which became the epilogue to *Green Sneakers*, and she said, "You know, when Jeffrey dies, the love will not die. Your love for him is not in him; it is in you." She was scared for me.

They didn't ask much of me. They just wanted to be there as a buffer, take me out for meals, and pamper me, and I was grateful they were there. We looked at paintings, sat in the Rothko Chapel, and perused hundreds of Native American artifacts. Susan lived with the Cherokee Indians on Alcatraz once, to write about them. They loved her and gave her beautiful jewelry. One day, when Susan was taking a bath at the boatyard, Sheila's friend Linda Klaff, a heroin addict who once, when I was little, chased me around the house with one of her turds in a napkin, came in and stole all of Susan's and my mother's jewelry. Susan was still hurting about it, and she was always looking to replace it.

I don't know what they thought of the opera. I consider *Tibetan Book* my most difficult opera to warm up to because of the subject matter and its general abstractness, though each time it is performed, that fear is not borne out. A few years ago, the Eastman School of

Music revived it in a truly beautiful and provocative production that took place in a perfectly reproduced New York City subway station, where the graffiti was all Tibetan imagery. I hadn't seen the opera since 1996 and I was scared. Would it hold up? Would it make any sense? I was astounded at how powerful it was, considering the whole thing was practically written in an emergency room.

Speight and I were staying in the same hotel. We met for breakfast the morning after he had seen the production. He liked the opera very much and decided to commission a new opera from me. I had an idea I had been kicking around in my head for a while. I loved François Truffaut's 1981 movie, *The Woman Next Door*, and thought, with its story of obsession, suicide, and murder, it would make a great opera. Even the narrator, missing a leg from her own suicide attempt years before over a painful breakup, is a great character. It is high romanticism à la Truffaut, everything he does best. Speight asked whom I might like to write the libretto, and I answered without hesitation, "Tony Kushner." Tony was the only writer I could imagine working with. His was the name on everyone's tongue in the theater. Jean Claude van Itallie, the librettist, said to Charlie Prince and me when he was in Houston for opening night of *Tibetan Book*, "I wish *I* had written *Angels in America*." I cataloged it. Tony, a great admirer of Jean Claude's, was his student at one point.

I am competitive, and not always in a good way—although, is there ever really a good way? Competition, according to Krishnamurti, is violence. I believe that, because I see what it does to me and others, as well as the world. But the competitive side of me wanted to say I was working with Tony Kushner, the most famous playwright in the world at that moment. I liked the idea of it; I thought it would give me cachet. I liked wrapping my mouth around it. "I'm writing an opera with Tony Kushner," though it was more than that. *Angels in America* was the cri de coeur of my generation, defining our experience of the AIDS crisis from within. When Jeffrey and I saw it, we were overwhelmed, shattered, and exhilarated.

After Jeffrey died, I walked to Central Park one day to weep at the Bethesda Fountain, because Tony had given it to me as my own

monument, our monument. I have never been able to walk past it
again without thinking about that. I wrote to Tony about a thousand
times. He is the only person who rivals Tina Landau and Audra Mc-
Donald in their reluctance to return emails. But eventually, he got
back to me, saying he was interested. We met at a diner in Chelsea to
talk about the commission. I had met Tony once. Craig Lucas brought
Tony to a New Year's Eve concert I did with Angelina Réaux at Mer-
kin Hall, the concert where we surprised Jeffrey, who didn't know I
had set "Sleep" to music.

We premiered it on the radio that afternoon for John Schaefer's
program on WNYC. That night, Angelina just said, "This is for Jeffrey." Craig was sitting in front of Jeffrey, though they didn't know
each other. During the song, Craig began sobbing. His own lover,
Timothy, had just died. Jeffrey leaned forward and held him from behind. That moment allowed me, inconsolable one day, to call Craig
after Jeffrey died, knowing he knew, and that fact alone would comfort me.

SLEEP

We have never seen a meadow together,
never seen sheep—
but sometimes, when I watch you sleep . . .

I see the Great Expanse, the Archipelago,
the Dolomites, the Himalayas,
hung with snow
do you know
that we have made
a universe of moments?

A ferry ride we took
across the rolling bay.
The sunset glowed so bright
it took our breath away.

I sang to you, and held you
from the evening's chill,
It resonates inside me now.
It always will.

A film we saw,
a beach in France
all soaked with rain.
My favorite kind,
a brooding blend of love
and pain.
After which, we danced
across the urban plain . . .
Always I will see you
through French movie rain.

Jeffrey
not a night has fallen,
not a star.
That I was not reminded
of how warm you are.
Warm you are in sleep
and dear!
Without a trace of meadow
or, of sheep near.
Sleep, dear.

Tony is an extremely charismatic individual. I felt lucky whenever I was with him, which probably, in the end, got in the way, but this was the beginning.

We talked about my Truffaut idea. I could see this did not interest him, not that he didn't like the idea, but it was clear in order for him to be truly excited about an idea, it needed to be generated by him. Tony and I were born in the same year, I, in May, a Taurus; he, in July, a Cancer. In Chinese astrology, this means we are both fire monkeys, strong-willed and stubborn, though I can be crippled by my insecurity, not that he doesn't have it, but I don't believe it ever cripples him. He asked me to read "St. Cecilia; or, The Power of Music," by Heinrich von Kleist. The story, about three Dutch brothers who go mysteriously mute and their poor mother who tries to understand their silence and bring them back to speech, though intriguing, did not ring bells for me, but I was so enamored with the idea of working with Tony I left the door open.

Then Tony came up with a much bigger, Kushneresque idea, even calling it "an operatic idea for Ricky Ian Gordon," about the day Louis B. Mayer "furloughed" Judy Garland from her studio contract including all future projects because of her profligacy and outrageous unreliability. Judy, who was married to Vincente Minnelli at the time, went home, broke an ordinary drinking glass in the bathroom, and slit her own throat, potentially ruining her voice. Mayer pleaded with Minnelli to allow Katharine Hepburn to whip Garland into shape the way she had with Spencer Tracy when he was bottoming out on alcohol. Minnelli agreed. After hours behind closed doors, Hepburn persuaded Garland to go to rehab in Lenox, Massachusetts.

Tony's intent was to imagine that conversation, but then it becomes a fantasia. In the dining room of the Red Lion Inn in Stockbridge, Massachusetts, the Dionysian, out-of-control Garland is represented by Herman Melville, and the Apollonian, practical Hepburn is represented by Nathaniel Hawthorne. There is a big scene between the four of them. The title was "Melville Loves Hawthorne; or, Katharine Hepburn Drives the Demons Out of Judy Garland's Soul."

Eventually, Judy Garland wants back in Hollywood, but Minnelli visits her and gingerly informs her it may not be so easy. "Other actresses have been coming up through the ranks," he tells her, at which point Tony has an absolutely radiant Grace Kelly come forward and sing "an exquisite little aria."

Judy makes a comeback, discovering a whole new voice, the big, belty voice she sang with toward the end of her life in songs like "The Man That Got Away" and "Come Rain or Come Shine."

I had an idea for the ending I thought would be great. I worried having an opera singer imitate Garland could be awkward. So, when Judy opens her mouth to sing with her new voice, a whole chorus would soar out of it like birds. Rather than one voice, a hundred voices would be hers. Tony liked that idea too.

David Gockley wanted to be in on the commission, as did Harvey Lichtenstein from Brooklyn Academy of Music. Because I was broke at that time, having an opera commissioned by three major opera companies was a big deal and I banked on it saving me. Tony and I went to meet with Harvey at BAM to talk schedule and commission. But there were too many things working against us.

I was still decimated by Jeffrey's death. I could maybe have managed the Truffaut adaptation, I already heard music for that, and the material at least existed, but this was huge and unwieldy. I couldn't fathom it. It scared the shit out of me. I did nothing to sabotage it, but I'm sure I sent out smoke signals of terror and ambivalence.

Then Tony was busy with a million projects. It was hard to gauge when he could ever actually *write* our libretto. Also, Tony was like a martian to Speight. He never even referred to him by name, calling him "that guy" instead. Nothing seemed to impress him, not the Pulitzer, not the Tony. Speight's preferred idea was for me to write an opera about his favorite human being who ever lived, Richard Wagner, but I had to explain to him that for my second opera outing, to write about perhaps the most celebrated and prolific opera composer of all time, who had written enough notes for thirty lifetimes, might be daunting, seem pretentious, and could easily be a self-destructive invitation for critics to feast on. I reminded him as well that I was Jewish and wasn't so hot on writing an opera about one of the most virulently anti-Semitic artists of all time.

David Gockley, who could be an extremely cool customer, maybe a tad on the spectrum, even brutal when necessary, telling singers when they had gotten too fat, or were singing flat, started picking up on the smoke signals. He intuited the commission was getting away from me, the idea was too large. Having just gone through *Tibetan Book* with me, my crying numerous times in his office, the trip to the airport to pick up Jeffrey and Jeffrey's subsequent tragic departure, well, let's just say the green lights had turned yellow, and it was obviously they would soon be turning red.

It's interesting, thinking about it now, why didn't David and Speight want to meet Tony? He was going to be writing half the opera. Wouldn't that have helped? I have never written an opera where the impresario wasn't interested in the librettist.

In Florida to visit my parents, I went with my mother to see the movie about Cole Porter, *De-Lovely*, starring a perfectly miscast Kevin Kline and a floundering Ashley Judd, with perhaps the worst script ever written. My mother loved it, but I nearly tore my hair and nails out during it. Earlier that day, the whole commission fell apart and I was suicidal. Now I had a dead lover, no future, no money, and no commission. Life was not de-lovely at that moment.

Tony and I tried to get back on track. He felt guilty it all fell apart and was trying to come up with something that would repair the damage. He even gave me some money. He wrote a treatment of "St. Cecilia" for which he scheduled a reading at the Public Theater with Betty Buckley, Marian Seldes, Michael Cumpsty, and many other superb New York actors. The reading, though truly affecting, lasted five hours. That night, in a state of panic, I called Tony to discuss cuts, and Tony screamed, "I can't believe you're even talking about cuts now!" But all I could think of was *all those words* I'd have to set to music and how the opera would be longer than Robert Wilson's *Ka Mountain*, which lasted three days! Maybe I should have written the Wagner opera? I felt as if my life were falling apart.

I set one lyric from the libretto, though, "Yolanda," which Tony didn't like. We had a tiff about it, and he called me at Cafe Luxembourg, where I was in the middle of a business lunch, and had me paged at my table so he could apologize.

Then he wrote *Caroline, or Change* and showed me the libretto. I loved it, with wonderful little touches like the washer and dryer singing. I thought I would do a great job with it, but just as I was gearing up to do it, he gave it to Jeanine Tesori to write. Everyone loved the score, it went to Broadway, Tonya Pinkins won a Tony, and the rest is history.

I think the truth is, the water surrounding the dream of us writing together was polluted, impossible to navigate. I knew it. I assumed the blame, feeling sad, embarrassed, and lost, like a loser. To feel important to someone in one moment and not the next . . . I had let Tony Kushner slip through my fingers.

We were still friends for a while. Tony had a new play opening at the Public, his version of *The Dybbuk*. We had read scenes from it together when we did our joint evening together at St. Ann's, "Words Spoken, Words Sung," where I sang and played from my work and he read from his. I surprised him by setting two of his monologues for that evening, first, Agnes's exquisite "Hands" from *A Bright Room Called Day*:

> *This hand to make*
> *a frail moon-cup,*
> *protective patch*
> *over the weak eye,*
> *the eye that cannot bear to see.*
> *Five fingers has this hand.*
> *With five I can . . .*

Even setting it in a way that I could display whichever hand was being addressed while performing it, which I thought was quite clever. I also set Harper's final monologue from *Angels in America*, "Night Flight to San Francisco":

> *Nothing's lost forever. In this world, there is a kind of painful progress. Longing for what we've left behind, and dreaming ahead.*

Angelina Réaux sang it.

Tony got me tickets to see *A Dybbuk* and called me really early the next morning to see what I thought before I had formulated what I was going to say. He heard ambivalence in my voice and blew up at me, unfortunately, another nail in the Ricky Ian Gordon/Tony Kushner coffin. I felt so bad, because the last thing in the world I wanted to do was hurt him. Now the thing is, I don't think I even knew if *A Dyb-*

buk was a good play or a bad one. It was the kind of play I would never normally go see, and I was an improper judge. *Angels in America* was about me, my world, my friends, my life, my "feast of losses."* Even *Homebody/Kabul* felt as if it were about the world at that moment, the chaos, the danger, the division, and I found it riveting. I love Tony's work! But *A Dybbuk* was Tony's take on an old Jewish theater classic that unfortunately had nothing to say to me that night and might never. I am not, nor have I ever been, an observant Jew.

One of my birthdays, when we were still friends, we met at a coffee shop on the Upper East Side. He showed up with all kinds of completely wonderful books by Virgil, Charles Simic, Whitman, Robert Duncan, and more, a treasure trove of riches, but something was wrong. I can't explain it, but we seemed to be dissipating.

Another time, we had coffee down by Union Square. This was a hard time for Tony as well. He was having trouble moving on from the immense success of *Angels in America*, and everyone, including me, I guess, was measuring everything he did against that. His friend Michael Mayer, the director, had a hit on Broadway and Tony was jealous. He said, in the sweetest, most downtrodden voice, like a little boy, "I want a hit on Broadway again."

When the light of our friendship dimmed, what I used to beat myself up about was that I was not smart enough to be friends with him. The *I Ching* talks about "no blame." I don't think it is either of our faults. Even when I decided I wanted to write with him, the idea was inorganic, born out of my alcoholic grandiosity. I didn't even know him. I loved his work. I admired him. But I couldn't see myself as his equal. Even now . . .

Almost two years ago, I ran into Tony in the street at dusk. It was winter and snowing. He seemed genuinely happy to see me, which made me feel overjoyed. We decided we'd get together, but that could have been a felt obligation on his part. We didn't. I had just recorded a CD with Jennifer Zetlan, the soprano who sang the titular role in the world premiere of my opera *Ellen West*. On it were the world

* From "The Layers," by Stanley Kunitz.

premiere recordings of my monologues from *Angels in America*, Harper's "Antarctica" monologue, which Tony had never heard, though I tried several times to get him to come over and hear it after I wrote it, and "Night Flight to San Francisco." At his request, I sent him the CD. I never heard back from him.

A month or two later, I was walking down Broadway, and I saw him on the corner of Sixty-Ninth Street. As I approached, he told me he was talking to Oskar Eustis on the phone. I didn't care. I shouted, "You're mean! Mean, mean, mean!" and kept walking. That night, my friends Mary Jo and Ted Shen took Kevin and me to the New York City Ballet for Wendy Whelan's hypnotic farewell performance, which was spectacular. I was sitting right behind Jeanine Tesori, who was there with Steven Spielberg and Kate Capshaw. They were working on the new *West Side Story* together, which of course made me jealous. Tony had written the new screenplay. Like a child, I blurted out to Jeanine how angry I felt at Tony. She rolled her eyes blasély and purred, "Oh, she gets soooooo busy."

That little tidbit of camp made me feel enormously vindicated.

A few days letter, I got an email from Tony:

Dear Ricky Ann,

You have to find a way to forgive me for being such a hideous feckless ingrate of an asshole. I can try to explain to you why I couldn't bring myself to listen to the cd, though I'm not sure I understand it myself, I kept meaning to but some combination of feeling completely overwhelmed with personal mishegas and a monstrous amount of work and I don't know guilt about not having been a friend to you and knowing that unlike most music I have to make actual time and space to give yours a listen, and probably also at this moment attending to Angels-related anything excites the worst of my terrifyingly potent powers of avoidance.

And the longer I failed to behave well the harder it got to do the obvious and of course pleasurable thing and listen to your music, I mean how nice that would be, so what is the matter with me, am I just mean? And then I ran into you and that was horrible.

I'm really really sorry, honey. I've hurt your feelings and I'm ashamed of myself and I hope you can forgive me.

I flew to San Fran yesterday for Tony Taccone's farewell party and on the way I listened to Your Clear Eye. I can't imagine that after all this you'll believe me when I tell you that I love it very very much, it's incredible. The Dickinson songs are utterly gorgeous. I can't recall having heard "You cannot put a fire out"—is that new? I don't even remember having read the poem. Dear God, it's an amazing text and your setting enlarges everything in it, the bald remorseless truth of it and the wit and the scary joy. I cried listening again to "Will there really be a morning" and of course all the way through "Night Flight." "Antarctica" is as magnificent a pocket epic of madness and liberation as ever it was. It's like you moved through the text setting off electrical storms! Ms. Zetlan is a beautiful singer and perfect for your music—open-heartedly emotional but with something reserved, something going on always under the surface, powerful and smart. I'm gonna have future Harpers—if anyone does the play again and if I ever feel I can go near it—listen to your reading of her because you get the edge she walks along and you've realized it perfectly. I'm a very lucky writer.

I'm around all summer filming West Side Story gevalt. If you feel you can retrieve me from the recycle bin, let's have coffee.

Much much love, and again, with deepest apologies,

Tony

It is entirely possible, even probable, I overinflate my own importance in Tony's life. I might have just been a blip on the computer screen, but for me it was enormous. The title of this book could be

Ruminations on Past Hurts or *Am I the Only One Who Is Thinking About This?*

In the summer of 2005, I walked into a bookstore in whatever city I was in that day. I was perusing the shelves and noticed there was a new book about Tony, by Jim Fisher. Like all writers with equally huge and fragile egos, I checked the index to see if I was in the book. I was. Mr. Fisher mentioned the setting I had done of "Night Flight to San Francisco," and because he had clearly never heard it, nor clearly had any curiosity to, he just quoted some snotty thing Anthony Tommasini said about it in *The New York Times*. I went ballistic. Mr. Fisher didn't even ask Tony about the monologue to see what he thought, because the *Times* is the be-all and end-all final word on everything. Yes, I know, like a child, I have peppered this book with all kinds of quotations from my great reviews, but it is to give a balanced picture. I have been revered *and* reviled. *Some* people have liked my work. Anyway, I wrote Tony a letter in a state of extreme rage and sadness, after writing to Mr. Fisher, who never had the balls to write back. After I sent it, I wrote back and apologized for what might have been indecipherable muttering.

Tony, in what might as well be an excerpt from Rilke's *Letters to a Young Poet*, wrote back:

Dear Ricky Ann,

No, no, it was only too decipherable. I have been all those places myself, in fact every day . . . oh well never mind. This life of ours is so hard and not so much fun a lot of the time and then at moments I suppose it gets fun enough to keep us going, and yes, yes the critics. I don't know which book you are referring to—is there a new one, or is it JIM Fisher's book? Anyway whoever quoted whatever critic saying whatever nasty thing about your gorgeous setting of the monologue, fuck em and fuck the critic and I hope when

they slam right into one another screaming in hideous torment as they run, each blind with terror and remorse and
pain, their hair eyeballs flesh burning in whatever pit of hell
they find themselves, this writer and the critic he/she cited,
I hope they fuse together and form one big shrieking lump
of mouldering smouldering tissue and burn together for all
eternity, and the writer cites the critic's shrieks and the critic
criticizes the way the writer is writing his/her perditional
agony. Every time I open a book if there's something bad in
it about me the fucking thing will fall instantly open to the
page on which the bad thing is printed, and the words will
leap out and sear themselves indelibly on my optic nerves. A
book or a newspaper or any printed matter.

It all sounds very lovely what you are doing, and I can't
wait to hear it all. When is the O&E piece happening? Will
you tell me how it goes in Dallas?

XOXOXOX

T

Probably not much later, in a fit of paralyzing jealousy concerning
someone who shall remain nameless (admittedly, I am high mainte-
nance), I wrote Tony a series of emails again, because Mr. Kushner
gives good counsel, and again, in the spirit of Rilke, he wrote,

Dear Ricky Ann,

Thank you for sending me the amazing heartrending letters. We must talk my darling. A few salient points. 1) Forget ——, he isn't real, he's just the bogeyman they invented
to make the rest of you stop writing, he has his own problems and they want you to stop writing for one reason: they
are the devil and they want the world to end and you mustn't
let them win—and that is the only reality, the only one,
it's NEVER about talent or prizes or success or failure, it's

about the devil wanting to stop the voice of the world from singing its song so that the world will die and the devil will win. POSTERITY doesn't give a flaming fuck about the opinion of any critic, not even the greatest who ever carped can expect his or her opinion to shape what posterity, the future, will like or dislike. POSTERITY also doesn't care about what you want or need, and you'll be dead when it arrives, and neither you nor I nor fucking —— can control it, all we can do is write and hope a few people in the future will like what we've done, and if they don't, well, we'll at least be footnotes. So we must write write write and help the world sing its song as best we can, adding our own little sound to the general chorus of exultation and rage and despair.

I will leave you with this. Last night, Kevin was working, so I decided to watch Rainer Werner Fassbinder's film *Fox and His Friends*. I've already seen it twice, but what I found out during the pandemic is how little I remember of films and books, so sometimes it's better to revisit things I remember liking, rather than try new things I will just forget, so I can affix into my brain until I forget them again what it was I liked.

There is a scene in a mud bath where Fassbinder, who plays Fox, walks out of a locker room butt naked with his rather formidable penis swinging around like a sturgeon undulating in the sea. Besides marveling at this important new or *refreshed* information about my beloved Fassbinder, inconveniently forgotten either out of shock or because my subconscious wanted me to be pleasantly surprised every time I watched it, I had this thought: it is important for me to be *that* naked in the world, in my work, because self-censorship means safe, less dangerous, and consequently less interesting.

AFTERTHOUGHT

Yesterday was Tony's birthday, July 16, and I sent him a little birthday wish, to which he replied, "Awwww Ricky Ann!!" I was overwhelmed with warmth for him. I was just walking around the lake with Lucy, and I remembered that when I knew him, Tony had two of my favorite poems, Paul Goodman's "Lordly Hudson" and Robert Duncan's "My Mother Would Be a Falconress," blown up and framed above the desk where he wrote. The idea that anyone could be so in love with words, their impact, their effect, their beauty, and frame them like paintings to inspire them . . .

> *And I, her gay falcon treading her wrist,*
> *would fly to bring back*
> *from the blue of the sky to her, bleeding, a prize,*
> *where I dream in my little hood with many bells . . .*

MARCH 14, 2022

Tony went to see my opera *Intimate Apparel* the night PBS was taping it for *Great Performances*.

> Hey Ricky Bicky Boo!!! I just saw your gorgeous glorious, lush romantic sexy heartbreaking opera!!! The music is so beautiful, surprising, complex, surging, haunting, filled with yearning and foreboding and suffused with terrible loss, even at times unnerving (in the best way), propulsive and suspended, horizontal and vertical, both at once. Really a magnificent achievement, doll, with such a huge encompass-ing heart. I love you and I'm so proud of you and proud to know you.

Of course I love him.

PART VIII

SELECTED WORKS, PART TWO

(Premiere, June 14, 2014, Opera Theatre of St. Louis)

The genius is in, at 27, rue de Fleurus.
—from Royce Vavrek's libretto for *27*

⌒⌒⌒⌒

One year, during a particularly cold and snowy winter at Carnegie Mellon, I got a terrible flu. My throat swelled as if I had strep, and all I could eat were tangerines. One of my roommates on Filbert Street, Kate Stainton, a soft-spoken, Brearley-educated intellectual who behind her little wire-rimmed glasses could be quite funny and macabre (knowing I was obsessed at that time with Ingmar Bergman's movie *Cries and Whispers*, in homage to a harrowing scene wherein Ingrid Thulin, after a perfectly awful dinner with her starched, frigid, boring, and homely husband, brings a shard from a broken wineglass up to bed and, staring at him, cuts herself in the vagina, muttering repeatedly, "A tissue of lies," while smearing blood on her lips, one afternoon Kate scrawled the word "lies" in red ink on a white tissue and taped it to my door) gave me a book I admired in her room one day, *Charmed Circle*, by James Mellow, about the life and times of Gertrude Stein and her salon at 27, rue de Fleurus, in Paris.

I read the book from morning to night between sneezing, coughing, and blowing my nose. It was one of those moments where the book, your mood, what you are thinking and feeling, and what you need all mesh together. My room seemed to turn into the damp and cold gray Paris of a Utrillo painting.

I needed a role model. I am not saying I was looking to become a stout Jewish lesbian in Paris, but Gertrude Stein was committed to her own muse, ruggedly individual, unswayed by the opinions of others, uninhibited in terms of being who she was, loving whom she loved, weighing what she weighed, having bold opinions, and facing the repercussions of her outspokenness.

Stein loved beauty and was constantly interpreting and reinterpreting what she thought was beautiful. Mostly, she believed in herself with such rigor it fascinated me. And her world—the habitués of her salon, Picasso, Matisse, Hemingway, Fitzgerald, Satie, Rousseau, everyone and anyone who was doing anything of interest and thinking anything worth thinking—came through her Paris salon at 27, rue de Fleurus, until finally it was Alice B. Toklas, who stole her heart. Until then, I don't think I had any idea of who I was in the world. I was floundering. But I knew I wanted a life where I was surrounded by artists, and I was one myself. Still a piano major, I hadn't even figured out that I was a composer yet.

I started collecting art. I would go to showings at the Forbes Street Gallery, the school gallery, which had shows every Friday night for the artists at school, and I would buy things, or bargain, or trade, or beg, or sleep with people for them. I bought a Robert Patla drawing of strange creatures wriggling all over the page in colored pencil. You couldn't miss Robert Patla, because he weighed about twelve pounds and would paint his shoes bright colors, like mint green, with ordinary house paint. I bought two incredibly evocative and beautiful drawings of East Liberty, a run-down Pittsburgh neighborhood, from a show by a guy named Ron Wiggins, my friend Stacey Robin Kimball's handsome WASP nerd with glasses boyfriend for a while, and Doug gave me two of his elegant silkscreens as gifts. One was charmingly called *X's Trying to Be Butterflies*, and the other, a lovely scene of colorful umbrellas and beach chairs, which made me think of *Death in Venice*, was called *Beach Club '74*. Wendy Storch gave me *St. R and the Fishes*, which was supposed to be me. Wendy is whom I hired when I needed a paper on Emily Dickinson and doing a paper was as far from my possible accomplishments as playing football. Dennis Koontz gave me a few insane drawings of his grids with Scotch tape, watercolors, ink, dead flies, and postage stamps. When Bill Turner wrote the music to that incredible production of Brecht's *Jungle of Cities* directed by Greg Boyd, who ended up running the Alley Theatre for many years before allegations of sexual misconduct and just plain meanness dethroned him, I bought the fantastic poster, a wall sculpture made out of muslin designed by Calvin Tsao. I was amassing my own art collection for the salon I was eventually going to host. Gertrude Stein was showing me how to live and savor a life, what I wanted my life to look like, and who I wanted to be inside it.

I did not yet know that one of the professors in the drama department was Leon Katz, a Stein scholar whom Alice refers to in her letters in *Staying On Alone* as Mr. Katz when she spent time with him after Gertrude died. Mr. Katz shows up quite a bit in Janet Malcolm's wonderful book *Two Lives*. Leon made an opera libretto out of Gertrude Stein's somewhat inscrutable thousand-page novel, *The Making of Americans*, which the Reverend Al Carmines set to music. It was performed at Judson Memorial Church, but then I started setting it to music because Leon wanted to hear a different take on it and I loved the words.

Finishing something as massive as that was far from my capabilities then, though I did get some lovely arias out of it. One day I was speeding, and I spent the day in my carriage house setting to music the final words from the opera, "Living Dying Being and Existing, anyone who ever was or is or will be living, shall be knowing and remembering, some such thing," and it is not hard to decipher I was on drugs because the music is obsessive-compulsive and insane like the rolling Catherine wheel. I set Gertrude's opening monologue, "I Write for Myself and Strangers," and when Ira Weitzman presented me in a cabaret in New York at the West Bank Cafe in the early 1980s, I opened with it.

In 2009, the Virginia Arts Festival, in collaboration with Virginia Opera in Norfolk, was looking for a composer to create an operatic work to commemorate the sesquicentennial of the Civil War. Kelli O'Hara and Rob Fisher, the conductor, were down there doing a concert and, having caught wind of this, kindly recommended me. I knew immediately I wanted to do a smaller piece than *The Grapes of Wrath*, because I was winding up a tour of it and I was exhausted. I suggested five singers and seventeen players, and they liked the idea. I approached Mark Campbell to be my librettist. We had both arrived in New York City in the late 1970s to conquer the musical theater, and though we constantly crisscrossed, we had never worked together. I thought this was a perfect opportunity to engage him. *Rappahannock County*, a theatrical song cycle, was made up of twenty or so musical snapshots of the people and events that took place in one Civil War county. Some of them were authentic. Mark sketched them from their own journals and historical documents. Some of them he created by collagistically culling various sources to create wonderfully unique and poignant characters, such as an embalmer, a wounded soldier trapped on a snowy battlefield, a woman liberated from slavery, living in squalor at a contraband camp where her baby succumbs to typhus, and a baker who sells her pies to the Confederate soldiers in order to surreptitiously spy on them. Kevin Newbury was the director, Rob Fisher conducted, and Wendall Harrington did the set and projections. Kevin Newbury talked constantly about his friend Jim Robinson, the artistic director of Opera Theatre of St. Louis, whom I knew about but had never met, and whenever Kevin mentioned him, I thought, characteristically, "Why the fuck haven't they commissioned *me*?" Lo and behold, almost as soon as I got home, I got a call one morning from Jim. "We'd like to commission you to write an opera for us starring Stephanie Blythe." I rarely come up with an idea so quickly, but immediately I said, "Gertrude Stein," because Stephanie is a formidable physical presence with a voice of great majesty unparalleled in its size in the whole world, and if you know her, you know, like Stein, she will naturally preside in any room.

She is a storyteller, a jokester, a ukulele player, an injustice collector, a disdainer, and a great enthusiast when she likes something and not at all if she doesn't. She is charming and fascinating. It came to me instantly, and I knew it was right.

At first, the road was a little rocky. I asked Michael Korie if he would write the libretto. We had already adapted Giorgio Bassani's novel *The Garden of the Finzi-Continis* into an opera (*way* more on that later) after *The Grapes of Wrath*, which, coincidentally, I worked on simultaneously with *Rappahannock County* while attending Civitella Ranieri, in 2009, an artist residency at a castle in Italy, and we were going to write an opera about Adèle Hugo, Victor Hugo's daughter whom François Truffaut memorialized in his film *The Story of Adele H.*, for the Met, a topic dear to my heart—someone crippled and derailed by an unrequited obsession.

Michael blew away everyone at the Met with his beautifully illustrated outline, and I thought we were on our way. In 2011, I returned from Virginia, after *Rappahannock County* premiered; not only had he not made any progress, but he had made no effort to and blithely informed me about all the other pieces he was working on that would have to take priority. I felt hurt and fired him. We didn't speak for a long while, but eventually we were back on track, détente, and I felt it was safe to get back into the water with him, so we talked about the subject matter and discussed the deadlines.

He missed all the deadlines, promising over and over again to deliver, until finally, and on the last day of the extension he asked for, I received a note from his agent saying he was dropping out of the project. The combination of rage, upset, and frustration I felt was so enormous I felt as if my head were exploding.

He kept writing to us all, me, Jim Robinson, and Tim O'Leary, about how well it was going, but he just needed more time. I didn't understand how someone could let me down in such a cruel way. I didn't even hear from him. I heard from his agent, who at one point was *my* agent. I was also scared, because I now had very little time to write the opera, no librettist, and dates that couldn't be changed because of Stephanie's schedule.

Kevin and I drove up to the country that night, and I couldn't speak; I just stared out the window and moaned. The next morning, the cloud had darkened. I was inconsolable. Kevin said, "You'd better go meditate. I'm worried about you." Like a dutiful child, I skulked off to my room. While in meditation, I remembered that Fred Lassen, the conductor of my *Sycamore Trees* at the Signature Theatre in

Arlington, Virginia, had brought Royce Vavrek, a young writer who wanted to meet me, over to my apartment the previous fall. I remembered Royce saying, "I would do anything to work with you," but I already had so much on my plate I couldn't imagine working with anyone new or taking on another project.

I called and told Royce about Stephanie, St. Louis, and the situation I was in, and then I said, "If you can read fifteen books and write me a libretto in a month, you've got the job." He said, "I can, I will, and *yay*."

We met Monday morning at my apartment. I gave him a list of many wonderful books, but highest on the list were *Charmed Circle, What Is Remembered* by Alice B. Toklas, and Gertrude's *Wars I Have Seen, Paris, France*, and of course *The Autobiography of Alice B. Toklas*. Because things with Michael had taken such a bad turn, I wanted to be as clear as possible with Royce about what I was looking for.

I didn't want this to feel like a Gertrude Stein libretto. She had written several, most notably, *Four Saints in Three Acts* and *The Mother of Us All* for Virgil Thomson, but, though delightful, they are nonnarrative and abstract, and I wanted something more linear with more of a narrative. I felt Gertrude and Alice were possibly the most inspiring gay couple of the twentieth century, and I wanted to celebrate their marriage. I didn't want to whitewash Gertrude, the speculation she might have collaborated to keep herself and Alice, Jewish lesbians, safe during World War II. The entire contents of the Louvre were emptied out and hidden all over France, but everything at the Stein salon including the art was perfectly intact. I wanted the paintings to sing, and the opera to feel like a one-act fantasia that sweeps you up on a delicious journey. And finally, my favorite line of Gertrude's was "Before the flowers of friendship faded friendship faded," and I would love if it showed up in the piece.

Royce made so many intelligent and sensitive decisions. He packed a truckload of seminal moments into one libretto with enormous inspiration and creativity. I had him do only one rewrite, not because it was flawed, but because he had read so much Gertrude Stein the first version of the libretto felt as if she had written it.

I told Royce to make it more his own language and he did.

Seeing how completely right Royce was for the piece made it easier to forgive Michael. Michael has a darker sensibility; Royce created a soufflé, filled with light, joy, and humor. Michael later admitted he could never quite get himself to *like* Gertrude.

Royce decided on a cast of five, two women and the three men who have multiple functions in the course of the evening, playing Leo Stein, Pablo Picasso *and* his girlfriend Fernande Olivier, Henri *and* Madame Matisse, Marie Laurencin, another painter and member of the avant-garde as well as the girlfriend of Guillaume Apollinaire (the famous poet and Picasso's best friend), the paintings of Picasso, Matisse, and Juan Gris, the empty frames, soldiers in both world wars, a doughboy, F. Scott Fitzgerald, Ernest Hemingway, and Man Ray.

Royce, clearly a writer for the theater, understands pacing, beats, dramatic arc, and variety. He divides the opera into five acts and a prologue without an intermission. In the prologue, "Alice Knits the World," Royce uses Alice's isolation and loneliness after Gertrude's death as the imperative for her to furiously knit the salon back to life.

Out of the yarn the three men emerge, the paintings. They introduce us to the world at 27, rue de Fleurus, and then Gertrude appears, haughtily addressing the audience as the denizens of the salon, with the line "De la part de qui venez-vous? Who invited you?"

In act 1, scene 1, Gertrude has invited everyone for the unveiling of Picasso's famous portrait of her. Matisse mopes jealously, seeing Picasso as his replacement, as his early fauvist masterpiece *La femme au chapeau*, with a streak of bright blue going straight down the face of a lovely young woman, was Leo and Gertrude's first big purchase and the prestigious start as well as scandal of the salon.

Picasso's portrait is unveiled, lauded adoringly by Gertrude and Alice, and loathed by Matisse and Leo, who sing, "It is very . . . brown," under their breath contemptuously. Royce gives Matisse one very funny nod of approval, though, with the line "The corduroy is correct."

Scene 2 is a flashback. Gertrude is sitting for Picasso's portrait for the hundredth time. Supposedly, Picasso one day, in a fit of frustration, wiped out Gertrude's face and proclaimed, "I can't see you anymore." She comforts him with the words "To be a genius, it takes a lot of time doing nothing." He later added her face alone in his studio one night, and unlike anything else in the portrait, in its angularity and primitiveness it heralds his beginnings in cubism. Gertrude decides to do her own portraits in words.

Back at the salon, Leo, sickened and jealous of Gertrude's relationships with Alice and Picasso, denounces her portrait of Picasso, "If I Told Him," taunting her with his lack of faith in her talent.

Matisse calls it all a circus, and a vaudeville ensues in which the three men hilariously transform into the wives or girlfriends of the geniuses, and Alice enacts her entertaining of them. Leo announces his departure with Matisse and a stack of paintings, slamming the door, in a reenactment of the moment when Gertrude and Leo parted ways and never spoke again. Passing him on the street once, she tipped her hat, and that was that.

Alice B. Toklas said she heard bells upon meeting Gertrude, Picasso, and Gertrude's friend Alfred North Whitehead, who wrote the book *Adventures of Ideas*. She considered them the chimes of genius.

As Picasso admires his portrait of Gertrude, Alice comforts Gertrude over Leo's leaving with the "Chimes Duet." People seeing the portrait would say, "It doesn't look like Gertrude," but Picasso, knowing the work would become synonymous with her name, said, "It will." He was right. As the act ends, we hear the sirens and explosions of World War I.

Royce illustrated the libretto with key paintings, and for act 2 it was three Juan Gris paintings that hung in the salon. Gertrude always said, referring to Picasso and cubism, the person who "invents" the thing has to make it ugly, but then someone comes along and makes it beautiful, and for her this was Juan Gris. It is probably for this reason that Gertrude Stein wrote in *The Autobiography of Alice B. Toklas*, "Juan Gris was the only person whom Picasso wished away."

Act 2 is a tango. Gertrude tries to write, but there is no coal, so she and Alice are freezing. The constant bombs keep them terrified, and food is scarce.

Gertrude befriends a doughboy who clandestinely supplies her and Alice with coal and cigarettes. Gertrude asks for some eggs. As he leaves to look for them, there is a huge blast, and Gertrude sings, "He'll never return with the eggs, another boy lost," coining the term "lost generation."

In act 3, Gertrude has turned her attention away from painters and toward writers: Ernest Hemingway in all his exaggerated masculinity; and F. Scott Fitzgerald, insecure and alcoholic. As Gertrude begins her condescending and even castrating critique of their work, the music becomes a foxtrot.

Hemingway and Fitzgerald vie for Gertrude's approval, while the photographer Man Ray takes his iconic photo of Gertrude and Alice. After Hemingway and Fitzgerald wrestle for Gertrude's approval, Hemingway has had enough. Castrating her back, he denounces her with his aria "She Calls Us Lost, Bullshit."

The disgruntled paintings complain about being insensitively sold for food when the cupboards were bare, and Gertrude's portrait becomes her conscience, questioning how she and Alice stayed safe, fed, secure, and even happy during World War II. With speculation about her friendship with Bernard Faÿ and her translations of the speeches of Marshal Pétain, both Nazi collaborators, act 4 attempts to get inside Gertrude's head and heart, the doubts she may be harboring.

In "Jury of My Canvas," she asks to be remembered for her volunteer work during the war and the good she has done for the world of letters and painting. Seeing Gertrude worrying about her legacy, Alice reassures her, "You are historical."

Exhausted and dispirited, Gertrude has a vision. She sees the doughboy on his way back with the eggs, luminous in their basket. Alice sings her a lullaby as she dies.

In act 5, Alice is alone on the day the Metropolitan Museum is coming to pick up the Picasso portrait to take to America. She invites Pablo to come say goodbye to Gertrude. Alice sings of how deeply she misses Gertrude, "Will she ever shut up?" and Picasso acknowledges Alice, "You are good. Good Alice."

Alice puts the flowers Picasso has brought in a vase, "these are the flowers of friendship," and Gertrude's portrait comes to life. She sings "I've Been Called Many Things" and invites Alice into the portrait with her, and Alice, Gertrude, and the paintings reprise the "Chimes Duet."

I was listening to Verdi's *Falstaff*, an explosion of energy that suddenly turns tender, lyrical, and profound in the gentlest way toward the end. *Falstaff* might be Verdi's most sophisticated opera compositionally, in that, rather than being an opera about set pieces, it is a through composed, brilliant, and economically told story, and is often considered the Verdi opera for connoisseurs.

Motifs and fragments substitute for the full-throated melodies Verdi was known for. I was fascinated by the way the piece moved, but I will always be a "set piece" composer, being a sucker for arias, duets, trios, ensembles, and choruses. I look forward every time I see it to the final trio from Strauss's *Der Rosenkavalier* or "Che bel sogno" from Puccini's *La rondine*, and I love writing them as well. But the energy of *Falstaff*, the skill, the rhythm, and the dazzling, unbelievable final fugue I find thrilling.

I was also having a love affair with Britten's *Albert Herring*, his chamber comic opera. Britten wrote it after his somber *Rape of Lucretia*, and though it deals with society's reaction to an outcast, a big theme for Britten, it does it in a lighthearted, almost twee way, though as a composition it is complex and brilliantly written, evoking the world of childhood in a small English village and even including a pennywhistle in the orchestra.

Before I write an opera, when I am in the thick cloud of terror and excitement before starting a piece, or the profligate misery of procrastination, a shadow slowly starts pressing against my back, telling me what the opera will be like. I don't hear specific notes and sounds, but it is an energy, a force, and when I finally put my hands to the piano and my pencil to the paper, the shadow begins to become whole, vivid, and detailed. It's as if it always existed and you were being readied for its passage *through* you.

Some of my favorite music growing up was by the composers I

would enjoy accessing for 27, Poulenc, Ravel, Fauré, Satie, Ibert, and Milhaud. Royce's instincts about where and what the moments should be and amount to were impeccable. He gave me a great gift at the beginning of the process. I invited him over to hear the prologue and act 1. Giddy and overjoyed, he said, "Oh my God, it's so *you*, Ricky. Just keep being *you*, it's perfect."

Barry Singer wrote an article on "muses" for *Opera News*, and Elizabeth Futral was mine. Her silvery, shimmering sound, her beauty, her depth, and her honesty on the stage made her a consummate artist. She came perfectly prepared the first day and for the entire rehearsal period brought one idea after another to the floor, a dream collaborator for everyone in the room.

I loved watching her evolve and create Alice and adding details for her, asides for when she was crossing the stage, because she made the tiniest details come alive. For the moment of Gertrude's death, Royce wrote a lullaby for Alice, "Before We Say Goodbye," freely incorporating the last two things Gertrude famously uttered to Alice before she died. "What is the answer?" she asked. When Alice didn't answer, Gertrude then said, "In that case, what is the question?" We turn it into their final dialogue.

Alice sits on the arm of the chair, holding Gertrude as her hand drops. On the very first day we ran the scene, Elizabeth, instinctively, slowly closed each of Stephanie's eyes and planted a long, sensuous kiss on Stephanie's mouth. No one directed her to do so. It was so startling, and so right, the whole room burst into tears.

At the first dress rehearsal, when we finally ran the whole opera with orchestra, sets, costumes, wigs, and lights, Stephanie came offstage afterward and said, "This is the biggest role I have ever done." Then she went and collapsed in the greenroom as we all received notes. I did what I was asked to do. I wrote an opera for the great Stephanie Blythe, and I was proud of it.

Michael Christie led the St. Louis Symphony through the orchestrations Bruce Coughlin and I fashioned with fierce commitment. Through the entire process he was collaborative from start to finish, enlisting my help and guidance, wanting to make sure he was helping everyone in the room convey exactly what I meant. I was grateful because not all conductors are that humble and egoless in the process.

In general, the reception to the opera was spectacular, my favorite review being one titled "A Hit Is a Hit Is a Hit," by Jim Sohre, for *Opera Today*. *27* has been done in Montreal, Detroit, Pittsburgh, Las Vegas, and Montana. I created a new version of *27*, adding the Master-Voices chorus, and Ted Sperling conducted it at New York City Center with the Orchestra of St. Luke's in the spring of 2016.

Morning Star

(Premiere, June 30, 2015, Cincinnati Opera)

Until I got sober, I could never have written an opera. It's too big a commitment, a lengthy process with twists and turns demanding entirely too much concentration. Also, opera is collaboration, and there are so many personalities that have to be navigated, you have to be at your optimum or the weight of the endeavor will pull you down.

In the late 1990s, I was invited to be the composer in residence at the Lyric Opera of Chicago. Having written only one opera, I was too scared to start a new piece, so I mentioned what I was writing about my family.

In Chicago, I played a bunch of the music for the Lyric staff. Everybody was pleased and "The Family Piece" it was.

Then I came to my senses. I realized how spotty my work for "The Family Piece" was, unstrung, without even an implied narrative; writing an opera on my own without a librettist was too ambitious. I called William Hoffman and asked him to work with me. Bill had written the libretto for *The Ghosts of Versailles* with John Corigliano at the Met.

One day, I got a call from Richard Pearlman, the overseer of the project. He had seen a revival of Sylvia Regan's play *Morning Star* at Steppenwolf and thought it might be perfect for Bill and me.

I was astonished at what an apt project it was for me. It concerns an immigrant family, the Feldermans, on the Lower East Side of New York City in 1910. Becky, after her husband's murder, escapes the rising anti-Semitism in Europe with her three daughters, a son, and her husband's best friend, Aaron Greenspan, and they come to America. They live together in an extremely cramped tenement. The constellation, a young son, Hymie, and his three older sisters, was just like my family, so it felt as if I could write about my family *through* the Feldermans.

Esther, the youngest daughter, a starry-eyed romantic, works at the Triangle Shirtwaist Factory. Fanny, the middle daughter, a "showbiz"-style singer, works as a ticket taker in a theater where she falls in love with the usher, Irving Tashman, a talented songwriter trying to break into vaudeville. Sadie, the oldest, is a shrewd businesswoman and sells hats. Once Irving marries Fanny, he won't let her sing in public. Sad and frustrated, a caged bird, she feels unjustly pressured to hide herself in housewifery. Harry, the handsome history teacher, comes to tutor the women once a week, including Becky. Sadie is in love with him, unaware that he and Esther are *already* in love, and all hell breaks loose.

The central tragedy of the opera is the Triangle Shirtwaist Factory fire in 1911. The bosses had locked the seamstresses in for increased productivity, and they all perished. My mother's mother, Rebecca Lieberman, worked at the Triangle but was home sick on the day of the fire. Her mother rushed her over to see her friends and co-workers flying out the window, their shirtwaists flapping like wings on fire. At the pier where the bodies were laid out, she helped identify their charred remains. She was suicidally depressed for the rest of her life. Bill, personalizing the story, made the city they escaped from Riga, Latvia, where his people were from. That is a big step in collaboration, when the "mine" of a piece becomes the "ours." We were now pregnant with the same child.

Bill was great; funny, naughty, and personable, but he was not always easy to work with. He could go so far off in a direction I felt was wrong and I would have to rein him back in. He went off to write Sadie's big aria, "Three Loving Sisters," in act 1, but the first draft was about five pages long and included kings, queens, ogres, princesses, dark clouds, spells, thunder, poisoned apples, and mirrors. "Bill," I said. "What the hell is this?!" feeling it would be longer than the "Liebestod" from Wagner's *Tristan and Isolde*. But that was his process; he had to go way far afield to get to the center.

I felt stretched by what Bill gave me to set to music. The first thing was the world coming to life outside and inside the tenement. Becky Felderman studies for her history lessons. Fanny tries to learn

"Morning Star," a song Irving wrote for her. Esther stares into the mirror, trying on her beloved Harry Engel's last name. Hymie studies for his Bar Mitzvah, and Aaron sleeps on the couch dreaming in Yiddish. Pearl and Prince, African American fishmongers, peddle their wares out on the street, and Kathleen O'Fallin, an Irish neighbor, warns her daughter Mary about the evils of men, and it all builds into a solo for Becky and the cast called "The Promised Land." I had never written anything with so much simultaneity before, but I loved what we came up with, and it helped me to understand Bill's style. Bill was a vertical thinker rather than a horizontal one, and he saw everything in layers. He was building clear and specific characters and inviting me to paint in broad brushstrokes to define them.

We did two workshops at the Lyric. Everyone loved it. Then something happened.

The opera was supposed to be a co-production with the Goodman Theatre. However, Robert Falls, the artistic director of the Goodman and our would-be director, was supposed to direct a production of Massenet's *Thaïs*, starring Renée Fleming, at the Lyric. His concept and design were delivered late, and when they finally arrived, the Lyric didn't like them, so like a twelve-year-old, Bob pulled out of his contract with the Lyric, which meant our opera was canceled, too.

In writing *Morning Star*, I leaned into my childhood, where my mother spoke Yiddish and everything she cooked—brisket, blintzes, black radish with schmaltz, lokshen kugel, and latkes—was old-world. Like my mother, Fanny is trapped and bemoaning the loss of her singing career. When she and Irving sing their duet "Morning Star," it taps into my past life in vaudeville, and the opera ends with the Jewish prayer for the dead, the Kaddish, for the victims of the Triangle. One day, sitting on a stoop outside, I asked Tony Kushner to recite the Kaddish into my tape recorder, and I set it exactly as he spoke it. It is that recording I played at the star magnolia tree the day Jeffrey's ashes were buried beneath it.

———

Robin Guarino from Cincinnati College–Conservatory of Music and Marcus Küchle from Cincinnati Opera developed Opera Fusion: New Works to develop new operas combining the resources of both institutions. They invited me to do something, but I didn't want to create something new; I wanted to look at *Morning Star* with fresh eyes.

Jim Robinson recommended the director Ron Daniels, who had directed the production of Christopher Bond's play *Sweeney Todd: The Demon Barber of Fleet Street* in London, which inspired Sondheim to write the musical. Ron has brilliant dramaturgical instincts, brusquely saying things like "Put that in act 2," "Cut that!" or "That doesn't work," and Bill and I rewrote a lot, based on Ron's suggestions. Though it was productive, a tragedy was looming.

Bill had been clean and sober for many years, when a doctor prescribed OxyContin for his chronic back pain. Quickly, he became addicted. The combination of the drug, the secret, and his guilt about the loss of his sobriety made him unreasonable, bordering on insane.

Ron suggested two new set pieces Bill and I thought were great ways to traverse the inner lives of our characters, an ensemble for the women where they sing of their dreams, and a counterpart for the men. One morning, Bill invited Ron and me down to his hotel room to see the lyric for the women's ensemble. He handed us a sheet of paper with columns for each woman's character, inside of which was a word or two, but nothing that made sense or strung together a single idea. Bewildered, we asked, "Bill, what is this?" "It's the lyric!" Bill yelled, almost enraged. "But there's nothing here!" I cried. "Then I have no idea what you want!" he shouted. Calmly, Ron said, "Bill, we need more than a graph with a few words in it."

We left Bill's room, and in the elevator I said despairingly, "This is not going to happen, Ron. Bill is either not up to this, or he's lost his mind." We realized we had to present what we already had, without trying to generate anything new. Luckily, we had plenty to show.

The presentation, conducted by my friend Steven White, was beyond all our expectations! You could tell from the feeling in the room everyone knew we had something. That night, Cincinnati Opera decided to do the opera.

Bill ended up in Payne Whitney after suffering a nervous break-down. It was sad and scary, but when he got out, it was as if his brain had been scrambled, and his new vision was exactly what we needed, offbeat and idiosyncratic. He wrote lovely lyrics for the two new ensembles. Here is an example of what he wrote for Prince's dream:

PRINCE
(In front of his fish stall on the street)
Prince dreams of catching yellow pike on Prince Street,
And nets fresh carp down on Grand,
And by five he grinds white fish at Broome and Bowery,
And pounds the fins and gills into floating boats.
Prince picks his mushrooms on Prince Street,
Pearl snips her dill on Ludlow.
Together they find horseradish on Allen
And cry onion tears for their Jewish fish.
Silvery, swiftly, they slide down the alley ways,
To sell jars of ocean.
Prince will make a fortune in mullet, smelling like the sea.
Carp is his caviar.

My friend Mary came from Akron for the room run, a fantastically bittersweet show with everyone knowing they were saying good-bye to the special intimacy of the rehearsal space to move into the theater, where, inevitably, the show would fall apart at first and they would have to adjust to a thousand things. The move was devastating.

It became apparent immediately we were in trouble. Ron had approved a design from the set designer Riccardo Hernández that was sculptural and symbolic, a triangular raked wooden floor and a triangular back wall Wendall Harrington could project onto, but essentially it was one big open space, no surfaces for the voices to bounce off, so you could barely hear anyone, especially with the orchestra.

Then I was erroneously told how many players we could have in the orchestra, but they were tight in the pit, so the orchestra manager just started plucking people out of the pit randomly without consulting me.

Christopher Allen, the conductor, and I had to go through the score reorchestrating and bargaining with him for which players we could keep and which ones we could let go of. Consequently, the score never sounded as good as it did in the sitzprobe, because we never had the complete orchestra again. Fortunately, there was a sound system and a skilled soundman that came with the theater, so he saved us.

In the *Chicago Tribune*, the headline was "Chicago-Born Opera 'Morning Star' Shines Powerfully." And John von Rhein wrote, "Was the long pull 'Morning Star' had to undergo before finally emerging into the blinding light of performance worth it? Most emphatically, yes."

The workshop of *Morning Star* before the premiere was chronicled in a documentary by the Academy Award–winning documentarians Julia Reichert and Steven Bognar called *Making Morning Star.*

Eric Einhorn, the artistic director of On Site Opera, a company out of New York City with no theater of its own that imaginatively comes up with locations that glorify the opera and the place, elected to do *Morning Star* in the Eldridge Street Synagogue on the Lower East Side for the centenary of the Triangle fire. Built in 1887, it is where many of the victims worshipped. Bill was gardening in his yard in Beacon, New York, one day, and he collapsed before the production and died. A week before, I got to tell him, "Bill, when you enter the synagogue, you are greeted by a magnificent circular stained-glass window with an image of a morning star emblazoned on it!" He wept. I think he knew he'd never see it.

The production was surreal, as if everyone were a ghost. We had entered a world that had never ended, and this was its continuance. The last matinee was on the day of the centenary. All around the neighborhood, in front of every house where one of the victims of the Triangle lived, were chalk markings on the sidewalks. Before the performance, in the snow, a parade of people walked past every marking, intoning their names.

PART IX

THE THREE SISTERS, CONTINUED

The Three Sisters, Continued, Concluded 𝄇

OLGA (Embracing both sisters): The music plays so merrily, briskly, and we want to live! Oh, my God! Time will pass, and we'll be gone forever, they'll forget us, forget our faces, our voices, and how many we were, but our sufferings will turn into joy for those who live after us, happiness and peace will come to the earth, and they will bless those who live now and remember them kindly. Oh, my dear sisters, our life isn't over yet. We will live! The music plays so merrily, so joyfully, and it seems before long we'll come to know why we live, why we suffer . . . If only we could know, if only we could know!

—Anton Chekhov, *Three Sisters*, translated by Richard Nelson

To report the circumstances of my sisters' lives, what they did, what happened, seems all I can do. We strove, all of us, to make something out of our pain, both succeeding and failing miserably. They were who I wanted to be until I knew better, when acting like them made conditions for me in the world perilous. But they were, and in Sheila's case continue to be, so interesting to me, like birds in high branches, elusive, beautiful when you catch sight of them, their fabulous plumage, but tragic when they fly into windows.

SUSAN

Being driven around Los Angeles with Fred Astaire at the wheel for an article in *Rolling Stone* about the fragility of idols, writing about Joni Mitchell at the start of her emergence, or Randy Newman when no one had yet, just before his solo Philharmonic Hall debut, and Mark Spitz, the Olympic gold medalist swimmer whose willingness to be commodified and exploited for advertisement she found tawdry (that article really upset my father, who saw no merit in destroying a Jewish hero-icon in the press that way) for *The New York Times*, or her friendship with Country Joe McDonald, and Shuna's with his daughter, Seven Anne, and of course David Getz. I got a lot of mileage out of her. She was the ticket to cool I used constantly and unabashedly. I bragged about her unmercifully as if it were *my* life I was bragging about. She seemed to know everything and I worshipped her. She even saved my life, because hearing the panic in my voice the night I called her in Oakland in 1989 with my heart beating out of my chest, she said, "Honey, you're bottoming out," which drove me to my first AA meeting, changing my life forever. I read every book she told me to read, saw every movie she told me to see, listened to her opinions as if they were dogma, so how had this happened to her, this fiery, indecent disintegration? My Vassar graduate, activist, enlightenment-seeking, world-famous journalist sister had become a down-and-out, in-the-gutter, sometimes-gun-toting addict, thief, prostitute, and degenerate.

Susan met David Getz at a party at Jerry Garcia's house. David was Janis Joplin's drummer in Big Brother and the Holding Company. Funny, with self-deprecating Jewish humor, he could be lacerating, according to Susan, but I never saw that side of him. Everybody blames David for getting Susan on heroin, but how could he know Susan was a can of gasoline and heroin was a lit match? For David, heroin was an occasional pleasure; for Susan, it was the beginning of a viselike grip, a cataclysmic descent. They were part of the Arica School of Knowledge, founded by a Chilean man named Oscar Ichazo. I don't really know what Arica was all about, but I didn't think it did anything to change Susan for the better, and she slept with Oscar, which seems a little unboundaried to me.

In the late 1970s, when Susan was living on East Seventieth Street, she would shoplift from places like Bergdorf Goodman, Saks Fifth Avenue, Henri Bendel, and Barneys, then sell the merchandise at discount to support her habit. She accrued fifty thousand dollars of debt. I was cleaning her apartment once a week, and often I'd have to take eviction notices off the door. My niece Shuna basically had to take care of herself. I opened the refrigerator one day, and mold was flourishing as if it were being cultivated. Shuna, rail thin, hid food she bought for herself to eat, like a bag of radishes or a head of lettuce, wherever the mold hadn't gotten to. Sometimes our aunt Sylvia would drive into the city from Rego Park with Tupperware full of Jewish food like chicken soup and flanken, but the situation was dire. If you walked into the bedroom Susan and her boyfriend Paul, also an addict, with the added burden of extreme and very messy alcoholism, slept in, you entered a smoke-filled opium den that stank like an ashtray. Susan, editing the Arica paper, *The No Time Times*, would be sitting on the bed cross-legged, piles of papers surrounding her, with more than one cigarette lit.

Only lucid on occasion, she had mostly become a phantom. My friends referred to her as "the reptile" because of her tendency to lash out like a lizard snapping its tongue to devour a fly. When she visited the boatyard, she would sit on the corner of the wraparound sofa, staring at the water, and cry. Guests never understood how we could stand by so impassively, but we had become inured to it. Shuna went to live with Lorraine's family, and Susan moved in with my parents at the boatyard.

One night, my mother tried to intercept her when she caught her stealing money from my mother's purse. Susan shoved her down on the floor and ran out with her wallet. She crashed my father's car on the way to Freeport to buy crack.

Another time, my mother took the train in to meet her at Macy's for lunch. Susan excused herself to go to the bathroom and never came back. Did she go shopping, becoming so mesmerized trying on clothes the world dropped away? Did she forget she was with my mother and stagger home after she peed? Did she nod out in a filthy shit-filled alleyway? We will never know; they are both gone.

My parents went to one Al-Anon meeting, but my mother said

she could never "detach with love." My father, who by now always looked as if he had swallowed scissors, would have stayed. He was ill-equipped for a dream gone *this* awry.

Susan and Paul were supposed to be at Shuna's graduation and take her out afterward for a celebratory dinner. They never showed up. Paul drove Susan to the Lower East Side to cop. Susan would give blow jobs to ultraorthodox Jewish men in an old abandoned synagogue, for money to buy drugs. Paul was waiting for her in the getaway car with his hands on the wheel when a thief reached through the open window and put a razor to his throat. Accidentally, he put his foot on the gas, and his throat was slit. Holding it together, nearly bleeding to death, he raced to the nearest emergency room.

Susan seemed to head the charge wherever she was. In the call for women's liberation, she was on the front lines, not just as a demonstrator, but as a spokesperson. I always say Susan did for the clitoris what Bernstein did for Mahler, exposing it to the world for reconsideration, with her essay "The Politics of Orgasm," from the first book of essays to come out of the women's movement, *Sisterhood Is Powerful*. In her cover article on Deborah Harry for *The New York Times Magazine*, her focus on Ms. Harry's engagement with heroin and yoga was something probably no one could have understood as well as Susan, a regular pedestrian of the precipice.

Lorraine met someone who worked at a rehab in Albany called Conifer Park, and they accepted Susan, even giving her a "scholarship." At Penn Station, beyond my mother's lexicon of anything whatsoever, Susan begged my mother to let her cop one last time, but they made it there by nightfall, and Susan stayed a year. Afterward, they sent her to an outpatient facility in Boston called Women Inc. for another year, where tough love meant cleaning toilets with a toothbrush. She was the only white woman there. When she got out, she spoke exclusively in Ebonics as if she were from "de hood."

Susan wrote three memoirs after she got sober. *Take the Long Way Home*, a harrowing account of her childhood and descent into addiction, started as an article in *The Boston Globe* when she was getting ready to "graduate" from Women Inc. Knitting began to dominate her life. Keeping her hands busy was essential to prevent idleness, disastrous for addicts. Entering a sisterhood of craftswomen around the world, which included my mother and her two younger sisters, from sweater makers in Scotland to Navajo weavers on the plains, she immersed herself in brilliant colors, sensuous textures, and beautiful patterns and designs she always had fantasies about creating, which brought her healing and a greater connection to her infinite self. She wrote *The Knitting Sutra: Craft as a Spiritual Practice*, after she had broken her arm tripping on someone's front step in California and she needed something to do *other* than knit until she was healed.

In the summer of 2005, before she came east to Florida to die, Sheila and I went out to California for the publishing of her astonishing last book, *Knitting Heaven and Earth: Healing the Heart with Craft*, in which she knits through our father's dying and her own devastating diagnosis of stage 4 cancer. When she started getting cancer, first the kidney, then the breasts, then the colon, though God knows she did everything other than swallow rat poison to get it, I still think the main cause was smoking. At certain points, she smoked three packs a day, and this, since she was a teenager.

Toward the end, we met at Ucross, the arts colony in Wyoming we both loved. I worked on a song about envy for a cycle about the seven deadly sins Audra McDonald was going to premiere at Zankel Hall, and Susan finished her book. Every night we would search for the sandhill cranes she had heard were in Wyoming that spring, but we never found them, only the Canada geese she loathed. "They scare off all the good birds!" She knit me a hat and scarf while we were there because it was snowy and cold. She said she was knitting Wyoming into them.

LORRAINE

There is a temptation, a shallow one, to be sure, to try to paint my sisters as equally enthralling in the same way, to idealize them, to pretend they were exciting and I was exciting at all times, and that's how I turned out so fabulous. Susan's life was obviously, outwardly, the most colorful, but clearly the colors of her inner palette were dark and shaded with enormous despair. Lorraine was so afraid of the external world, so tentative in it, half-blind and groping, only her discovery of an inner life, a connection to something "spiritual," or "divine," allowed her to thrive as long as she did.

There is a night I will always remember when I saw Lorraine at her neediest and most insane. She had met Harry Hughes, a Vietnam vet, and an immediate obsession began. She decided that night that she needed to get to him wherever he was on Long Island. It was pouring rain at the boatyard. The water outside was churning, banging up against the bulkheads like a typhoon. Begging, sobbing, cajoling, screaming, to get Susan and her friend Robert Christgau, the rock-and-roll reviewer for *The Village Voice*, who was visiting at the time, to drive her. She would not take no for an answer. At moments like this, Susan could delight in having such power, and she was clearly delighting in torturing Lorraine with her indecision. I don't remember if she got there that night, but Lorraine did marry Harry.

Harry, who at the time had waist-length somewhat greasy hair and looked as if he had just left the Manson cult, was Lorraine's longest-lasting relationship. For about five years, she was the happiest she had ever been. They moved to Selden, on Long Island, so they could study at Stony Brook. When they settled there, she developed allergies to everything. Anything suddenly had the power to close her throat and make her stop breathing. She cultivated a new relationship to food, her voice becoming hushed around it, spinning pendulums above it, testing her muscles around it, as if it had strange powers to kill her and needed to be curated with great care. It seemed to be the beginnings of agoraphobia, but eating with her became incredibly strange, as if she were tiptoeing to her own funeral at all times.

When they were finished with Stony Brook, my parents bought them a lovely little house just blocks from the ocean in Long Beach. Lorraine got pregnant, and my mother helped Lorraine with the birth of Gabriel. They stopped eating meat, and Lorraine became a fantastic vegetarian cook. Gabe was adorable, and I resumed my mission to turn my niece Maggie, now in her early teens, into a genius, reading poetry, Sylvia Plath, Anne Sexton, Dorothy Parker, and Edna St. Vincent Millay, to her, just as my sister Susan had done with me. I bought her books, and whatever I told her to read, she read. Harry and Lorraine became Yogis, turning one room in the house into a Yoga studio. Harry started working with my father to make a living, a fate worse than death, and started disassembling with serious PTSD from his time in Vietnam. The marriage started disintegrating, and after Yoga and a haircut made Harry quite handsome, like Sheila's Patrick, he slept with some of Lorraine's girlfriends.

A disciple of Swami Satchidananda, in 1979, Lorraine moved down to his ashram, a huge lotus that appeared to be growing out of the ground, in Yogaville, Virginia, with Gabriel and Shiva, her two sons. She did it to get away from her failed marriage, selling the house in Long Beach, an incredibly bad decision financially because, much like the building my father owned and sold in Brooklyn, both properties would be worth a *lot* of money now.

Soon after one visit to Sheila in Oceanside, she called to say she was marrying a man she had never mentioned to any of us the whole time she was there. We rolled our eyes in a special roll we saved for Lorraine, who was now Leela, her Yogi name. We were invited to the wedding. Maggie, who was still at CCNY and living in the city when Lorraine married Kurt "Mohan" Wenzel, didn't attend the wedding, because she hated the ashram, which felt neither spiritual nor serene to her, more "a haven for dropouts who couldn't make it in the world, worshipping an opportunistic nut." Mark Weiner, Lorraine's son Shiva's father, whom Lorraine never married, drove us down. I insisted no one eat on the journey, assuming we were in for a magnificent vegetarian feast. After the nine-and-a-half-hour drive, we found the picked-at remains of an already eaten iceberg lettuce salad and some cold leftover pizza. The next day, the wedding outdoors overlooked a spectacular view of the James River. The marriage lasted about five minutes, enough time for Lorraine to have a son, Gopal. We later found out Swami, for reasons we never discovered, had advised Lorraine to marry Mohan, whom she had never even met. She now had three sons and however many children Mohan had and was a new mother and a servant, doing all the cooking and cleaning.

After the divorce, she met Bill, the antithesis of Harry, who thought the ashram and all of that were a crock of shit. Lorraine met him when she was performing at a local club after having learned to play the tabla and getting involved with a Black drummer named Houston. She would keep her guitar close by and sing the occasional folk song. A big, swaggering galoot, Bill swept Lorraine off her feet because the sex was great, and—my hypothesis—he was the closest thing to my father she could find. He was also a way out of Yogaville and poverty. He was the founder and president of a motorcycle gang called the Hell's Henchmen, which started because they didn't think the Hells Angels were tough enough. He drank, rode his motorcycle, and bred game birds for hunting. Lorraine, a devout vegetarian, now lived on a game farm with a man who shot birds and sold them for others to shoot and had the temperament of Stanley Kowalski, violent and bullying, pushing her head down to his crotch, saying things like "Blow me!" and meaning it; it was hard even for her sons not to think she had gone off the deep end. Not surprisingly, my father got on brilliantly with Bill. He and my mother would drive up to Virginia, and my dad would help Bill fix things around the house. Then my parents would take the three boys back to Florida for weeks at a time. My father had fun with them in a way he never could with me, and because they had no history with him, and he was old, they weren't the least bit afraid of him. He was just their irascible cur of a grandpa.

She left Bill's wild game death camp and went back to Yogaville.

After the divorce, she fell in love and married Jai Heard, a healer and fireman from Texas who came to Yogaville after getting sober to become a Yogi and find God. On the afternoon of Good Friday, they were making love in his trailer. The phone rang. She got up to answer it. There was nothing on the other end but what sounded like wind and an eerie crackling. "Hello?" she kept repeating, but there was nothing. She hung up. When she got back to bed, Jai was heaving and gasping, having had a massive coronary. Lorraine tried to call an ambulance, but he wouldn't let her. He died while she held him. She believes he sent his spirit out to make the phone call, to protect her from having to see the onset of his paroxysms.

Though each of her boys had at least one name that meant God (Ram, Shiva, and Gopal), it wasn't *their* God, nor was Lorraine's spirituality theirs. They wanted to get as far away from Yogaville as possible, eat cheeseburgers and French fries, and lead normal lives. They became Gabe, Jeremy, and Josh.

Maggie got into Oxford for grad school summa cum laude. She wrote a master's thesis on James Joyce's *Ulysses*, Virginia Woolf's *Waves*, and Yeats's "Lapis Lazuli," which she called "The Articulation of Silence," but eventually decided Oxford, though beautiful, was cold—and not just the temperature. She met a handsome philosophy student named Martin Ball, married him, and moved to Australia.

Whatever misfortunes Susan and Lorraine incurred or brought upon themselves were at least partly the gifts of being fathered by my father, the rotten fruits my sisters thought they deserved. They lived in perpetual impenetrable unrealities, running away from something without knowing what they were running toward, which was usually, and unfortunately, grueling pain.

Lorraine could lie to herself and sometimes to others, even when she didn't know she was doing it. She so wanted to see another reality. But you had to either go along with the charade or call her bluff and risk rebuke, which could be intense. I was probably the only one who could call her on it, because she trusted me and I could somehow say things to her without stinging her.

I don't remember how she met him, or when or if she fell in love with him, but Lorraine then married Joe Garnett and moved into his house in Charlottesville, Virginia. Joe was kind and warm and terrified. I feared for her. Newly and loosely sober, Joe was in a state of perpetual grief, because his wife, also an alcoholic, had been in a terrible car accident and died less than a year before. There was no way he was capable of taking care of anyone. He was a broken-winged bird with two children of his own. Susan joked that Lorraine "married Joe for the house," which is mean, especially with the way she cackled after saying it; however, it is not entirely impossible to imagine, because, as I have said, need could and did impair Lorraine's judgment. But she also had three sons she wanted to leave something to. Joe's use of drugs and alcohol engendered the need for a liver transplant, and in that way she certainly got to repay Joe for the house her boys did *indeed* inherit after she died in 2014, because taking care of a liver transplant patient is no small feat.

She was in the midst of voice lessons with a teacher she had found whom she loved. I've never heard her so excited about anything. Every day she'd call me to talk about the mechanics of the voice and all the things she was finding out about her larynx. Her teacher was a fan of mine, and she started singing my songs, calling me to ask all kinds of questions about them, which was a new and greatly appreciated conversation for us. It was lovely to hear her so joyous.

A lump growing on Lorraine's neck turned out to be thyroid cancer. No friend of Western medicine, she treated things like chemo and radiation as poison, so she was terrified imagining any of the available treatments, but she finally relented to having the surgery. Maggie went down with my mother to look after her when she was in the hospital. Lorraine was tiny and looked so frightened and vulnerable that Maggie fainted on the first visit. The surgery was successful, and all she had to do when she recovered was take Synthroid, a thyroid drug my mother was on as well that replaces a hormone normally produced by the thyroid gland to regulate the body's energy and metabolism. But she could no longer sing.

Looking back on it, I feel bad, because I think I fed and encouraged some of Lorraine's delusions. She started having fevers every afternoon, but we allowed each other to think it was because she spent so much time in meditation she was burning karma. Somewhere inside myself I knew this wasn't true.

She was practicing homeopathy and psychic healing. I sent my friend Tommy Krasker, the record producer who worked with me on Audra McDonald's first album, *Way Back to Paradise*, and my *Bright Eyed Joy*, as well as *My Life with Albertine*, *Only Heaven*, and *Dream True*, to see her when he was weak and sickly from an almost fatal reaction to the antibiotic Cipro, and he swore by her. When Kevin's mother died tragically and suddenly at the age of sixty-four, very possibly an alcohol-related death, Lorraine met her (literally) in her meditation, describing her in detail to Kevin, knowing her name (never having met her or heard about her), and had a very logical and specific message for him from the numinous, which brought him enormous comfort. She said that his mother was prouder of him than he could ever know, and that she always knew what he was afraid to tell her (Kevin didn't come out until he was forty-six), and that she could do more for him from where she was than she could when she was in her body, because she simply could not stop drinking. A few years later, when I told Kevin's father about it, without balking, he said it made perfect sense and sounded exactly like something Dianne might have said.

But when blood started showing up in her urine, even her friend Audrey, the psychic healer I had sent Lorraine Hunt Lieberson to see when *she* was first diagnosed with cancer, said, "You'd better go to a doctor, now." She was diagnosed with stage 4 renal cancer. They said she needed to have one of her kidneys removed immediately, and within the week, on a Thursday, she was in surgery. Not long after she was out of surgery, Sheila called to tell me the news. The doctor told her the real cancer, the worrisome one, was behind the kidney and had metastasized and spread. He said, "If I were you, I'd be in the chemo chair first thing Monday morning." But again, my sister, who wouldn't even eat a raisin if it wasn't organic and Himalayan, was not going to put chemo into her body. She decided to just have localized radiation. Sheila went back to Florida to regroup. We were going to meet in Charlottesville for the treatments.

I got there a day before Sheila. Lorraine wasn't in bad spirits the first day. She was so happy I was there. I had never been to visit her in Charlottesville before.

Looking at all of Lorraine's things—her plethora of crystals, her lavish orchid-colored bedding with big, beautiful flowers in the Japanese style, the pretty colors she had painted her walls, her bright yellow chintz-covered sofa—I thought, knowing what I already knew, is this what it is all for? We work like dogs to pay for things we don't take with us when we die. We form attachments, only to have to let go. I asked myself, did Lorraine ever think she'd have to say goodbye to all this *stuff*?

Something happened that first day that was slightly awkward and uncomfortable for me, but I'm glad it did. When I was little, I used to climb into bed with Lorraine in the morning to cuddle. She was the one I went to in crises and emergencies, when I had my bad acid trip at twelve, or the morning after Jeffrey died, when the shock abated and I called her screaming, realizing he was gone. She just breathed with me.

I went to take a nap on the bed she had prepared for herself, in the living room by the window, and she got into the bed with me and wrapped herself around me like a little girl while I slept. It almost felt incestuous. I had grown up and didn't sleep with my sisters anymore. But I look back at that moment with almost unbearable tenderness.

The next day, when Sheila arrived, we went with Lorraine for her first radiation treatment. They drew a black circle on her where the radiation was supposed to go. She did fine and it all seemed so simple. The next morning, I was awakened by horrible sounds and whispered murmurs. When I went out, she was on all fours, moaning in agony while her son Jeremy, looking completely panicked and helpless, tried to comfort her. We got her to the hospital, where they firmly explained how she had to stay *ahead* of the pain, hard for her because she hated taking pills unless they were little white pearly homeopathic things that went under your tongue and didn't seem to do anything. But we got her on a schedule with the pain meds, and things calmed down considerably.

Sheila and I were able to relieve some of the burden, cooking, shopping, cleaning, trying to get Lorraine to drink and eat, and just bringing the warmth of family to a difficult situation. Sheila sang her to sleep every night as if she were her mother. Joe lived in a sort of lair downstairs and at that moment was barely allowed up because she was punishing him for having pocketed some of her painkillers when he was supposed to be clean and sober. Toward the end of the week, Sheila went by herself for a walk, and I took it upon myself to be clear with Lorraine about the diagnosis. I worried she'd squander this time living in a fantasy she would be here for a long time. She still seemed to be denying herself so many pleasures, and I wanted to say, "Honey, you're dying! Just enjoy yourself!" All I could think about was Jeffrey with his cinnamon bun and coffee the morning I told him his body was failing. She cried bitterly but accepted it. I left with the intention I'd come back.

About a week later, Kevin and I packed up our dog, Lucy, and drove to Charlottesville. The night we arrived, Lorraine, in great distress, was again on all fours, howling in agony. I decided to take control of her pain meds. About a week before, I called her from the country one night while I was walking Lucy through the fog and drizzle. She was disturbed and upset because people were visiting her and she didn't feel she had the energy or lucidity to entertain them. "Lorraine, no one expects you to entertain them right now. They just want to be with you. Just allow them that privilege." But clearly, and stubbornly, she was not staying ahead of the pain. Though this was the first time Lucy was meeting Lorraine, she seemed to sense what was happening. I put her in Lorraine's bed, and she nuzzled gently against her back. We decided Kevin would sleep in the little guest room that was also Lorraine's office and I would sleep on the couch next to her, with Lucy's little bed right below me. I decided to read to Lorraine, but I wasn't sure what to read. Kevin went into her office and pulled out the Bhagavad Gita, which was perfect. I seemed to open to the most comforting passage—"Because death is certain for the one who is born, and birth is certain for the one who dies. Therefore, you should not lament over the inevitable"—and she fell asleep. In the middle of the night, she was in great distress again. Lucy jumped onto the arm of the couch overlooking her bed with hypervigilance. I should say this. A week or two after we got Lucy, she was sleeping in bed with me and Kevin. I woke up in the middle of one night to Lucy staring at me, and I thought of that line in Rilke's "Requiem on the Death of a Boy," "And mother, who was that dog *really*?" At this point, I decided to try a new tack: I ground up two of the painkillers in a spoon and added water so I could give it to her that way. She thought I was over-drugging her the next day, which made me feel guilty. But was I? What was better, her writhing in agony or sleeping? I knew the drill, having been through it with Jeffrey. The patient may crave lucidity, but if they are in agony, what they experience may be not lucidity but hysteria.

Kevin and I took Lucy for a walk in Charlottesville, which was hilly, and when we got back to Lorraine's, Lucy went under the table and coughed and coughed. The same thing would happen when I walked her around Central Park.

Audrey spoke with sadness and frustration about how all along she knew Lorraine had cancer, but Lorraine was stubborn and didn't want to get the tests, like the one where they shoot dye into you and then X-ray you to see what's happening, but Lorraine decided without any evidence that she was allergic to the dye and wouldn't undergo it. By the time she *did* get any test results, she was too far gone. Maybe on some level she didn't want to be here anymore. But I wish I had screamed at her to go to the doctor the summer before when I stupidly agreed with her about meditation causing the fevers and burning up her karma.

I had a teaching engagement in Tallahassee I had to do because I needed the money. There was a blizzard, not bad enough to prevent the plane from taking off, but I was to change planes in Atlanta, where there was an ice storm, and Delta Air Lines stupidly sent all their planes to Atlanta, so the Atlanta airport was *mayhem*; no planes could take off, and wall-to-wall disgruntled travelers. My flight was booked, rebooked, delayed, and then canceled. I never made it to Tallahassee. They booked me on a plane back to New York, and I got to our apartment at 3:30 a.m. Sheila called in the morning. Lorraine had died at 7:30 a.m. It was January 30. Dad was gone, Mom, Susan, and now Lorraine.

Kevin was up in the country. We decided I would get myself up there. There was nothing I could do to get myself down to Charlottesville. Right before I got off the phone, Kevin said, "Do you think you can handle some bad news?" I barked, "Really?!" When I got upstate, he told me Lucy tested positive for heartworm and had an enlarged heart. This accounted for her horrible coughing after all the long walks when I was unknowingly endangering her life.

SHEILA

All Sheila wanted was to be my mother, not the "bullied sex slave," but the mother and wife. What she didn't allow for is that kids grow up and leave, and husbands cannot shield you from the peril of your own thoughts and feelings or the world. My mother thought Sheila suffered the most inside, and I wouldn't dispute it. She has always battled depression, boiling constantly below the surface. This may be what makes her so lovable. Anyone can tell she's been there.

Sheila is alive, so I don't have to draw her story to a close. But a few pertinent details, especially since, when Don Katz was about to publish *Home Fires* and we all read the proof for the first time (except for my father, who never read it), Sheila nearly had a nervous breakdown at what she felt was her deliberate absence from the book. "I was disappeared in my own family. I am not going to be disappeared in Don's book! Didn't any of you talk about me?" she asked tearfully and accusingly. We had, but it seemed to fit the thesis of Don's book that the most normal (or seemingly normal) one got the least space. I won't make that mistake here.

In 1973, Sheila's marriage to Patrick imploded, because she found out how many of her friends Patrick had slept with. Defensively, she slept with another high school sweetheart, Jay, which blew everything up. They were supposed to move to California together, but Patrick moved there with Polly, a tall, blue-eyed blonde he was suddenly seeing. So, Sheila went out there alone. While she was staying in Susan's house on Telegraph Avenue in Berkeley, Susan stayed with David Getz in Marin County. I was sent there to cheer Sheila up.

One night Patrick showed up to claim the Fisher stereo he had decided was his. Sheila agreed to help him get the stereo to the car, but I could tell by the look on her face she was up to no good. Dutifully carrying the speakers out one by one she smashed them through the roof of the Volvo they had bought together but that he had *also* laid claim to. He chased her back into the house, and as they were punching each other, I got shoved into the fireplace trying to stop it. I started to develop a pain in my abdomen as if someone were disemboweling me from the inside. Sheila had to rush me to the emergency room, where I writhed and moaned on the floor. They diagnosed me as pre-ulcerative. Two days later it happened again, only worse. I had to go back to New York and live on Mylanta and oatmeal for the rest of the summer. Sheila's pain was so all encompassing I couldn't express how upset and heartbroken I was. I felt as if I had broken up with Patrick as well.

David Getz slept with Sheila in an effort to be as elastic in regard to fidelity as all the other men in my sisters' lives. Then, with her self-esteem smashed to smithereens, she moved back to New York, into the boatyard with my parents, and lived in the laundry room.

She was working at a bakery in Long Beach. My father, in an uncharacteristic act of kindness, decided to surprise her one afternoon when her shift was over, picking her up at work. In the car he asked her why she never dated Jewish men, but he wasn't looking for an answer; he was looking for a fight. They circled each other like enemy soldiers for a long time.

In 1977, Jon Wolff drove up one day on his motorcycle and strutted into Higher Grounds, the coffee, tea, and spice store Sheila had opened the year before, where she looked like Little Orphan Annie behind the counter with her new perm. After some wooing, Jon proposed. She knew Jon would love only *her*, never *cheat* on her, take *care* of her, and give her *children. And he was Jewish!*

Jon lived with his mother, Dorothy, in a house overlooking a canal in Oceanside, one town away from Island Park. They had a family business called Cinderella Flower and Feather Company, on West Thirty-Eighth Street, which provided all the great Broadway costumers with feathers and silk flowers. The monochromatically arranged boas fluttering out in every color of the rainbow were a drag queen's dream.

Dorothy, the meddlesome manager, was beautiful like Frida Kahlo, but severe looking, as if she did her makeup and hair with a black Magic Marker. Jon's father, Nat, lived in Florida, in their Palm Beach house, because he and Dorothy got along better when they were nowhere near each other. He had a philandering problem, and later in life Jon discovered he and his brother, Peter, had a stepsister.

Dorothy was no homemaker. You could have legibly written the Constitution with your index finger in the thick dust on the lid of the grand piano. Her recipes, usually found on the backs of boxes, always combined ketchup, pineapple, mayonnaise, Velveeta, and Ritz crackers, inedible for Sheila. But Sheila liked Cinderella and, as long as she was at a safe distance from Dorothy, enjoyed having a job and customers to interact with.

Not yet thirty, Sheila was complaining to me about her empty and meaningless existence. Probably hungover, I screamed, "Sheila! You're pathetic! You need something that engages you!" She called me a "consciousness terrorist," but she found painting. She started coming into the city every week to study figure drawing at the Art Students League, and she found a teacher on Long Island, John Murray, who taught old master technique painting.

She had a daughter and a son. Danielle seemed wise for her age, as if she remembered clearly a conversation she'd had with God before she was born. Daryl developed attention deficit disorder. Loving machines, he would take apart everything, intending to put it back together, but then lose interest before he was finished, so there were loose appliance parts scattered all over the house.

After "Jeffrey's Birthday," the concert I did at Symphony Space on March 10, 1997, Sheila painted a startlingly realistic portrait of me that hangs above my piano. Like van Gogh painting Gauguin's room royal blue, filling it with dazzling paintings of sunflowers in preparation for his visit, Sheila sent me enough flower paintings to adorn every wall of my studio on Wolf Lake. She lives in Boca Raton, Florida, where she shows her work, portraits, still lifes, landscapes, and plein air in local galleries and continues to study painting in workshops all over the world. Kevin (whose sister Kerry and her husband, Dylan, live nearby) and I go there as often as we can for holidays, where Sheila and Jon give us our own little wing of the house. Sheila's house is home now, when I say I am going "home" for the holidays, because the heart and soul of everything I mean when I say "family" now resides in her.

PART X

SELECTED WORKS, PART THREE

The Garden of the Finzi-Continis, or Bad Behavior, or a Difficult Birth

(Premiere, January 27, 2022, co-production, New York City Opera and the National Yiddish Theatre Folksbiene, at the Museum of Jewish Heritage, New York City)

After the success of *The Grapes of Wrath* at Minnesota Opera, the company started the New Works Initiative, and it was decided that Michael Korie and I would write the first new work to kick it off. I was proud to be part of what looked like a renaissance in new American opera. We'd made a splash and were being asked to do it again.

If *The Grapes of Wrath* had a relatively easy, albeit *long*, birth, *The Garden of the Finzi-Continis* had an excruciating one.

But how did it begin? Michael and I had to find our next project.

One day in 2008, I was looking for a video for my date with Kevin that night. I thought, "I wonder if Kevin has ever seen *The Garden of the Finzi-Continis*, Vittorio De Sica's 1970 Academy Award–winning film. I saw it when I was fifteen in East Rockaway and have never been able to shake it. Having watched it every few years, I could tell you my favorite shots, my favorite lines, my favorite parts of the score, which I knew every note of (composed by De Sica's son Manuel), and I thought Kevin would love it. I rented it and I could never have predicted what would happen.

It never hit me like this. I was heaving and sobbing, inconsolable by the end of it. I was overwhelmingly swept up in it. Suddenly it was about me, my people, and their history, more than it had ever been. It felt like a sign. I called Michael and told him I thought I found our next project. A fan of the movie, he didn't hesitate, saying yes immediately.

We bought Giorgio Bassani's 1962 novel, written twenty years after the Jews of Ferrara, Italy, were deported for extermination under the Nazis, because we wanted to go back to the source material the movie was based on. In its elision of historical and personal agony, Bassani's heartbreaking novel depicts people trying to live their lives, just as their rights to live them are slowly being demolished by Mussolini's racial laws. Catastrophe looms. Death is certain. But the quotidian continues. Dishes need washing, beds need making, Shabbas candles have to be lit, the heart wants, the body needs, and people go on with their lives, trying, for as long as they can, to push the inevitable back.

When Jews are no longer allowed to do their banking, go to the library, have servants, commingle, or play tennis in public, the wealthy Finzi-Contini family, beneficent and naive about the power of their wealth and assimilation, open up their tennis courts and their magnificent garden to a number of youths Micòl and Alberto Finzi-Contini have either grown up with or gone to university with.

If it were just a story of unrequited love—Giorgio loves Micòl, who doesn't love him back, and Alberto loves Malnate, who lusts for his sister instead of him—that would be one thing, but it happens against the backdrop of the greatest catastrophe of the twentieth century, the Holocaust, which amplifies every hurt in the story. We have no idea who will even be alive or dead by the end, much less together and in love. The opera company approved heartily and helped us to get the rights from the Bassani family, and we began work on it.

I have a feeling this story was harder for Michael to dramatize than *Grapes*. Well, I know it was. *Grapes* is jam-packed with events, and its bones, its three-act structure, and its symbolism are clear, whereas *Finzi-Continis* is a much moodier and internal story with always a foreground portraying one thing and a background looming, another. Right from the beginning my own behavior was bad. I was anxious and cranky about Michael actually getting the work done. He was taking longer than usual to get me anything to work on. It is something that is naturally difficult about collaboration. You are completely dependent on your collaborator.

For me, it is the words that inspire me, and in most cases I must have the words to start. Michael doesn't always share the struggle, the wrestling, so I'm prone to taking it personally if I have to wait too long before I have anything in my hands. I immediately assume the work he's doing with other collaborators is more important to him than whatever he is doing with me, prone as I am to jealousy, and that's why I'm constantly fretting and resentfully waiting.

I immediately started triangulating, complaining with Eric Simonson, our director, about Michael, enlisting him in my anxiety, which is never a good thing. It sort of pollutes the water. So, there was an atmosphere of divisiveness already building. I think I also knew we were going to have less time to write this opera but more pressures, seeing it was our second, so I was extremely agitated and nervous to start.

Finally, I wrote a prelude because I didn't need Michael for that, so I could get into the mood, the heart of the piece, put some notes down on the page, but then Michael heard it and decided it should be Giorgio's first aria in the graveyard, so he did what he did with the act 3 prelude to *Grapes,* turning that into Ma and Tom's "I'll Be There" duet, and he lyricized the melody of the prelude, which ended up being a good thing. It was good to have at least some words and music down on paper.

There was one trip scheduled for Minnesota where Michael and I were meant to speak on some panels about the piece, do some press, and share a bit of the music. I played the prelude without words, and Karin Wolverton, one of our young artists from *Grapes,* learned one of Micòl's arias, called "Trees," unfortunately not one of our best efforts, not terrible, but perhaps too much of a list, like a catalog aria, and focused on the trees and not enough on the overall arc of the story, or the subtext. It would soon be gone from the opera.

The strangest thing about that trip was that there was an organized screening of the movie at a local synagogue, but basically they got a VHS and projected it onto a big wall. Because it is already a quiet movie dependent on the crisp beauty of its imagery, it looked and sounded terrible, like a small image blown up and over-pixelated and being played through a mediocre sound system. I should have seen that as a portent, for it was.

In 2009, an invitation came in the mail saying that I was invited to an artists' colony in Italy called Civitella Ranieri, an incredible castle in Umbria surrounded by fields and farmland. There were artists of various disciplines from all over the world, including Fanny Howe, the great American poet.

Fanny and I would have our own Al-Anon meetings in her room every Friday focusing on recovery and gossip at a table she kept next to the window overlooking the stunning views of the castle grounds. She would come for tea at my studio, a house next to the castle called Pizza because it contained the remains of an old pizza oven. It was a cold autumn, and the castle was freezing, so everyone staying in it including Fanny caught colds. Pizza was heated.

One day she lay on my couch and listened to the unreleased recording I was editing of a piece I had written for Jeffrey called *Green Sneakers*. "You write with a nail," she said, when it was over. Fanny accidentally set her room in the castle on fire, and though the damage was minimal, the fiasco added to her wonderfully nutty allure.

While I was there, I alternated between working on *Rappahannock County*, the Civil War piece I was writing with Mark Campbell, and *The Garden of the Finzi-Continis*. It was a fertile time, and I was excited about what I was doing.

When I returned to New York from Italy, I had already sent Dale Johnson, the artistic director of Minnesota Opera, the first act and at least half of act 2, and he seemed really pleased and excited. He sent me back a one-word email, "Fabulous." A workshop was planned, and we had to audition tenors for the role of Giorgio. We met on the Upper East Side for the auditions, and hearing Giorgio's arias in my head, I was looking forward to hearing who was available. Act 1 ends with an aria for Giorgio called "Eternal Flame," which I was excited about, and I imagined them singing it.

A donor event was scheduled after the auditions where Kevin Puts and Mark Campbell were also going to be, because they were writing *Silent Night* to premiere a year after our opera. My insides were churning when we got to the party. Something had happened earlier.

The auditions were okay, but the only tenor who was even remotely right for the role was Eric Margiore. He was handsome, had a beautiful and clarion voice, and even looked a little like Giorgio Bassani. He was the one I wanted, and we were all in agreement. Happy and triumphant, we were wrapping up, but before leaving, I made the mistake of sharing my excitement about the opera with Dale, who suddenly looked like a venomous snake about to strike.

He singled out an entire scene that took me weeks to write, a big scene I felt strongly about both libretto-wise and musically as being pivotal to act 1, and said, "Yeah, but that scene has to go." I said, "What? Are you crazy? I love that scene." To which Dale replied, "No. It's too Jewish." Which caught me off guard. I doubt he meant it as an anti-Semitic comment, but something in the scene made him uncomfortable, and instead of saying something reasonable like "Can we talk about that scene?" he just tyrannically decided that it had to be cut with a total disregard for the hole the excision would leave.

I was enraged but said nothing, not wanting to put a damper on the evening. I did think, though, "How can an opera about Jews, adapted from a novel by a Jew, and written by two Jews, be too Jewish?" Wasn't it a little late for that concern? But never mind. The scene, by the way, was this: Jews, no longer allowed to have gentiles as domestics, can hire only other Jews, and Jews are known for being a great many things, but not domestics.

So, Mamma is grappling with a disaster of a servant, the half-deaf and inept Signorina Ricca Cohen. The scene, as Michael wrote it, is wry and devilishly funny, and then tragic, because it portends the full weight of what the Jews of Ferrara will have to give up before they actually give up their lives. I went into survival and protection mode. "Dale doesn't get it," I thought. "I'll just have to convince him."

Walking down Fifth Avenue with him to get a cab, I couldn't help myself and brought up the scene again. Dale snapped at me, "I *knew* you were going to get like this when I brought it up. Why do you always have to be so sensitive?" I stared into space. Now I was really upset and confused. What happened to negotiation or collaboration?

The next day, I did something that might well have been what hammered the nail into the coffin. I called Kevin Smith, the general director of the company, and told him how upset I was, that Dale was not allowed to speak to me that way ever again, and that Kevin had to defend me. It was something I would *never* do now. I was a tattletale, too afraid of confronting Dale myself. It was divisive and triangulating, because my anger was illogical and out of control.

Kevin was understanding, saying he would talk to Dale, and he did. Dale was sweet and came to New York to apologize, but something was ruined. We had dinner to talk it through, but we were walking on eggshells; the damage was irrevocable.

When, before an opera is even completed, someone starts discussing what they think should be cut, it eats into you, eroding the delicate shell you have built to protect your confidence. For one thing, to put it simply, you feel as if you were off on the wrong foot. Dale bit a chunk out of my self-esteem that evening. Then I had to act happy at the party, but I was sick and just wanted to go home.

Then came the workshop. Now, a workshop is supposed to be a safe space where you look at a piece, see what you have, and hear the score for the first time. Usually, everyone has had their scores ahead of time so they can learn it, the conductor has studied it and has a pretty organized idea of how he or she is going to approach it, and the director has a sense of what he'd like to accomplish and communicates that to everyone in the room.

You can get a sense of the pacing, hear if an aria is too long or too short, and assess what it is you need to do when you go back to the drawing board. The director might stage a scene, or a moment or two, to see how it feels on its feet.

Let me try to describe what happened that week. Absolutely no one was on the same page, and there was an air of meanness in the room from the start that was positively demoralizing.

First of all, the opera company decided to open every session to audiences of patrons, so in your most delicate and vulnerable state you always felt as if you were in a fishbowl auditioning your baby before it was born. Second, Michael Christie was new to the world of opera and theater, came from the world of symphonic conducting, and had no idea what a workshop was, so he arrived not knowing the score or the story we were trying to tell. Eric Simonson, who was magnificent on *Grapes,* seemed out of it, bored even. The chorus let me know they were disgruntled because they were hugely featured in *Grapes* and played a lesser role in this opera.

Bill Murray, an intern when we did *Grapes,* working with the young studio artists, had climbed the ladder. "This just makes me miss *Grapes,*" he said, at a tableful of people with an audience in the room. The feeling in the room was bad, and every day it got worse. It was too hard to see the piece in any way because everyone and everything was out of whack. I tried to take matters into my own hands.

I called an early morning rehearsal with Michael Christie and the two pianists, Eric and Mary, to go through the score and teach them the tempi and the dynamics. I had made very well-prepared MIDI files, which are audio computer files meant for everyone to listen to with the score in hand as an aid to learning the piece, because they are full of pertinent and important information about tempi and dynamics.

They take weeks to prepare and are copiously detailed, but no one had listened to them. Dale, the artistic director, even pooh-poohed them, never listening to them at all. So, we started from scratch, and I at least felt as if we could now proceed. Eric Simonson tried for about five minutes to stage one scene and gave up, as if ineffectuality were a virus and it was sweeping the room.

The tenor, Eric Margiore, singing the lead role of Giorgio, had allergies, so, after about one day of singing, he lost his voice altogether, and the day of the workshop he couldn't sing. He seemed beleaguered by insecurity and doubt, beyond allergies. I liked him, and it was sad to see him plummet.

We had to do a little presentation for donors at the home of Garrison Keillor and his wife, Jenny Nilsson, who plays in the orchestra and is lovely. I had to sing the tenor role. I am not a tenor.

Kevin Puts was friendly at Garrison and Jenny's and wanted to talk about my skill with ensembles, but I couldn't tell if it was authentic or obsequious, because by then I had no perspective and wanted to slit my own throat, and he is smart, so he knew what was happening.

The poster idea for the opera looked like the cover of a dime store romance novel with no sense of what the story was about, just two silly-looking local models posing under a tree. It looked as if someone at the company took the photo with their iPhone.

I knew from the beginning I wanted the tenor Charles Castronovo, whom I had met early in his career, to play Giorgio. I was told his agents had been called, but nothing seemed to materialize in that department. Vagueness surrounded the topic like a cloud of nerve gas. I invented: they decided the opera wasn't good enough to hire someone as top tier as Charles, and I felt ashamed. Frustrated, I called his agent, Bruce Zemsky, whom I knew since we were opera nerd kids in the standing room at the Met together. Bruce came over to hear the opera and was very moved, which was a boost, but he said he had never heard from anyone at Minnesota Opera about Charles. I asked Charles himself, who knew nothing about the opera and was never approached. I felt like Ingrid Bergman in *Gaslight*.

When Michael and I left Minnesota, we were battered, upset, and discouraged. We felt twenty years older.

After weeks of disgruntlement, we started rewriting the piece. We took the whole thing apart, examined every moment, and slowly put it back together again, creating whole new sequences that we were both really proud of. At one point, Dale even came to the city to hear some of the rewrites and seemed truly happy.

I asked the designers lined up for the production, Michael Yeargan, the set designer, and Jane Greenwood, the costume designer, over to hear the score. They loved it. We were all feeling great about it, and the meetings were a sheer delight, which only served to create further mystification about the way things turned out.

In the summer of 2011, after Michael and I had sent the new scores to Minnesota, my agent, Beth, received a note from Dale that they had decided to "pass on it." But I was curious, did they even look at or listen to the rewrite? In 2014, Michael Christie was conducting my *27* in St. Louis, and we were becoming good friends. We were at dinner one night, and I broached the subject.

It was so good to finally talk about the whole saga with him because I was a volcano of erupting lava. I asked him about the rewrite, and he said he knew nothing about a rewrite, and he couldn't imagine anyone else had either, because absolutely no one mentioned it. I had sent not only the scores and the new libretto but an entire new MIDI version of the opera to listen to.

What went wrong?

I think one has to begin with the cliché about the unlikelihood of lightning striking twice in one place. What was golden for *The Grapes of Wrath* turned to ashes with *Finzi*. Maybe the strength of that success made us all cocky? We were tackling a difficult topic, and it was proving to be a difficult and painful process.

But there is this too, though this is just speculation, but there might be something to it. When we premiered *Grapes* in 2007, everyone had money. The next year everybody lost money, but Michael and I were writing a big piece for the previous economy. We can't know for sure, because no one seemed to be telling the truth.

A few years later, I was at Banff, in Canada, when I got a call from David Ng, a reporter for the *Los Angeles Times*. He was interested in doing an article on why *Grapes* hadn't been done in California, where most of it takes place. Mark Swed, the music critic, had written glowingly about it three times in the *Times*, so why no productions? We were supposed to open at Opera Pacific, in Orange County, in 2008, but the night Obama got elected, Opera Pacific went bust. Ng started talking to Michael Korie and me for the article, but our disgruntlement over *Finzi* became the topic. There was so much heat pouring from us David Ng became more interested in that than in *Grapes*, but then our agents notified us that we had signed a nondisclosure agreement with Minnesota Opera, so the story couldn't be published. We couldn't even *talk* about what had happened to us. Then I found out that Kevin Puts had won the Pulitzer Prize for *Silent Night*, which premiered in Minnesota a year after *Finzi* was to premiere, and I folded into a cocoon, slipped into a deep unfathomable depression, and didn't write another note of music at Banff.

Sometimes, the only antidote is work.

In 2012, I got two commissions, from Opera Theatre of St. Louis and Houston Grand Opera, to write *27* and *A Coffin in Egypt*, a vehicle for the great mezzo-soprano Frederica von Stade, based on a one-woman play by Horton Foote.

On September 13, 2013, after Oussama Zahr wrote a big feature on me for *Opera News*, "Ricky's Moment," out of the blue, I heard from Dale, congratulating me on the article and the upcoming work it mentioned, saying the praise was well deserved and that he looked forward to hearing the new operas.

The next spring, I wrote to Dale:

Dear Dale,

Last night I dreamed I was in two cities in Germany, Hamburg, and I believe the other was Berlin. I had a different opera happening in each city. I ran into you in Hamburg, and we were very cordial . . . I was even going to say how lovely it was to run into you, but I went into a sort of panic because I couldn't remember which or what was opening in either city, and then it turned out I was there by mistake or maybe false hopes, and I had nothing opening in either city. I listened at the door and heard someone else's music. Then I had to go to the restroom and there was only a lady's room, and I couldn't find the men's room!

It has been a very strange year mainly because my sister Lorraine became very ill and died at the end of January which makes for almost my entire family dying in a small space of time. It happened quickly. We were very close, and I am somewhat lost. You met her at Carnegie Hall.

It seems time to bury hatchets.

I'm sorry our last collaboration disintegrated in the way

it did. I'm sure we both held responsibility in many ways. It takes two to tango. It's funny, because I have played the finished version of Finzi-Continis for many people and it gets a wonderful response, though I imagine it is written for an old economy . . . it is big. Even writing this to you now, though, I feel the sting of what was for me the most painful professional period of my life. Isn't it strange, after something as wonderful as Grapes? I suppose it is as simple as you can't strike oil twice in the same place, though I imagine it is more complicated and we all have big personalities and probably entered that collaboration with baggage based on a previous experience, and each of us were in a different place and hadn't figured out how to navigate the new territory. Sometimes something is not right from the very beginning.

Whatever it was . . . I am happy that together we made, in Grapes, something that seemed to usher in a renaissance for American opera, nothing should sully that, and I wish you the best with all your new projects. It was good to see you in Germany and I imagine one of these days I will run into you where one of my new operas is being done and this note can at least serve as an ice breaker.

Best,

Ricky

I heard back from him two days later, on April 15: "This was a stunning and wonderful e mail to receive. I was hoping I would receive it." He sent heartfelt condolences about my sister Lorraine. He told me how important I was to him: "We have created a masterpiece together, you and I. That is extraordinary and not an everyday occurrence"— and agreed to "bury the hatchet." He said he was going to see my opera *27* in St. Louis—"Michael [Christie, the conductor] says it is terrific"— and ended with "we must meet up and talk and cry and share."

Then, on June 27, I heard from Dale again. He had just seen *27*, which he called "delightful." He praised the performances, and Jim Robinson's production as well as Michael Christie's conducting, and at the end, he said, "at the heart of it was your beautiful score. Thank you for creating this exciting and moving evening of music theater."

It was as if he had applied cool and soothing aloe to my burn. It was nothing short of tragic how our relationship had disintegrated, and now, finally, the past was the past.

When I began composing *Finzi*, my intention was to create my Italian opera with soaring vocal lines and lush romanticism. It is perhaps harder to cast for this reason and may be another contributing factor to the Minnesota debacle. Giorgio has to be a leading man, an A-house tenor, and Micòl, a superb soprano. We need to be drawn to them physically. This is true of Alberto and Malnate as well, because sexual chemistry and obsessive animal attraction are very much built into the story, so the casting of the opera has to be impeccable in order for it to be believable. Each role is complex emotionally and psychologically, so it would be a hard opera to just throw up on its feet. Even the parents are rich and complex roles that require excellent singing actors.

I think it took a while for Michael and me to figure certain things out, like, for instance, we had too many kids in the first draft, which made the cast too big. Micòl's first aria, "Trees," was too baroque, list-like, informational, Handelian, and *long*. Micòl and Giorgio's first duet, "When We Were Children," was not quite right energy-wise or in the chemistry department. Micòl's dog, Jor, was too highly featured and getting a trained dog for the production would have proved costly. We didn't have anything menacing enough yet to introduce Mussolini's racial laws, and eventually the ending wasn't quite right, not sad enough, and that is because we were so intent on adapting the book and not the film that we were being emotionally cautious, which we had to abandon. We had to be braver and less afraid in our writing. Some things I was really proud of. Alberto's homosexuality is definitely in the book and the movie, but with all the yellow lights the times would impart on that subplot. I think Michael, in his libretto, updated what could be expressed now in the most elegant way, and I am very proud of the scene in act 2, "Alberto's Studio," where Alberto shows Giorgio around the studio he has designed and Malnate shows up for a visit. Malnate, whom Alberto went to college with and with whom he is obsessed, toasts Alberto and Giorgio with a jocular and jazzy "To College Days," and then Malnate and Giorgio freeze. Alberto then sings "Before I Die" about his smoldering love for Malnate and his devastation at his sister being the object of Malnate's love instead of him, taking the same melody as Malnate's jocular "To College Days" and filling it with sadness and longing.

Other than addressing and replacing the things I mention that went into the new version, which apparently no one at Minnesota Opera knew about or heard, there is a scene in both the book and the film that I knew had to be just right. After Giorgio finally gets up the courage to make a move on Micòl in her bedroom, the scene in which she spurns and emasculates him, banishing him forever from the garden, he goes home, and his father can see right away that something is terribly wrong. His father too is bereft, having been listening to the radio, finally figuring out what is *really* happening politically in Italy, what the fate of the Jews will be under Mussolini. He is by now afraid and utterly abject. He tells his weeping son he has to let himself die in order to be reborn, reborn into whoever he is going to be next, if he lives. Michael knew how I felt about this scene, and this is where I must pause and say this about Michael: Michael can be difficult, he can be late and vague about deadlines, he can be imperious, he can disappear, he can be cranky, overmedicated, and all of it, but when he gets his work done, it is well worth waiting for and everything is forgiven.

PAPÀ

> *Let yourself die, my boy.*
> *Let yourself die.*
> *Die of despair.*

Once every life
Everyone learns
Life isn't fair.

Now while you can, my boy,
Let your dreams go,
So that a true dream
To believe in can grow.

Time passes by, my son,
And you will live.
Will you forget?
Probably not,
Though you'll forgive.
While you are young and strong,
Let yourself die.
When you are old
It will be too late to cry.

I never learned, my boy,
How to move on,
Waving my flag
Of a New World
When it was gone.
Better to die than live
Chasing a lie.

When you are old
It will be too late to cry.
Cry. Cry now.
When you are old
It will be too late to cry.

In the new version, Michael did something he does really well with the introduction of the racial laws. He combines Papà being thrown out of the bank, Ernesto being thrown out of the library, Mamma's servants quitting on her, and the young tennis players being excluded from the tennis club into one huge sequence called "The Law Is the Law," a sequence whose antecedent might be "Not My Fault" from *The Grapes of Wrath*, but in its incredibly deft lyric and construction, and its spilling out into the first invitation by Perotti, the Finzi-Continis' manservant, to the Finzi-Contini estate to use the tennis courts, which is an important plot point, it is wholly original. I was very happy to receive it and excited to set it to music.

I love this opera. I love the score with such tenderness, as much as anything I have ever written. When Michael and I finished act 1 with the aria "Eternal Flame," which Giorgio sings in the ruined synagogue, confused about whether it is what is happening in the world that devastates him or what is happening between him and Micòl, I knew we had something, the heart was beating wildly, and I felt we had written something for our people.

AND FINALLY . . .

Opera in the Time of Covid, or Everything but the Hounds Snappin' at Her Heels

I felt neither lucky nor excited. From the moment I arrived in the city, January 3, 2022, I felt I had entered one big intensive care unit, where the last thing anyone could possibly care about, including myself, was opera. It was freezing cold, and the streets were empty. Whoever *was* on the streets was wearing one, two, sometimes three masks at a time, and there was a sense that everyone had a runny nose and couldn't wait to get home out of the disease-riddled, snot-covered streets. We had already lost our star tenor, Victor S., a wildly handsome and charismatic artist, who for two years had been slated to sing the lead role of Giorgio in *The Garden of the Finzi-Continis*, already triumphing in a workshop of the opera last spring, because, as a boy, he was diagnosed with a dangerously placed, inoperable brain aneurysm, and he is forbidden to take even an aspirin, much less a vaccine, so the Museum of Jewish Heritage, where we were to premiere the opera, would not allow him to sing, even if he had various lawyers, state counselors, and legal papers guaranteeing he would be tested twice a day and was willing to subject himself to any and all medical protocols and procedures in order to keep himself and everyone else safe and healthy. The answer was just a flat no, and that was that. We had to find another Giorgio, someone capable of the kind of high-flying vocal writing required in the Italian operas of Verdi and Puccini. They are not easy to find, especially when they have to be young, handsome, good actors, and believable. We found Anthony Ciaramitaro, a young tenor with the Los Angeles Opera, a lucky break, because his voice was stunning and he was fully capable of navigating the role's demands, as well as grateful to have been chosen. Our Micòl, Rachel Blaustein, sang as if spools of silk were unraveling from her throat. She was delicate and ferocious all at once. Also, pretty soon before I left the country for the city, the baritone for whom I wrote the role of Papà, Giorgio's father, a pivotal role, perhaps the moral center of the piece, canceled, because he didn't think he was getting enough money and he didn't feel the contract treated him importantly enough. We exchanged a few sour embitterments and then parted ways. We recast him with Franco Pomponi, a baritone on the roster of the Metropolitan Opera, who ended up being excellent.

Our director, Richard Stafford, who for a year had been working with a production team on bringing his concept to life, had a personal catastrophe, his partner of forty years was diagnosed with stage 4 cancer, and he had to bow out of the piece, so the head of the company, Michael Capasso, had to take over the directing of it, which he did with enormous skill and aplomb, but he was taking over someone else's entire concept, so it was making the best of a not ideal situation. I was crestfallen about Richard, with whom I had spent a year discussing the opera. *Then*, just before I got to the city, our pianist, whom I had handpicked, fell down a flight of stairs and hurt his wrist, so he couldn't play the opera. He had spent months getting the opera into his hands, and anyone we would be lucky enough to find would have to start from scratch, and the score is difficult to play. For the whole of December, practically every day there was a different pianist sight-reading the score, so our poor conductor, Jim Lowe, had no one anywhere near knowing the score. One day, he himself even had to step in and play the score and conducted and taught from the piano. When we were finally supposed to welcome our pianist Dmitri, whom I liked and I knew because he played my opera *Morning Star* when On Site Opera did it at the Eldridge Street Synagogue, before we could even sigh with relief, he tested positive for Covid, and we had to wait another week; so even into January, no pianist.

Rehearsals for *Intimate Apparel* had not yet begun, but I was less anxious about that than *The Garden of the Finzi-Continis*, because before Covid closed all the theaters in New York City on March 12, 2020, we were almost three weeks into previews, so *Intimate Apparel* was at least a known quantity to me.

The Garden of the Finzi-Continis was a wholly new animal. Though we had a workshop the previous spring, the piece had never been staged, the orchestrations had never been heard, and we had a lot of new cast members whose voices were unfamiliar to me. I already had enormous trepidations, only compounded by the likelihood of every cast member getting sick, being out for a week, not having enough time to learn and absorb the music, having to be tested every day, sometimes waiting for hours outside in the cold to do so, no one buying tickets, and the fact that I still had a lingering cough that refused to go away since November, when I returned from a trip the Dolomites, in Italy, bedraggled and sick, and no matter how many times I waved my hands between heaves and gasps from behind my mask, and said, "Not Covid, not Covid," the singers would scowl at me as if I had come there to murder them. At that point the only thing that was helping me was a codeine-based red cough medicine, and though I have thirty-two years clean and sober this year, I felt at all times the warm seductive arms of opium-based love around me as well as a possible burgeoning addiction. But the persistence and insistent discomfort of this constant cough made the horrible possibility of becoming an addict again worth it. It was such a sickening time, on every level, I would pray during my morning and evening meditations that both operas would be canceled. Certainly, the disappointment of no operas at all would be better than this growing dread that everyone including me was going to die and no one was going to come anyway. When you work for years writing an opera, it is essential you feel you are doing something meaningful and important, that you foster thoughts that keep the flame flickering. But in this climate, it was impossible to feel important. There was not yet any press, and everything that *was* playing in the theaters, including my collaborator on *Intimate Apparel* Lynn Nottage's very well-reviewed play *Clyde's*, starring Uzo Aduba, was limping along, playing to three-quarters empty houses. Her *MJ*, about Michael Jackson, which had sold out its previews, was suddenly half-empty, faces full of masks, and starring countless ill-prepared understudies, because inevitably the stars were sick and in quarantine.

On the first day of rehearsal for *The Garden of the Finzi-Continis*, which the head of the company could not attend and which was supposed to entail a full read through of the score, there was the sight-reading pianist stumbling through the score, cast members who did not yet know their music, and several singers who had been hired without my ever hearing them, and for whom it was quickly evident this was beyond their capability, while singers I loved from the workshop had not been hired for reasons that were mysterious to me. I felt sick very deep in myself, but I knew enough not to cave in yet. There was plenty of time for that. Michael Korie, Jim, and I met with the head of the company, now the director, for an emergency meeting to at least insist that the singers who couldn't sing the piece be immediately replaced. Luckily, no one balked, and at least that task was set in motion.

When things *did* start coming together, when we finally *had* a pianist and the cast could feel as if they had something buffeting and consistent underneath them, the piece started to take shape as we heard and envisioned it, and I started emerging from my psychopathic depression. We finally had a wonderful cast, engaged, committed, invested in their parts and the story, and rehearsals for *Intimate Apparel* were going great, with Bart Sher doing a considerable overhaul from what we did two years earlier. We had all grown considerably in those weird and difficult two years. One thing that was strange, though, for both rehearsals no one ever took off their masks. One day, Elisabeth Vincentelli from *The New York Times* came to a rehearsal for *Intimate Apparel* at Lincoln Center, and with masks on it was hard to tell who was singing and *what* they were singing. I invited her over to my apartment to play her excerpts from both operas so that way she could at least *see* the words.

So how did it all turn out? I would say *Intimate Apparel* was a smash. We got a lot of press leading up to it, including a big profile about me in *The New York Times* by Vincentelli focusing on the two-operas-at-once phenomenon. When we opened, the first review in *The New York Times*, by Jesse Green, was a rave calling the show a "knockout," and for the most part the rest of the papers followed suit, so we were pretty much set. We sold out, scalpers were charging a thousand dollars for tickets, and PBS decided to film it for *Great Performances.*

With *The Garden of the Finzi-Continis*, there are many good things to be grateful for and some, not; the set was beautiful, a simple fluid structure designed to be projected on, with projections that were all photos from Ferrara our set designer, John Farrell, took himself, the run sold out pretty quickly, we got to see our piece on its feet, a lot of love was heaped on it by everyone involved, and our cast was incredible. But, once again, for me, as is *always* the case in the opera world, something was set before the public before it was ready. We had the orchestra *just long enough* for them to play through it a few times, but not enough to know it and make a piece of music feel lived in and confident until a few performances in. Whatever the needs of the piece were, we found out at the first dress rehearsal, could not be addressed, because there was no time. I heard in that absurd space not designed for opera that there were drastic balance issues, the orchestra being off to the side, right smack in the middle of the theater, which has no pit, so I just panicked and had them turn the mics on to save us; no sound design, just turn them on or we won't hear the children who play the younger versions of the lead characters and don't sing loud enough for the space. The mics helped but somewhat unnaturally augmented the sound of the singers whose voices *were* big enough for the space.

The critics were invited on opening night and started reviewing the piece, when, for me, it was *maybe* ready to be reviewed by the fourth performance. At the third performance, a Sunday matinee, no less, which was the day *The New York Times* came, one entire scene in act 2 fell apart from the start when the conductor waved his baton and no one came in. They didn't play again until the next scene. It is just the way it goes, folks. There are things we composers are helpless over. It is a miracle, given all that, it came off as well as it did. The baby I loved and nursed ran the gauntlet and made it across the river, perhaps a little bruised and battered, but alive.

Intimate Apparel, though, was ready to be seen. If you didn't like the piece, you didn't like the piece, period. But we got to work on that piece the way a piece for the theater should be worked on. By previewing in front of an audience, you get to make adjustments that make a remarkable difference. Bart Sher was constantly restaging scenes to play with where the focus lay, Lynn and I were always cutting and reshaping, Jennifer Tipton would sit everywhere in the house to see if everyone was seeing the same show under her glorious lights; it is endless. We met in the lobby of the Mitzi E. Newhouse Theater every day at 11:00 a.m. to talk about what we could do to the piece to make it better. If we had been able to *watch Finzi* even a week more . . . but, spilled milk.

That said, in the end, I was incredibly happy and proud of both operas. *The Garden of the Finzi-Continis*, just as I predicted, started getting wonderful reviews after the first few performances, including being called "the best new opera of the year" by Chris Ruel in *Opera-Wire*, and if anything, I can't wait to do it again, hopefully in Italy, where it received all kinds of lovely press as well.

Ellen West 𝄆

(*Co-production, Beth Morrison Projects and Opera Saratoga, premiere, June 30, 2019, Little Spa Theatre, Saratoga Springs, New York, and Prototype Festival, January 14, 2020, Gelsey Kirkland Arts Center, New York City*)

In the fall of 2017, I was at Houston Grand Opera getting ready to open *The House Without a Christmas Tree*, the opera I had just written with Royce Vavrek. We were to premiere in the theater Houston Grand Opera uses for more intimate pieces, the Cullen, but Hurricane Harvey flooded out the entire city including the opera house, which looked like a patient in the intensive care unit, tubes coming out of every orifice. Instead of canceling their season, they decided to create an alternative theater space in the convention center, which was huge, dead, and unwieldy, and though we managed to make it look beautiful in the space, and a sound designer saved our asses in terms of the disastrous sound, Houstonians were not necessarily ready to come back to the theater yet, and we had whole rows of empty seats, which was dispiriting to say the least. For some reason, the disappointment of that, and the first snarky review in one of the stupid smaller Houston papers, sent me into a dark tunnel that was only going to get darker. My sister Sheila and Kevin came to Houston for the premiere, and I felt I had a secret I couldn't tell either of them, that I was sinking inside myself. I became psychologically ill and vomited all night after our opening.

While we were there rehearsing, I felt I had to begin *Ellen West*. As if in a trance, I would awaken at 4:00 a.m., like Sylvia Plath writing "Ariel" while Nick and Frieda were asleep in their beds, to enter the disquieting world of Ellen and the Doctor before rehearsals.

In 1996, Michael Klein told me to read Frank Bidart, a poet whose
work I didn't know. I read this poem first:

THE YOKE

don't worry   I know you're dead
but tonight

turn your face again
toward me

when I hear your voice there is now
no direction in which to turn

I sleep and wake and sleep and wake and sleep and wake and

but tonight
turn your face again

toward me

see   upon my shoulders is the yoke
that is not a yoke

don't worry I know you're dead
but tonight

turn your face again

I had never read poems like his before. Everything about them,
from the way they were arranged on the page to their use of CAP-
ITALS, "quotations," and *italics*, felt new to me. Three of his poems
read like libretti. One, "Herbert White," is the harrowing inner

life of a serial murderer, in bald, ruthless, and uncompromising language, much of it while desecrating the body of the girl he has recently murdered. "The War of Vaslav Nijinsky," in which, among other things, Nijinsky, the legendary maniacal dancer who choreographed Stravinsky's ballet *The Rite of Spring*, considers his complex and sometimes sexual relationship with the head of the Ballets Russes, Diaghilev, who was obsessed with him, and his own descent into madness, while his wife, Romola, watches helplessly.

But the poem that called the loudest to me, haunted me, wrapped around me like a serpent and would not let go, was "Ellen West." Based on a case study by the Swiss psychiatrist Ludwig Binswanger, "Ellen" was a woman in a Swiss hospital in the 1930s suffering from an eating disorder before there was a language for such things. The agony of her struggle with gender, embodiment, and appearance, and the doctors' helplessness in light of her situation, felt familiar to me, laced as it is with grief, bitterness, longing, and entrapment. I shuddered every time I read the poem.

I called Beth Morrison, the producer of Prototype, a new opera festival. She had expressed interest in my doing something for her, and I told her the only thing I was interested in doing was "Ellen West." I invited her over to read her the poem. Immediately, she gave me the green light.

I knew I wanted a baritone for the Doctor and a soprano for Ellen, and I had decided the piece would benefit from a smaller orchestration because I wanted it to be portable, so I decided to use a string quartet with an added bass, one C glockenspiel bell, and a piano.

I wrote to Frank Bidart on April 17, 2015, asking for permission to set the poem:

Dear Frank,

I hope it is ok to call you this! I met you once at a fantastic reading you did. I was with poet friends Michael Klein and Marie Howe . . . I write you in a way as a sort of plea.

There is a new opera company called Prototype which

has been getting a lot of press in NYC because of its in-
novations and its explosively broad aesthetic. They have
been interested in my doing something for them, and I told
them my dream project—the only thing I am interested in
doing—"Ellen West."

I am 25 years sober off of drugs, alcohol and most importantly Frank, I have always dealt with an eating disorder. I
know the inside of this story. I know the crippling "ideal." My
therapist says, "Perfectionism is the outer manifestation of
shame." I understand this. I believe I will make something very
beautiful and moving. Important. I don't intend to change a
word of what you have written. Please allow me to Frank.

May I send you some of my music?

It has begun inside of me, I hear it, but I cannot begin
writing it without permission.

What do you think?

You are a genius.

Please.

Best,

Ricky Ian Gordon

(I wanted to write love)
When my lover Jeffrey died, "The Yoke" was a lifeline. It
still is.

On May 6, I heard from Frank.

Dear Ricky,

You can have permission to set "Ellen West."

I'm grateful for your letter and two CD's. The CD's are
beautiful. I am eager to see what you do with "Ellen West."
Your letter moved me a great deal.

I hope we can stay in communication.

I too want to write "Love,"

Frank

How strange it was to be rehearsing *The House Without a Christmas Tree*, this family-friendly Christmas opera, during the day while writing this tempestuous tornado of a piece before the sun even came up. Characters call inside you to be born. They are separate from you and a part of you. You need something from each other. I needed a deeper understanding of the Ellen in me and the doctors' impotence in the face of the severity of her crippling ideal: I and my ruthless inner tyrant. How often I have nearly destroyed myself in the attempt to be more or different than I am. The music of *Ellen West* is an attempt to come to terms with that struggle.

It is hard to break down something you have created note by note, but, for example, in the center of the poem there is an extended section in which Ellen likens herself to Maria Callas, the great opera singer, at the point when she felt she needed to lose weight to look as beautiful as her voice sounded, which ultimately, sadly, resulted in the loss of her voice. Because I have listened to Callas for so long, I felt instinctively that I needed to conjure her up with the aria that I feel is most associated with her singing, "Casta diva," from Bellini's *Norma*, though the poem refers to her in Puccini's *Tosca*. "Casta diva" is the snake charmer conjuring Callas into existence. This allowed me entry, and then, having internalized so much of *Tosca*, I could start pouring the various references from the poem, especially Tosca's aria "Vissi d'arte," into the section, and it was like building a house made of all my favorite things. There was a moment writing it that feels important to recount.

Dear Frank, I was struck this morning, in setting it, by the brilliance of the moment,

—Perhaps it says: The only way
to escape
the History of Styles

is not to have a body.

I never understood, IN READING IT, that what happens at that point in the poem (at least, in the way I am setting it) is, she realizes what she must do. Her fate seems to me, in that moment, sealed. I am humbled, setting these words . . . grateful to live here for a while . . . though sad too.

Happy Holidays O Great one. xxxooo Ricky

Dear Ricky,

That's exactly the import of that moment for me. When she is talking about Callas, she is thinking out her own fate. When she says the words you quote, she has decided no longer to have a body. I think that's the only way the long Callas "detour" could not be a detour. She is imagining the options that she faces, and as she articulates them, she comes to a drastic, tragic conclusion. But a conclusion that allows her to take possession of her fate. She is basically resolved from that point. I'm so glad that reading seemed inescapable to you as you came to set it. It means you're in touch with the "subtext," however painful. What a journey you've been on.

Love, Frank

When I came to the end of the poem, the theater writer in me felt strongly that what I had written was a Greek tragedy. Therefore, I felt I needed a prologue and an epilogue. I felt pretty ballsy asking, but Frank understood, quickly writing me a prologue with new material, lines culled from older poems, and sections of a newer one called

"Writing 'Ellen West.'" For the epilogue, we went back and forth, and I infuriated him, because I was *sure* the epilogue needed to be "The Yoke" and would not let up on trying to convince him, only irritating him further, to my utter frustration.

Ricky,

Your letter today prompts me to write. I should have written earlier. I was hoping the idea of using "The Yoke" would die without my prompting.

From the beginning, I haven't understood why using "The Yoke" is necessary. The poem (and presumably opera) is only in the most peripheral way about the love story between Ellen West and her husband (or Ellen and her doctor). She's a diva. She's a diva who (like Callas) becomes linked to, becomes one with metaphysical ideas: the idea that she is tormented by the question "WHY AM I A GIRL" (questioning the necessity of gender and its enormous force in our lives) and the idea of the mystery of the link between mind (or voice or spirit) and the fact we have bodies. The two ideas are obviously related. She is crucified on the cross of these ideas, on the incompatible demands of mind and body. Linking this to "The Yoke" seems to me to sentimentalize these ideas. It undermines her grandeur and the grandeur of the question she raises.

Maybe I'm wrong. When I first heard about adding "The Yoke" to "Ellen West," I was told that you wanted to put it at the beginning AND END of the opera. That seemed to me terrible. Now the suggestion seems to be to put it at the beginning only. There presumably it would serve as an invitation to Ellen West to visit the listener of the poem/opera once more. That she is a yoke THAT IS NOT A YOKE, a yoke that is desired once more. Conceivably there it could work. I still don't see why it's necessary. The reader/listener should be assaulted by the grandeur of her initial metaphysical

assertion: WHY AM I A GIRL? Why begin with the
lament of someone left behind who was never at the center
of her feelings, who was married out of a desire to escape the
radical nature of one's desire?

I can understand if you have an important male singer
who is interested in this project, and you want to make his
role more important. But obviously the price of this can't be
to throw the initial focus of the whole project off.

There. I've said it.

I hope you will read the original essay by Binswanger
where I first found the story of Ellen West. It's in a collection of papers on phenomenological psychotherapy, "Existence" (published by Basic Books). The essay is long and
profound—and may suggest feelings and colors in the instrumental accompaniment, the "ground" Binswanger goes
into at great length and that I have her in the end briefly
allude to.

Of course, I'm willing to listen to anything you come up
with. I should have articulated before this my deep qualms.

Frank

One day, I was at jury duty, and Frank called, genuinely excited; he
had decided a poem of his, "Hymn," from his Pulitzer Prize–winning
collection, *Half-light*, would be the perfect epilogue. Luckily, I was on
my lunch break, because he read it to me a couple of times and I fell
in love:

HYMN

Earth, O fecund, thou. Evanescent when grasped, when

Venus drives all creatures crazy with desire
to couple and in coupling fill the earth with presences

like themselves
needful, ghostly.

Earth, O fecund, thou. Electric ghosts

people the horizon, beguiling since childhood
this son of the desert about to disappear.

They are no less loved and feared because
evanescent. Earth, O fecund, thou.

It is both exciting and exceedingly vulnerable for me when the librettist is seeing and hearing what you have done with their work for the first time. I sent Frank the video of the first workshop. After Frank's letter below, we rewrote the prologue, and I began to sew the role of the baritone into the piece *much more*. Frank's response was correct, and we both had work to do.

> Ricky, you've done it. The opera is beautiful. Eloquent, gripping, passionate. I've just heard—seen—it once (I watched the first run-through). I'm too wrung-out to say much now or to see it again right away. I love the score. It's often gorgeous. The soprano is magnificent—rising to tremendous eloquence particularly in the second half. The conductor and instrumentalists also seemed to me superb. The opera starting with the Callas scene seems to me hair-raising—really tremendously gripping. Something hasn't settled down about the Prologue. Right now, the Prologue is a little lumpy. Something stylistically doesn't seem quite focused—of course, insofar as the author is the speaker, that's not like anything else in the opera. Maybe the Prologue should be a little shorter (or a little longer). We have to talk about this. Now I have to recuperate.
> You've done it.
>
> Xo Frank

Larry Edelson of Opera Saratoga heard about the piece and came over to hear it, deciding he *also* wanted to do it. He worked out a co-commissioning deal with Beth, and we premiered it at Opera Saratoga in the summer before we brought it to New York City for the Prototype Festival in January, which was great because, though it was a full-blown production, Saratoga was a relatively safe place; we could watch the piece repeatedly and think about what we might want to improve or change before we entered the lion's den of New York City.

Larry suggested—in light of the subject matter, a good call—it might be beneficial to the piece and everyone in the room, especially Jennifer Zetlan, our Ellen, if there were primarily women working on the piece. We got Emma Griffin to direct, whose idea was to include two dancers who could serve the piece both narratively, as orderlies in the hospital, and abstractly, as figures in the imaginary psychic and emotional space. Their presence created a sense of witness to the tragedy.

Emma found an inspired way to open the piece up and give it a kind of movement on the stage that, I felt, took it into another realm. With her set designer, Laura Jellinek, and her lighting designer, Josh Epstein, a space was created for the piece to happen in that could be both literal, a doctor's office, and abstract, a kind of desert of the mind. Her costume designer, Kay Voyce, brilliantly created twenty of the same exact flesh-colored dresses for Ellen to endlessly take on and off, sometimes all at once, illustrating Ellen's discomfort in her own skin. Our conductor was Lidiya Yankovskaya.

Jennifer had gone on a strict diet before and continuing into rehearsals, which made her both diminutive and fragile, and because she is a superb singing actress, she went where the piece needed her to go, meaning that a lot of her own issues about her body came to the fore and it was a turbulent, delicate, and tear-filled process. The patience and maternal presences of Emma and Lidiya were not only helpful but essential.

Keith Phares, the baritone, is gentle, loving, generous, and surprisingly nonthreatening for someone as handsome as he is, so the feeling in the strange rehearsal space, a converted empty store in a half-abandoned shopping mall, was extremely safe.

Frank came to town right before the dress rehearsal. Though I had met him once, years ago in the late nineties, I had not seen him with his voluminous white beard that made him look like a cross between Walt Whitman and Leo Tolstoy. It was moving to sit with him. We had done everything, expanded the prologue, created the epilogue, addressed the balance in the roles, and worked on the first section of the piece before the Callas section. I tweaked the instrumental parts, and I was feeling really good about it. He wrote,

> As you say, now I know what the piece is! I know how brilliant and moving the piece is. The whole is a tightly strung bow, an arrow *aimed* with great penetration. I think I will seem a good librettist whereas all I did was make a poem as good as I could make it almost fifty years ago. It's "stage-worthy," riveting, compelling. Ellen rides a storm at sea and then is drowned in it.
>
> It's weird to have words one heard in one's head so long ago suddenly surrounded by the majesty and tumult of the ocean in "The Flying Dutchman." Which I saw in Wolfgang Wagner's brilliantly stylized production at Bayreuth.
>
> Something triumphant in Ellen at the end, even as she is consumed.

Every time you open a piece, you are running the gauntlet, and you are rarely unscathed. If you come out of it bruised but not battered enough to need intensive care, it's a coup. I didn't know how *Ellen West* would be received. I was so involved with my own engagement with the poem I rarely thought anyone else would feel anything but what I felt about it. We got enough good reviews (Heidi Waleson called it "riveting" in *The Wall Street Journal*) to make the move to New York all the more exciting. Keith Phares as the Doctor and the Husband was magnificent. His astonishing beauty is contrasted with a heart so transparent he always looked as if he were going to crack apart on the stage. When the Doctor, facing that there is nothing else he can do for Ellen, sends her home with her husband, a harrowing train ride ensues, wherein the Doctor becomes her husband traveling with her. He doesn't sing a note, only observing her in horror. It was unbearable to look at him, so clearly distraught about what faced the two of them; he looked gutted. Jennifer Zetlan was resplendent, a jar of jitters and exposed nerves with a voice like a shining silver mallet.

Nathan Gunn in New York was wholly different from Keith. Older, edgier, a more burnished sound, and the father of five, he brought an innate paternal protectiveness to the proceedings, which was harrowing in another way. It is a godsend to see truly talented artists bring something new and different to a role, making it feel fresh and alive.

What drew me to creating this piece, more than anything, was Ellen's final letter to her friend in the hospital, before she commits suicide. I wrote this first, knowing it had to be beautiful (to me) before I could write the rest of the piece. I had to be satisfied with the end. It is the line "when I was not yet truly thin" that is the shiv, the knife in the back. I took speed so I wouldn't eat, and I exercised compulsively. There was nothing that made me hate myself more than eating too much and feeling fat. Even now, I am always thinking of eating, or not eating, or penance for eating, or exercise, or any number of ways to work off what I have eaten.

I have lived every day not wanting to rest until I am good enough, constantly disappointing myself.

> *Dearest.—I remember how*
> *at eighteen,*
> > *on hikes with friends, when*
> *they rested, sitting down to joke or talk,*
>
> *I circled*
> *around them, afraid to hike ahead alone,*
>
> *yet afraid to rest*
> *when I was not yet truly thin.*

When you set a text to music, you are its servant. It takes hold of you, commanding you to do what is best for it. I was a changed person when I was done setting *Ellen West*. It had me by the throat. Finding what felt like an authentic voice for these extraordinary words meant turning myself inside out, and when I was done, well, for one thing, I needed to go on antidepressants.

Something that had been building in me for years was unleashed, and I needed help. Loving the poem with the weight and velocity I did, living within the intensity of its perimeters, collapsed a wall in me. I have been rebuilding.

Intimate Apparel

(Premiere, January 31, 2022, Lincoln Center Theater)

Let him go.
He ain't real,
He is an unanswered letter.
He just a feather on the wind.
Open that door
And we be chasing him forever.
　　—Lynn Nottage

In 2007, after *Grapes* premiered at Minnesota Opera, I was in Houston doing an AIDS benefit that Houston Grand Opera was producing when I got a call from my friend Paul Cremo at the Metropolitan Opera saying Peter Gelb at the Met and André Bishop at Lincoln Center Theater wanted me to be a part of their new commissioning project. To my knowledge, it was the first time these two monumental companies were collaborating, and they wanted to commission a new body of work wherein each piece would be a modest commission with the promise of a full workshop to see if any of the new pieces could fit in either institution. To tell the truth, it was a little like hearing they were going to throw spaghetti at the wall to see what would stick, but they were the two most powerful producing organizations in New York, so who the hell was I to argue. I was happy to be asked, though there is a backstory. I was not in the first rounds of commissions to be asked and, rightly or wrongly, I was terribly hurt. There was even a party to honor Mary Guettel right around the time the first commissions were announced. Mary made a beautiful speech, much of which was about her pride in recognizing and bringing me and Michael John LaChiusa before the public.

André was at our table, and I wouldn't look at him once the entire night. It was deliberate and willful. I am as hurt writing it now as I was then. It felt as if someone had scratched my name off the list at a board meeting when someone had to be eliminated, and I was marked "Possible alternate." When I got to my hotel room that night, lo and behold, there was a beautiful email from André saying I should have been on the first list and there were mistakes in the logistics and part of it was his fault, and he apologized profusely, and not only did I feel vindicated and comforted, but my fragile ego also started to heal, and I began to get excited.

There was even, a year before *The Grapes of Wrath* opened, an Opera America conference where Peter Gelb was the keynote speaker and he read proudly the list of all the composers being commissioned that I was not on, and I felt sick. Now, you could say, "Who the fuck are you to say you should have been on that list and someone else shouldn't have?!" and you would be right. But here's the thing, I knew everyone involved, the whole cast of characters, they were my colleagues, my friends, and it felt like such a deliberate pointed omission that I was devastated. I am certainly not the first artist this has ever happened to, but that thought didn't ease the pain. Nowhere near was my humility. Buck it up, you weren't chosen. No. There is so much pain in the world of the arts. You are bolstered and then easily dismissed. You are forever being criticized and compared with others. People including critics never look deeply enough into your work to actually see what you were trying to do. Critics *never* ask for scores. Would a book reviewer review a book without reading it? Yes, music is an auditory language, but I do not believe *anyone* can know what a composer is trying to say on the first hearing, *especially* something as long as an opera! A look at the score can speak of the integrity, the order in the writing. But it is what it is, and my grousing about it will not change anything. Nevertheless, it can be ego and soul crushing, and if you are the least bit sensitive, which you are if you spend your life creating, it can be very upsetting and hard on the stomach, but I was finally commissioned, finally included, and I felt alive again.

I have written elsewhere about how my first idea was, naturally, to work with Michael Korie, since I had just written *The Grapes of Wrath* with him to great success. The opera I always had a fantasy about writing was about Victor Hugo's daughter Adèle, whose crippling and unrequited obsession with Lieutenant Pinson impels her across the ocean to Nova Scotia and then to Barbados and eventually into a high-end insane asylum in France where she outlives the rest of her family. Adèle Hugo was the inspiration for François Truffaut's harrowing film *The Story of Adele H.*, which moved me greatly. Michael liked the idea and did one of his gorgeous illustrated treatments for our opera that we were going to call "La Misérable," and we met at the Met in Peter Gelb's office and got everyone excited. But it wasn't to be. I returned from the world premiere of my opera *Rappahannock County*, at the Virginia Arts Festival and Virginia Opera, and excitedly called Michael to check in on his progress with the libretto. I could see immediately; Michael had said yes to too many projects and was simply too busy to work on ours. Hurt, and perhaps insulted, I had to let Michael and that idea go. I thought, or perhaps was *given* the thought, of Lynn Nottage. I knew Lynn a little bit. At one point, Michael and I had met with her for coffee, to see if she might be interested in writing the book to a musical we were planning. Also, in 2006, when my *Orpheus and Euridice* won an Obie Award, Lynn had been on the selecting committee. So, I bought all of her plays and began to read them. I was blown away by their power, the strength of her narratives, her simple and clear storytelling, and by the way she wasn't fooling around; she was *always* saying something. So, and here is where it is sort of comical, because I remember the story one way and she, another, but you can ask her for hers, and I will tell my version. I remember Facebooking her and saying, "Hey, would you be interested in writing an opera with me for The Met?" and she replied, "Yes, and it's interesting, I've always thought my play 'Intimate Apparel' WAS an opera!" To which I remember replying, "Bingo! Because that's the one I want to do." Her story has us knocking around various ideas for a while before we settled on that, but what does it matter? What matters is what we chose in the end.

Intimate Apparel takes place on the Lower East Side of Manhattan in 1905. Esther, an excellent, highly skilled seamstress, lives in a Black boardinghouse run by Mrs. Dickson, where mostly prostitutes live. She sews their intimate apparel, and her work is exquisite and impeccable, and that's how she makes a living and earns her keep. To save money for her fantasy of a "beauty parlor," she stuffs and sews money into a patchwork quilt she keeps on her bed. Her work is so good white Upper East Side matrons even take notice, and one of them, a Mrs. Van Buren, hires her to make lingerie as sexy as what Esther makes for Mayme, her prostitute friend, in order to lure Mr. Van Buren back into the boudoir. Esther buys her fabric from an orthodox Jewish man on Orchard Street, Mr. Marks, whom she clearly has a deep connection with that can be expressed only through fabric, and in act 1 a man named George Armstrong starts writing her very romantic letters from the Panama Canal, saying he heard about her through her deacon's son. Esther writes back, but only through Mayme and Mrs. Van Buren, because she can neither read nor write. By the end of the act, he comes to New York City, and they get married. In act 2, all hell breaks loose.

The first thing was, Peter Gelb and André Bishop wanted to meet with Lynn, to see how she would open up the play, which is all scenes for two people. Lynn had really thought this through, and she charmed and delighted them, and we got our commission. Because Lynn found a way to include an ensemble in the production, it worked beautifully for me, because I used all the extra voices throughout the piece as a sort of orchestra to accompany and augment my two-piano score.

Lynn, for someone who had won two Pulitzer Prizes, a MacArthur Award, and every possible playwriting award, brings very little ego to the table. She had not written an opera libretto before, and she just wanted to get it right. Paul Cremo, the dramaturge from the Met, and I would go through each draft with her, mostly to get her to trust

how much of a role the music has in telling the story. The first draft
had too many words, and I told her it would be as long as Wagner's
Ring. The second draft was much better but still too dense. I can tell
just from looking at a page whether it will be a pleasure to set to music
or simply obligatory because I will be having to think about so many
words and too little music. Understandably, this task of boiling her
not only beautiful but tremendously successful play down to a rich
stock was not only difficult but painful. By the third draft, she had
figured it out. Her libretto was lean, crystal clear, and essential. She
found a way to keep everything necessary from the play, but also a
new lyrical language for it, so the words became inherently musical.

The first thing I composed for *Intimate Apparel* was a two-step. I
got a residency at Banff in the Canadian Rockies, and I worked for a
couple of weeks on it, thinking it would be the prelude for the piece,
but really, it just ended up being the door in, though I kept a lot of the
thematic material and embroidered it into the body of the opera.

I don't always write from beginning to end, in order. I have written about how in *The Grapes of Wrath* I picked hot spots that would
get me going, partially so I could feel as if I had stones to build with
and mostly to quell my fear of creating something so large. But with
Intimate Apparel, I started from the beginning. Lynn's set pieces are
seamlessly sewn into the fabric of the piece, so instead of singling
them out, I wanted to arrive at them organically so that I was at that
point in the story and ready to write it as if I were living it. It created
an urgency for me, an excitement in writing it. I felt the story deeply,
and I fell in love with the characters, wanting to animate them, enno-
ble them. If there is always one character in an opera you encode with
your own DNA, I would say I embroidered myself into the character
of Mr. Marks, making him a version of myself, my family, my history,
so that there is for me, in *Intimate Apparel*, a larger conversation going
on, a dialogue with my own history. Lynn's beautiful play, even as a
libretto, was large enough to absorb such personal subplots. However,
this does not mean I didn't relish musicalizing the maternal protectiveness of Mrs. Dickson; the cynical, slightly naughty street smarts
of Mayme, the prostitute with a heart of gold who unwittingly falls

into a trap, devastating her dearest friend; the hot, almost matronly lostness and yearning of Mrs. Van Buren, imprisoned by her station in society; and of course Esther, Esther, like Lynn, around whom the universe circles, while she quietly spins her thread into diamonds.

In many ways, Lynn and I are very different. Lynn has been very awarded, very heralded, very celebrated, and though she in no way lords this over you, it expresses itself as a quiet dignity and security I don't share with her. I have a hard time ever feeling I've earned a seat at the table, so sometimes I acted like a noisy and frantic little satellite crazily circling Lynn's steady solar system, but we balanced each other out, and in the end I felt really good about what we had created. Once, though, I felt Lynn wasn't giving me material quickly enough. I would get to the end of a scene and have to wait sometimes weeks before she had what I was supposed to write next. This is, by the way, a librettist problem, not necessarily exclusive to Lynn. After I slightly badgered her at one point about this, while she was vacationing with her family in Barbados, she texted me, "I will not be bullied." I was shocked! I even worried it was racial! Where had I overstepped? I just wanted to write a great opera! Suddenly I felt so shaky around her. But on the opening night of *Porgy and Bess* at the Met, which our friend Jim Robinson had directed, there was a party afterward. Tony Gerber, Lynn's husband, was sitting at the big banquet table Peter Gelb had set for us all, and standing next to Lynn, I said, "Tony, Lynn called me a bully." He blithely said, "That's okay, she's called me worse." We all laughed and that particular blip in our collaboration passed.

For the first workshop of act 1 of the opera, Gayletha Nichols cast it, and after teaching everyone the music in my studio using the detailed MIDI files from my computer, we went to the Met, and in List Hall, for an audience of about twenty, I conducted the singers from my computer, and they sang along with my files! It went surprisingly well, but that's when I found out that opening with my almost six-minute two-step overture was unnecessary. Those are the things you find out quickly, pacing issues. I remember, when I was a little boy, I got a black-market pirated recording of an opera by Marvin David Levy of Eugene O'Neill's *Mourning Becomes Electra*. I loved it so much, and even to this day find it was pivotal in my shaping as an opera composer, but there were so many orchestral interludes I loved then, though I completely understood when years later they were cut when the opera was revived in Chicago. Dramaturgically, nothing happened during them, and though thoroughly interesting musically, they most probably felt superfluous in performance. Now, there are the incredible Sea Interludes and Passacaglia in Britten's masterpiece *Peter Grimes*, but they are so thematically sewn into the fabric of the story that their elision would create great gaps; not so in the Levy.

When I finished act 2, and it was time for Peter Gelb and André Bishop to hear it, Peter wanted me to come to his office, but I knew that wasn't possible. The only and best way for them to hear it was to walk up to my apartment on West Seventieth Street and sit in front of my computer, watching the music scroll by, hearing the MIDI files, with me singing all the parts. I knew that was how it would sound the best and would be the most entertaining. Plus, it is how everyone hears my music for the first time now. I knew I was asking a lot, but I was pretty insistent. I had to control the situation for the optimal experience of hearing the score for the first time. One thing I have learned as I have gotten older is to be judicious with your yeses and brave with your noes.

The day they arrived, they both seemed uncomfortable, like fish out of water. I went to get them glasses of water, and when I got back to my studio, André was even pacing, and said, "Ricky, can't we just sit on the couch?" Here I was squeezing them onto my little piano bench with their asses touching, but I knew there was no other way. "I'm sorry, André, but you have to *see* the music as it scrolls by so you know what's going on!" Once I got them to calm down and behave, though, things went really well, and they seemed to love act 2! I will always remember that day, though, because I can't believe I forced those two bulwarks of culture to conform to my own way of doing things.

The next step was a workshop of the whole opera. I requested we workshop it in Cincinnati, where I had workshopped *Morning Star* with Opera Fusion, a collaboration between Cincinnati Opera and Cincinnati College–Conservatory of Music, then run by Marcus Küchle and

Robin Guarino, that is extremely helpful and useful. The two institutions share their resources, so you pretty much have everything you need to look constructively at your piece. Opera Fusion actually arose out of a seminar held at Opera America on the topic of workshopping operas in the opera world, and Robin and I happened to be present for it. It is useful and exciting because you have experienced professionals in the room, but also students who are eager to help something come to life, so the air is charged. There was one moment in Cincinnati, though, where we were running the second act, and suddenly Lynn looked ashen and blurted out, "We left something *major* out of the act! The dramaturge dramaturged something very important right out of the act!" Poor Paul Cremo! Lynn wasn't really blaming him; she was just exasperated. "How could we do that?!" she exclaimed. It was a moment, after George has gone about as far as he can in fucking Esther over, when he goes to touch her and she screams, "No! Don't touch me! I ain't gonna let you hurt me. I'm a good decent woman! Worthy! Yes, worthy!" I calmed her down, promising, as soon as I got back to New York City, I'd add it, and I did. When we were ready, we were flown back to New York, where we did two presentations, one at the Armory, where Lynn is an artist in residence, and then at Lincoln Center Theater, where André, Peter, our director, Bart Sher, and everyone else involved could see it. There was a lot of excitement in the room, and an extremely warm feeling afterward with lots of hugging, *even* from Peter and André, and I would definitely say Lynn and I were very happy.

Sometimes I would call Lynn at 8:00 a.m., when I had just finished writing something, irrepressible in my excitement, and wake up her whole family, to insist she come over that minute to hear what I had written. I wanted to please Lynn. I knew how important her play was to her, and I wanted her to feel as if I were celebrating it, anointing it with my music, not diminishing it in any way. I knew I had a precious jewel in my possession.

It can actually feel false and pretentious to try to describe building something that is in essence instinctive, because it makes you feel as if you were pretending so many decisions you made were deliberate, when in fact you were following some impulse, some taste, some aesthetic that just felt right. I am always just trying to find the right music for the story, but music I can stand behind as well. But one thing I can break down fairly easily in terms of the score of *Intimate Apparel* is the way I approached the character George, and again, this was most probably unconscious, but I am still proud of it, and don't feel self-conscious citing it, since it was a musical response to what Lynn was very specifically doing in the play. George, in act 1, exists only in his letters to Esther as they are being read to her, so he is her fantasy of who he is, "Dream" George, if you will. In act 2, he becomes real, who he really is, gruff, aggressive, and insensitive, coarse, really. So, in act 1, his music is all legato, very lyrical and dolcissimo, like a romantic obsession come to life, whereas in act 2 his music is percussive, angular, and abrupt, in keeping with who he reveals himself to be. This is something music can illustrate perfectly, and something I feel is truly successful in the opera.

I admired Bart Sher in watching him direct our opera. Perhaps the first day or two, I was wary and a little afraid of him. He was too quick to cut something I felt attached to, and I went and sulked behind the piano. At the break, he came over, sensing something was wrong, and we quickly found a way to navigate the delicate terrains of two fragile egos. He is, at least in our piece, a great director for opera singers, intuiting exactly what they should be doing with their hands so they never have time to telegraph or announce physically what they are singing about. It seems to take them to a richer place in themselves, to the truth. We had an immensely talented cast, and Bart coaxed stunning performances out of them. He worked assiduously on transitions, and I got to see I didn't have to resolve everything; instead, I could bleed things into one another cinematically as he was doing with his staging. It was an inspiring collaboration.

Oddly, we were nominated for all kinds of theater awards, and they kept calling it a "musical," which really irritated me, but André convinced me they only wanted to recognize it in any way they could and they had no categories for opera. He said I should just be grateful. So, I was.

PART XI

DOWN THE ROAD A PIECE

Deaths

With Susan's well-earned tolerance, they had to pump enough morphine to kill an elephant through her veins in hospice. She held on for a long time, and we think it's because she was enjoying the legal high. On the day before she died, my mother and I sat in her hospice room for hours, singing. At one point, my mother sang a setting of the Lord's Prayer that I had never heard, and an Irish nurse, hearing it in the hallway, came in and sang with her. When Sheila got the call at four in the morning, I felt as if we had sung Susan out of this world, as I had with Jeffrey.

When Lorraine died, she didn't want her body moved for three days, a Tibetan ritual because they believe it takes three days for the soul to make its journey. Friends and family gathered around her bed, telling stories, sharing memories, chanting, meditating, and singing. Her three boys met in Long Beach to scatter her ashes, and Maggie has written one beautiful poem after another commemorating her.

Sheila sent me a photo of Lorraine dead, but it was upsetting. She had become skeletally thin, and her teeth seemed much longer. When Jeffrey died, his mother, Yvonne, wanted a photo of him dead. I think it is because her son Gary died so violently and so suddenly; Jeffrey's death was at least something she was *present* for. But I couldn't look at it; it was excruciating for me.

Theodore Presser Music just published my string quartet called *Lorraine* and a cello and piano piece called *Samba for Susan*.

For My Father 𝄞

My father died on August 22, 2001. My mother thought it was merciful my father died before September 11; she thought that would have dispirited him in a way that would have been worse than dying. About three weeks before he died, I was getting ready to go off to Ucross, an artists' colony I found in a catalog. A gigantic ranch in Wyoming, with writers' cabins, artists' studios, and little houses for composers all facing running streams or plains that fill with deer, pronghorn antelopes, mink, beaver, golden eagles, great horned owls, and birds of every variety including the western blue, in the middle of nowhere, just before the foothills of the Bighorn Mountains. I wanted to go there because going out west, after Jeffrey died, was the most healing thing I did. I wanted to be back in that landscape, smell the sage, and scream into the endless nowhere, the silence where no one can hear you. I was supposed to be there for three weeks, but while I was there, they had to put my father into hospice in Florida. He was getting up all hours of the night careening through the house, and my mother was ill-equipped to handle it. My sister Lorraine was visiting them and decided it was time, which Susan and Sheila thought was bossy, but someone had to. He had congenital heart failure, which made his testicles swell up to the size of grapefruits and only made his lumbering more difficult.

❦

I arrived late at night in Florida. My nephew Daryl picked me up at the airport and took me straight to the hospital to see my father. He was in a coma, but when I kissed him and said I was back from Wyoming,

Mecca for my father, who was a cowboy at heart, he heaved, almost leaping at me out of his coma, even opening his eyes. Then he fell back again, forever.

Those days in Florida were both sweet and comical, as well as sad. My sister Sheila set up her easel in the hospice room and painted the landscape out the window. Susan knit, Lorraine anointed my father with oils, massaged his feet, and acted as his health advocate, while my mother sang, kibitzed, and told jokes.

The third day, my father started looking scary. He was making rattling sounds when he was breathing, his mouth agape. My mother, in distress, said, "That's no longer my husband." I said to the nurses, "Please. If there's anything you can do," but they said, "We do not hasten demise," but he was gone a couple of nights later and I suspect they did.

Sheila walked into my room at 4:00 in the morning. "Ricky. Daddy's gone."

Before he died, my father asked me if I would go to synagogue and say Kaddish for him every year on Yom Kippur. I feel bad, but I can't get myself to do it. When I was little, there was nothing I would call holy in synagogue for me, no sign of God, no particular light, nothing, not even on the day of my Bar Mitzvah. It was just oppressive. What I got in Sunday school was not a spiritual education but an empty, rote-driven memorization of facts. So no, I can't suddenly go to synagogue, pretend it means something, pray for my father in that way. When Michael Korie and I were writing *The Garden of the Finzi-Continis*, I said, "Michael, why don't we dedicate this opera to our fathers?" He agreed, and we did. That feels better, a monument.

When I wrote *Morning Star*, with Bill Hoffman, I knew the final Kaddish for all the women who died in the Triangle Shirtwaist Factory was for my father as well.

FLEA MARKET

One day, in Florida, most probably in the mid-1990s, my parents were going to the flea market. They loved to tool around consignment shops and flea markets, looking for bargains. Their whole house was furnished with stuff that belonged to someone else before them. They were getting out of the car, my mother from her side stepping out into the sun. Assuming they would separate and shop for the things each of them liked, as they usually did, she asked, "What time do you want to meet for lunch, honey?" He replied, "I don't give a fuck if I ever see you again." She was stunned, wounded, having no idea what she had said or done to precipitate such a demonic outburst, but she was also used to it. You never knew what was going to set my father off. I have moments of flash rage that are usually related to self-loathing. A sudden reflection on my own uselessness, any tidbit about someone else's good fortune, who *did* get a Guggenheim, who *was* inducted into the American Academy of Arts and Letters, who won a Pulitzer, who received the MacArthur *this* year and will now forever until they die be referred to as a genius, Emmys, Tonys, Oscars, everything set up to make one artist feel better or worse than another. A critical review, a look in the mirror at the wrong moment, it doesn't really matter; when it comes over me, I want to kick my dog, scream at Kevin, and destroy something, anything.

We never celebrated our father's birthday, and he never celebrated ours. I at least knew the day of his birthday; he never knew mine. I never heard my father utter the words "Happy Birthday." Sometimes my mother would take me shopping for my birthday, which was lovely because it was fun to have a day alone with her, to be doted on, to get some nice clothes, and she liked to stop for coffee and cake frequently throughout the day, so it was like five birthdays in one. But my father never had anything to do with our birthdays. I think he felt bad about this before he died, though I think he felt bad about everything. He said to my mother with a grief that was unprecedented for my father, "I missed my children's lives," to which she replied, "You have now, Sam."

I think, after all the life my father was destined to miss, from the Depression, the war, the role he felt consigned to as a provider, we were a burden, an intrusion on a life he hoped for and never lived. He wanted to do something important, to be somebody, just like all of us, but exigencies thwarted him. He didn't even go to college. How could he *not* resent us? We got everything he never had. No wonder he never knew our birthdays; they were probably sad days for him, another nail in the coffin of his freedom. We were wedged between him and my mother, the only relationship he valued or wanted to have. My father was the shadow in our house. He could block out the light. But what did he want to be? What did he intend to be?

Every once in a while, love letters my father wrote to my mother during the war would surface, and they would always be shocking, written in a voice that was unrecognizable. There were pressed flowers and "dears" and "darlings" and clever little drawings with hearts and valentines. Where did his tenderness go? Where did his ability to *articulate* go? Sometimes you just associated him with snarls and grunts.

But then he discovered email.

In the most jerry-rigged, duct-taped office you could possibly imagine, when it was AOL and dial-up and "you've got mail," he taught himself how to email and became a whole new person. It was as if he had been waiting all his adult life, since the war, to reacquaint himself with himself and words. He started writing to all of us, loving, caring, idea-filled, advice-giving emails. Where was this person when I was growing up? But now he was Ann Landers! Dispensing all the wisdom he had been secretly saving for that moment. He sought to get to know us, and he allowed us in. Suddenly we all had relationships with my father we never had before. My dad definitely loved Sheila the most and was fascinated with her painting. He couldn't fathom how she had become so good at it. He started taking painting lessons himself and hanging out in Sheila's studio discussing the tricks of the trade as if in a few months he fancied himself a Rubens. He framed and hung everything he painted on the walls, and my mother treated him with the respect a great painter deserved, swooning every time he completed something. That was unchanging in my father, his need to be a know-it-all, only now it was endearing, even funny, because he was growing out of being unyielding and intractable to a floppy and lovable puppy dog. He started giving things away. He gave Susan a beautiful pair of ruby earrings, keepsakes she always admired. She was so shocked she cried. He gave me his Masonic ring, the Bulova watch his mother gave him during the war, inscribed with the words "To Sammy, With love, from Mother," and his 22-karat gold Nivada Grenchen watch. The morning Jeffrey died, I dialed Florida to tell my mother, but he picked up. I panicked. He was the last person you wanted to trust with your emotions. As soon as he picked up, I was intending to say, "Dad, can I talk to Mom?" but I began to howl into the phone, "Dad, Jeffrey's gone, Jeffrey died." He listened. "You did good by that guy, Rick. Don't ever let that guilt shit get the best of you. You did good by him." His acknowledgment of my love, of the care I took with Jeffrey, instantly melted the permafrost from the tundra of our relationship. Like the day in the 1970s I called him, risking his advice: "I feel like I have no idea what I'm doing, Dad. I feel like a fraud." And he said, "Nobody knows what they're doing, Rick. Everybody's bluffing," which was all I needed to hear.

My father wanted taps played at his funeral, and a Masonic service, so all the Masons did some kind of ritual over his coffin, the specifics of which I can't remember, but it was deeply stirring. I read a poem I wrote for him:

> *Like cowboys, my father swaggered, walking into rain*
> *Bearing pain with courage clearly modeled on John Wayne . . .*

Ending with the lines

> *Giddy-Yap! My father swaggers off into the night.*
> *His holster holds his gun, and if his horse is saddled right,*
> *he rides him like a cowboy, screaming, "Yippy Yi Yo Ki Yay!"*
> *It warms my heart to see him that way.*

> *Shoot 'em up dad!*
> *Howdy partner,*
> *and anything else they say.*

For My Mother 🎵

When my mother died, on June 27, 2012, and I wonder if this is un-avoidable, I felt the weight of Flannery O'Connor's last line in her mighty story "Everything That Rises Must Converge": "The tide of darkness seemed to sweep him back to her, postponing from moment to moment his entry into the world of guilt and sorrow." Why wasn't I the kind of son who moved in with my mother when her death was imminent, or moved her in with me? Why, in the last few years of her life, did we put her in the place she never ever wanted to be—a nursing home? She hated them so much; she wouldn't even visit anyone who was living in one. It's almost as if she held it against them, as if she were angry at them for getting old and saw them as if they'd been incarcerated. But there were major issues with her health that seemed unmanageable.

Her skin was like tissue paper, her bones were brittle, and she was always falling and hurting herself. Kevin and I went to Florida to visit her on her birthday. We wanted to take her shopping for new clothes and to the beautiful outdoor pavilion at the Four Seasons for lunch. We bought her all kinds of colorful V-necked T-shirts, because she still loved to feature her ample bosom, and purple-and-green cotton pants that looked as if they had been batiked. They were happy clothes, and with her little open-toed sandals she looked cute in them.

The next morning, we went to pick her up to take her to breakfast. There was blood on the bottom of her right pant leg, and it was pooling in her shoe and spilling onto the white tiled floor. It looked like a murder scene. She had somehow scratched her calf on the sharp corner of a table without knowing it and was bleeding all over the place. This could mean months of wound care because of her diabetes, and it meant getting her to doctors' visits, into the car and out of the car with a walker, and then, at a certain point, a wheelchair, several times a week.

Because I didn't live there and Sheila did, it was she who shouldered the burden of my mother's care, and it was becoming overwhelming. So that she and Jon could go on a cruise they had booked months before, I went down to Florida and stayed in their house, visiting my mother during the days. I got a call from my mother's friend Ann late one night. My mother had fallen in the shower. She was okay, but she had bruised her ribs. When I got there, she was shaken up and in pain. I stayed over for two nights, but then I behaved badly. It was time for me to go back to New York, and I left my niece Dani alone with her. I was afraid of being sucked into a whirlpool.

By then, the cycle of caring for the ill seemed never ending, and I just wanted to get back to my life. But there is no excuse. I am to this day haunted by my mother's pained and astonished face that I was leaving. She, who had taken care of me so much of her life. When Sheila and Jon got home from the cruise, it was clear she couldn't live alone anymore. The home she normally kept clean was becoming the kind of dirty where her black hairs were everywhere and the sheets were the final place of rest for what was always leaking out of her. If she made herself oatmeal for breakfast, she would take a portion out of the pot and leave the rest to fester for weeks. She would close the shades and watch television all day, waiting . . . for what? My beautiful, talented, wildly alive, funny mother.

After *The Grapes of Wrath* premiered in St. Paul in 2007, Kevin took me to Ireland. We were staying in a house our friend Sinead was watching for a family that looked out over the dazzling coast of Connemara. One night I called my mother, who I thought would by now have adjusted to the nursing home, but she was in a state, shuddering as I had never heard before. She was screaming and crying into the phone, "How could you do this to me?" Normally, she never let on she had needs. A stoic, she hid her feelings, never wanting to be a burden. It was unbearable hearing her sound so miserable, victimized, and disempowered. I was so distraught I made Kevin drive me all the way to a church that is practically on the way out of Connemara to pray for her, for her serenity, for her surrender. A church.

It didn't matter; it just had to be a space where I felt God could hear me. Casa Del Mar was a really nice, really high-end assisted-living facility with two lovely dining rooms and extremely attentive nurses, and she had her own room with an outdoor screened-in porch. Sheila, Kevin, and I helped her fix up her room with paintings and furniture she liked, including her favorite red-velvet love seat, and filled the outdoor porch with plants and places to sit to enjoy the sunlight.

But here's the thing, my mother only liked being around people when it was her choice. She turned on her big borscht belt personality, but then she'd spend days alone regathering the strength for her next act. Here, she felt "on" all the time. Also, she was always saying, "These aren't my people." Frankly, it was basically that they weren't Jews, more specifically, shtetl Jews, who'd grown up poor and uncultured and had to claw their way from nothing up into the middle class. I think she felt the pressure to impress because she felt inferior there.

I wrote to her doctor, "Isn't there anything you can give her to make her happier? It's awful at this point in her life she should be so miserable." The doctor never wrote back to me, but she added Lexapro to my mother's arsenal of medications, and within weeks she was her old self again, smiling, entertaining. She even got herself a younger boyfriend, Michael, whom she called her "boy toy," told us he had a small penis but was a good kisser, and started showing off her cleavage again.

Years before all this, in 1994, Jeffrey and I, with Jim Mahady and Tom Piechowski, drove to Wildwood, New Jersey, where Jeffrey's mother had a condo on the ocean. It was such a sweet weekend, but one moment was agony for me. We went out for ice cream one night, and there was one old lady sitting by herself in the parlor, eating a hot fudge sundae. She looked so lonely I started crying. It was unbearable for me to *ever* think of my mother alone or lonely.

All through this period, from Casa Del Mar to the Atrium, which she preferred, I would always bring my piles of old songbooks. No matter how far gone these people were, they always perked up and, most amazingly, remembered the lyrics of the songs. I would place my mother next to me facing out so she could feel like the star, and we'd sing "I'll Be Seeing You," "You'll Never Know," "That's My Desire"; Kevin would stand in the back and weep. He gave her a beautiful photo he took of me and her one day when we took her to the sea. "Who is that?" she asked. "You!" he replied. "No," she said, and pushed it away. My sister Sheila persuaded her to stop dyeing her hair because it was too labor-intensive getting her to and from the beauty parlor. But she gave up and stopped looking in the mirror. In the photo Kevin gave her, her hair was gray.

The Atrium was more her style, less expensive, and filled with shtetl Jews like her, but by then she was in a wheelchair. When they moved her to the second floor with the Alzheimer's patients—she called them "the Alzies," insinuating she hadn't sunk that low—sometimes I would find her alone in the kitchen asleep in her wheelchair with spilled food all over her velour tracksuit—Ensure, mashed potatoes, Jell-O—and nearly die of sadness. If I said, "I love you, Mom," she'd say, "I love you more," staring off into the distance toward wherever she was going next.

Right across the street was a little park with shaded picnic tables and a labyrinthine area where you could amble a path through twisted tropical greenery and trees. I would stop at Flakowitz's, the local deli on Federal Highway, and buy her an egg salad sandwich, a black-and-white cookie, and a coffee to go. We'd sit and eat, and then I'd wheel her through the brush, singing to her.

Sometimes I would recite poems to her. One day, I recited Stanley Kunitz's "Layers"—"Live in the layers, not on the litter"—and she was reflective after it, so much so she felt the need to sum up her entire life's philosophy in one fell swoop: "If you can reside in your own body without panic, without anxiety attacks, just taking the day as it comes, that is the meaning of happiness." I was stunned. It seemed so unlike my mother. Then, in her most Fanny Brice borscht belt accent, she said, "I'm a philosophizer!"

Another time, she came out with the sentence "My heart is a heart for nourishment."

One of the last times I saw her, when she was still conscious, I brought a big container of chocolate frozen yogurt, got into bed with her, and spoon-fed it to her. It was such a happy time. It was like feeding a hummingbird, broken-winged, but still humming.

The nurse wanted me to remove her wedding ring. I made up a story that I was going to get it cleaned, but she smelled the truth and wouldn't let me. When her bedsores got so deep they exposed her bones, the hospice nurse who put her into a morphine-induced coma volunteered to take it off. Although she greased the finger to get it over the arthritic knuckle, my mother nevertheless winced, crying out from her coma like a wounded animal. I believe she thought she was no one without that ring.

Sheila gave it to me to sell, but I won't.

We played tapes of her singing and telling jokes on a boom box for everyone to hear, and marvel at, until she left the world.

In our first house, 221 Lincoln Avenue, in Harbor Isle, every day during the summer we'd go to the Beach Club. I would swim or catch killies in towels we dragged like nets through the water, and she would play mah-jongg with the Girls. She called the other moms the Girls.

One time, upstairs in their bedroom at dusk, I was watching *The Three Stooges* on TV. Suddenly, inexplicably overcome with panic and dread, I ran downstairs to the kitchen, sobbing.

"Where do we go when we die?" I cried.

"To the Harbor Isle Beach Club," she said, after only a moment's pause.

"Just like here. I'll have a game with the Girls, and you? You'll be playing shuffleboard."

Comforted, I ate my dinner, my existential angst subsiding for at least a year or two.

Yahrzeit

My mother always kept
A pile of sewing in the kitchen,

Darning late at night
When she couldn't sleep.

Sipping coffee, she'd mend
Worn socks, torn seams,
Holes in knees of pants that now
You'd never keep.

Sew Mama, sew,
And thread the stitching through slow.
Sew slow.
Breathe Mama, sing
A song of mourning
For what's long ago.

My mother always kept
A bag of worsted by the sofa,
Knitting afternoons
When disquiet came.

Clicking needles, she'd bring
Forth warm wool things
Blankets, scarves, or hats
From fine merino sheep.

Knit Mama, knit,
And purl the yarn with your fears.
Loop tears.
Dream Mama, sing
A song of yearning,
For the passing years.

She knit me once, a poncho,
When ponchos were in style.
The colors were effeminate.

I wore it for a while.
But only out the door
And once I got within a mile,
I took it off,
Avoiding all the rancor
It would rile.

She knit herself a suit once,
Striped gold lamé and cream,
Adorned the cuffs with rabbit fur,
It fit her like a dream.
She knit a teal blue jacket,
Sewed crystals on the seams.
They clinked when she would dance, and caught
The light like laser beams.

My mother kept a jar
Of coarse and kosher salt for cooking
Pinching in a dash,
Enhancing every dish.

In youth, Mama learned,
Food comes hard earned,
When her father dragged in spent
From smoking fish.

Cook Mama, cook.
Imbue the stock with latent grief.
Life's brief.
Wish Mama, sing
A song of sorrow
For the falling leaf.

Through busyness, my mother learned
To keep at bay her crying.

She vacuumed after she had pinned
The laundry up for drying.
She started every meal by cutting
Onions up for frying.

For Jeffrey,
she crocheted a throw
For warmth, when he was dying.

Her loss is like
An albatross, an incomplete.
What will I wear now?
What will I eat?

PART XII

 KEVIN

In Terence Davies's movie *The Deep Blue Sea*, Rachel Weisz leaves her husband and a staid marriage for a young and dashing retired RAF officer who is sexy, unstable, and bad for her, but she calls it "passion" and attempts to kill herself over it. Her landlady, discovering her almost dead with the gas on in her flat, tries to drill some sense into her: "Love is wiping someone's arse and cleaning someone up when they've pissed the sheets and letting them keep their dignity, so you can both go on." When you are young, you think chemistry is everything. Everything hinges on how attracted you are to someone, how much you want to sleep with them. As you get older, you start to want to replace the hysteria of young passion with trust, serenity, reliability, a love that is deeper and more meaningful.

When I first hugged Kevin, after a gay AA meeting on the Upper West Side, I knew this was someone with whom I could have *that* kind of love. A love more defining of the adult me, born out of maturity, a place I could only have gotten to after the younger me was carved away, honed by chasing the same sharp pain of flawed thinking over and over again.

In 2001, before my first date with Kevin, I was walking uptown with my friend Mary and saw Kevin at Fifty-Seventh Street with his friend Michael Burg, crawling around on all fours loudly muttering any number of "fucks" and "shits," freaking out about something. Michael was laughing, egging him on. I stopped and asked what was going on. "I lost my keys," he said. Quite boldly, I said, "You can stay at my place."

I was half joking, but I also meant it. I saw Kevin two or three times a week at meetings. We would say hello before the meeting, and afterward, in the spirit of fellowship, we would hug. Kevin's body gave off an unearthly heat. It felt as if his heart had assuring arms. I felt inexplicably safe around Kevin.

After the meetings, a bunch of us would go out to a diner with turquoise Naugahyde booths or to La Dinastia, the Cuban Chinese restaurant where the waiter Mike called what we ordered every night "gay chicken," simply because we ordered it. "Ricky, you want gay chicken?" "Yes, Mike, with a side of sweet plantains and bok choy."

Kevin says he heard me talking one night and thought I sounded smart, special, or something. For three years, we threatened to go out for dinner, sometimes even getting so close as to call each other to make the plan, but each time it got nearer, we'd chicken out. In 2001, I got back to New York after my father died and September 11 happened. I went to a Sunday night meeting, all of that swimming in my head, and shared that I was feeling unhinged. After the meeting, Kevin, no doubt pitying me, said, "Let's have that dinner we've been threatening to have."

Our first date, September 26, we went to Ernie's, a spacious restaurant on Broadway and Seventy-Fifth, and I did Kevin's numbers. I do this often because, for one thing, it breaks the ice. Everyone likes having the attention on them, and I am liberated from the panic of what to talk about.

Kevin seemed fascinated and amused, and it was clear we were unusually comfortable together. Our second date, we went to see David Lynch's *Mulholland Drive*, but I was too aware of every time our bodies made even the slightest contact to concentrate on the movie.

The city still smelled of the acrid, tar-like smoke emanating from the Twin Towers, still smoldering downtown, which added a kind of haunted quality to our burgeoning relationship. Next, we saw Satyajit Ray's *Middleman* at the Lincoln Plaza Cinemas. Kevin's palms were sweating, which I had never experienced before, so I knew he was nervous, but he seemed open to anything I threw out.

He lived on 123rd Street, near a highly sophisticated video store, so on our first movie date in bed with Chinese food, I asked him to rent Mikio Naruse's *When A Woman Ascends the Stairs*, and he barely balked. This was followed by all the movies of Yasujirō Ozu and Kenji Mizoguchi. He was such a good sport. I could request the most obscure titles, and he would watch them. The only time he ever got upset about anything I made him see was our first Valentine's Day together, when I suggested we see Maggie Gyllenhaal in her new movie *Secretary*.

In a kind of sexual cat-and-mouse game, she is enslaved by her sadistic boss, played by James Spader, even peeing herself at her desk when he won't let her leave it. I wanted to see it because a friend of mine wrote the screenplay, but it sickened and offended Kevin, and twenty years later he still mentions it every Valentine's Day.

On October 31, the first version of my piece *Orpheus and Euridice* premiered downtown at Cooper Union. I told the story of Jeffrey and me through the myth, and it was scored for clarinet, soprano, and piano. Kevin came, and I could feel his quiet gravity filling the room. He came backstage just after Ned Rorem expressed how moved he was, which made me happy.

I don't think Kevin knew what to make of my music then, and I'm not sure even now, but he comes to everything I do and is always encouraging, and I know he is proud of me. We go to tons of operas together, and he buys subscriptions at Carnegie Hall, so we hear a lot of music together. One of the things he missed most during quarantine was live music. I feel guilty about this, but I was happy for the respite.

So, the night he lost his keys, a voice in my head said, "You are going to end up with Kevin Doyle," and it was right.

Everything about getting to know Kevin and falling in love with him was different. It felt real. There was nothing addictive or obsessive about it. This scared me, because I thought obsession meant love. If I didn't feel sick, as if I were in excruciating pain, I didn't know where I was. Kevin was one big "yes." It was so normal, so easy. I was so confused; I was afraid to even kiss him.

Kevin was working at *Condé Nast Traveler* as the ombudsman, and shortly after we started seeing each other, he had to go to Paris for business. We wrote each other tender, slightly cautious emails, skirting our feelings through news and gossip, and I couldn't wait to hear from him every day. An astute editor—in fact, eventually, he became the executive editor of the magazine (before some creepy women took it over and fired everyone)—he is also a meticulous writer with a great deal of acquired wisdom, so any written communication from him is beautiful. A rich backstory was being constructed, and a foundation that felt solid and real, not a fantasy stuck in my head.

When he got back, after we had dinner at a Greek restaurant on my corner, he presented me with an extravagant, beautifully packaged box of chocolates. We were standing by the piano, and Kevin said, "Are we ever going to kiss?" And the relationship was consummated.

I was at the tail end of my obsession with the violist I met when he was hired for the recording of my *Bright Eyed Joy* CD, Michael Nicholas, and still reeling from Jeffrey's death, so I was a veritable panoply of tics and neuroses—all of which Kevin seemed pretty patient with and even confident about weathering. He is a Capricorn. He brings stability to my hysteria.

One morning, though, we woke up in my bed, and he seemed really disturbed, on the verge of tears. "What's going on?" I asked. He pointed to my bookshelf, at the five framed photos of Jeffrey, and said, "When I wake up in your bed, the first thing I see is Jeffrey. When I sit at your piano with you, I see Jeffrey. When I hold you in your kitchen, I see Jeffrey, staring at me from the refrigerator door."

There was nothing to say; I knew it was time to put those things away. I cleared the highest shelf of my kitchen cabinet and made it an archive of Jeffrey's photos and all the condolence letters and cards I received after he died.

One of the perks of our early courtship was that we went all over the world, places I would never have gotten to on my own: Thailand, Cambodia, Laos, Vietnam, Turkey, New Zealand, the Dolomites, the Himalayas, Switzerland. My life became immeasurably bigger with Kevin in it.

Kevin was raised Catholic, which still has enormous meaning for him. He has scattered periods of going to church regularly. In fact, he is quite inspired by the priest up here in Wurtsboro, New York. But he has a searching spirituality and a hunger for God that is deep and rich and helps me on my own journey. We meditate together every day, and often, on the major holidays, I go to church with him. I don't mind, because I believe in prayer, and prayer's power only increases the more people there are in a space designated for contemplation.

Kevin traveled with Hillary Clinton in 2012, when she was secretary of state, and wrote a cover story for *Condé Nast Traveler* about the trip. Watching how she dealt with people and her unyielding dedication to service and her own faith was meaningful and inspiring to him. On that trip they went to China, Bangladesh, and India. Kevin went back to India in 2013 on assignment to write about the Kumbh Mela, a gigantic Hindu festival that is the largest gathering of human beings on the planet.

One night, he was stricken with terror before going. He is claustrophobic, and there were supposed to be upwards of eighty million people there. I told him he had to go, sensing it would be deeply transformative for him. My sister Lorraine, whom he bought various sacred relics for while he was there, said he would never be the same after it, and she was right.

I was in Manhattan, Kansas, doing master classes with singers at the university, when Kevin sent me a photo someone had just taken of him after he dunked himself three times in the Ganges River with all the other pilgrims, despite dire warnings from friends in Delhi about ever going *near* the river. He looked beatific and said the water tasted sweet, like honey.

I've always had a fantasy of having a house on a lake. One weekend, in 2008, Kevin took me upstate to a beautiful little cottage he found on a place called Wolf Lake. Though it was perfect, I was terrified, because a house signified deeper commitment to me, which made me feel trapped. But the closer we got to living there, the more my reservations turned to gratitude. It was a tree house on a promontory above the lake. Kevin was Daniel Boone, chopping logs for the fire and shoveling the snow, and I thanked him a lot, making him feel good about doing it.

The first night we slept there, it snowed several feet. In the morning, I opened the back door to look out at the snow in the woods, and about fifty deer scattered like fireflies. Apparently, the previous owner fed them, but to me it might as well have been God dancing. We see bears, butterflies, rabbits, otters, snakes, eagles, blue herons, owls, and foxes. Boats with motors are not allowed, so the water is pristine. I swim in it all summer long—only now in a bigger house we moved to because we needed more room. Kevin and Lucy, our little rescue dog, are my family. Kevin is stability, safety, and love. I always want to be with him. We are married now.

Having always been looking for a father, at one point I titled this book *Will* You *Be My Father*. With Kevin, even though he is eight years younger than me, I found a stable, lasting relationship with a man who is grounded, durable, inspiring, sensible, and consistent, who thinks about our future, who is able to manage my immense mood swings, and who has an almost paternal need to nurture.

He is the oldest child, I, the youngest. We fit. We have been together twenty years, a miracle.

Last weekend, with Lucy in her knapsack (she is older and can no longer walk the four-plus miles with me) on another walk around the lake, I saw something white in the street that looked out of the ordinary. Approaching it, I saw it was a baby bird. It looked up at me as if to say, "Help me." I put my hand out, and it jumped on my finger, accompanying me for nearly forty minutes, until I got home. With this wildness in my hand, I summoned Kevin out of the house, bursting with excitement about my rescue mission.

I was going to look for milk, worms, water, anything, like a veterinarian or a falconer. Kevin, remaining calm, disappeared for a minute, then came out of the house and said, "Get in the car." "What?" I said. "Why?" "Where did you find it?" he asked. In about five minutes, Kevin had researched what needs to be done with a baby bird when you have found it outside its nest. We slowly drove around the lake until I found the approximate place where I found it, and I placed it on a tree stump so its mother would hear it chirping and take it back to the nest.

I am enthusiastic; he is serene. I couldn't see past the shoebox and the heating pad. Kevin repairs things, follows directions, follows recipes. I do none of those things. I am excitement followed by torpor, all bursts of inspiration and then periods of indolence, even misery sometimes. We watched a series about Julia Child on TV, and they kept talking about a cake she liked to make called Reine de Saba, so for my birthday Kevin made it flawlessly. It was unbelievably delicious, rich, and extravagant.

The wonderfully rustic lamp in my studio with the moose and fir trees on the lampshade broke, and I was going to throw it away.

Kevin fixed it.

Kevin is a fixer.

He fixed me.

PART XIII

NOW

I am working on *This House*, a new opera for the fiftieth anniversary of Opera Theatre of St. Louis in 2025, with a libretto by Lynn Nottage and her daughter, Ruby Aiyo Gerber, about the life of one brownstone in Harlem through a century. The house sings, as do its inhabitants— and its ghosts.

Intimate Apparel will be recorded by Time Life. My *Huit Chansons de Fleurs*, commissioned by Tony Lee and So-Chung Shinn, with poems by Emily Dickinson, William Wordsworth, Jane Kenyon, Dorothy Parker, Donald Hall, Telmo Dos Santos, and me, will premiere with Erin Morley, soprano, and Gerald Martin Moore, pianist, at the Kennedy Center, on May 13, 2024, and they have recorded it for Orchid Classics for a 2024 release. *The Grapes of Wrath* will again be done by MasterVoices at Carnegie Hall in April 2024 to celebrate Ted Sperling's tenth anniversary with them, and I just premiered my *Marvin Gaye Songs*, to poems by Vievee Francis, commissioned by the Tucson Desert Song Festival for the magnificent baritone Justin Austin.

My chamber opera, *Autumn Valentine*, which uses the works of Dorothy Parker, was just performed in a shiny new version with orchestrations and added songs in San Diego, with its original stars, Angelina Réaux and Michael Sokol, produced by Bodhi Tree Concerts.

The publication of the scores of *Intimate Apparel*, and *The Garden of the Finzi-Continis*, by Theodore Presser Music Company, is imminent.

In the first version of this book, which was eight-hundred single-spaced pages, I had many poems and lyrics that all had to go in the effort toward brevity. It is my hope to publish them in a separate collection.